ROSWELL GARST

A BIOGRAPHY

ROSWELL GARST
A BIOGRAPHY

HAROLD LEE

THE HENRY A. WALLACE SERIES
ON AGRICULTURAL HISTORY AND RURAL STUDIES

IOWA STATE UNIVERSITY PRESS ● AMES

TO MY WIFE, **ANTONIA GARST LEE**

Composed and printed by The Iowa State University Press, Ames, Iowa 50010

First edition, 1984

Library of Congress Cataloging in Publication Data
Lee, Harold, 1933–
    Roswell Garst: a biography.

    (The Henry A. Wallace series on agricultural history and rural studies)
    Bibliography: p.
    Includes index.
    1. Garst, Roswell, 1898–1977. 2. Agriculturists—Iowa—Coon Rapids—Biography. 3. Coon Rapids (Iowa)—Biography. 1. Title. II. Series.
S417.G26L44 1984   630'.92'4 [B]   83-26452
ISBN 0–8138–0796–4

CONTENTS

v

    Background: Living with the Surplus, 169
    First Agricultural Exchange: 1955, 174
    First Trip to Eastern Europe: 1955, 186
    Whose Iron Curtain?, 196
    Months of Progress, Days of Disappointment: 1956, 203

8 Starting Again, 215
    Aftermath of Hungary, 215
    Conversation with Khrushchev, 220
    Khrushchev in Coon Rapids, 223

9 The Sixties, 229
    Agriculture on the New Frontier: 1960–63, 229
    Bringing Cattle to the Corn Belt, 236
    Russia Again: 1960–64, 250
    El Salvador Experiment, 265

10 The Last Years, 282

    Sources, 287

    Index, 301

EDITOR'S INTRODUCTION

THE HENRY A. WALLACE SERIES on Agricultural History and Rural Studies is designed to enlarge publishing opportunities in agricultural history and thereby to expand public understanding of the development of agriculture and rural society. The Series will be composed of volumes that explore the many aspects of agriculture and rural life within historical perspectives. It will evolve as the field evolves. The press and the editor will solicit and welcome the submission of manuscripts that illustrate, in good and fresh ways, that evolution. Our interests are broad. They do not stop with Iowa and U.S. agriculture but extend to all other parts of the world. They encompass the social, intellectual, scientific, and technological aspects of the subject as well as the economic and political. The emphasis of the Series is on the scholarly monograph, but historically significant memoirs of people involved in and with agriculture and rural life and major sources for research in the field will also be included.

Most appropriately, this Iowa-based Series is dedicated to a highly significant agriculturist who began in Iowa, developed a large, well-informed interest in its rural life, and expanded the scope of his interests beyond the state to the nation and the world. An Iowa native and son of an agricultural scientist, journalist, and secretary of agriculture, Henry A. Wallace was a 1910 graduate of Iowa State College, a frequent participant in its scientific activities, editor of *Wallaces' Farmer* from 1921 to 1933, founder in 1926 of the Hi-Bred Corn Company (now Pioneer Hi-Bred International, Inc.), secretary of agriculture from 1933 to 1940, and vice president of the United States from 1941 to 1945. In the agricultural phases of his wide-ranging career, he was both a person of large importance in the development of America's agriculture and the leading policymaker during the most creative period in the history of American farm policy.

Wallace had significant ties with the subject of this book, another fascinating man who had a great impact on agriculture. The second in the series, it is a thoughtful, probing book that defines the man and his contributions with precision and flair. In these pages, we learn many things about Roswell Garst. We learn that he was not humble; we learn also that he was colorful, enthusiastic, energetic, gregarious, and persuasive. He made some contributions to the New Deal for agriculture; he contributed even more to the development of our modern highly mechanized, sparsely peopled, and abundantly productive farming system. He promoted the adoption by farmers of hybrid seed corn, synthetic fertilizers, and new types of feed for cattle. To use terms Garst employed, he was one of the architects and builders of a "farming revolution" and a "new agriculture." Although he preferred the "egalitarian nature of Iowa farming" to California's "feudal" system, he was, as the exchange with the agrarian economist, Paul Taylor, suggests, more strongly committed to the modernization of agriculture than he was to the agrarian tradition with its preachings about the value of a large number of land-owning family farmers. And his horizons were not limited to Iowa, the Middle West, or even the United States. He worked to bring the new agriculture to other parts of the world. The story of his activities in the Soviet Union and Eastern Europe and of his visits with Nikita Khrushchev is one of the most exciting parts of the book and one of the sides of Garst's career that reflected the influence of Henry Wallace.

Focused on an extraordinary man, this is an unusual book. Written by a son-in-law who is also a scholar, it benefits from the perspectives supplied by both family membership and professional training and experience. The result is a book that should be read by all who are interested in a subject of enormous importance: the recent history of American agriculture.

Richard S. Kirkendall

FOREWORD

ROSWELL GARST was a pure example of the American tradition of brilliant individualism, a man who though not a scientist himself was a salesman of science, not a diplomat he became a remarkable instrument of diplomacy, a thorough pragmatist he won as much respect for his views in Moscow as he did in Iowa.

The role which Garst played on the international stage was almost unique for his time, that is the 1950s and to a lesser extent, the 1960s and early 1970s. It was most effective in the Sovient Union and Eastern Europe but he also left a mark in Latin America.

Garst was far from being the first of an unusual American species – a man really larger than life, a virtual genius in his field, an excellent businessman who became an evangelist in pursuit of his conviction that great national and world problems could be solved – or at least alleviated – by new technology – specifically, by new farming techniques.

Although there was no one in contemporary American history just like Garst he had some prototypes – Thomas Campbell, the Montana wheat farmer who introduced the Soviet Union to his dry farming methods in the late 1920s and Hugh Cooper who built some of the Soviet's early great dams. In his internationalism and iconoclasm Garst somewhat resembled Henry Ford without Ford's negativism – antisemitism, antilaborism, and the rest.

It is impossible to imagine Garst or Garst's character evolving in any land but America and probably nowhere but Iowa could have nourished such a personality as his.

By an accident of history Garst was moving onto the world stage with his evangel of corn, hybrid corn, and other advanced agricultural technologies just as Nikita S. Khrushchev rose to power in the Soviet Union. The two men had much in common. Each was expansive, earthy, verbal, given to broad gestures, and passionately interested in land, soil, crops, animals, and food. It was Khrushchev and his top-flight agriculturists who had the wit to understand what it was that Garst was preaching and to dare to pin the agricultural hopes of the Soviet Union on Garst's doctrines and practices. It was an experiment which paid off—both for Garst and for the Soviet Union. But first it had paid off for Iowa and for the American agriculture of the Midwest. What Garst did was to take the remarkable experiments and discoveries of that complex Iowan Henry A. Wallace and prod, push, preach, and convince Iowa farmers and then farmers throughout the Midwest and beyond that in this lay the pattern of the future. It was an extraordinary success story and could not have been achieved without Garst's total belief in the new approach and his extraordinary gift for words and images. It is easy to imagine decades passing without application on a mass scale of the Wallace discoveries had not Garst been there to take the tale to the fields of the Corn Belt.

Garst's success in implanting his hybrid corn in the Soviet Union and Eastern Europe was equally spectacular. They joked from one end of Russia to the other about "cornball" Khrushchev but as the painful deficiencies of Soviet agriculture became more and more evident with the passing years the extent of Garst's contribution to the Soviet resources of protein became more and more apparent.

Garst was an exuberant, outgoing man. No one could fall within his orbit without coming under the spell of his passion—for better farms, better corn, better land cultivation, better living, better nutrition, a better life. Nor was his vision narrow. Of course, he put his own country and his native Iowa first but his gospel was one which he took to the whole world and he pursued it as avidly in Bucharest as he did in El Salvador. To him food and hunger knew no boundary lines.

While Garst was and remained a citizen of Iowa and of his beloved Coon Rapids he imperceptibly became a citizen of the world. Wherever he went his views were solicited. And not only on farming matters.

Garst suffered only one real setback in a life so packed with activity that reading about it one thinks sometimes it must have been lived by more than one man. This was in the failure of his effort to slow the pace of the arms race, to get some sanity into the competition between the United States and the Soviet Union in the production of nuclear weapons. He tried and tried to convince Khrushchev that this was the No. 1 priority in the world. He did not succeed. He tried and tried to make it the No. 1 American priority. If he had for a time a bit more success in Washington in the end not much was achieved in his lifetime and the question is still No. 1 on the world agenda.

No one ever mistook Roswell Garst for anything but a capitalist but even Communists like Khrushchev had to confess he was best of his breed. In fact, the Communists never quite got over Garst's humanity, his willingness to share his techniques and his secrets—at a reasonable price, of course—with his nominal enemies. Garst never really believed he had any enemies. And if he did have one now and then he was always certain that given a chance to talk to him a bit he could bring him around. And he was probably right about that. He could bring almost anyone around if he talked long enough.

It was ironic that in his last years cancer deprived Garst of his vocal cords. But it was typical of the Garst spirit that this did not stop him in his endless preaching. He learned to use a voice box and after a few months was back in business, travelling the world, talking to the great statesmen and the ordinary Iowa farmers, with as much vigor as ever.

To one who knew Garst it is almost impossible to imagine Iowa without him. Unfortunately the genetic techniques to reproduce new clones of Garst do not exist. Perhaps that is just as well. One Garst on earth could kick up enough storms — good storms though they were. A clutch of clones would possess such high energy levels that the world might not be able to survive it all.

Harrison E. Salisbury

PREFACE

"I've always been a showman," Roswell "Bob" Garst liked to say of himself, and it is that part of his personality that is most remembered. Everyone who knew him has stories of his entertaining, flamboyant, and occasionally outrageous performances as the greatest agricultural salesman of his time. Proud of his commercial success, Garst was vigorous, combative, and often controversial as a promoter of innovations in farming methods, persistent and aggressive in argument. His style was a colorful mixture of calculated gesture and spontaneous improvisation, born out of wit, a natural gift for teaching, and an abundance of that brazenness known in Yiddish as *chutzpah,* which Roswell called "having good guts."

The most memorable and well-known exhibition of this truly public personality occurred in the fall of 1959, during Nikita Khrushchev's visit to the Garst farm in Coon Rapids, Iowa, when Roswell was in his prime at a vibrant sixty-one years of age. For twenty years his body had a shape rather like that of Alfred Hitchcock, larger in frame but marked by a swaybacked posture to balance a stomach that made him look like a man who had just swallowed a watermelon. ("A very difficult shape to fit," his tailor once remarked.) In contrast to Hitchcock's soft features and pixielike expression, Roswell had a leathery complexion, an angular nose, and thrusting strong jaw; a face, as John Dos Passos once described it, "that comes at you like the prow of a ship." He had not yet lost his larynx to cancer, and as he escorted Khrushchev and an entourage of politicians, diplomats, bodyguards, and curious locals around the farming operation, his voice was strong and resonant, his repartee equal to Khrushchev's own gift for showmanship. To the reporters and photographers whose numbers jeopardized the educational aspect of the visit, Roswell was imperiously angry and abrasive, engaging at one point in pitched battle against the swarming press corps with threats and handfuls of silage, an episode captured in a memorable photograph that followed him to the obituary pages nineteen years later.

Such moments in his showman's life have tended to obscure for all but a specialist audience two important but thus far less fully explored aspects of his extraordinary career: the quality of his mind and the range of his contribution to the advancement of agricultural theory and practice. "Generally, over the years," John Kenneth Galbraith has written, "Roswell Garst has been the source of more straight-forward, unadorned information on agriculture than anyone else with whom I have been in touch." His facility with information was but a part of a larger gift. "His mind," Galbraith explained, "works through a problem, makes great use of the relevant technical information and does not pause before the logical or necessary conclusion." When a necessary conclusion called for new directions, Roswell went into battle armed with an arsenal of persuasion ranging from brilliant analysis to a style of aggressive argument he used to call "the diplomacy of exaggeration."

Roswell lived, thought, and talked agriculture all of his life. His practical accomplishments in the field, sustained by a personal vision of America's agricultural potential, spanned forty years and ranged from the introduction of hybrid seed corn in the thirties through the pioneering of protein-enriched cellulose for cattle feeding in the forties to a central role in the fertilizer revolution of the fifties and sixties. "The contributions you and Henry Wallace have made to American agriculture in this century," Hubert Humphrey wrote to Roswell in 1977, "are unequalled by anyone I know."

The Khrushchev episode highlights another dimension of Roswell's work which, although in this instance well known, has also not been much explored. "He was one of the most important figures in the establishment of East-West relations," Silviu Brucan, former Rumanian Ambassador to the United States and later to the United Nations, has said of Roswell, "something that hasn't been appreciated in America, even though Khrushchev came to visit him." Brucan is right. The scale, the persistence, and the motives with which Roswell pursued his personal campaign for rapprochement with Eastern Europe in the fifties and sixties require several chapters in the telling.

The opportunity to see more of Roswell than we have seen before comes in large part from his voluminous correspondence, which is now at the Iowa State University Library. It constitutes a remarkable body of evidence for the multiple and simultaneously conducted levels of his professional and intellectual life. It has influenced not only the content of this biography, but also its organization. Because it is impossible to portray the simultaneity of Roswell's rich intellectual life, I have elected to trace his interests within each decade in a thematic fashion. It is itself a tribute to Roswell that the papers of a private individual have to be approached in a manner normally reserved for the papers of those who have held high office.

Other sources have been important for this book, and in citing them I must at the same time acknowledge my great debt to the people who provided me with them. My wife Antonia, to whom this book is dedicated, searched through fifty years of the Coon Rapids *Enterprise* to provide all my citations from that admirable newspaper, shared most of the interviewing, performed various research tasks, and consequently may lay claim to partnership in all that follows.   John Chrystal, Roswell's nephew, helped at every stage of the project with material and advice, giving generously of his time. In England, Geoffrey Wadhams located, translated, and summarized many of the documents in Russian, and Eve Spear did much of the typing. Those people who contributed interviews are acknowledged in the endnotes. Their tapes and transcripts are now at Iowa State University.

The *Enterprise* files were made available by Drexel Nixon, who sadly did not live to see the fruits of his kindness. The management and staff of Garst and Thomas Hybrid Seed Corn Company (now Garst Seed Company) allowed me access to Roswell's correspondence in the basement of their main office and were unfailingly helpful. I am especially indebted to Aden Owen, Pete Oliver, and Cathy Headlee. The Iowa Savings Bank, Jo Garst, and Elizabeth Garst provided typewriters and work space at various times. Consequently, the writing of the book was in itself largely a Coon Rapids enterprise.

ROSWELL GARST A BIOGRAPHY

CHAPTER ONE

Town and Family

"The name of this city is not one that will impress the stranger favorably with the place," wrote publisher and editor S. D. Henry of the *Coon Rapids Enterprise:* "there is not much poetry in it." Henry wrote these lines in 1883, and during his career as chronicler and chief publicist of Coon Rapids for more than forty years, chafed periodically over the name of his beloved town, carrying on an intermittent and ultimately losing effort to change the name. Henry confessed that when he first came to have a look at Coon Rapids he kept its name secret from his friends and in the same issue of the *Enterprise* printed a letter from a lady whose little girl had exclaimed: "Please don't go to Coon Rapids. A place with such a horrid name I know will not be a nice place to live!" Coon Rapids, Henry concluded, "is not a name that possesses a large amount of magnetic power in the way of attracting people."

But Henry was not a man to dwell overlong on the defects of his town, for Progress resided there, disguised though she might be with humble name and rustic garments. "It is customary," he commented,

for persons who have located in a new country to portray its beauties and advantage with a pen dipped in the liquids of poesy—with an imagination inflamed in the inspiration of the Muses, and those attracted hither are destined to meet with disappointment. We frankly admit that no Naiads bathe within the classic waters of the river Coon, nor do Nymphs revel in our forests, meadows or plains. No Seraphs charm the disconsolate, but we do claim some practical, genuine inducements.

Foremost among these inducements was the railroad, for in 1882, during a decade when 70,000 miles of track were laid in America, the Chicago, Milwaukee and St. Paul railroad pushed West just south of the old town of Coon Rapids. The citizens of old Coon Rapids moved or rebuilt their homes and businesses, and what had been a village of fifty-four inhabitants in 1880 became a booming town of six hundred by 1883.

So many people came at the same time to settle in the new town that lumber and carpenters were in short supply, forcing many to camp out for a season or crowd into buildings "as thick as three in a bed." "It was a year of general rush and hurrah," he continued, and of scramble and inconvenience, but a year after the railroad was completed, "all were comfortably situated."

Henry was delighted by the prospects for the new town. Surveying this splendid new creation in 1883, he saw

no indication but that this summer will be a season of marked growth and prosperity. Our businessmen are enterprising, our farmers are thrifty, and all are full of life and snap and there is no cause for even a whisper of doubt as to its future.

Coon Rapids already had one of the largest grain elevators on the Chicago and Milwaukee road, two banks, two hotels, and a variety of businesses. A new school and church were going up, the Masons and the Odd Fellows were already organized, and the town itself lay in the center of one of the richest farming areas in the state. No young city had a brighter future, in spite of its name, and even the name showed no signs of further discouraging prospective young ladies and their families from settling here. Or, as another poetically minded citizen put it in a later issue of the *Enterprise,*

> Just let the growth be rapid, still,
> And we'll try and bear the Coon.

The old town of Coon Rapids was scarcely more than fifteen years older than its successor, but the site itself had entered recorded history as early as 1855, when Obadiah Niles settled on the land embraced by both the old and the new towns. Niles, characterized enigmatically by Henry as "a peculiar character," was elected justice of the peace for the small settlement that began to take shape and acted for his neighbors as an agent in the purchase of supplies in Des Moines, seventy-five miles to the east. A mill was built in 1855, burned down, and rebuilt in 1863, followed by a store and blacksmith shop. By 1865 a proper town was laid out. The inhabitants of the new town petitioned Washington for the establishment of a post office, with the community it served to be called Fairview, but Washington replied that the name was already in use. Niles Grove and Ribbleton were contenders, but Jacob Cretsinger's suggestion of Coon Rapids—the town having been established on the middle fork of the Raccoon River—won the day.

In 1868 Edward Garst journeyed on horseback from Boone, Iowa, to have a look at the little town, liked it, and in 1869 returned with a wagonload of goods with which to go into business with his cousin, Crockett Ribble, who had built the new mill in 1863. Ribble and Garst set up a general store across the street from the Fort Sumter Hotel, but within a few months the partners quarreled, dissolved the partnership, and divided up the stock. Edward took his half and moved into a building on the Fort Sumter side of old Main Street and went into business on his own, with the aid of a loan of five hundred dollars (at 10 percent interest) from his grandfather. This was the first general store in the village, supplying groceries, dry goods, clothing, hardware, and a few drugs and remedies.

In 1875 Edward's brother Warren came to Coon Rapids, and the partnership of E. and W. Garst was formed. According to S. D. Henry, Warren had just returned from California, "where he has chased the phantom of a great fortune in a quicksilver mine." The mine, however, proved to be "a delusion and a snare," Henry reported, "and although it is not recorded whether Warren came back afoot or on horseback," he never went on another such chase for wealth. Indeed, there was no need, for E. and W. Garst proved to be a bonanza more substantial than most mother-lode digs. The new partners rented the lower floor of a new building, whose second floor was occupied by the Masonic order. The Garsts also built an addition to the hall, furnishing the public with "a commodious hall" on its second floor for dancing and other occasions. When the railroad came through, the Garsts were among the first to plan a move to the new site, but the Masons refused to budge. Exasperated by such lack of foresight by the brotherhood, Edward sawed the building in half, moved the Garst's part to the new town, and left a braying jackass in the lower floor of the part of the building they were still renting. The Masons soon capitulated, and the whole building appeared in its new location.

The new town grew without interruption until 1886, when a cyclone destroyed thirty-seven buildings, mostly residences, but also the town hall, the Presbyterian and Christian churches, and the school. It was a severe test for the young town, but within a year "the fated portion" was rebuilt and prosperity resumed. By the 1890s the population had leveled off at a little more than one thousand, and although the town elders worked hard to induce a railroad to build a north-south line through the town, the effort failed. However, as the new century approached, Coon Rapids was attaining maturity as a quietly prospering small town, the hub of a fertile farming area, and proud possessor of the largest grain elevator between Council Bluffs and Marion, Iowa. In 1904 Henry boasted that Coon Rapids was the only town of its size in the state that supported three newspapers and three banks. In addition to fifty-three business establishments, it had an opera house, a waterworks system, an electric light plant, and a telephone exchange.

For Henry, the centerpiece was the emporium operated by his close friends Edward and Warren Garst. Described by Henry in 1892 as "the

town's pioneer business firm, the strongest financially, and possessed of
the most extensive stock," E. and W. Garst carried practically everything
in clothing, dry goods, cloaks, boots, shoes, hats, caps, general furnish-
ings, and groceries. Their goods were selected with "keen and unerring
judgment" by the two shrewd businessmen and were attractively displayed and well advertised in the *Enterprise*, furnishing Henry with fresh
copy almost weekly. The store continued to improve and expand; by 1907
it had electric lights and a cash system of vacuum tubes "as is used in the
large city stores." Before 1907 an addition called the Coon Rapids
Clothing Store was built next door, and in 1907 the upstairs rooms of the
two buildings were made into one. The area over the clothing store was
used for excess stock, carpets, and other goods; the balcony of the
general store was made into a rest room for ladies, "where mothers can
take their children"; and salesmen were employed for each department of
the store. The effect of such managerial brilliance confirmed Henry's
faith in progress and perfectability.

ALTHOUGH the Garsts, Henrys, and a few other families were the social
leaders of the town, the general nature of its entertainment and cultural
life reflected the cohesion and intermingling of a small town thrown very
much on its own resources, self-conscious and proud of its youth and
independence. Its most representative and most important public celebration was the Fourth of July, an event whose first recorded occurrence
took place in 1859 at Tuttle's Grove and was attended by a group of
people from Coon Rapids. Lawson Mingus, reportedly barefooted, read
the Declaration of Independence under an oak, after which a dance was
held at a house on Brushy Creek. However, in 1883, that momentous year
that had seen the building of the new Coon Rapids, Edward Garst and his
committee organized a móre grandiose affair. An out-of-town state senator, known for his rhetorical gifts, was imported because, as Henry put it,
"in point of oratorical entertainment, Coon Rapids is determined to excell
any of her neighboring towns." Between speeches the Coon Rapids brass
band played "stirring music," and during the day there were races, a
greased hog and slippery pole contest, a fireworks display which cost
$150, and in the evening a ball at the Harris Hall.
    In the summer the community made use of its one geographical at-
traction, the five-mile stretch of the Raccoon River, which could be navi-
gated from the old mill dam in a northwest arc to the Galloway farm. The
enterprising purveyor of boats advertised that it was "well proven by all
who have been boating on Coon River at this place that there is hardly a
lake in the west more picturesque and with finer scenery on its shores."
About 1897 a boat christened "The Belle of the Coon" was built, hand-

powered at first, but later equipped with a steam engine and a leaky boiler. The Belle made two trips daily to a landing at the Galloway farm, where a dance pavilion and resort area had been established; the Belle was also available for daily charter by picnic parties. The 50-foot barge moved at the stately pace of 10 miles per hour, filled with fifty or even sixty passengers, who for the price of ten cents sat under its canopy and pilot house enjoying the scenic delights of "the rippling waters of the River Coon."

The most common entertainment of the town was the "sociable," usually organized around food. Strawberry and ice cream suppers were frequent events in the summer, corn roasts and pumpkin pie socials were popular, and there was even a "mush and milk" festival recorded in 1887. Another kind of sociable, held after the completion of a large barn at the Pingrey's, provided the occasion for a party consisting of dancing, games, and a midnight lunch. In the winter other occasions were invented: in 1898 the husbands of the members of the Women's Club surprised the ladies one Monday evening by inviting them to a sleigh ride and afterwards to an oyster supper at the Ellsworth Hotel.

Entertainment existed further afield, and Coon Rapids society was by no means exclusively insular. The railroad provided excursion fares and easy access to events in the cities. In the 1880s "a large number" of people, according to Henry, travelled from Coon Rapids to the state fair at Des Moines, a somewhat smaller number to Nebraska, and in surprising numbers attended the Chicago Exposition of 1885, the World's Fair of 1893, and the Omaha Exposition of 1898.

At home, musical and dramatic entertainments were a mixture of the home grown and the imported. "Coon Rapids wanted a band – a brass band," Henry wrote in 1883, and "she raised the necessary money to procure it." Twelve instruments arrived, including a big bass drum, and were "turned loose with a number of our young men, some of whom have conquered the animals before." The music man hired to train the band was "a gentleman from Des Moines," who rehearsed it diligently for its first performance at the great Fourth of July party of 1883, for which it had been organized. The band got uniforms in 1884 and remained a town institution throughout the first half of the next century. In 1895 the singers of Coon Rapids gathered at the Henry house to organize a chorus; the aspiring pianist could buy a piano in Coon Rapids and take lessons from Mrs. Gaynor; the singer had Miss Monarch to take his voice in hand; the Presbyterian ladies organized a quintet club to raise money, and the home musicale was a regular event on the social calendar, especially at the Edward and Warren Garsts and the S. D. Henrys. Touring performers appeared in the opera house, among them the Salisbury Orchestra in 1906 and the Grinnell College glee club in 1914. The most popular entertainer, however, was Blind Boone, a blind Negro singer and musician who appeared regularly at the opera house.

Women were the leaders in the formation of the town's more serious cultural institutions. The Women's Club, originally eight but increased to twelve by 1896, decided that their principal study for that year would be Russian history, and each of its members prepared a paper on the topic. Current events were discussed at every meeting, and at least one gathering during that year attracted thirty guests. Women's suffrage was taken up early: in 1884 a group of Coon Rapids ladies forwarded a petition to the legislature in Des Moines in defense of their right to the ballot, and in 1898 a Political Equality Club was founded. A Literary Society appeared in 1885 and attracted fourteen members, whose inaugural debate was entitled "Should Foreign Emigration Be Encouraged?"

Finding the books to pursue these activities was a problem for a small town. Families such as the Garsts and the Henrys acquired modest private libraries, and Henry sold books as a sideline to the publishing business. In 1885 he gave the following notice:

I have lately received a full stock of books, including Boys' and Girls' Chatterboxes, histories, Bibles, dictionaries, poems, story books, and novels, bound in cloth, also the standard poems bound in alligator, sets of Dickens, Elliott, Macaulay and Gibbon, Carlyle and Irving, which I have for sale at the gallery and will sell them so cheap that everybody can have books to read these long evenings.

In 1884 a semipublic library was established whereby each shareholder would give one dollar, which would buy one book. A library association was subsequently formed from this cooperative, and more than one hundred books were acquired. In the 1890s the state created travelling libraries, thirty-nine in all, which were placed in the residences of designated townspeople for three months. But the town wanted its own library, and beginning in 1908 there was much discussion and agitation on this issue. Finally in 1913 a subscription library was founded, and Garst Hall in the store building was remodeled and opened as a public library room.

EVEN at the turn of the century, Coon Rapids was still an island of settlement in a vast river of westward migration towards the still unbroken lands of the West and Southwest, and it was partly for this reason that its population leveled off in the 1890s. The railroad promoted the westward move by offering excursions to the new lands and cooperated with land agents in assembling groups of new settlers from areas such as Iowa and

Illinois. In 1895 twenty-one families from Coon Rapids planning to move met in the Garst Hall to discuss arrangements, ate a dinner provided by the local Dakota land agent, and left by train on 15 March. A train leaving from Perry that year carried two hundred people in seventy cars, with coaches for women and children, baggage cars for men, and wagons for livestock. "Many have previously gone from here," the *Perry Advertiser* reported, "and their satisfactory reports of crops, climate and soil have induced a yearly exodus that at once transformed a renter here into an owner there, and the land yields freely and meets their expectations."

Some of the local residents were skeptical about what they had seen on their excursions to look over new land. In 1900 eighty-four potential emigrants from Coon Rapids took the train to Chamberlain, South Dakota, and reported that although it was "a beautiful country," the crops "are not up with those in Iowa." The Coon Rapids area occasionally picked up new settlers from among the waves of European immigrants, and in 1913 a large number of Danish families settled on the relatively poor land south of town. Henry approved of these new settlers because "the Danes are a very prosperous people and make the best class of citizens. The Community can't have too many Danes." He took a less charitable view of Mormons, observing that the occupants of a train passing through Coon Rapids on its way to Salt Lake City "were a hard-looking lot of citizens."

Coon Rapids also gained a few new citizens through the curious institution of the Children's Train, filled by churches and benevolent societies in New York with orphans and children from parents too poor to support a large family and sent West in search of foster homes. In 1904 B. W. Tice, the agent travelling on one of these trains, arrived in Coon Rapids with seventeen boys and girls from age two to fifteen. Tice spoke in the opera house, presented the children for adoption, and managed to dispose of eleven. The children who came to Coon Rapids had varying fortunes; some were adopted merely to provide free labor on local farms. On the day he came of age Ted Bonney, one of these children, threw down his hoe and walked off the farm on which he had been impressed.

There were population levelers other than emigration, and chief among them was disease, especially among children, who were struck down by such afflictions as diphtheria and whooping cough. Henry also had frequent occasion to report that people had "suicided," especially in the lonely rural regions, and from time to time reported the commitment of people to the insane asylum. Nor was everyone moving West. There was a small but steady movement eastward of failed homesteaders, unable or unwilling to try again after a bad experience on a land that could be barren, inhospitable, and lonely, giving back nothing in return for the labor expended upon it.

Henry was not only the historian of the vicissitudes and triumphs of
Coon Rapids and its immediate area; he was also its chief moral arbiter,
the public upholder of the virtues of the respectable citizenry of Coon
Rapids, pronouncing judgments on a spectrum of issues that touched
Christian morals, the business community, and progress. His most sustained effort over the years was his campaign against liquor, and in this he
was foursquare with the business and social leaders of the town. By 1887
the aroused citizenry had managed to eliminate saloons in Coon Rapids,
the chief source of solace for those who did not share in the social and
cultural activities heretofore described. This effort "has created some
little feeling," Henry conceded, although nobody had actually been hurt.
He awarded most of the credit to the Women's Christian Temperance
Union, whose determination he found both "surprising and admirable"
and announced that even though situated in a noted liquor county, Coon
Rapids was without saloons, "not closed temporarily but permanently."

The victory was short-lived, however, for taverns began to reappear
and after 1900 hung on through attempts to tax and vote them out of
existence. The economic facts of life began to shift in favor of the wets,
and in 1910 Henry defended the decision to license at least one saloon in
Coon Rapids because "there is not at present any other way to raise
sufficient funds with which to conduct the town's business."

Henry was also offended by the saloon-crashing tactics of the Anti-
Saloon League, finding himself in the position of "a reformer trying to
reform the reformers," and was deeply hurt by the league's condemnation
of Coon Rapids as a "vile and lawless town." Certain as he may have been
in his moral convictions, Henry was not a zealot. He knew when to let a
thing go, when to laugh, and when to exercise tolerance and common
sense. His sense of community was strong and productive, and if his
notion of the morality that should prevail in Coon Rapids seems rigid in
retrospect, there existed in the man a delight in the company of his fellows and great faith in their capacity for achievement. Of his love for the
town he served so well for a lifetime, there is no doubt.

MORE than one hundred years before Edward rode his horse to the banks
of the River Coon, De Walt Garst and his wife Maria emigrated to
America from Alsace-Lorraine. Like many Lorrainers, De Walt was of
German lineage and had no desire to serve in the army of the French king
Louis XV. To escape conscription by the king's agents, De Walt emigrated three years after his marriage, taking passage to the English colony of Pennsylvania in 1753. In 1775, doing for General George Washington and the colonies what he would not do for Louis and France, he
became a private at the age of fifty in the Eighth Company, Second Bat-
talion of the Lancaster County Militia and was among those who, as the

Pennsylvania Archives phrased it, "assisted in establishing American independence."

Maria died in 1788, De Walt in 1789. They left five sons; the two eldest, liable to a draft for service with the British Army in 1775, reverted to the earlier family tradition and disappeared into the mountainous wilderness of southwestern Virginia. After the deaths of their parents, the three younger sons followed their brothers into Virginia, where presumably they farmed. In the early years of the nineteenth century, some of this second generation and most of the third left Virginia for Ohio and Indiana. Family biographer Horace Garst attributed this movement to an aversion to slavery, a motive for westward movement that occurs rather frequently during this period, but we cannot discount an aversion to mountainous wilderness or simply to worn-out land.

Two third-generation brothers, Elias (1807–59) and Michael (1815–1901), were especially close. Elias moved to Ohio and took up the practice of medicine; Michael, Roswell's paternal grandfather, followed his brother to that state and also into a medical career. Working his way through college by teaching in country schools and doing odd jobs during vacations, Michael took his medical degee in Pennsylvania at Jefferson College in 1837, went into practice, and married in 1840. He and his wife Maria had six sons and two daughters.

Considering their time, place, and circumstances, the most remarkable achievement of Michael and Maria lay in sending five of their children to universities or military academies. Maria was chiefly responsible for this effort; she journeyed to Washington to obtain from her senator the two military appointments that brought a free education, placed one son in an eastern university, and two other children in the newer schools in the Midwest. Roswell's uncle Perry graduated from Annapolis, distinguished himself in the Spanish-American War, and retired with the rank of rear admiral. Uncle Charles graduated from West Point but gave up a military career to devote his life to missionary work in Japan, where he died. Uncle Julius attended the Johns Hopkins University and became a doctor. He then worked in a room behind the Garst Store to perfect pheno-caffeine, a headache powder, which made him a rich man; subsequently he became a land speculator. Aunt Mary was among the first women to graduate from Northwestern University, and Edward, Roswell's father, graduated from the University of Michigan. Those of Roswell's uncles and aunts who did not go to college were also an uncommon lot: Laura married a career army officer, Morrison became an extremely successful salesman and man of property, and Warren went on from E. and W. Garst to state politics and eventually to the governorship of Iowa in 1908.

In 1857 Michael's medical practice in Dayton, Ohio, began to suffer, apparently because of the financial panic of that year. He decided to leave his profession, move to Illinois, and take up a commercial life. He sold some land he acquired when times were good, used the proceeds to buy a stock of merchandise for a general store, and went into business. However, the new venture failed to improve his fortunes; Edward later wrote of his father: "having had no experience in that line, the venture was a failure. We soon had a stock of remnants on hand." Michael was one of the few Garsts with neither luck nor a knack for business.

However, his son Edward possessed these gifts in abundance. Born in 1843 when the family still lived in Ohio, he moved with them to Champaign, Illinois, and was sent to the University of Michigan in 1861. In the spring of 1862 he enlisted in the Union Army, in which his father was already serving as a surgeon, contracted malaria, and after a year's illness was invalided out of the service. He returned to Michigan to complete his degree at war's end. At the same time Edward's father moved further west to a farm near Boone, Iowa, in another attempt to recoup his affluence, and it was here that Edward rejoined him for a time before setting out for Coon Rapids.

Years later, looking back on his friend's career, S. D. Henry remembered that Edward

came to Coon Rapids in 1869, a comparatively poor man but by being long-headed, an excellent judge of human nature, capable of seeing a good thing a long way off, possessing uncommon tack and an abundance of "mother's wit," he climbed up along with the growth of the country, making money and friends rapidly.

With some goods in hand and the five hundred dollars borrowed from his grandfather, he moved into what he described as "a plank storeroom" for which he paid no rent, slept on a mattress under his counter because he could find no lodgings in the little settlement, and spent money only for meals. He sold at a profit of 50 percent, and, as he wrote in 1903, "my stock began to thicken from the start."

Edward looked back with nostalgia on those early years in the old town. "During these years I was one of the people," he recalled. "I attended the dances, kissing bees, singing schools and revivals. I had as much fun as anybody." In Edward's view, James Whitcomb Riley's poem "The Little Town O' Tailholt" captured Coon Rapids in the period before the railroad came through, and he reprinted the poem in the booklet he and Warren published in 1919 to celebrate the fiftieth anniversary of the Garst Store. Two stanzas seem particularly pertinent:

> They hain't no style in our town—hit's little-like and small,
> There hain't no churches neither—jes' the meetin-house is all;
> There's no sidewalks, to speak of—but the highway's allus free,
> And the little Town o' Tailholt is wide enough for me.

> Some find it discomodin'-like, I'm willing to admit,
> To hev but one Post Office, and a womern keepin' hit,
> And the drug store, and a shoe shop, and a grocery, all three,
> But the little Town o' Tailholt is handy 'nough for me.

In a letter to Roswell in 1929, Horace Garst provided some verification for these lines as a description of Coon Rapids:

About 1872 I was travelling through Iowa selling dry goods for a wholesale house in New York City. That was before the railroad was built through Coon Rapids. I got off with two big sample trunks—from the cars at Glidden and engaged a team to take me down to Coon Rapids. Oh, but the mud was soft! I think there was only about two buildings there at that time and everybody wore rubber boots.

In the great debate over the town name Edward told S. D. Henry that the name Coon Rapids "suits me just fine," a sentiment echoed as well in Riley's poem:

> You kin smile and turn your nose up, and joke and hev your fun,
> And laugh and holler "Tailholts is better holts n'none."
> Ef the city suits you better, why hit's where you'd ort a be,
> But the little Town o' Tailholt's good enough for me.

During these years Michael and Maria were struggling along in the aftermath of yet another business failure and came to rely upon Edward more and more. He had numerous calls from them for help, and he was always able to send what they asked for. "They fell under the delusion that I had a gold mine at Coon Rapids. It cost me something to keep up the delusion," he admitted, "but I rather enjoyed it, and as I had no other expense, I let the money go rather freely."

As his profits mounted, Edward began early to acquire the abundantly available land in the surrounding countryside. In Illinois and Iowa alone, federal surveyors had platted 71,500 acres of land, which in the 1840s and after could be bought in 160-acre lots or more from the government for as little as $1.25 per acre outside of transportation grants to the railroad and $2.50 within. Consequently, homesteads could be purchased for as little as $100.00 or $200.00, with a further small outlay for building a log cabin and buying a plow and horses. As late as the 1860s and 1870s land around Coon Rapids was available for from $5.00 to $8.00 per acre because it was still relatively distant from a railroad and lacked timber for building cabins and fences. It was a hard life and a number of early settlers around Coon Rapids gave up, often coming into Edward's store, where they bought their supplies, to announce that they were moving back to Ohio or Indiana. Edward would frequently either buy the land from them for cash, or offer to outfit the family with new clothes, trunks, and suitcases to enable them to arrive home with dignity, taking in return their title to the farm and assuming the debts they owed. Roswell estimated that his father owned approximately 10,000 acres of land by the time the Milwaukee Railroad came through Coon Rapids.

By his own account, when the railroad approached Coon Rapids in 1882, Edward had about eight thousand dollars worth of stock and had gathered in "two or three pieces of land." A former classmate of Edward's at Michigan supervised the engineering work for the Milwaukee road, and through him Edward learned the location of the station for the new town. He bought 120 acres around the spot and acted as confidential agent for the railroad in securing land for town sites and selling lots. He estimated that he earned about ten thousand dollars in this capacity. According to Roswell, during this period Edward sold 5,000 acres of his farmland, used the proceeds to pay off the mortgage on the remaining 5,000, and bought land himself in the new town and further afield. Because of the rise in prices that accompanied the prosperity brought by the railroad, Edward could now buy a farm, hold on to it until prices rose, borrow on the increased value, then buy another. Within fifteen years he had become a substantial landholder but remained always a speculator rather than a farmer.

Although Edward's humor ran to laconic understatement and droll irony, it could also be the weapon of a man who did not like to be interfered with in the pursuit of his interests, as the Masons discovered when he moved his part of the building to the new town. In 1871 Edward became the town postmaster, an office that he held proudly but informally by keeping the mail in a cracker tin, allowing the residents to sift through the contents to find their own letters. When he joined forces with Warren in 1874, however, he built a proper mailroom. When a change in administration (though not in party) brought with it a rival for the post, Edward took steps to dispose of this challenge to his position in the town. Seeing his rival dressed for a day's fishing in overalls with turned-up legs, a straw hat perched on his head, and a fishing pole resting on one shoulder, Edward—with his unsuspecting opponent's permission—took a photograph, sent one copy to his rival and one to the central post office in Des Moines. "This is the fellow running against me for the postmaster job," he scrawled on the back of the card to Des Moines, and he kept his job until the election of a Democratic administration in 1885.

Edward was willing to devote time to dealings in land, to advertising, and to the physical improvement of the store but not to bookkeeping and the trivia of administration. According to Lee Miller, one of the earliest employees of the store and later an owner, when it was time to take inventory, Edward would walk up one aisle and down the other, look around a bit, then say, "Well, it looks like we're just about the same as we were last year." He brought this informal and ambulatory manner into town affairs as well on one occasion at a meeting of leading citizens who gathered to plot the length and width of the new main street. Edward noticed a man driving a carriage and horses, called the man over, and told him to turn his team around in a tight circle. "That's how wide main street ought to be," he told his fellows, and that is how wide they made it.

Edward used his wealth for further investment in land, a comfortable house and modern store, and for helping his family, but in his personal habits he remained a frugal man. In his store he wore inexpensive clothes and a little skull cap, but his second wife Bertha saw to it that he was presentable for their social life. She insisted that he buy good quality clothes, and Lee Miller remembers Edward picking out a one-dollar straw hat in the store to wear to a social function. "Well, Bertha won't like *this*," he said, looking at the price. He marked it up to four dollars and wore it home.

He first met his second wife in 1879 during a visit to Northwestern University to see his sister Mary, whose education he may have been helping to finance. Bertha Goodwin was her roommate. "I took a shine to her," Edward wrote, "and hoped as she was so friendly to my sister she might be a little bit friendly to me." But it was not yet to be, Edward admitted, and he "went back to Coon Rapids and kept on sawing wood." He was a bachelor for the next eight years, but in 1887 married Nettie Burton, a union that lasted only a year, cut off by Nettie's death in childbirth in 1888. A pious and respected lady, she had during her brief time in Coon Rapids organized the first Chatauqua Circle and had been a pillar of her church and community.

A year later, in 1889, Edward once again proposed to Bertha, who had been teaching for ten years in Illinois, and this time he was successful. "Circumstances over which I had no control," he wrote,

brought me again to the home of Bertha Goodwin in 1889. Whether it was because I now lived on a trunk line railroad and was worth thirty thousand dollars or what, I don't know. At any rate she weakened and so we were married.

Bertha was born in Oxford, England, in 1855, to the wife of Samuel Goodwin, himself born of a prosperous merchant family of Kidderminster and partner for many years with his father in the grain and flour mill operated by his family for two hundred years. In 1854 he had married a woman of a lower social class, and two years later, angered by his family's hostility toward her, emigrated to Chicago to enter the grain business. Once in America he bought a 325-acre farm instead, near Rockford, Illinois, and purchased as well 15 acres of land near the town center. Samuel lived to the age of ninety-one, until May 1917, and was a frequent visitor to Coon Rapids. Editor Henry explained that "in politics Mr. Goodwin was a republican and became intensely American," so much so that on his eightieth birthday he was presented with an American flag, with the inscription "Presented to a Good American Made of English Stuff."

Bertha cared as much about education as had Maria Garst, and was proud of her place in the first class at Northwestern that had graduated women. Speaking at a reunion in Des Moines in 1910, Bertha recalled that her class of 1878 consisted of twenty-three men and four women. The women had lived in Willard Hall, named after Frances Willard, the distinguished educator and dean of the Women's Department of Northwestern, whom Bertha had come to know through older students. The student body was a close-knit, happy society, proud of the quality of their institution. "Northwestern," Bertha recalled,

was even so long ago considered a strong and rich institution. It owned valuable property in Chicago, yielding good income so that tuition was not high and the school well equipped. I tell you these things that you may understand it was a good college though our numbers were few.

Her first refusal of Edward seems to have been rooted in a strong feeling of vocation and a determination to pursue an independent professional life. When she finally accepted Edward, a similar sense of the responsibilities as well as the privileges of her education fortified her in her role as a social and cultural leader in Coon Rapids. She had intelligence, energy, and a degree of compassion and humor that were perhaps overshadowed at times by her rather formidable public manner. She was certainly not overbearing physically, but rather was slight in build and crippled by one short leg. She was handsome rather than pretty and brought into the family the characteristic square jaw and strong features of the Garst face.

Within a year of her arrival in Coon Rapids she was well established in civic and religious affairs, all fulsomely reported by Henry, who was one of her greatest admirers. She took a keen interest in the school, entertaining the new teachers, and in the Presbyterian church, raising funds for the minister's salary. She entertained often, not uncommonly in large numbers. She also travelled for extended periods to Rockford to care for her parents or with Edward, and in 1904 she took her father and her three oldest children to the World's Fair in St. Louis.

As guardian of the public good, she was as active as Henry, and perhaps even more effective in her mode of operation. Advised that the local butcher was failing to maintain adequate standards of hygiene, she visited his shop and told him to clean it up within three days if he wished to avoid an official visit by the health authorities. He complied, and Bertha returned to pronounce the shop in order. On another occasion at the opera house she refused to allow a play to begin until the rear exit, blocked with pasteboard boxes and therefore inadequate as a fire escape, was cleared out.

Of his uncles and aunts, it was Warren who most influenced young Roswell, not only because of his proximity, but also because of his personal qualities and political convictions. Although Edward and Warren always remained friendly, their interests began to diverge after an initially close working relationship. Edward was content with his land speculation and his store, avoided politics, and did not engage in controversy unless it affected these specific interests. In their business relationship especially, Warren complemented his brother: he was the buyer for the Garst Store; he took matters such as the inventory more seriously; and he was also interested in property speculation, acting often as seller of the land he and Edward had bought.

However, Warren's social and political ambitions exceeded those of Edward. In the debate over the town's name, Edward, it may be recalled, thought that Coon Rapids "suited him just fine"; Warren, on the other hand, declared the name to be "utterly outrageous" and stood behind Henry's efforts to have it changed. Once he acquired a firm economic base, Warren began to look beyond the town, and by 1888 was a regular member of the Republican state congressional convention. In 1893 he was elected state senator, which meant among other things residence in Des Moines for six months every two years. In 1894, the year the Garst Store celebrated its twenty-fifth anniversary, Henry reported that "Senator Garst had the pleasure of attending the McKinley banquet in Des Moines last week and reports it a grand affair." Warren served with distinction as chairman of the senate committee on appropriations and rose steadily in the estimation of his party and his constituency. In 1904 approximately one thousand people gathered in the Coon Rapids opera house to pay their respects to the senator and Mrs. Garst. In 1906, after twelve years in the senate, he became lieutenant governor, and when Albert Cummins resigned his governorship in 1908 to become a United States senator, Warren became governor.

Warren's wife Clara was another formidable country lady, hostess, and lecturer. She entertained on a more extensive scale than Bertha, lectured at Sunday schools, and was an ardent clubwoman. Henry reported that the Des Moines *Register & Leader* contained a three-column picture of her, "and also an extended history of this excellent and much loved woman," of which Henry offered his Coon Rapids readers a condensation. When Warren's term as governor ended in 1910, he and Clara remained residents of Des Moines, returning in the summer to what was now a vacation residence in Coon Rapids, travelling at times to Lake Okoboji with the Edward Garst family.

Warren's political career coincided with the growing split between the conservative and progressive wings of the Republican party, a struggle that in the first decade of the twentieth century made Iowa second in

political ferment in the Midwest only to Wisconsin, the home of Robert
M. LaFollette. The victory of the Republican party under McKinley in
1896 defeated not only the Democrats but struck down the Populist
movement as well. The fate of such proposals as a more plentiful currency, reform of the railroads and their rate structure, and other Demo-
cratic/Populist initiatives now lay with the progressive wing of the Republican party. In Iowa, Albert Baird Cummins became the spokesman
for such reforms, and in the United States Senate, John Dolliver of Iowa
led the Republican progressives.

Cummins began his career as a corporation lawyer in Des Moines,
and first attracted attention when he represented the Grange against a
firm controlling the market in barbed wire in 1884. He became a state
legislator in 1888, began to support progressive causes, and gathered
around him a group of influential supporters including Warren Garst,
Fred Maytag of Newton, and Frederick M. Hubbell, founder of the Equitable Life Insurance Company and the wealthiest Iowan of his time. Cummins, also wealthy, had no special ties to small farmers or laborers and
was by background and temperament, according to Leland Sage, "a
rather aloof, fastidious man of elegant tastes and patrician manner," a
member of Des Moines' most exclusive clubs. However, after he was
elected governor in 1902, he set in motion a program of reform that
brought important changes in the direction and spirit of state government
in Iowa. He sought to impose heavier taxation upon the railroads, sharply
curtailed the free-pass system affecting important local citizens (among
them Edward Garst), banned contributions by corporations to political
candidates, regulated – with the approbation of Hubbell – insurance companies more closely, and established direct primary elections. In Washington, Dolliver led the fight for federal regulation of the railroads and at the
Republican national convention campaigned unsuccessfully for a moderate tariff plank in the party platform.

In 1908, Cummins won the Senate seat that became available when
William Allison died, and Warren served as governor for the two years of
Cummins' unexpired term. Warren carried on the Cummins program in
state government, devoting particular effort to legislation for workmen's
compensation and insurance, but was defeated in the party primary election of 1910 by a conservative Republican and held no more elective
offices. However, in the next government he organized the state's first
Department of Labor and became its first commissioner, working for this
hitherto unrepresented constituency in the face of strong opposition from
elements of his own party. During his political career, Warren supported
the passage of laws enabling farming areas to be drained, legislation
which was especially helpful for the development of northwest Iowa, the
last area in the state to become intensively farmed.

Shortly before his death in October 1924 Warren made one of his regular visits to Coon Rapids and mused retrospectively to Henry about his political career. He could have made more money by sticking to his business, he said, but told Henry that his terms in office had been "socially and educationally enjoyable and valuable." When he visited Roswell and Elizabeth in the early twenties, he would talk politics occasionally, but preferred to socialize, sing, and recite poetry. He made a point of visiting during threshing season to taste the food and to make much of Elizabeth Garst's cooking. In the lengthy obituaries occasioned by his death, he was praised for his fairness, honesty, good humor, and ability. Until the end, the Des Moines *Tribune* noted, "and in a quiet, logical, impressive way," he remained "a force for humanity, optimism and faith in democracy."

Warren was the only uncle to live in Coon Rapids, but by no means the single relative available to Roswell. In addition to the parents on each side of the family, all Edward's remaining brothers and sisters visited the town at one time or another, and Edward reciprocated. Roswell grew up in a family often widely separated geographically, but always close-knit and interested in one another. In Coon Rapids the collective interests of the Garsts centered on land and commerce but also encompassed a family ethic of civic responsibility, political reform, activism, and ambition. They attached great importance to participation in community life, upon whose resources they drew and to which they contributed profoundly. Roswell, steeped in affection and respect for both town and family, was nourished by that dual influence throughout his life.

C H A P T E R   T W O

The Earliest Years

Growing Up: 1898–1922

Edward brought Bertha to Coon Rapids in 1889. In October 1891 their first son, Goodwin, was born, followed by Jonathan in 1893, Dorothy in 1895, and Roswell on 17 June, 1898. On the occasion of Roswell's birth, S. D. Henry, who had recorded all the Garst births in the *Enterprise,* noted:

A nice little boy was born to Mr. & Mrs. E. Garst Monday morning. Of course Mr. Garst is greatly delighted and presumably will name it Dewey or Hobson. However, it might be best to wait till the war is over and then name it after the greatest hero.

Edward, perhaps taking up Henry's badinage, chose a name for his youngest son that reflected the delighted father's commercial interests. Following his brother Julius's example, Edward had just purchased land in Roswell, New Mexico, and named his son with this latest piece of speculation in mind.

Goodwin and Jonathan were sent to Rockford for their grade and high school educations; Dorothy and Roswell followed them for some period but appear to have spent more time in the Coon Rapids schools. Bertha had taught in Rockford for several years and thought well of the quality of the school. Furthermore, her parents and her sister Ida still lived there and could provide a foster home for the children. There has always been speculation in the family that the strain of the children on the nerves of their elderly parents may have been part of the reason for the sojourns in Rockford, which may be true. However, Edward and Bertha cared very much for their children and wished to give them as broad and humane an education as possible. In 1903, Edward wrote of his children:

We have three sons and one daughter. Our two older boys go to school in Rockford, Ill. They sing in the Episcopal choir, dance in the Union Church and practice in the YMCA gymnasium. They help their grandfather raise strawberries and their aunt raise incubator chickens, and market the same. We think they are absorbing useful knowledge right along.

If there is a pedagogical theory behind these remarks it might be summarized as a sufficiency of education, a modicum of work and religion, an amplitude of fun, and the acquisition of practical business sense. These rules embody Edward's personal development and, along with his affection for his children, are to be found in other comments of his on education. In 1908, while mastering the typewriter, he wrote seventeen-year-old Goodwin in Rockford:

You need not feel bad that you do not stand at the head of your class. I never did but at the age of sixty-four I believe I stand near the head. Our class poet started out rich but went broke within five years after he graduated. Some of the others started poor and got rich; but I think I stand well to the front, so take it easy and don't worry. . . . I hope you manage to have some fun somehow. I think it is more important than great learning. We do not want you to be a school teacher.

Edward asked Goodwin to send him any church or theater programs and inquired about his son's horse-back riding. He approved of Goodwin's interest in good clothes and noted a five-hundred dollar trade in his store the day before. "I wish you had a typewriter," he concluded, "this is an Oliver number 5. They claim it is one of the best made."

By 1908 ten-year-old Roswell was going to school in Coon Rapids, and Edward wrote to Bertha's sister Ida that "Roswell had a fine teacher and we think she will be promoted up with him." To Roswell, his father was a grandfatherly figure, a man of leisurely habits, given to aphoristic lectures. When Roswell was fifteen, his father was seventy, which Roswell recalled many years later as "exactly the right age differential for lectures to be impressive." Although he was undoubtedly an active man intellectually and physically, old age and recurring malaria slowed him down by the time his children were growing up, and he affected a philosophy of leisure to match his condition. "I received your letter," he wrote to Goodwin in 1908,

stating that your grand-father was going to put out more strawberries. I think that it is a mistake. It takes too much work to raise strawberries; I would put the place out to grass. What is the use of working ourselves to death? We die soon enough anyhow. I would keep a few cows and a few chickens and put in most of my time buggy-riding or automobile riding. What time is left for your grandfather should be spent hunting and nothing else.

The aphorisms voiced by his father that Roswell most liked to quote were "never stand up when you can sit down, never sit down when you can lie down," and "the day is for rest—the night is for sleeping." In addition to such pronouncements on the human condition, Edward's lectures contained the distillation of his business experience and his knowledge of land values. His business activities during the last years of his life con-

sisted of going to the store at 10 A.M., looking at the mail, and taking a
deposit of cash to the bank twice daily. His other daily occupation was
that which he had suggested for his father-in-law, a buggy ride known as
the four-mile drive–a route which took him north to the George farm,
over to the old Galloway bridge, around the back of the town, and home.
The duty of driving Edward fell to Lee Miller when he worked in the
store, occasionally to Bertha, and eventually to Elizabeth during the last
two years of his life.

Edward was liberal with his children's educational expenses and
spending money, usually giving them more than they asked for. He taught
them to swim, hunt, and recite poetry, while he sang, whistled, and spent
a considerable amount of time on his front porch in a rocking chair. The
children shared his sense of humor and interest in the vagaries of human
behavior, which remained with him to the end. One of the last entries that
he made in his journal repeated a story he heard from his daughter
Dorothy, then living in Oklahoma with her husband Jack Chrystal.
Dorothy reported that in their town there were two newspapers–one was
Republican in its editorial policy, the other Democratic; both were owned
by the same man. Edward was much amused.

Bertha took the central role in organizing the household and regulat-
ing Roswell's duties, with the general approbation of Edward. In the
evenings, when supper and chores were completed, Bertha would call
Roswell and the remaining children home to sit with their father to hear
her read Dickens, Shakespeare, and other writers for her husband's pleasure and the children's edification. One of Roswell's duties was to take the
family cow to pasture just outside of town every morning and bring her
back in the evening; another was to meet the 4 A.M. train on Sunday
morning, which brought the preacher to Bertha's church. Bertha prohib-
ited corncob fights between Roswell and Jonathan but encouraged the
appropriate kind of cardplaying. "We had a game of whist last night,"
Edward wrote to Goodwin. "The last hand Roswell had six trumps and
swept the platter." Roswell at the age of six travelled with his father to
New Mexico and Illinois and that same year was taken by his mother to
the World's Fair in St. Louis.

In 1912 Roswell entered Coon Rapids High School, did well in his
studies, performed in school plays, and became captain of the football
team. He was generally gregarious and especially friendly with Charley
Rippey, a farm boy. Together they took their girl friends by horse and
buggy to barn dances around the countryside, to lantern-slide shows in
country schoolhouses, and occasionally by train to other towns. They
embarked on the Belle of the Coon, which operated on Sundays and on
the Fourth of July, taking passengers to the dance pavilion at the Gallo-

way bridge. There were more journeys with his parents, brothers, and sister, and in 1915 he travelled with Charley Cretsinger to the World Exposition in California.

Roswell grew up in harmony with his town and his family. He slipped comfortably into the social patterns of life in Coon Rapids and in general accepted its mores, with certain exceptions. Although he did not drink at home, he was never puritannical about liquor in S. D. Henry's fashion and would take refreshment when the social context required it. He did not "take up" religion. However, he was an admirer of the aging Henry, especially of his wit, and he liked to quote from the *Enterprise* one of Henry's best known bits of waggishness: "An airplane flew over Coon Rapids last Thursday. There was no apparent motion of the wings." As a young man, Roswell was already interested in the history of Coon Rapids, and that of his family; for the rest of his life he was an authority on both. He seems to have found in his circumstances fertile seed ground for growth. His memory of his youth was of "an easy, lazy life."

His relations with Dorothy and Jonathan were close, but not so with Goodwin, whom he remembered as something of a loner. In the pages of the *Enterprise,* Goodwin appears to be at one with the social, business-oriented nature of his family. He gave parties, did some singing, went to a college in Illinois for a time, then graduated from Grinnell in 1915. He came back to Coon Rapids, took his place in the Garst store, married, and with his wife entered into the social and cultural life of the town. However, just before his father's death in 1923 he sold his interest in the store to John Miller, moved to Rockford, then to Chicago. He became increasingly radicalized in his political opinions, rejected his background completely, deserted his wife and children, joined the Communist Party, and disappeared in the East, not to be heard of again until 1943.

Dorothy graduated from Grinnell in 1915, after an unhappy term at Rockford College, and four years later married Jack Chrystal, the son of a U.S. Marshal in the Oklahoma territory, a gifted story-teller, and eventually an Iowa state senator. A cheerful, engaging person, Dorothy was very close to Elizabeth until her own untimely death from pneumonia in 1936. She left a daughter, Virginia, and two sons, John and Tom. Jack later married Julia Shaefer, a high school Latin teacher.

Roswell formed his closest brotherly relationship with Jonathan. Brilliant, personable, witty, and tall, with a square jaw and aquiline nose similar to Roswell's, Jonathan was away at the University of Wisconsin while Roswell was in high school. In 1915 he graduated, announced he was going to be a farmer, and took a job on a farm in Illinois at twenty-five dollars per week. Shortly thereafter he returned to Coon Rapids, where — joined for a time by Roswell in the summer of 1916 — he farmed

200 acres just outside of town that his father had owned for some time, known then as the Apple Farm, later to become the Garst farm. Johnny's earliest surviving letter was written to his father during his sophomore year at Wisconsin. Entitled "A Strictly Business Letter," it read: "Dear sir, Your son Jonathan needs some money. (signed) Your Son Jonathan." Such requests became a regular event in Jonathan's early life, and, in later years, were addressed to Roswell.

Johnny later described his farming with Roswell as "old-time Americana" in style and speculated that Thomas Jefferson would have felt "very much at home" on Apple Farm. Farm implements had improved since Jefferson's time, but they were still pulled by horses in 1915, Johnny explained, and Jefferson "would have had no trouble in understanding how every tool worked." Johnny and Roswell planted oats with clover in April and corn in May. They harvested the hay in June and cut the oats with a binder in July. Corn picking started in October and lasted "half the winter." It was not entirely a rustic society, Johnny noted. "We had books and read them. If someone started quoting a poem, there was someone around who could finish it."

In the fall of 1916, Roswell left Jonathan on the farm and entered Iowa State College at Ames along with three of his classmates, described by Henry on their departure as "stirring and promising boys." However, compared with his practical work on the farm, he found the agricultural course uninteresting and his fraternity brothers dull. After one semester he came home and told his parents that Ames was not sufficiently challenging. In January 1917 he tried Johnny's school, Wisconsin, but by April had once again lost interest. War was declared during the term, and Roswell discovered that if he could prove that it was necessary for him to return to the farm immediately, he could get credit for a full semester. Jonathan wrote a cooked-up letter to him about their need to increase the acreage and livestock, and Roswell came home to farm from April to August.

That summer of 1917 Johnny enlisted and was sent to France with the Thirty-fifth Division. There followed an anxious period in which the family heard nothing from him. "Jonathan Garst has not been heard from for sometime," Henry reported somberly. "He has been in the heaviest fighting for months." When a cable and letters finally came, Bertha was ecstatic. "We have been crazy to hear," she wrote to her sister Ida. "Really had a notion to telegraph to you." Always a prolific letter writer himself, Jonathan spent the next year and a half writing to his relations as regularly as he could, asking for scientific books from his parents, describing flowers for his aunts, and relating agricultural practices he had seen to Roswell.

Jonathan and Roswell had discussed a farming partnership at least as early as 1916. Of their experience during that year and the next, Jonathan wrote in 1917 from France: "We have had a lot of fun and good experience and not unprofitable labor there. We ought to be ready for bigger fields when we start again." They discussed in letters their next start throughout Johnny's term of service; Roswell was especially interested in Canada. Early in 1918 Jonathan advised that they temporize:

I do not have any idea how long this war will last, but it is pretty safe to say I will not be ready for anything until 1920 and you probably a year after that. . . . You know if we spend any time over here after the war I am going to try and get a permit to go to Oxford so as not to waste my time in the Army.

After Jonathan enlisted, Roswell, probably under pressure from his parents, decided to try Ames again, entering as a sophomore in the fall of 1917. Iowa State was a land-grant college and required two years of military training for all its graduates. Roswell quickly lost his patience over a foolish difficulty with his uniform—he had brought a cap from the different uniform at Wisconsin—and refused to take military training, renouncing his intention to graduate. He stayed on as a special student in agricultural journalism, which enabled him to take whatever courses he wished. He returned home in the spring of 1918.

By now, food production had achieved a high priority. With Jonathan away, Roswell was able to farm for a year with his parents' blessing until the following spring of 1919, several months after the end of the war. His parents still wanted him to get a degree, however. This time they suggested Northwestern, Bertha's alma mater, which in Edward's view offered the practical inducement of proximity to Chicago, a city he thought Roswell should get to know. Roswell dutifully set off in 1919 but stuck it out for only one quarter. Meanwhile, after a year at the University of Edinburgh instead of Oxford, Jonathan returned home and travelled to Canada to farm. Roswell went back to Ames in the fall and remained until the spring of 1920 but still did not take a degree. He left in the summer to join Johnny in Canada.

For the Roswell anxious to strike out into the commercial agricultural world, the move to Canada must have been a relief after his collegiate comings and goings. For the Roswell who wished to please his parents and valued education himself, his failure to obtain a university degree was a matter of regret for the rest of his life. He made a good story of it, yet spoke often and with pride of the general level of education in his family. This lack of a college degree made him eager to prove himself as good as or superior to academicians; it generated much of his sometimes excessive belligerence towards academic authority on agricultural matters and helped make him the iconoclast he often was in his field. However, beneath this bravado lay envy and at times excessive respect for

education, especially for the labels of degrees. Fortunately, these conflicting feelings produced positive achievements rather than destructive deni-
gration. He created lasting personal and professional relationships with
university researchers, did more than any other farmer in the Midwest to
see that the fruits of academic research were put to practical use on the
farm, and in the process he matured as an independent thinker.

In 1919, however, his aim was simply to farm with Johnny in Canada.
The choice of territory was similar to that of Edward and Warren, who
had bought property east of Winnipeg before the war and later sold it at a
good profit as prized farmland. As soon as he returned from Scotland,
Johnny bought 1000 acres at thirty dollars per acre, making a down payment of ten thousand dollars. It was a promising venture; agriculture was
still in its wartime boom, and flax (his principal crop) was selling for three
dollars per bushel. The two brothers broke the new soil, planted their
crops, and settled in as homesteaders. In the evenings they talked and
read. Johnny brought along a set of the *Encyclopedia Britannica,* and
during his stay in Canada got through the letter *M.* Roswell's reading is
not recorded.

The collapse of the agricultural market in 1920–21 brought an end to
this idyll. Flax dropped in price to one dollar per bushel, and land values
dropped just as precipitously. Roswell apparently saw the end coming
more quickly than Johnny and returned home in the spring of 1921, less
than a year after his arrival. He repurchased his machinery and corn on
the Garst farm from his tenant for considerably less than he had sold
them and started farming again at home. Jonathan stuck it out until 1922
and then gave up. He persuaded the Iowa investment company from
whom he had purchased his Canadian land to keep the down payment and
take back the land, an easy way out of a potentially greater financial
difficulty. During the year he farmed while Jonathan was in the army,
Roswell made ten thousand dollars, so they came out about even financially. Although Roswell would from time to time hope otherwise, it was
the first and last cooperative farming venture in which the brothers
engaged.

Marriage and the Des Moines Years: 1921–30

By spring 1921 Roswell was back home on the 200-acre farm just out
of town, looking for opportunities to make money in a farm economy that
had declined severely after the loss of the wartime export market. He
discovered he could sell milk to Jens Jensen at the Coon Rapids creamery
for $2 per hundredweight, which would earn him about $160 per year per
cow, and went into the dairy business with a herd of sixteen or eighteen
cows. He milked his cows by hand, loaded the milk cans in an old pickup

truck, and delivered them to the dairy. He lived alone on the farm, cooked for himself after a fashion, and consumed prodigious amounts of milk and butter. He travelled to Wisconsin that year with some other Coon Rapids farmers to purchase more cows and took a fishing trip to Minnesota with Lee Miller.

That summer he also paid some attention to a girl from Spencer, Iowa, who attended summer school at Harlan. Accompanied by Lee, Roswell drove to Harlan later in the summer to visit her, only to find that she had become engaged to someone else. However, Elizabeth Henak, a blind date arranged for Lee, proved a far greater attraction for Roswell, and after he returned to Coon Rapids, he embarked upon his first significant campaign of persuasion—the courtship of Elizabeth. Elizabeth Henak was of Bohemian stock, born and raised in the Czech colony of Oxford Junction, Iowa. She had not known her father, an alcoholic of violent temperament whom her mother had left when Elizabeth was a small child. She grew up with a brother, sister, and her strong, hard-working mother in straitened financial circumstances. After high school, Elizabeth borrowed enough money to enroll in a small college, then transferred to the Iowa Normal School at Cedar Falls (now the University of Northern Iowa). After two years at the normal school she left to teach and eventually returned to the University of Iowa to take her B.A. degree. She had been teaching for two years at Cedar Falls when she met Roswell, and during the summer of 1921 she taught in the summer school. Her education and professional competence were doubtless part of her attraction for Roswell. Elizabeth was immediately attracted to him as well, but at the same time she was a reluctant participant in Roswell's speedy and aggressive courtship of the next few months.

After their first meeting, Roswell made a date to drive the fifty miles from Coon Rapids to Harlan to see Elizabeth, but heavy rains made the roads impassable. Instead, he sent a telegram from the railroad station telling her that he had been looking at the moon but discovered that one pair of eyes was not enough for such a sight. When the roads dried, he concluded on a practical note, he would be down. The telegram reached Elizabeth's principal, who could not resist calling her out of class and reading it to her. Elizabeth was furious and immediately wrote Roswell demanding that he send her no more telegrams. Roswell replied—by telegram—that he did not care who knew his feelings for her but agreed that Western Union should have given the telegram to her alone. However, these exchanges were merely the opening salvoes in a campaign of telegrams that continued to arrive after she returned to Cedar Falls and her regular teaching job. She got a night letter every Sunday morning, and Roswell acquired an ally in the person of the telegraph operator at Cedar Falls, who would often preface the Sunday-morning call to Elizabeth

with, "Hey, I got a really good one tonight, Miss Henak, listen to this!"
Roswell travelled to Cedar Falls as often as he could, quoted poetry, sang
the ballads of his favorite songwriter Jerome Kern, and did a lot of fast
talking.

Elizabeth began to soften, but, made uneasy by Roswell's confident
personality and doubtful about giving up her career for married life on a
farm, she postponed a decision. She asked for six more months to pay the
last of her school and medical bills, but Roswell was in no mood to temporize and finally obtained from her an affirmative answer to his proposal.
However, she almost reneged after the invitations had been sent, calling
to say that she had to see him. When they met in Des Moines, Roswell
asked her what was wrong. "It's your . . . shirts," she said, in a paroxysm
of doubt, "I just can't marry you." His practice of wearing a plaid shirt
over a white one, tucked into his trousers, was for him a mark of his
individuality, and, as Elizabeth recounted later, "symbolic" for her.
Roswell chose to take her statement at face value and walked her to the
nearest clothing store. "This girl is going to marry me," he told the clerk,
"but she's decided not to because of my shirts. So get out the shirts and
we'll let her pick them out." Elizabeth capitulated, and they were married
in January 1922.

Life in Coon Rapids did not begin without difficulties for the bride. In
preparation for her arrival, Roswell had his bachelor's house on the farm
painted and wallpapered, but when Elizabeth looked inside the little
house and saw the ill-matched and slap-dash decoration, she burst into
tears. Roswell promised that she could redecorate the house to reflect her
own taste. She also discovered she would be the driver for Edward's daily
buggy ride, a chore irritating in principle but enjoyable as she grew to
know her father-in-law. Bertha took an annoyingly close interest in the
new household and insisted that the Roswell Garst laundry be done by
Bertha's hired girl. Such irritations were minor; Elizabeth established an
affectionate working relationship with her new in-laws and took her place
in the social life of Coon Rapids. Dorothy Garst Chrystal was still in
Oklahoma in 1922, but she and Elizabeth would become close friends
after 1924, and the newly married Garsts spent a great deal of time with
Charley and Vivian Rippey. There were summer holidays in Minnesota,
visits to relatives, and extended business trips together. Children began
to arrive — Jane in December 1922 and Stephen in 1924.

While Elizabeth improved the house, Roswell improved the farm,
taking on Henry Moore as hired man and doubling the size of his Holstein
herd. Even Edward, retired from business but not from luck, made a final
financial contribution to the family wealth. Some years earlier he had
taken 40 acres of poor land in Oklahoma in lieu of an unpaid debt; Christmas morning, 1922, he learned that a prospecting company had struck oil

on an adjoining property. Because the field lay partly under his 40 acres, he was entitled to one-eighth of the field's production. At the time an amusing windfall, the oil became a valuable source of income in the later lean years.

However, there were darker events in 1922 and 1923. In the fall of 1922, Bertha became ill and entered a lengthy period of depression. Apparently she believed she had cancer, from which her sister Ida had died. According to Elizabeth, Bertha feared she would be unable to care for Edward or continue her work in the town. Elizabeth, pregnant with Jane, tried to cheer her and told her how much she would be needed as a grandmother. Such efforts were of no avail. In October 1922, presumably to avoid what she expected to be a long and eventually terminal illness, Bertha killed herself by taking a large dose of weed killer.

A year later in the fall of 1923, after a brief illness, Edward died peacefully in his sleep during the night while Jonathan sat at his bedside. It was not his death but rather his will that provided a shock by its revelation of his hatred for his son-in-law Jack Chrystal. Edward was known to have disliked Jack, possibly because he believed Jack had misrepresented his education and background when he was courting Dorothy. Whatever the reason, the antipathy Edward felt was so strong that in spite of his equally evident fondness for his daughter, he virtually disinherited her by giving her far fewer of his abundant possessions than he gave to her brothers. In the morning when Goodwin, Jonathan, and Roswell discovered the contents of the will, they walked down behind the barn where Edward kept his horses, decided that Dorothy had been unfairly treated, burned the will, and sorted out the property among themselves to give Dorothy her fair share. Clyde B. Fletcher, a friend of the family, who along with Warren Garst had been named an executor of the estate, disposed of the property according to the wishes of the brothers.

By 1925 Roswell and Dorothy were the only family members staying close to their roots in Coon Rapids. A month before his father's death, Goodwin sold his interest in the store and shortly thereafter moved to Rockford. He returned with his family for a summer visit in 1924, but he had begun the Eastward movement that would eventually cut his family ties entirely. Warren Garst died in 1924, and Johnny, his academic interests now dominant, returned to Scotland for further education and agricultural research. Roswell continued to enlarge his dairy herd and in 1925 became a town benefactor by donating land and labor for a public swimming pool and changing rooms.

However, life as a dairyman and prominent Coon Rapids citizen did not fulfill Roswell's interests and capacities or his financial ambitions. Salesmanship fascinated him, and when the opportunity presented itself, he left Coon Rapids and formed a partnership in Des Moines with two men he admired greatly for their talents as salesmen and promoters. One friend, Clyde B. Fletcher, had helped with the disposal of Edward's estate; the other, Bill Clemens, was an earlier friend of Fletcher. Roswell knew Fletcher especially well and took him as his earliest model outside the family of the commercial traveller and entrepreneur.

Clyde Fletcher was in his early teens and working for the Garst store part-time when Roswell was born. He worked full time for a few years after high school and moved north to Storm Lake in Pocahontas County to open his own variety store. There he met Bill Clemens, who had taken over his father's livery barn but was also looking for wider commercial horizons. After a few years in Storm Lake, Fletcher sold his business, moved to Des Moines, and began selling socks wholesale for the Rollins Hosiery Mill. An admiring customer in Oklahoma invited him to sell township lots in what was still Indian Territory, which involved the creation of new towns similar to the process practiced by the railroads. Fletcher sold lots for several townships, became a land agent for the railroad, later bought and sold land from the Indians, each of whom had been given 80 acres when Oklahoma became a state, and eventually reappeared in Des Moines as the owner of a hosiery factory. The factory burned down, impressing Fletcher with the possibilities of selling fire insurance, which he did throughout most of the twenties. When Roswell took up with him again, Fletcher was in the real estate business, largely on the basis of an inheritance from his father-in-law. He would eventually found the Home Federal Savings and Loan Association, on whose board of directors Roswell would one day sit.

Fletcher's idea of selling lots in a new subdivision of growing Des Moines attracted Roswell into a partnership with him in 1926. Fletcher bought a subdivision of 120 acres on contracts, found himself overextended financially, and approached Roswell as a potential investor. Roswell, along with his cousin Morrison Garst, Jr., purchased 80 acres from Fletcher and established the Garst Land Company. He platted the first 10 acres, gave over the running of his farm and dairy to his hired man Henry Moore, and moved to Des Moines in 1926. Bill Clemens, already embarked on a salesman's career, was brought to town to assist in selling the lots. The subdivision promotion gave Roswell a chance to see both Fletcher and Clemens in action, to learn from them, and to discover his own talents as a salesman. "If it's sound, it can be sold" was the maxim impressed upon him by his mentors, and Roswell began to practice his newly discovered talent with success.

For Elizabeth, the years in Des Moines were among the most satisfying of her life. She and Roswell were provided a connection with Des Moines society and cultural life through Warren Garst's daughter Louise, a painter of some talent, and her husband Micko McBroom, a successful architect with a sharp tongue, a taste for liquor, and a habit of dunning people for their bills in public. The McBrooms brought the Garsts into their wide circle of acquaintances, among them Henry Wallace and his wife Ilo. Another set of cousins, the Merrills, also lived in Des Moines, as well as an old classmate of Roswell's, Harold Brenton, on his way to becoming the state's most prominent banker. The transition from farm wife to urban matron was a welcome change for Elizabeth. An easier life as the wife of a city businessman, a varied and interesting group of friends, a comfortable house, and the wider choice of cultural activities made her time in Des Moines deeply satisfying.

It was a pleasant time for Roswell, also, and he established social and business connections that kept him in touch with Des Moines for the rest of his life. Although he was heavily in debt with his subdivision, it was a prosperous time in the main. He had an income from the oil well in Oklahoma, from his rented farm and from the Garst store, and every prospect of success in the rapidly growing real estate market. However, he did not embrace city life as completely as Elizabeth; he kept in close touch with his farm and Coon Rapids and travelled regularly around the countryside. He talked agriculture a great deal with his new friend Henry Wallace, and after a trip to the country he would drop in to visit Wallace, now editor of *Wallaces' Farmer,* to report what he had seen. Wallace occasionally printed tidbits from Roswell about new farming practices and other observations from his Coon Rapids acquaintance.

His friendship with Wallace was the most significant event of Roswell's years in Des Moines. Through Wallace he discovered a focus for the apparently disparate threads of his abilities and interests. In the infant hybrid seed corn industry he found a challenge for his salesmanship, a means to bring agriculture back into the center of his life, and ultimately the opportunity to discover and fulfill his potential as educator and innovator. Through Wallace he would awaken to the economic and political issues posed by the decline of the farm economy since World War I and begin to view agriculture in its international context. Roswell considered Jonathan Garst and Henry Wallace as the two most brilliant men he had ever known. "All of the economic theories I ever learned," Roswell once remarked to an Iowa governor, Clyde Herring, "I learned from the Editorial page of *Wallaces' Farmer* when he [Wallace] was editing it."

Henry Agard Wallace was the third generation of a distinguished Iowa family. His grandfather, "Uncle Henry" Wallace, left a career as minister in Pennsylvania to move to Adair County, Iowa, in 1869. He founded the *Iowa Homestead,* a farming newspaper that became a forum for his popular editorials on modern farming methods, morality, and politics. He helped turn the agricultural college at Ames into a respected scholarly institution, established himself as a champion of agrarian re-

form in the 1880s, and dedicated himself to progressive Republicanism in
the Teddy Roosevelt era. Roosevelt appointed him to the National Commission on Country Life in 1908, and in 1916 Wallace spoke privately to
Woodrow Wilson about his hopes for peace in the world. His son, Henry
Cantwell Wallace, achieved prominence as the editor of *Wallaces' Farmer,*
as an educator at Iowa State College, and as secretary of agriculture in
the Harding administration. His son, Henry Agard, followed a similar
path, teaching at Ames and joining his father on the family journal. By
1930 Henry Agard Wallace had made his special mark on American agriculture in three areas, all of which were to affect Roswell profoundly.
These three contributions were made in the genetics of hybrid corn, in
the mathematical relationship between feed grains and livestock production (the corn-hog ratio), and in the relationship of tariffs and war repara-
tions to the agricultural economy.

Henry Agard – "H. A." to his friends and associates – was a teenager
when he became interested in corn genetics, influenced by Perry G.
Holden, a frequent visitor to the Wallace household and founder of the
largest seed-corn business in Illinois. Holden was the originator of Reid's
Yellow Dent corn, and at that time in 1904, director of the extension
program at Iowa State College. Holden's "corn show," sponsored by the
college to improve the quality of corn raised in Iowa, toured the state by
train; its arrival in Coon Rapids in 1910 was prominently advertised by
the *Enterprise.* Holden taught that high quality seed could be judged by its
looks and trained farmers to choose seeds from ears of corn that had
straight rows of kernels, well-filled tips and butts, deep wedge-shaped
grains, and rich yellow color. He maintained that it was actually possible
to see the vigor and virility of the kernels on an ear of corn. Consequently,
farmers would walk through their cornfields before the harvest and
choose their most splendid specimens to save for seed; during the harvest
they would often keep a box on the side of the husking wagon for setting
aside choice ears they had missed the first time through. Holden was the
most effective, but by no means the only, proponent of this view, which
prevailed among farmers for another twenty-five years.

In 1904, when he was sixteen, young Wallace voiced his doubts to
Holden about this method of choosing seed corn. Holden listened and
suggested that H. A. run a yield test with corn that Holden would select
and whose performance Holden would predict. Henry took up the challenge and laid out 5 acres of seed from the kernels from 33 ears of Reid's
Yellow Dent corn. In order to keep track of the productivity of each ear of
corn Holden had chosen, he numbered each ear. Wallace shelled half of
each ear by hand, laid out two rows each of every ear of corn, and planted
and cultivated by himself. When the plants were sufficiently mature in
the summer, he performed the task that twenty years earlier had been

shown to increase yield and quality significantly, the crossing of different varieties of corn by detasseling.

Every corn plant contains a "male" part, located in the tassel at its top, and a "female" part, located in the silk, which grows out of the central part of the stalk and actually produces the ears of corn. When the tassels on top ripen and open, they release pollen, which floats down to the silk on the stalk or is blown to the silks of neighboring plants. When left to take place without interference, this process of fertilization is called open pollination. In 1881 Holden's teacher at Michigan Agricultural College, J. W. Beal, following work done by Darwin, planted different varieties of corn in close proximity, removed the tassels of plants he chose to be exclusively "female", and thus ensured that they were pollinated only by the varieties he planted (but had not detasseled) in an adjoining row. By making this controlled cross of varieties, he discovered in the superiority of the corn produced by the detasseled plants what he called "the buoyancy of hybridization."

On his 5 acres, Wallace detasseled in the north those rows representing even-numbered ears, and in the south half the rows of odd-numbered ears, so that one row of each variety would be detasseled. Wallace harvested the corn, weighed it, and computed the yield of each row in bushels per acre. Too anxious to wait for the corn to dry, he calculated the moisture loss and cob weight and arranged his figures as relative acre yields of air-dried shelled corn, figures that were later proved to be correct. His results showed that although all the ears looked alike, in the manner Holden had prescribed for the best quality seed, they varied in their yield from 33 to 79 bushels per acre, and the ear Holden claimed to be the best potential producer was among the ten lowest-yielding ears. Shape, size, and color, it was clear, did not offer correct guidelines for the production of seed corn.

About the time Wallace was disproving Holden's widely shared views on corn, other researchers were further revolutionizing the genetics of corn by investigating the process of inbreeding and its relation to crossing, or hybridization. In 1906, while Wallace was a freshman at Iowa State and Roswell was an eight-year-old schoolboy, Dr. George Shull of the Carnegie Institution Station for Experimental Evolution on Long Island and Dr. Edward East at the Connecticut Experiment Station began experimenting independently with the inbreeding of corn plants, a process which at that time was thought to produce a severely weakened strain of plants. Both Shull and East tied bags over the tassels of each plant, collected the pollen, applied it only to the silks of the plant from which it had been obtained, then repeated the process with the next generation. Shull went one step further than East at this point and crossed the inbred lines. Shull announced the results of his experiment in 1908; East then crossed his own inbreds and was able to confirm Shull's work. Both men found that plants inbred, then subsequently crossed, produced "a genetic explosion," which, according to Wallace family biographer Russell Lord, exhibited "the widest, most amazing variations." Some effects were good, some bad; the most impressive effect was an increase in yield significantly larger than that obtained by Beal. Shull called the vitality achieved by crossing varieties that were first inbred "heterosis," from the Greek word "alteration," now more commonly known as "hybrid vigor."

Shull was less interested in the practical possibilities of the discovery, but East, H. K. Hayes, and later Donald Jones, all of the Connecticut Experiment Station, worked to isolate and fix the genetic characters of high yield and other desirable effects. Wallace told *Farm Quarterly* editor Grant Cannon that he heard of Jones's breakthrough from East, who encouraged him to concentrate on the commercial possibilities of hybrid seed.

In 1913 Wallace made his first crosses of inbred lines of corn, decided that practical application of hybridization was possible, and in 1914 and 1915 began working on a method of producing seed commercially. Wallace set himself a correspondingly practical objective. The experiment station researchers, he commented,

were rather too much concerned with comparing the yielding power of the cross with the parents, rather than with the best yielding variety of the locality. Could I find some cross which in Iowa would consistently beat Reid's Yellow Dent?

To that end, he grew almost 300 crosses of the standard North American strains, mixing them with strains from other parts of the world. He bred inbred after inbred and continued to cross them until he found a "nick" of desirable genetic characters that would continue to reproduce themselves. Finally, he achieved a nick between Reid's Yellow Dent and certain merged Mexican varieties, achieved more successful crosses of inbreds between 1919 and 1923, and in that year entered a variety called Copper Cross in the Iowa Yield Test. It did well in 1923 and in 1924 won a gold medal as the highest yielding corn in its district. Wallace grew only 15 bushels of Copper Cross seed, but it was apparently the first hybrid developed from inbreds to be produced and sold in the Corn Belt.

The age of hybrid corn had arrived, but just barely: there were still formidable practical problems. The excessive cost for the small quantity produced by a single cross was partially solved by the introduction of a second, or double, cross (first accomplished by Donald Jones), which enabled Wallace to produce a hybrid that had almost as much hybrid vigor as its parents, was consistently higher yielding, and had stronger stalks than any open-pollinated variety. However, the process was still expensive, and there remained the difficulty of selling a product which, although in a much inferior form, was still available free to the farmer in his own cornfield. Finally, there were problems in the design and construction of dryers, sorting machinery, and storage facilities: in short, in the creation of a whole new industry.

In 1926, the year the Garsts moved to Des Moines, Wallace formed the Hi-Bred Corn Company (the word "Pioneer" was added in the thirties after other hybrid seed companies had been formed). Wallace had been writing about hybrid corn in his newspaper for some time, made speeches about it, and was beginning to attract attention for his product in the annual corn-yield contests. Raymond Baker, a plant breeder, joined the company in 1928, followed by Jay Newlin, who took over the management of the company's installation at nearby Johnston. Roswell followed these developments with interest and before 1930 began to plant some of Wallace's new corn on his own farm.

Between 1917 and 1920, while he was trying to develop a suitable commercial strain of hybrid corn, Wallace regularized the traditional method by which farmers calculated the profitability of raising pigs—that balance between the price of corn used to feed pigs and the price of the finished product known as the corn-hog ratio. Ever since the 1870s, Corn Belt farmers had calculated that they would make a profit raising hogs if the sale price of hogs per hundredweight was equal to the price of 10 bushels of corn at the time of sale. Put another way, the price the farmer received for every 100 pounds of pork had to be 10 times the cost of 1 bushel of corn that was fed to the hogs. Thus, if corn was worth $1.50 per bushel when the farmer sold his hogs, he would expect to get at least $1.50 times 10, or $15.00 for every 100 pounds on his hog. It was the ratio that was important, because the price of corn could fluctuate a great deal, primarily in relation to its availability.

In 1917 the government wished to increase the national production of pork so that larger quantities could be sent to Europe to ease the ever-worsening food shortage. Herbert Hoover, wartime food administrator, established a commission to set a national price for hogs that would encourage greater production. Accordingly, in November 1917 a seven-man commission began work on the project and selected as its statistician Henry A. Wallace.

During the summer and fall of 1917, H. A. had already published notes and articles on the ratio approach to price determination in *Wallaces' Farmer* and would enlarge and develop the theory in his book *Agricultural Prices* in 1920. He convinced the committee that simply fixing a set price for hogs would not constitute an incentive because of local variations in availability and cost and other market considerations. "There is no such thing as a standard cost of production," he maintained. "It is a will-o-the-wisp." Instead, he chose to refine the corn-hog ratio to a higher degree of statistical rigor by taking into account the varying price of corn throughout the year and the varying amounts actually fed to a hog each month. Wallace calculated that 2 percent of the corn went to the pig or its dam in the first three months of feeding, 3 percent in the fourth month, and so on, up to 20 percent in the tenth, then down to 15 percent in the twelfth. He matched these amounts with the prices of Chicago Number 2 corn at each stage and concluded that the way to ensure an increased supply of pork for the coming year was to offer a price per hundredweight of pork equivalent to 13 bushels of corn rather than 10. Thus if his corn was worth $1.50 per bushel at Chicago prices when he sold his hogs the next year, a farmer would get $1.50 times 13, or $19.50 per hundredweight, rather than the $15.00 at the ordinary ratio of 100:10. Hoover accepted the ratio approach, although he preferred a minimum guaranteed price. However, Hoover did not mention Chicago prices for both products, as Wallace had specified, and when the Wallace calculation produced an even greater abundance of hogs than he had wanted, Hoover equivocated on the price. The Food Administration refigured the data in light of corn prices on the farm rather than at Chicago and eventually offered a fixed price that cut the farmers' payment from the 100:13 ratio down to 100:10.8. The angry protests from the Corn Belt were ignored.

From this affair came the establishment of the corn-hog ratio as a tool of agricultural economics. For H. A. came the lesson that farmers would have to employ trained experts to look after their interests or become better trained themselves. Henry Cantwell was even angrier than his son about Hoover's handling of the ratio; in an editorial in *Wallaces' Farmer* he accused Hoover of juggling the figures and fooling the farmers. "Mr. Hoover's deceit in dealing with the farmers," he wrote, "was in fact the impelling motive for the organization of the Farm Bureau in its later and stronger form."

The third area in the agriculture of the twenties that Wallace influenced derived from his fight against high tariffs, a battle that initiated his disenchantment with the Republican party. His contribution lay not in victory, but in educating his readers on the consequences for agriculture of high tariffs and in formulating an agricultural policy to cope with economic isolationism.

Wallace's antitariff rationale was summed up by President Woodrow Wilson when he vetoed a Republican tariff bill in 1921: "If we wish to have Europe settle her debts, governmental or commercial," the president wrote, "we must be prepared to buy from her." However, the succeeding Republican administrations thought differently. Beginning with Harding's presidency, they introduced in 1921 a tariff with prohibitive agricultural schedules during a period of agricultural surplus caused by the collapse of the wartime export boom. In 1922 the Fordney-McCumber tariff established the highest rates in American history; in the succeeding years Europe could no longer acquire American dollars through its exports to the United States, which in turn would have fostered sales of American goods and products abroad. Europe subsequently took reprisals by imposing retaliatory rates. In 1927 France and England increased duties on wheat and meat, accelerating a decline in U.S. foreign trade that caused serious misgivings among many Republicans over their own party's inflexible tariff plank.

The younger Wallace's disaffection with the Republican party began as early as 1922, during his father's term as secretary of agriculture under Harding. Taking up his new job during the 1921 agricultural depression, the elder Wallace pressed for and was finally allowed to convene a conference in January 1922 to consider remedies for the plight of the farmer. H. A. attended as secretary of the Corn Belt Meat Producers Association and intended in his speech to strongly condemn the Fordney-McCumber tariff. His father had to tell him Harding had forbidden any mention of tariff policy at the conference and that the speech had been rewritten by two USDA economists. Years later, H. A. told the Wallace family biographer Russell Lord that the process taking him out of the Republican party had begun that week. If he could not be against high tariffs openly, and if the secretary of agriculture could not obtain an open hearing for such views, he told Lord, "old-time Republicanism had become too hidebound for any good use."

American agriculture in the early twenties faced a surplus; both Wallaces began looking for ways to live with a postwar tariff policy that denied an export market to this surplus. Consequently, they decided to press for a reduction in acreage and launched a campaign in *Wallaces' Farmer* with the slogan "Less corn, more clover, more money." On the editorial page they argued month after month for voluntary acreage reduction, setting forth the latest figures on corn supplies and emphasizing the diminishing world markets. In an agricultural economy still geared for maximum production, the Wallace proposal that farmers plant 8 million fewer acres of corn and 8 million more acres of clover to restore the fertility that was lost during the wartime boom was a new departure, foreshadowing by a decade the major agricultural themes of the thirties. In 1924 the new tariffs and the fiasco over the unpaid war debt, in H. A.'s view, required that "during the next decade or two the United States must adjust herself to her position as the world's greatest creditor nation." Economic forces now stood against exports, he told his readers; consequently, he argued, "we must reduce our surplus."

The inauguration of a new administration in 1928 promised the possibility of change, but in April 1930 the Hoover administration enacted the Hawley-Smoot Tariff, which raised the barriers even higher. By 1932 twenty-five countries had established retaliatory tariffs and foreign trade continued its downward slump. Between 1920 and 1932 total farm income declined from $15.5 billion per year to $5.5 billion, cereal prices plunged, and the foreign market collapsed. Farm cooperatives were established by the administration, but further attempts to get the government more actively involved in agricultural support for the farmers were vetoed as too socialistic both by Coolidge and Hoover. In June 1929 Hoover signed the Agricultural Marketing Act, authorizing a new Federal Farm Board to extend loans to cooperatives and to buy surpluses, but the act was never fully utilized until the Roosevelt administration. Wallace believed in 1929 that Hoover was merely perpetuating a situation that was eroding agricultural prices. He told biographer Lord that year he thought Hoover's ideas about agricultural recovery and even general recovery were in his estimation

about 99 per cent wrong. They by-pass the tariff issue; they sidestep the debts. They'll never work. The smash we've had already isn't anything to the smash that will come.

Hybridization, corn and hogs, tariffs and surplus: these were the things Wallace wrote and talked about to Roswell. They were the stuff of Roswell's intellectual life during the Des Moines years, and, along with his personal devotion to Wallace, formed the basis for much that he achieved later.

By 1930 Roswell's immediate practical concerns were the selling of hybrid seed corn and the effect of the crash on his personal fortunes. Still in debt over his subdivision, he soon found himself without liquid assets and with a considerable amount of property which, no longer being sound, could not be sold. Although the lots on which they had actually built houses were paid for, Fletcher and Garst were still contracted to the Wakonda Country Club for the bulk of their subdivision. However Fletcher, by some ingenious process of reasoning, argued that the club had misrepresented its intentions to him, and after much wrangling got them to take back the undeveloped property. Consequently Roswell owed less than he might have on undeveloped land. He also owed money on his house in Des Moines and on capital he had borrowed. But his property at Coon Rapids was intact, and there were now good reasons for returning to it. The years in Des Moines were over.

CHAPTER THREE

The Thirties

Founding Garst and Thomas: 1930–33

Roswell's decision to enter the hybrid seed corn business coincided with, but did not follow from, the Great Crash; it simply made the enterprise more difficult and caused him to move back to Coon Rapids perhaps sooner than he might have. Fond as his father of a neatly turned phrase, Roswell liked to say that he and Elizabeth moved to Coon Rapids because they preferred to be peasants on the farm rather than paupers in the city. It was a sensible choice in view of their rapidly disappearing assets. But Coon Rapids was also the only place where Roswell could have planted his corn in 1930, on the 200 acres just south of town. Departure from Des Moines was one of the prices to be paid, from Elizabeth's viewpoint, for going into the business; they would have moved to Coon Rapids even had there not been a depression. For Roswell, however, the move was a response to the attraction of the land with which he had kept in touch throughout his time in Des Moines. He never became citified by his urban years; like Edward, Coon Rapids suited him just fine.

Roswell observed Wallace's operation from its beginning in 1926, and for the following three years took a bushel of hybrid seed to his tenant Henry Moore to plant on the Garst farm. The first year the corn yielded well, but the plants were too tall and towered above the 6-foot–4-inch Moore. The next year there were no such side effects, and the yields continued to be substantially higher than for open-pollinated corn. In 1929 Roswell asked his old high school friend Charley Rippey to grow a stand of the new corn and discovered a further quality of hybridization. "Bob lived in Des Moines at that time," Charley recalled,

but when he came to Coon Rapids he would visit us, you know, and we kept watching that corn. We were watching it and there came a wind and it blew all of mine down, but the hybrid corn was still standing. I had planted it two rows, and

39

two rows, so there were two rows down and two rows standing up. That just amazed Bob.

In 1930 Roswell acted. He asked Wallace for foundation stock so that he could make the final cross and produce hybrid seed under franchise. Wallace readily agreed to let Roswell have seed but asked for a 25 percent royalty to help underwrite the great expense of research. Roswell argued that such a figure was acceptable only if a small amount was sold, but that a higher volume of sales should bring royalties down substantially. With the help of Clyde Charleton, a Des Moines lawyer and friend, Roswell worked out an arrangement that lowered the royalties in inverse proportion to an increase in sales up to 50,000 bushels. "Bob, I just love you," Wallace exclaimed after he had read the agreement, "You are such an optimist. There won't be 50,000 bushels of hybrid corn sold in your lifetime or mine." Roswell thought differently. "I'll hit 50,000 bushels in five years," he replied. The agreement was not signed, but concluded with a handshake. A simple contract was drafted and signed a year later.

Roswell planted his first seed field of 15 acres on a plot of land west of his house along Spring Branch Creek in the spring of 1930. The first business crisis occurred in the summer, as detasseling time approached without the thousand dollars it would cost to pay for the job. Elizabeth came to the rescue by organizing a farm camp for city children in July and August, earning the money that allowed Charley Rippey, assisted by Russell Carpenter, to get the job done in July. The crop was harvested in the fall and sent to the Wallace plant in Reinbeck to be processed and sacked. When the sacks were brought back, they were stored on the screened porch of the house and were watched over by Elizabeth, whose main task was to keep the children from playing among them and impairing the germination of the seed.

Roswell's 15 acres produced 300 bushels of hybrid seed corn, a modest amount, yet at the same time approximately 10 percent of all the hybrid seed being grown in the United States in 1930. Wallace grew much of the remaining acreage, other companies were springing up as well, and the experimental station at Iowa State was ready to test its own hybrids. Joe Robinson, in charge of crop experiments at Ames, sent samples to farmers, asking them to plant two five-pound sacks and report the results. Closer to home, the Guthrie County Farm Bureau sponsored test plots on five farms throughout the county, one of them near Coon Rapids. However, the sum total of such activity was small, and in 1930 hybrid corn was as yet unseen by the vast majority of farmers and was even unheard of by equally substantial numbers.

Hybrid corn was not only new, it was expensive. Consequently, the salesman for this product faced two challenges: he had to persuade a group of people conservative by nature and cautious by experience to give up a traditional and cheap method of selecting seed and to do it in a period of rapidly worsening economic crisis. Farm incomes, which had been declining since 1921, dropped sharply after the Crash, and by 1932 would be one-third of what they had been in 1929. Ordinary commercial corn was plummeting in price, down to $0.50 per bushel in 1931, and $0.10 per bushel in 1933. A bushel of the new seed corn, which would seed seven acres, cost $9.00 per bushel in 1931, $6.75 in 1932, and $5.25 in 1933. "Now you'd go out to sell," Charley Rippey said,

and if they would listen to you at all, they wouldn't know anything at all about hybridization. That was a foreign word; farmers didn't know just exactly what it meant. But if you could interest them at all in it, sooner or later they were going to ask you the price of the corn. And if you would say six or seven dollars a bushel you could almost see them reaching around to their hip pocket to get the gun. Because you could buy the first-prize bushel at the county fair that looked just wonderful for a dollar.

Roswell and Charley also tried to sell round kernels from the tip of the ear for $4.50 per bushel, which to many farmers seemed out-and-out chicanery; they had been taught to throw those away in the belief that they were inferior in quality and germination. This particular mythology about kernel shape and size dogged the seed industry for years, and well into the fifties small round kernels were always the last to sell.

In the winter of 1930–31 Roswell loaded 20 bushels at a time into the back of his Buick and drove until he sold them. He worked the area fifteen miles north to Glidden, turned west on Highway 30 through Carroll and then to Denison, Manning, and Manila. In subsequent journeys he drove north into the rich farmlands of north-central Iowa to Pocahontas, Humboldt, and Webster counties. It was hard going—usually he sold 1 or 2 bushels at a time, perhaps 5 if he was lucky, often none at all. He had one big sale that season, just west of Glidden off Highway 30, to a farmer who had planted some of Wallace's hybrid seed the previous year. Roswell asked him how much he needed this year, the farmer thought for a moment, then replied "20 bushels." It was Roswell's entire load for a journey of several days.

During his second year of production in 1931 Roswell and Elizabeth faced another financial crisis. Elizabeth held her summer camp again that summer, but the prospects of acquiring capital for expansion were not encouraging. Roswell's worth on paper that year was approximately $7400, his assets were largely nonliquid, and his borrowing capacity nil. Moreover, he was still struggling to pay the money he owed for his real estate venture. Roswell needed a business partner who had some capital and who could borrow. He found his man in Charley Thomas, a high-school acquaintance who had become a highly competent and successful farmer but who had fallen into a corn picker in 1929, damaging his right arm so severely that he was unable to farm. Roswell invited Charley to drive to Chicago with him one day, and, as Charley recounted it,

said that he was very interested in hybrid seed corn and that he thought that it was going to develop into more than a one-man job and he would like to have a partner and I was the one he would like to have. "You won't be able to farm again because of your arm injury," he said, "I'd like to invite you to go into the seed corn business with me." I knew the condition that I was in, too, and I was wondering what I would do since I couldn't farm anymore. I said I'd be glad to do that. Actually, there was hardly any discussion about it.

Charley was also aware of Roswell's financial condition and addressed himself immediately to the problem of raising money for the newly created Garst and Thomas Hi-Bred Corn Company. Because seed companies are not paid for their corn until it is delivered to the customer in the spring, they need large amounts of cash for harvesting, processing, and distributing their product. Consequently, it is essential to borrow money. In those first years of the depression Charley found that trying to borrow money was a difficult business, even from a government agency devoted to business expansion. One year he went to Omaha to borrow eight thousand dollars from a governmental loan agency and explained his business to a committee reviewing applications. "One of the guys looked around at the others, and said, 'It sounds like one of those alfalfa deals to me.'" But Charley got his money, and when he returned to repay the loan in the following spring after the corn had been delivered, he created a sensation in the loan office. "God, I didn't think we'd ever get it back," the loan officer told his colleagues, whom he had assembled for this auspicious occasion.

Both Charley and Roswell committed their assets and their energies to the new business. Charley and his wife Bertha put the inheritance from Bertha's father into the partnership, and in 1932 Roswell auctioned off his dairy herd and mortgaged his farm. He spoke to interested groups in the state and with Charley Thomas took farmers to Iowa State, which now had extensive hybrid test plots and a seed-testing laboratory that farmers could use to determine the germination potential of their seeds. There were changes in Coon Rapids. Editor S. D. Henry died in early 1930 after forty-seven years as publisher of the *Enterprise* and it fell to his successor Tom Rogers to report on Roswell's latest enthusiasm. "If you ever saw anyone who was 'sold', it's Roswell Garst on this hi-bred seed corn idea," Rogers wrote in 1932. "Bob talks seed corn all the time."

However, in the spring of 1931, the year in which the partnership began, a considerable amount of corn was still sitting on Roswell's porch and sales resistance showed no signs of abating. In the course of working Pocahontas County in May, Roswell returned to Des Moines to urge Clyde Charleton, who owned a farm in that county, to buy some seed and to split the cost with his tenant. Charleton argued that the tenant, who knew nothing about hybrid corn, would need a guarantee that the hybrid seed would outyield open-pollinated corn. Roswell agreed, but said that if he were to guarantee the yield he should get an extra price if the yield went up. It was finally agreed that the tenant Hoskins would plant twenty rows of hybrid and twenty rows of open-pollinated seed. As payment for the seed, Roswell would take one-half of the increase in yield produced by the hybrid seed over the open-pollinated seed at the market price of the corn when it was sold.

The tenant readily agreed to this plan, and planted 6 bushels of hybrid seed corn, enough for 42 acres. In September when the crops were harvested Hoskin's 42 acres of hybrid corn yielded 80 bushels per acre; his open-pollinated corn yielded 58. The increase was 22 bushels— Roswell was entitled to 11 bushels per acre on 42 acres, or 462 bushels, and Hoskins got the same. In the fall of 1931, corn was worth about $0.50 per bushel, which meant that Roswell earned $115.50 and Hoskins had earned $115.50 in addition to his ordinary income from the crop. On a straightforward sale of seed, the farmer would have paid $54.00 dollars. It was this ordinary sale price that Roswell actually charged, rather than taking half the increase. Consequently, for an investment of $54.00, Hoskins made a net gain of $177.00 on the increase ($231.00 less $54.00). A return of more than three times the investment spoke volumes, and Roswell found he had an effective new sales method.

He had planted 1,000 acres of seed in 1931, and during the winter and spring of 1932 Garst and Thomas put out their entire acreage on half-the-increase agreements. The corn was bagged in 8-pound sacks, just enough to plant 1 acre. Aided now by Dick Caswell, Roswell and Charley Rippey set out through north-central Iowa, sometimes in pairs, sometimes alone, to distribute the corn to any farmer who would take it. Often, they would catch the farmer in the field, planting. If the proposition appealed, the farmer, who customarily used a two-row planter pulled by a team, would tip out the open-pollinated corn in one of his planter-boxes and replace it with hybrid seed. With one box filled with open-pollinated corn and one with hybrid seed, he would plant thirty-two rows, sixteen of open-pollinated, sixteen of hybrid.

In the fall of 1932 Roswell and his two salesmen took to the fields again, this time equipped with scales to demonstrate, they hoped, the greater yields of the hybrids. "We went out and checked the corn that fall," Charley Rippey recalled, and we'd go to the fields with the scales and explain how it would be the difference of the poundage. We'd say, we'll go here so many rows and then we'll start counting. Now, we'd say, if there was a missed hill, of yours or ours, you couldn't make that up because it was probably no fault of the corn. We'd go to three places if they wanted to, then asked them to pay us market price for one-half the increase in their yield. Well, until we weighed it, they thought that they had got some pretty cheap corn. But gosh, we had an average over 10 bushels over them and we would get 10 bushels at say 20 cents or whatever corn was worth that year, and it mounted up to be 20 to 30 per bushel. By golly, that was a different story and they would begin to wonder about it. They would be wanting to weigh it over again and they'd be wondering if we used the right kind of scales, or measured at the right place in the field, and so on.

Convinced finally that the hybrid seed had outyielded the open-pollinated seed, the farmer would often forget that he owed for 7 acres of corn rather than just 1 acre. If Roswell had beaten the farmer's ordinary yield by 15 bushels per acre, he would have to remind him that he was owed for 7 bushels times 7 acres, or 49 bushels. However, instead of the price of 49 bushels, he would, as he had with Hoskins, charge only the price of the seed, which averaged one-third of the price of the agreed bargain. "So then," Roswell said,

I would say to them, "how much do you want for next year?" They wouldn't dare say it was too much. . . . even though commercial corn was hardly worth picking, he could hardly refuse to order seed for the next year's spring planting when one-half of his increased yield had actually been worth more than we were charging him.

Roswell believed it was the best method ever devised to illustrate that a high price per bushel "does not mean anything." It was adopted as well by Pioneer Hi-Bred in Des Moines as their principal sales technique during the thirties.

The corn was proving its soundness in other ways. As it had on Charley Rippey's farm in 1929, the corn stood straight and firm when open-pollinated corn blew down, preserving a high yield and making mechanical harvesting feasible. Its extensive and deep-root system made it more drought resistant and able to ingest more nutrients than open-pollinated corn. During 1932 Roswell and Elizabeth checked the yield of a farmer who had bought 5 bushels. When Roswell asked if he saw much difference in the plants, the farmer replied,

My God, Bob, even Blind Boone could tell the difference. You pull up one of my stalks, and there aren't any roots on them at all. You put your hands on the hybrids and try to pull them up, and by God you can't budge it.

Another sales technique used by Roswell was to persuade the leading farmers in each district to use hybrids. Charley Rippey found such a customer, F. A. Miller, in Grundy County. Miller owned a large number of farms, rode with Charley while he weighed yields, and ordered 300 bushels for his own farms. "I was the most excited fellow you ever saw," Charley said. "I drove clear to Coon Rapids to tell them about it." When you began with the big ones, Charley confirmed, "the little ones gradually fell into line."

The major group of big ones were the insurance companies, whose local and national representatives Roswell assiduously courted. By 1932 these companies owned approximately 20 percent of Iowa's farmland, in large part through foreclosures and because farmers were losing heart and selling even when the company was willing to overlook defaulted payments. In seeking to sell seed directly to these reluctant landowners, Roswell was seeking a change from the tenant's traditional obligation of furnishing all of the seed to a fifty-fifty sharing of this new burden between landlord and tenant.

Roswell's first approaches met with failure. Insurance executives and the managers they now hired were skeptical of hybrid corn and saw no sense in increasing production when the government was attempting to curtail the surplus. Barney Trullinger, an early salesman, remembered an exchange between Roswell and the president of an insurance company. "Wouldn't you rather grow as much corn on 50 acres as you normally grow on 80?" Roswell asked him. "No!" the executive emphatically replied. Roswell found an apparently more sympathetic listener in Fred Hubbell, head of Equitable Life Insurance Company of Iowa. After Roswell explained all the advantages of hybrid corn, Hubbell said: "That sounds fine. Now what will the discount be?" "Just the same as on life insurance," Roswell replied, "nothing." Hubbell was not interested.

Roswell made a final effort. He and Charley Thomas invited the executives of every major insurance company that did business in Iowa to Coon Rapids, took them through fields of open-pollinated and hybrid corn, and pointed out the virtues of the hybrids. That afternoon they returned to the Garst farm for a chicken dinner prepared by Bertha Thomas and Elizabeth and for more talk. By evening, they had all agreed to buy hybrid seed and to share its cost with their tenants.

By 1933 Garst and Thomas needed more office and storage space; both Charley and Bob's homes were overflowing with bags of seed. They rented an old creamery in town, moved the corn from the farms and their office from the bank where Charley had been doing the payroll. Roswell, Charley Thomas, Charley Rippey, and Dick Caswell met on the weekends to "talk it over and ponder about next week," as Charley Rippey put it. When production exceeded 2,000 bushels, another move was made, this time to the Daly building on Main Street. Their first office worker, Vera Nelson, was hired to keep the books and dole out expense money. Capable, solemn, and straitlaced, Vera found it difficult to maintain a businesslike routine in an unorthodox and makeshift situation. Roswell's attitude toward the minutiae of administration especially annoyed her. "I wish you'd keep better account of your money," she admonished him when he failed to account to the penny for the money he spent. Roswell usually just laughed.

In those first years, Garst and Thomas was not large enough for a formal division of labor. July was spent supervising detasseling, September and October in harvesting and processing the crop. In the winter, when the corn was sacked, the sales season began in earnest (although Roswell kept at it all year around) and continued until detasseling time again. In the late fall Charley Rippey and Dick Caswell outfitted themselves with long underwear from the Garst Store and set out, as did Charley Thomas and Roswell, in cold automobiles to find farmers working in cold fields beyond muddy or frozen roads. Roswell wore his woolen shirt, a coat, but no hat and sometimes no gloves. It was long, hard work on the road for everyone, with prospects of success less than rosy.

Yet there was an excitement in the air; in spite of an overlay of romanticism, Roswell's reminiscences evoke his enthusiasm for the challenge of his work. "We had to sell corn," he wrote in the forties to Grace Carey, proprietor of a Pocahontas County hotel:

Many a time we left Coon Rapids with 3 dollars in our pockets and ten bushels of corn in the back end of the car. If we didn't trade the corn for money, we wouldn't eat or sleep. Knowing that, we were pretty good salesmen – and we always ate and slept.

Grace, he recalled, was buying corn for $.07 per bushel to burn in the hotel furnace in the fall of 1932, while he was selling seed for $6.50 per bushel. "We all laughed together – I sold corn so I could eat – and you fired that old furnace with ear corn." On her parents' twenty-fifth anniversary, Jane wrote that Roswell and Elizabeth had taught her by example not to fear a future depression; she had learned from them how to work hard and still laugh.

In the spring of 1933 Charley Thomas and Roswell contracted with farmers to plant 2,558 acres of seed corn, with 285 acres located around Coon Rapids. Fascinated by the new industry, Tom Rogers of the *Enterprise* went to look at the fields, remarking on their "peculiar appearance" after two rows had been detasseled and one left with tassels. Detasseling, he informed his readers, had to be thoroughly done in order to pass inspection by experts from Iowa State, who rode through the fields several times during the detasseling season to see that a proper cross was assured. This year's crop, he noted, would produce forty thousand dollars worth of seed corn. Henry had not lived to see the beginning of this new era, but Rogers had become its chronicler, and during that spring he hailed the appearance of "an industry of considerable importance to Coon Rapids."

Bringing in the New Deal: 1933

On election day in November 1932, Iowa was engulfed in a blizzard. Roswell, accompanied by Dick Caswell, spent the day in Lidderdale, a small community in northern Carroll County, campaigning for his brother-in-law Jack Chrystal, who was a candidate for the state senate. Late that afternoon, forced to abandon their canvassing in the face of snow and driving winds, Roswell and his salesman came to Carroll to the county court house to listen to the returns. Late that evening they set out south for Coon Rapids and about midnight slid into a bank of drifting snow. Caswell recognized the house of Louis Nagl, a farmer whom he knew, so they hiked through the snow and roused him out of bed. Louis put some coal in his stove, and the three men warmed themselves at the fire and talked about the election. Roswell told Louis that Roosevelt was winning everywhere; Iowa had gone Democratic and so had Carroll County. "How did Roselle Number 2 vote?" Louis asked of his own township. "Ninety-eight for Roosevelt, two for Hoover," Roswell replied. "I wonder," Louis mused, "who the two sons-of-bitches were."

Louis's strong feelings about the unfortunate Hoover were not unusual for Iowa farmers in the fall of 1932. In October, on the day the Republican incumbent opened his campaign for reelection, Milo Reno, head of the Farm Holiday Association, led an anti-Hoover parade of farmers in Des Moines. One of the demonstrators carried a placard that epitomized many farmers' sense of betrayal: "In Hoover we trusted," the placard read, "Now we are busted." The Farmers' Holiday Association and the Farmers Union represented that segment of the farm population whose frustration with foreclosures and financial ruin, and with a series of administrations whose policies seemed especially unjust to the farmer, had reached flashpoint, which by the spring would lead to violence. The most notorious incident took place in April 1933. With the new farm bill stalled in Congress and the state debtor relief laws unclear, violence erupted in LeMars, a small town in western Iowa. After a day of rioting, farmers dragged Judge C. C. Bradley from his bench, took him to a county crossroads, smeared him with grease, put a noose around his neck and stretched it until he fainted. On the following day, a violent confrontation took place at Denison between law officers and eight hundred farmers trying to halt a foreclosure sale. Governor Clyde Herring felt obliged to call out the National Guard to maintain order in a situation that was virtually a state of rebellion.

The Farm Holiday Association was pledged to a farm strike. In addition, both this organization and its parent group, the Farmers Union, advocated the old Populist objection to a scarce currency based on gold, asked for increased income and inheritance taxes, and in general opposed the prevailing economic policies of the Republican dynasty of the twenties. They wanted immediate relief for debtors, an end to foreclosures, and rapid legislation. At the heart of their economic program was the demand for the cost of production as a minimum guaranteed return to the farmer based on growing costs, seed, a percentage of the farmer's real estate investment, personal property and equipment, and one hundred dollars per month for labor and management.

Roosevelt did not underestimate the depth of feeling in the Midwest or the crisis that produced it, and in the interim between his election and inauguration he did what he could. Convinced that the general recovery of the nation depended on the restoration of purchasing power to the farmer, Roosevelt instructed his supporters to give new agricultural legislation priority during the lame-duck session of Hoover's Congress. However, January and February of the new year passed with no legislation, and as soon as he took office Roosevelt called a special session of Congress. On 8 March, Wallace and Rexford Tugwell asked Roosevelt to hold Congress long enough to pass a new farm program, which they were in the process of drafting.

Henry Wallace felt as deeply as anyone the injustices done to the farmers during the last ten years, and in his own way was no less an agrarian Populist than were the supporters of Milo Reno. However, his analysis of the ills present in the farm economy was more penetrating, his solutions were more imaginative and less parochial, and his anger was tempered by a realistic appraisal of what was actually possible. He was convinced that the basic difficulty was the greater vulnerability of agriculture in the marketplace than that of industry. Unlike businessmen, farmers could not reduce their output to meet reduced demand and therefore could not maintain price levels for their product. In the language of economics, agriculture is extremely inelastic; a relatively small surplus can reduce prices dramatically, and food production cannot quickly change its levels to meet reduced demand. "In agriculture, supply sets the price," Wallace had written, but "in industry, price sets the supply." Because of the loss of foreign markets and the onset of the depression, the farmer's dollar, based on commodities such as corn and hogs, bought fewer city products, while the city dollar, based on gold, bought more farm products than ever before. To raise prices and reduce goods produced in the farming sector, Wallace proposed four measures: (1) to reduce crop acreage through a domestic allotment plan, (2) to lower and refinance the debts of farmers, (3) to extend farmers' ability to pay through "controlled inflation," and (4) to search for new foreign markets using reciprocal trade agreements and a truce in the tariff wars begun in the twenties.

Since the early twenties Wallace had argued in *Wallaces' Farmer* that reduction of crop acreage was the key short-term objective, and by 1931 many others shared his view. Among economists, discussion of production control proceeded from William J. Spillman's *Balancing The Farm Output* through John D. Black's *Agricultural Reform in the United States* to a practical "domestic allotment plan" put forward by M. L. Wilson, a farm economist from Montana, at a meeting in Chicago in 1931. In addition to Wilson and Wallace, three agricultural economists who would achieve prominence in the New Deal were present: Louis Bean, Mordecai Ezekiel, and Howard Tolley. Later, Wilson was summoned to meet the Democratic candidate who, with the consent of his advisers, gave his approval to the plan. In the spring of 1932 a domestic allotment bill was introduced in Congress. The bill concentrated on wheat, cotton, tobacco, and hogs. It asked for a tax on processors of farm products to pay for land taken out of production by leasing and called upon farmers to organize and carry out the program within the framework of a central plan, but the bill failed to pass. One month after Roosevelt's election a delegation of farm representatives gathered in Washington to request the passage of a new domestic allotment bill, which the administration was already committed to provide. After his appointment as secretary of agriculture in March 1933, Wallace asked and received Roosevelt's permission to draft a crop allotment plan but allowing the secretary of agriculture discretion in its application. Wallace, M. L. Wilson, Mordecai Ezekiel, Frederic Lee, Jerome Frank, and others set about the task of drafting the legislation.

The bill, signed into law by the president on 12 May, 1933, was a brilliant combination of old and new ideas, whose centerpiece was Title I, the Agricultural Adjustment Act (AAA). The concept of adjustment, doubtlessly related to Wallace's ratio concept of the World War I era, would curtail output in the short run but would also achieve a balanced economy by shifting production from surplus commodities to other areas. The major provisions of Title I established the power to control the quantity of commodities released for sale through marketing agreements and quotas, the leasing of farmland by government in order to withdraw it from cultivation, the power to maintain prices through government loans on stored crops or through purchases, and the licensing and taxing of processors of agricultural products.

The bill also included the Emergency Farm Mortgage Act, which created the Farm Credit Administration that refinanced mortgages, loaned money, and in general eased the immediate conditions provoking mob action in 1933. Taken as a whole, the bill gave Wallace what he wanted: a good chance to restore farm purchasing power to its pre-World

War I parity with other sectors of the economy and various means of approaching the problems of farm prices and surplus. It also gave—indeed, demanded of—the farmers and processors a junior partnership in determining the shape and success of farm relief.

At the center of Wallace's farm relief program lay the proposition that men of good will and energy would come forward to embrace and implement his plan. In Iowa, two men and an institution were among the first of many to respond creatively to the necessity of meeting the challenge of depression on the farm. The men were Jim Russell and Roswell Garst; the institution was the *Des Moines Register.* In 1933 the *Register* was an excellent newspaper, possessing a strong editorial page (whose most sparkling attraction was the syndicated column of Walter Lippmann), a vigorous Washington Bureau, and a first-class farm staff headed by Jim Russell. With a large farming constituency and its favorite son the secretary of agriculture, agricultural innovations and the whole thrust of the New Deal were reported sympathetically and in depth. The newspaper also had easy access to Wallace, who in turn found in the *Register* a platform for disseminating with maximum coverage his public pronouncements.

Russell was a good reporter, a lucid and persuasive commentator on the present crisis, and himself committed to the kind of change Wallace envisioned. In May 1933 he was disturbed that although grain prices were finally beginning to rise, hog prices remained depressed. Wheat and cotton farmers had organized themselves, but movement on corn and hogs had thus far been limited to the formation of a state advisory committee. There was hope for action at a meeting to be held in Chicago, convened by C. V. Gregory, the editor of the *Prairie Farmer,* after pressure from Wallace, George Peek, the administrator of the AAA, and from Chester Davis of the AAA's Production Control Administration, all of whom, Russell noted, "are said to be desirous that the farmers agree on what they think can and should be done."

However, the May meeting proved a disappointment to Russell. The delegates, two of whom were from Iowa, asked Wallace to name a committee to establish control over corn acreage and over the amount of pork marketed in the fall. In Russell's view, the meeting fell short on two counts. The situation required far more drastic measures than the producers were yet ready to face, and, more significantly, they placed the burden of organizing a corn-hog program directly on Wallace. After a visit to Wallace to confirm his own appreciation of Wallace's attitude, Russell returned home to urge in his columns a more active approach than that presented in Chicago. "Farmers who expect to have some plan of action presented to them," he wrote, "are not going to get any such thing." A mechanism for federal action existed – meetings between producers, processors, and administrators; contracts with packers; even suspension of the antitrust laws so that duplication of activities could be eliminated. However, Wallace insisted that his role in the implementation of the new program was to help farmers who had worked out their own programs. He refused to force a plan upon them.

Russell knew that Wallace's postion created special difficulties for the Midwest because the existing farm organizations did not represent any single commodity. The Grange, the Farmers Union, the Farm Bureau, and the Farm Holiday Association contained dairy farmers, hog producers, as well as growers of corn, wheat, and oats. The organizations were jealous of each other's influence and bitterly divided on the merits of the new program. There was no special representation for the corn-hog producer, whose two commodities produced in tandem constituted the lifeblood of Midwest agriculture.

In his efforts to help his constituency respond to Wallace, Russell was constrained by the duties and responsibilities of his job. He used his position to great advantage by presenting the issues with perception and by keeping them before his public. He also must have spoken privately wherever he thought it would do some good. However, there was not much more he could do on his own. In any event, it turned out to be a private word with Roswell Garst on the streets of Des Moines that suddenly transformed the situation.

In May 1933 Roswell was one month short of thirty-five years of age. He was squarely and firmly built, well muscled and strong from his years of milking cows, hefting milk cans and barrels of butter, and more recently, bags of seed corn. He was a long way from acquiring his watermelon stomach; his face still had a touch of boyishness in the fatty tissue of his cheeks. During the three years in his new career, he had undergone a personal form of heterosis in which the return to Coon Rapids, the challenge, the hard work, and the exhilaration of his new enterprise combined to produce an explosion of vigor. Like many who discover their own capacity for an active, wide-ranging life, Roswell was ready to take any challenge that came along. It is the consciousness of this capacity and the enthusiasm for fulfilling it that lie at the core of his actions in the summer of 1933.

There were other motives, of course. With his farm mortgaged in the attempt to sell seed for a product worth only twenty-five cents per bushel and burning brightly in the furnaces of Pocahontas County, Roswell had a vested interest in agricultural recovery. Because so few farmers were planting hybrid seed corn as yet, even the reduced acreage Wallace hoped to achieve would continue to provide a huge potential market for the new product. Furthermore, along with his new acquaintance Louis in Roselle

Township, Roswell was strongly moved by FDR's campaign and thrilled by his inaugural address. Roswell was of an age and experience to respond wholeheartedly to the new president's call to arms, "We have nothing to fear but fear itself!"

But most important of all his feelings were those he held for Henry Wallace, who not only provided the means to his new interest, but also provided an economic and political education. He was schooled by Wallace himself in the program the secretary now put forward and helped H. A. lace a campaign speech with adjectives one evening in front of the fireplace on the Garst farm. He had already responded to a Wallace request for help in a campaign for an inflatable currency called "commodity money." If H. A. needed more help, Roswell was the man to ask.

According to Roswell, the opportunity to help came in late May, when he met Russell on the street in Des Moines and asked why there was not yet a corn-hog program. Russell explained Wallace's desire that farmers take the initiative in organizing a response. "Well, let's start the 'ask'," Roswell replied. He accompanied Russell to his offices at the *Register* to look at the calendar of organizational meetings and discovered that the Federation of Iowa Farm Organizations was meeting in Des Moines in a few days. Russell called the federation and received their permission to initiate a discussion on corn and hogs. Discussion there was. At one point, a shouting match between Charles Hearst of the Iowa Farm Bureau and Milo Reno of the Farm Holiday Association was concluded by a decision to call a larger, better organized meeting during the following week. On 31 May, Russell could report that "plans were moving forward early this week for action on the part of Iowa farmers to formulate some plan for applying the farm act to corn and hogs." Russell identified Roswell as an independent farmer and quoted him on the need for action. "We sit back and wait for somebody else to do something," Roswell said, "and if we let the 'New Deal' turn into a misdeal, we'll have no one to blame but ourselves."

Roswell and Jim Russell invited approximately forty people to the next meeting and devised a strategy to circumvent the rivalries between the farm organizations. They limited each organization to two representatives and stipulated that twenty individual farmers and other interested parties should be invited. Along with Guy Roberts, the president of a small insurance company who had turned up at the first meeting, they worked out the nominations for office and the organization of a Committee of Five to take the lead for the Midwest. (Elizabeth described the proceedings as "cooked up"; Roswell said "it just happened that way.")

The meeting took place on 16 June at the Kirkwood Hotel under the auspices of the Federation of Iowa Farm Organizations. A representation of fifty attended, of whom twenty-six were representatives of thirteen

Iowa farm and commodity marketing organizations; the remainder were farmers and agribusinessmen. Guy Roberts called the meeting to order and nominated as secretary Oscar Heline, president of the Iowa Farmers' Grain Dealers Association and a strong farm bureau supporter who according to Roswell had wanted to be chairman. Roberts then nominated Roswell as chairman and he, like Heline, was unanimously elected. After some argument over the merits of higher prices for corn or for hogs, a proposal to name a committee of five farmers to formulate a plan for both corn and hogs was put forward. Roberts moved that Roswell appoint three members in addition to himself and Heline to form the Committee of Five. Roswell named Ralph Moyer of Fairfield, a large hog producer; R. M. "Spike" Evans of Laurens, to whom Roswell sold corn, and George Godfrey of Algona. The conference adopted resolutions that called for the reduction of corn and hog production for the coming year and the payment both of direct benefits to producers who participated in such a program and a bonus for light hogs. The secretary of agriculture was asked to take steps through trade agreements with the packing industry to effect an immediate increase in hog prices.

While Iowa farmers were organizing themselves early in June, the government offered meat packers a trade agreement based on a scale of higher prices for medium weight hogs, so that farmers would be encouraged to sell their pork before it reached normal maturity. The packers seemed willing, and Russell reported Iowa farmers "heartened" by this news. By 16 June, when Roswell became chairman of the Iowa Corn-Hog Committee, a meeting was arranged between processors and producers by A. G. Black, an agricultural economist from Iowa State College who had been appointed national administrator of the corn-hog section of the AAA. Black set as his immediate goal a reduction of 15–20 percent in the tonnage of pork marketed and tried to arrange a trade agreement between the interested parties. After some delay, Black managed to convene a conference of producers, packers, processors, and consumers for Monday, 26 June, in Washington. He invited Roswell from the Iowa Corn-Hog Committee and Charles Hearst from the Iowa Farm Bureau to represent the producers.

Roswell received the invitation by telephone on the afternoon of Friday, 23 June, one week after his election, during what must have been the first meeting of the Committee of Five in Des Moines. The committee members had to make up the price of an unexpected and immediate ticket to Washington, and Roswell left via the Chicago train that night, without even a suitcase. His departure marked the beginning of what S. D. Henry would have called a summer "of general rush and hurrah, of scramble and inconvenience."

ROSWELL arrived in Washington at 9 A.M. on Monday and went straight
to the Department of Agriculture, where the hearings were just beginning. He spent the first hour listening to Thomas E. Wilson, chairman of
the Wilson Packing Company, present the processors' proposal for cutting
costs. Wilson suggested that packers eliminate duplication of effort by
dividing the trade carried by various railroads among themselves—
Wilson Packing could deal exclusively with customers on the Milwaukee
Railroad, Rath Packing with those on the Illinois Central, and so on. By
eliminating duplication of sales and shipping procedures, the processors
could cut costs, pass the savings on to the farmer, and accept a negotiated
fair return.

In midmorning Jerome Frank, general counsel for the AAA, asked if
anyone in the room represented the pork producers. Roswell responded
and introduced himself as a farmer. He had listened attentively to Mr.
Wilson's speech, he explained, but he hadn't had time to read Wilson's
proposal because he couldn't read and listen at the same time. "I'm just a
farmer," he remarked, tongue-in-cheek. Then he analyzed the problem of
determining "fair return," especially as the railroads applied the term, and
concluded that nobody ever knew exactly what a fair return was. Roswell
asked that the approach be shifted to the relationship between the cost of
raising pork and the price the processors received for the finished product. He was willing to accept lower costs for processors but asked that
they be reflected as well in the price the farmer got from them for the raw
product, that is, the hogs they had raised. He offered a variation on his
half-the-increase technique: if the processors narrowed the margin between their profit and the farmer's when they reduced their costs, "as a
farmer I would be willing to give you half of the savings."

"You did a wonderful job," Frank told Roswell after the meeting and
took him downstairs to meet Rexford Tugwell, assistant secretary of agriculture. Frank and Tugwell invited Roswell to spend the rest of the week
in the house they shared that summer, and they coached him on questions
to put to the processors. "Night after night," historian Arthur Schlesinger,
Jr., wrote, "stray lawyers, economists, newspapermen, and innocent by-
standers appeared at the house he shared with Tugwell, and indulged
heavily in conversation and bourbon. It was sometimes hard to tell which
was the more intoxicating." Frank found Roswell's "just a farmer" approach especially effective. "Act like you're a country boy in a whore-
house and don't quite know what to say," he advised his protégé.

Roswell attended meetings the week of 26 June, returned home that
weekend, and was recalled on 7 July, apparently because the packers
objected to the levying of a processing tax. He testified intermittently
during the rest of the summer but became increasingly reluctant to follow

the line Frank and Tugwell set forth. He found himself in the middle of a struggle within the department over what policies the AAA should follow. Peek, the single-minded crusader for the equality of agriculture with industry, insisted upon the primacy of marketing agreements to ensure a fair price for the farmer. Tugwell and Frank went along with the idea of agreements but suspected they were intended to fill the pockets of processors and farmers; instead, they hoped to use them to achieve a balance within the total economy. Furthermore, Frank thought that the processors owed the government something in return for their release from the restrictions of the antitrust laws and that the way to prevent excessive price increases was to obtain access to the company books.

Roswell balked over access to the books. His own business instincts led him to sympathize with and defend Wilson on this point; he believed Frank and Tugwell were going too far. He liked Wilson, admired the way he had conducted himself throughout the hearings, and the two became good friends. Wilson had enjoyed Roswell's performance. When he introduced Roswell to a friend, he would say, "I'd like you to meet Bob Garst. He's just a farmer."

During the week when Roswell was in Washington, Wallace was in Des Moines, at the end of a midwestern tour of speech making and opinion gathering. On 27 June he conferred with members of the Committee of Five who were in town and expressed his pleasure with Iowa's response to the corn-hog problem. In Washington he talked to Roswell and urged him to see that other states were organized along the same lines. That week, Russell wrote that Iowa farmers had assumed "definite leadership" in the formulation of a national corn-hog program.

SUNDAY, 2 July, Roswell received a wire from Washington announcing 12 July as the provisional date for a national conference to be held in Des Moines and confirming Wallace's instructions to organize the other Corn Belt states. The next day he left for Chicago and a meeting with A. G. Black, Earl Smith of the Illinois Agricultural Association and other Illinois producers on Wednesday, and spent Thursday meeting with processors. From Chicago he travelled to Washington, probably summoned to take part in the processing tax debate that was holding up a marketing agreement, then returned home around 10 July.

The national conference had been postponed until 18 July to give other states time to organize delegations, so it was probably during this period – 10 to 15 July – that Roswell and his Iowa Committee of Five did their organizing for Wallace. Spike Evans went to Minnesota and South Dakota, Roswell to Illinois and Indiana, and other members to Nebraska,

Kansas, and Missouri. In Indiana Roswell's visit resulted in the recruit-
ment of Claude Wickard, a state senator, soon to be national corn-hog
administrator and eventually secretary of agriculture. Roswell led the
meeting of Indiana producers at Indianapolis, told his audience that Wallace had sent him to arouse interest in the new farm program, outlined
the efforts that had been made, and announced the meeting to be held in
Des Moines on 18 July. "Now I think the way to proceed," Roswell said,
according to Wickard,

is to see what you want to do, if you want to do anything, and how you want to
approach it. The first thing to do is to elect a permanent chairman. I've filled my
mission here from Henry Wallace. Now if someone will make a nomination. . . .

The Indiana group was not unprepared for Roswell's visit; Claude
Wickard was immediately nominated as chairman and the nominations
were closed. "Garst smiled," Wickard reported, "and called for the vote."
By Saturday, 15 July, the delegations were organized, and a front-
page headline in the Sunday *Register* reported Garst's announcement that
ten states would send seventy-six delegates to the Des Moines conference. Earlier, Roswell urged that states be represented in proportion to
their total production of corn and hogs. Consequently, Iowa sent nineteen
delegates, the largest single representation. When the meeting actually
convened at the Kirkwood Hotel on 19 July, the large number of observ-
ers and interested parties brought the total to nearly three hundred, according to Tom Rogers, who covered the event for the *Coon Rapids Enterprise.*
Roswell called the meeting to order, then gave the chair to A. G.
Black. Plans for the orderly marketing of corn and hogs were agreed
upon, noted Rogers, "in accordance with the desires of the administration." The meeting proceeded smoothly for the most part, and committees
were appointed. Roswell, "administration leader in the movement and
perhaps the most influential man there," Rogers reported, got high marks
for his performance. Most of the farmers were poor speakers, Rogers
complained, and could not be heard in the rear of the room. "Garst, however," he said, "spoke clearly and well, giving the best farmer talk of the
day."
The National Corn-Hog Committee that emerged centered on two
bodies. The first was the Committee of Twenty-Five, which included all
the members of the original Iowa Committee of Five and William McArthur, a state senator from Mason City. From among this larger committee
a national Committee of Five was chosen, which would begin conferring
two days hence in Chicago with a committee of packers. This national
Committee of Five consisted of Earl Smith, president of the Illinois Agri-

cultural Association and chairman of the National Corn-Hog Committee; Ralph Moyer, secretary; Ed O'Neal, president of the American Farm Bureau Federation; C. V. Gregory, editor of the *Prairie Farmer;* and Roswell Garst.

With preliminary resolutions in hand for a processing tax and marketing agreements with processors, and with the authority to carry out specific negotiations, Roswell and his fellow committee members took the train to Chicago. There followed several days of meetings with representatives of the packing industry, during which the necessary agreements were put together. If final figures were not always reached, at least agreement in principle was achieved. The Committee of Five thus fulfilled its immediate charge; the Committee of Twenty-Five gathered as arranged in Chicago on 24 July and by the following night the National Corn-Hog Committee had a program for Henry Wallace.

During this apparently climactic week of progress in Chicago, other events occurred that forced the Corn-Hog Committee and the administration to lay aside their work on a comprehensive program and concentrate on the single problem of hogs. That same week, the grain market plummeted far enough and fast enough to be closed by Saturday on Wallace's orders, which also included a price freeze imposed on trade in all grains. Hog prices, which had started an upward trend earlier in the month, collapsed as well, along with the corn futures market. The immediate result of these misfortunes would be a rush by farmers to dump their pig crop as fast as possible. A huge surplus of pork was about to glut a marketplace already in distress and would continue to do so throughout the fall. Consequently, at the end of July a complete collapse of midwestern agriculture seemed imminent.

A month earlier, Roswell had been concerned by the June pig report predicting an 8 percent increase in the number of sows that would farrow in the fall of 1933. He had seen the report during one of his journeys to Washington in June. On his way to the capital after a weekend visit to Admiral Perry Garst, his uncle living in retirement in Virginia, Roswell stopped along Chesapeake Bay and swam to a duck blind to contemplate the problem of pigs. He concluded that pregnant or "piggy" sows would have to be slaughtered. He thought the government should buy them from farmers and perhaps sell the meat to Russia. Back in Washington, he persuaded Tugwell to make money available if such a proposal were accepted.

Roswell's suggestion was taken up by the national committee during their deliberations in July. They asked the Department of Agriculture to make payments to farmers who marketed piggy sows and certain "light" pigs, whose precise weights were as yet unspecified. However, by the time of the Chicago meeting, it was clear that disposing of piggy sows alone would not relieve the pressing problem that the present live pig crop constituted. John Wilson of Ohio proposed the immediate slaughter of virtually all light pigs. He made the suggestion to Roswell on or near July 24th and asked Roswell to present his proposal to the Corn-Hog Committee. Roswell did so; the proposal was accepted and passed to the administration for action.

Through the last week in July to 2 August, AAA administrators worked on a plan for intensive slaughter. Late that day, under growing pressure from the heavy marketing of hogs that had followed the collapse of the markets, George Peek announced a meeting on 10 August of producers, marketing agencies, packers, and wholesale and retail meat dealers to get an emergency program underway. The Committee of Five reached Washington Saturday, 5 August (Roswell by air, apparently his first flight) and began a round of meetings. By Tuesday the producers and administrators had a program drafted, and on 10 August it was accepted by the full meeting of all parties.

The plan provided for government purchase of 5 million hogs before October, of which 1 million would be sows about to farrow and 4 million would be little pigs weighing from 25 to 100 pounds. The sows were to be purchased at four dollars per head above the regular market price, and the little pigs from six dollars to nine dollars per hundredweight. The processors agreed that money for the plan would be provided by the proposed processing tax on hogs weighing more than 235 pounds. All the edible meat from the slaughter would be sold by the government at a moderate price to charity and relief organizations, which would help make the program a support for the market rather than simply a dumping operation. The plan was intended to reduce heavy marketing of hogs during the coming winter and spring, thereby raising the price level in the long term and giving a fair price to those farmers who would in any case be forced to slaughter their light hogs because of the feed shortage.

Garst, Moyer, Hearst, McArthur, Heline, and Evans stayed in Washington to work out the details of the operation and marketing schedule with the packers. By 16 August Wallace, Harry Hopkins, and Roosevelt agreed upon the final details, and on 23 August the slaughter began. "30,000 hogs die for Country," the *Register* reported on the first day, and on the next day reported almost 100,000 slaughtered. The AAA was well on the way to buying the entire 5 million hogs within forty days, as intended by the plan.

The response to the program was "beyond all expectations," Russell reported at the end of the first week of processing, but it had produced problems. The small pigs were glutting the markets and plants, and on occasion were even slipping through the stockyard fences to run loose. Consequently, the government temporarily suspended the purchase of hogs weighing less than 80 pounds. Speculators bought hogs from farmers and collected the benefits, and farmers held their sows in the hope that increased prices would make the litters even more valuable later. To curb these practices, the government granted permits that forced the farmer-owners to sell directly to the government and announced that sows about to farrow would be accepted at 240 pounds instead of at 275. Unless more piggy sows were killed, there would still be a surplus of pork in 1933. The AAA program "has not been running perfectly," the *Register* noted. "Probably no one presumed it would at the start."

Ultimately, not enough piggy sows were killed to reduce the number of pigs as much as the producers and the AAA had hoped, and hog prices rose only slightly. However, 100 million pounds of meat were distributed to the needy; 22 million pounds of grease and lard were sold, and the farmers got 90 percent of the $33 million the program cost at a time when they desperately needed the money. Furthermore, a prolonged and large-scale slaughter of light pigs would have occurred anyway, with little hope of benefit to the farmers or to the economy.

The killing of the little pigs raised a great outcry and for years afterwards was for many Republicans the first item in their condemnation of Roosevelt. Administrators, expecting some reaction if not what actually occurred, explained that all pigs were raised to be killed and their admittedly premature termination was amply justified by the economic crisis. Wallace pointed out that the plowing under of cotton and the slaughter of the pigs were emergency acts "made necessary by the almost insane lack of world statesmanship during the period from 1920 to 1932," defended the farmer's right to control his production just as industry controlled theirs, and reacted testily to the charges of inhumanity in killing baby pigs rather than only full-grown ones. People seemed to think, he said, that "every little pig has the right to attain before slaughter the full pigginess of his pigness. To hear them talk, you would have thought that pigs were raised for pets."

WITH the emergency program underway, the administrators, producers, and processors could now get on with a long-term plan for corn and hogs. The Iowa delegation was especially anxious to do something about corn because Iowa, largely untouched by the drought, still had large stocks on hand and its members were disturbed by talk in the other states that the drought had disposed of the problem of surplus corn. The pattern of negotiation continued: producers met to draft their proposals, processors met to discuss a processing tax, and administrators shuttled back and forth between the two groups.

Roswell attended a meeting of the Committee of Twenty-Five, held at

the Union League Club in Chicago on 6 September at which a program
was drafted calling for a 15–20 percent reduction in corn acreage and a
further 20 percent reduction in pork. On 8 September Moyer, Garst,
Smith, and a member each from Kansas and Missouri arrived in Washington to present the proposal to A. G. Black and Claude Wickard, now the
assistant corn-hog administrator. On 13 September, accompanied by
Wickard and Chester Davis, chief of production control, Roswell and his
colleagues returned to Chicago to work out details of the proposal.

The weeks of travel, negotiation, and persuasion on behalf of the new
program were stretching into months, taking Roswell entirely away from
his only livelihood, selling corn. To continue he had to find alternative
sources of money. He persuaded Wallace to pay his travel expenses and
five dollars per day while on corn-hog business, which took care of his
personal needs. To provide for Elizabeth, the children, and the farm, he
went for help to two Iowa insurance companies, Equitable and Central
Life Assurance. He farmed only 200 acres, he told them, they farmed
millions, but everyone needed a farm program desperately. He would not
act in their special interest; instead, he asked them, in the interest of
getting a program that would benefit everybody, to subsidize Elizabeth
three hundred dollars per month until he had finished his part in creating
a corn-hog program. The companies agreed, and Roswell could get on
with "saving the world," as his family, who saw even less of him than when
he was on the road, characterized his present burst of energy.

One month later on 18 October the corn-hog program finally
emerged. Described by Richard Wilson of the *Register* as "the greatest
agricultural production control measure yet undertaken," and from which
Iowa farmers alone could receive $75 million in benefits, the program
settled on a reduction of corn acreage by at least 20 percent and a reduction of hog farrowing of at least 25 percent. A compromise was reached
on the processing tax for hogs: it would begin on 5 November at $0.50
cents per hundredweight instead of $1.00 but would be raised to $2.00 by
1 February, 1934. The corn tax was not yet announced, but it was intended to be fixed at the producers' figure of $0.27 or $0.28. Milo Reno
denounced the plan as "an adroit way of bribing farmers to lie quietly
while the shackles of bureaucracy are more firmly placed on their wrists."
The same edition of the *Register* commented, "the new corn-hog program
strikes the shackles off the hands of the Iowa farmer and gives him the
chance to create for himself the greatest degree of agricultural prosperity
the state has ever known."

There was justice in the claim of Reno and others that the program
did not sufficiently alleviate the immediate problem. During mid-October,
corn dropped below $0.20 cents per bushel in country elevators through-

out Iowa; the grain market, in Russell's words, "had hit the toboggan." Other commodity prices were falling again, while farm implement prices were rising. In Iowa, farmers blocked roads and poured out milk; in North Dakota, Governor William Langer imposed an embargo on the shipment of grain; in Wisconsin, farmers occupied the state legislature. Five governors, led by Floyd Olson of Minnesota, came to Washington to demand that the government adopt compulsory production control and price-fixing for all basic commodities.

Although they could not accept the governors' demands, Wallace and Roosevelt were disturbed by the resurgence of unrest and discussed new measures at a cabinet meeting on 29 October. The most promising additional action seemed to be a loan on corn and wheat, an indirect form of price-fixing that had first been applied to cotton. Oscar Johnston, a Mississippi planter, suggested that the government make loans to cotton farmers at a rate above the market price and hold the cotton as security, an action that would keep the surplus from further depressing the market. If prices rose above the loan, the grower could redeem his cotton; if not, it remained in the possession of the government. State senator Louis Murphy of Dubuque had already urged a $0.60 corn loan upon Wallace, who by 22 October had endorsed such a program. On 26 October, after obtaining Roosevelt's approval, Wallace announced a rate of $0.50 per bushel to be loaned to farmers who cooperated in the corn-hog program and committed the government to taking up to 75 percent of the corn each farmer offered for sale. The precise manner in which the corn would be set aside, or "sealed," was not yet decided, but the program would make an additional $200 million immediately available to Corn Belt farmers.

On the day Wallace announced the loan on corn, Roswell appeared in his capacity as chairman of the Iowa Corn-Hog Committee at a conference held in Ames to introduce the new program to Iowa. Contracts for farmers, Roswell told Russell, had been drafted, but it would be two weeks before they were printed. When they did appear, Roswell called another conference in Des Moines to study them, and the Extension Department of Iowa State conducted statewide study meetings. The regional drive began the first week of November, attended by various officials of the farm administration. Roswell explained the workings of the corn loan, now at $0.45, to readers of the *Enterprise,* and in December was reported by Rogers to be one of a dozen men "in charge of the new set-up in the state," although not one of the four official administrators. In December Roswell was still travelling throughout the state explaining the program at farmers' meetings, as well as instructing field administrators at a meeting in Des Moines.

"EVENTS rather than theories, experience rather than doctrine, supply the reasons by which men are brought into line," commented Walter Lippmann in August about the impact of the New Deal. His words were especially appropriate for the sequence of events that occurred during the summer and fall when the corn-hog program emerged. No one knew whether the new measures would work, Lippmann explained, but even if they had to be reversed or modified, something important had happened. "We do know," Lippmann continued:

that in the spring we overcame the paralysis of government in Washington, and were able to achieve unity of action. We do know that we were able to sweep aside the obstructions of organized minorities and the influences of private powers. We do know that we have seen new energies, new faces, young men, enterprising and hopeful minds in the responsible posts. We do know that the national spirit has been revived, that frightened calculation is giving way to confidence and even to magnanimity.

The months devoted to the farm program widened Roswell's circle of friends and broadened his interests as he worked enthusiastically with other enterprising and hopeful minds. He developed a working relationship with the old and the new Midwest farm leaders, several of whom accepted jobs in the New Deal, and extended his business acquaintances to men such as Thomas Wilson. In Washington he got to know Milo Perkins, author of the food stamp program, and his aides Phil Maguire and Arthur Becker; economists Howard Tolley, Louis Bean, and Mordecai Ezekiel; and Gardner "Pat" Jackson and his wife, Dode.

Pat Jackson, one of the great liberals of his generation, inspired affection in all of his New Deal colleagues and became a favorite of both Franklin and Eleanor Roosevelt. He was a leader in the fight to save Sacco and Vanzetti, a man whose "abundant sympathy, courage, and curiosity," Arthur Schlesinger writes, "kept him in the middle of one fight after another for the underprivileged." When Roswell came to Washington, Jackson was working for Fred Howe on the Consumers' Council, which was also keeping a close watch on marketing negotiations. By Jackson, Roswell was further educated in liberal values and even liberal arts, and in the coming years Pat would serve as a rich source of new acquaintances, a great instructor in the ways of Washington politics, and, along with Dode, an intimate friend to himself and Elizabeth.

Roswell met Jackson through his brother Jonathan, who was working for the Consumers' Council. In 1926 Johnny returned to France to study geography at the University of Grenoble, moved to Edinburgh for a year, after which he taught for a year at the University of California at Davis. In 1930 he travelled to Edinburgh to complete his Ph.D., then worked in the Hebrides for two years helping the Scottish Department of Agriculture develop a process of extracting nitrogen from peat bogs. In 1932 he wired that he was "coming home to see the Depression," and in 1933 he arrived in Washington. Contemptuous of people who complained of intellectual fatigue, he used to laugh at Elizabeth when she claimed that people's brains got tired. After a few months in Washington, he admitted: "Elizabeth, you were right. You get positively brain-boggled trying to figure out what to do next." Johnny charmed the Jacksons, brought Roswell into their circle of friends and into the intellectual atmosphere of the most liberal wing of the New Deal.

His own brief but deep immersion in this world left Roswell with a choice in the fall of 1933 – to stay in the Department of Agriculture in some official capacity or return to the hybrid seed corn business. His commercial instincts and his desire to recoup for his children the patrimony he had lost in 1929–30 prevailed, and he returned to Coon Rapids. It was a decision he believed – or hoped – Henry Wallace would approve, providing the means to carry on agricultural change in a manner that suited his present ambitions and in the place where he felt most comfortable. The New Deal farm program was now sold – hybrid seed corn was not.

Building a Seed Corn Plant: 1933–36

Until the winter of 1933, all corn raised at Coon Rapids was shipped to the Wallace operation in Reinbeck to be dried, graded, and returned to Garst and Thomas. However, as production increased by several thousand bushels each year, and as corn was sold in eighteen counties by spring 1933, the new company decided to create its own processing system. During September and October 1933, Roswell's old dairy barn was converted into a sorting and selecting plant for the 10,000 bushels Garst and Thomas had grown that summer. "Under the new arrangement," Tom Rogers reported, "the corn will be kept here and local labor employed, all of which means more money in circulation in Coon Rapids." The new arrangement owed its creation to Ralph Wheeler, a self-taught mechanical engineer whose seed-corn processing machinery would become the prototype for much of the later industry.

The younger son of a respectable and God-fearing Presbyterian family, from the age of ten Ralph was taken out of school each year to pick corn during the harvest season, an act which produced a life-long bitterness over his conscription and a strong aversion to farming as a career. When he finished grade school, he left the farm in the hands of his brother, became an electrician by correspondence course, raised a great deal of hell, and eventually drifted into Coon Rapids in 1933 looking for a job. Charley Thomas hired him to do some wiring and to pitch in with the sorting operation at the Garst farm. Ralph asked for $0.40 per hour, a good wage in 1933, not caring much whether he got this particular job or not, because he did not think Garst and Thomas had much of a future. "Hybrid corn didn't seem like a very good idea," he recalled. "My dad wouldn't plant it because he wouldn't depend on a seed company to furnish him seed. Too many of them had been shysters before that."

But the processing of seed corn interested him, and he began contributing ideas for the sorting tables and bins that were set up that fall. As the harvest came in, approximately 400 bushels per day were husked at the Thomas farm, then brought over to the Garst farm, where twelve or fifteen workers sorted through the ears and culled the best. Late in October a shelling machine arrived, 300 bushels of ear corn were shelled and then driven to Reinbeck by Charley Thomas and Leo Watrous.

That fall there was talk about building a drying rig on the farm, but some Des Moines engineers were pessimistic about the prospects. However, Ralph decided that it could be done, and after about 7,000 bushels had been trucked to Reinbeck, Charley and Roswell told Ralph to do what he could. During November 1933 Ralph, with the help of Bill Kupka, installed an old furnace in the basement of the sorting barn that had three hot-air pipes running to the cribs overhead. Ralph borrowed the blower from an ensilage cutter and powered it with an electric motor, which forced hot air through the cribs. To eliminate the unpleasant hourly climb through the crib to determine the temperature (which at first turned out to be the wrong one), Ralph rigged up a brooder-stove thermostat with an indicator extension near the furnace, so that the fireman could see the temperature at all times. "This apparatus is still in the experimental stages," Rogers judiciously observed, but it convinced Roswell and Charley that they could do their own processing. Throughout December Ralph improved both the drier and the sorters on the Garst farm while Garst and Thomas made plans for a major expansion. Next year there would be no trucks sent to Reinbeck.

By December 1933 Charley and Bob advised farmers via *Enterprise* advertisements that they had better hurry if they wanted hybrid corn, and by February 1934 the company's supply was sold out. "We have instructed our field men to quit taking orders," Charley told Rogers. In the spring of 1934 they contracted 1,225 acres for seed corn, and in July they sent 350 men into the fields to detassel. Of this acreage, 500 was around Coon Rapids, 270 at Bayard, 350 near Lake City, and 350 near Sac City. The acreage was distributed to acclimatize the seed to the areas in which it would be sold and to begin the inbreeding of specific varieties for each area.

Work also began in July 1934 on the first brand-new Garst and Thomas building, a drying and grading plant. Charley and Roswell leased a part of the old gravel pit between the Milwaukee Railroad tracks and Muller's harness shop to the north, not for access to a railhead (Grettenberg Grain provided that), but simply because it was the cheapest land available. Micko McBroom, Louise Garst's husband, designed a three-story building of hollow tile, with two driers of 100-bushel per hour capacity. The driers and elevator machinery were on the top floor, the second was for grading corn, and the first for treating the corn with mercury dust and sacking it. Ralph, in consultation with Micko, designed the machinery for shelling, grading, treating, weighing, and sacking.

Throughout August two shifts worked seven hours per day to put up the building while Ralph worked on the machinery. The sacking and treating machine was built to his specifications by two local workmen identified as Bill and Storony; it held five bags and could be quickly rotated to allow the removal and replacement of the bags. "The machine looks just as good as any factory-built product," Rogers remarked. Ralph designed a belt-sorting system, a major improvement over the sorting tables he had seen at the Garst farm, but which he had to modify; a single long belt allowed some sorters to do less work than others. Consequently, Ralph changed to a series of short belts, each with an equal number of sorters, thereby achieving a considerable gain in efficiency. He also created mechanical shuckers and grading machines that worked by weight and specific gravity. In the beginning, only four sizes were graded – large and small flat, large and small round – but with specific gravity machines and length graders, ten kernel sizes would eventually be differentiated. Micko McBroom once told Roswell and Charley that Ralph was the finest engineer with whom he had ever worked.

"I wasn't an engineer," Ralph used to insist, "I was just a mechanic that was starving to death." He once described his method of engineering as getting acquainted with people who knew the things he needed to know. He cultivated an electrical engineer from Des Moines, an aerodynamics engineer who could tell him about the movement of air, and a steel engineer in Omaha. "In the meantime," he said, "I had learned an awful lot of swear words but also a lot of thumb rules that engineers never would let you catch them using." Above all, he improvised, juggling his knowledge with his materials, his method with the result required, often drawing his plans on the floor with crayon or chalk, constantly keeping in mind the limited means of the company. "I never made a mistake that wouldn't work at least the rest of the season," he said, although in the process he left a great deal of scrap lying around. Pointing to a pile of rusting metal behind a building one day, he remarked to Maurice Campbell, "There's the college education Garst and Thomas gave me."

Severe drought in August 1934 brought a major crisis to Garst and

Thomas. Roswell and Charley halted work on the new building and surveyed their fields to see whether there would be any corn to process. They found enough hybrid corn in north-central Iowa to provide at least for last year's customers and decided to finish the plant. By mid-September 1934 the motors, driers, graders, and miscellaneous equipment were installed, and the plant went into operation. Because of the drought, it would process only 10,000 bushels rather than the 30,000 originally anticipated.

John Parker ran the sorting plant, which was still located at the Garst farm, and Ralph managed the new drying and grading plant, moving from machine to machine, locating faults and modifying machines on the spot. He acquired a store-bought moisture-testing machine, which took a sample of shelled corn, ground it up, and produced a reading on a gauge within one minute. The corn came into the plant with a moisture content of from 14 to 17 percent. To ensure germination, the corn had to be dried accurately and uniformly to 12 percent.

A third operation was added in December, to ensure that as much seed as possible was salvaged from the diminished 1934 crop. Forty bean-sorting machines were installed in what had been Ballard's Garage, each consisting of a hopper that held about one-half bushel of shelled corn that was fed out slowly on a conveyor belt. This corn, which had been rejected in the earlier and cruder processing, was sorted again by forty women, who were able to save a large number of kernels.

Although he had no technical experience, Roswell involved himself deeply in the processing part of the operation. "Bob just had an idea a minute," Ralph said. "His mind was working all the time." Because he lacked knowledge of building strength, horsepower, or electricity, his suggestions were often impractical, and it became part of Ralph's job to pick out the practical ideas. If Ralph thought an idea was useless, he would tell Roswell that he needed to think it over. "I'd think it over for about two days and then we'd start over again. But if you argued with him, he would outtalk you. More words in five minutes than I can think of all my life." (When Roswell was preoccupied with a different aspect of the business, he would sometimes pass Ralph in the street without a word of acknowledgment, an idiosyncrasy that the staff of Garst and Thomas learned to accept.) Roswell also taught Ralph to spend more money on his machines than Ralph was at first inclined to do. About to build new conveyors some years later, Ralph recalled:

We had figured out a 24-inch conveyor, which cost around nine or ten thousand dollars. That sounded like a hell of a lot of money to me. A Farm. If I'd had that money I'd probably have bought a farm. But anyway we got it all figured out and then Bob asked how much more it would cost to make it 36 inches. God, it pretty nearly floored me. I never even thought of it. But it only cost 6 percent more than the 24-inch belt.

After that, Ralph ordered extralarge driers and expensive bearings, for which he was occasionally criticized by others. "We're not trying to save money, we're trying to dry corn," he would reply. In later years he concentrated on protecting the seed on its journey through the plant, and in 1940 he put rubber cylinders on his corn shellers. In succeeding years he installed rubber pads wherever the corn had to be dropped, put rubber floats on the conveyors, and padded boards on field wagons. "I think probably the greatest thing we did in the seed industry in my time," Ralph said, "was to learn to handle seeds carefully."

Roswell made plans in the spring of 1935 for a 30,000-bushel year, and to that end Garst and Thomas bought the Ford garage building on West Main Street as a warehouse. They replaced the Garst farm sorting operation by building a sorting, shelling, and drying plant as an extension and enlargement of the 1934 building. Micko McBroom was again the architect, Ralph Wheeler the consulting engineer, and McCorkle and Son the builders. Work proceeded throughout the summer, and on 27 September, 1935 Tom Rogers announced the new plant would begin processing corn within the next week. He commented proudly:

They have built in Coon Rapids what is without doubt the world's finest seed processing plant, capable of taking in 1500 bushels of ear corn containing a high moisture content each day, and transferring the 1500 bushels from the state of ear corn into sacked, graded and treated seed corn, ready for the planter. Approximately a hundred men will be given employment in handling their seed, and in so far as possible these men have been hired locally, which is a big boost to Coon Rapids.

The extension of the existing plant was a gamble, for other seed companies were building a series of local seed plants near their largest acreages, thereby eliminating the costly trucking. However, Roswell and Charley agreed they would retain greater control over the quality of their processing if they operated only one plant and the quality of germination achieved with the seed would more than pay for the additional expense and risk of trucking. They had only one Ralph Wheeler.

The new plant began operation about 1 October with a small shakedown staff looking for problems. They found one after two days; the arrangement by which air was forced from the furnace through the corn also forced gas fumes into the building. Ralph and his crew worked all night to change the location of the fans and reorganize the entire system to pull the hot air through the corn from above, which prevented the dispersal of fumes.

Meanwhile, new inbreds were being developed by Pioneer Hi-Bred. All new hybrids grown or sold in the state had to be certified by the Extension Department of Iowa State, which determined if they were grown under proper conditions for foundation stock, if they were isolated from other corn, and if they produced both a higher yield and a stiffer stalk in state yield tests. The college regularly compiled and released a list of hybrids that were certified. In 1935, 85 percent of those certified were Pioneer of Des Moines/Garst and Thomas; the remaining 15 percent were grown in small acreages by a number of producers.

It looked like a promising year. Instead of drought, summer rains soaked the crops and an abundant harvest of seed corn poured into Coon Rapids to be processed. On 4 October, a freeze, not uncommon for that time of year, produced no immediately noticeable effect. Rogers, on 11 October, sat down at his typewriter to write with satisfaction of a town in which there was work for all, new construction, stores doing a good business, "and even this old print shop humming like a factory with machinery going at top speed." The community would remember 1935 as a good year, with plentiful hay and corn.

By the third week in October, the situation was not so idyllic. After a month of processing early varieties of seed corn, Garst and Thomas turned to the late varieties, only to find that they had been seriously damaged by the freeze of early October. The corn looked perfectly good, but when the cobs were broken open, most of them were soft with mold and the kernels were severely damaged. The graders were instructed to break open every ear and discard the moldy cobs; the surviving ears were rechecked before going to the sheller. A large incubator was installed at the drying plant so that on-the-spot germination tests could be made. Iowa's entire corn crop had suffered; apparently the excessively heavy (although at the time welcome) rains of May and June had soaked the corn and caused it to mature too late to escape the October freeze. Seed corn dealers reported the situation to be the worst since 1917, and they predicted an acute shortage of corn that would pass germination tests. "The 1935 crop," Rogers had to report within two weeks of his earlier prediction, "apparently is going to be of a poor grade and good seed corn next spring will probably be at a premium save for the earlier and smaller varieties."

Although no jobs were immediately at risk, the freeze caused another crisis for Garst and Thomas. Salesmen were instructed to stop taking orders for seed until the extent of the damage could be determined and a new price set. In September seed had been sold for $8 per bushel, but after the freeze that price on the reduced amount of seed would have put them out of business. They had already borrowed $75,000 by 23 September, which was due on 13 November. This obligation was renewed and postponed until June 1936, and the price of corn was raised to $12 per bushel. Luckily, the sales campaign had been slow in starting that year, perhaps because the new plant took so much of Roswell's time, and the bulk of the corn was still unsold in late October. Consequently, they were able to sell enough $12 corn to show some profit and repay their annual debt. In 1934, government agencies had been reluctant to loan money to Charley Thomas; a disaster in 1935 could have cut off further credit.

Having run out of adequate hybrid seed, the company began processing open-pollinated corn to supply the demand for seed of any kind. As with the hybrids, germination samples were sent to the college for certification. Garst and Thomas also got business from the insurance companies, which were alarmed over the scarcity of seed corn and sent seed to Coon Rapids to be processed by a plant that was rapidly acquiring a reputation for careful work. In an attempt to salvage every possible bushel of hybrid seed corn, twenty additional bean sorters were operated, bringing the total number to sixty, while the processing of open-pollinated corn enabled the sorting season to continue at its usual level of employment throughout the winter.

The drought of 1934 and the freeze of 1935 also retarded the establishment of new hybrids, which required at least seven years of inbreeding and crossing to be developed and marketed. However, those that reached the market in 1935 had once again proved their superiority to open-pollinated corn, in spite of adverse weather. In February 1936 Iowa State announced that in the most extensive tests yet made, the yield of all hybrids was on average 10.8 percent higher per bushel. For the farmer, this meant an increase of from 21 to 36 bushels per acre for his crop. In addition to overall yield, factors such as percentage of standing corn, percentage of dropped corn, and percentage of damaged kernels were also measured. Pioneer had the consolation in this otherwise disappointing year of winning the college's Banner Trophy for variety 315, which produced the highest percentage above the average yield of all hybrid corn in Iowa.

There was also the promise of a large market for 1936–37, now that seed of any kind was scarce, and in the spring of 1936 Garst and Thomas planted 1,915 acres of seed around Coon Rapids, Lake City, Pocahontas, and Sac City. But the spring and summer were dry, and just as detasseling started in July, a blistering heat wave brought temperatures as high as 110°F and burned the corn more thoroughly than it had in 1934. In addition, the worst plague of grasshoppers in twenty years ate its way through alfalfa, red clover, and corn, in spite of a massive broadcast of poisoned bait. From 1928 to 1932, the average yearly corn harvest had been 438,700,000 bushels. The September 1936 crop forecast was for 196 million bushels, the lowest production since 1894, and 21 percent below the previous record low of 234 million in 1934. Although the quality of the seed corn was good, Garst and Thomas processed only 13,000 bushels. They were still in business, but only just.

Going West: 1936–39

"Our Hi-Bred corn is practically sold," Roswell wrote Jonathan in November 1936, three days after Roosevelt was reelected, "and I am going to start selling open-pollinated corn next week with all the power I have. I am going to start in Nebraska and western Iowa and if I do any good I am going to drive hard at it until I get stopped." The trip sprang from another risk taken. Roswell had traded three of his best counties in Iowa to Pioneer of Des Moines in return for the right to sell in Nebraska and all along the western and southwestern fringe of the Corn Belt, an area at its best just sufficiently moist for corn, but in those years parched and dust ridden. While the parent organization, Pioneer, moved east through the Corn Belt, Roswell began to move west.

Facing low stocks and a great demand for seed, Garst and Thomas made another decision, this time to follow Pioneer's lead and grow winter corn in Argentina. In December 1936 Ralph Wheeler sailed from New York to Buenos Aires and travelled fifty miles inland to the Dugan Ranch. Here he supervised the construction of a drying and processing plant for both companies. Because 315 was their best variety and probably the best drought-resistant variety of hybrid corn yet developed, they decided to grow as much of it as possible in Argentina. "We intend to give all of the 315 away," Roswell wrote to Johnny, "and thereby hope to put ourselves in a position of dominating the territory next year." Both 315 and 312 would be divided into seven-pound bags, to be distributed in the new areas and in the drought areas of western Iowa, where Garst and Thomas was beginning to lose customers.

To sell corn in Nebraska, Roswell had to find corn; consequently, he concentrated on the rivers, the largest of which is the Platte. Entering the northwest corner of the state, it shapes a path east in a lazy S, its axis moving southward until the river empties south of Omaha into the Missouri River. The Platte divides Nebraska into two unequal parts. In the larger northern section, a series of tributaries—the South, Middle, and North Loup, the Elkhorn, and others—feed into the Platte from the sand hills of north-central and western Nebraska. In the smaller, southern part of the state, Rock, Silver, and Salt Creeks feed into the Platte southwest of Omaha, while Weeping Water Creek empties directly into the Missouri. To the west, Medicine and Red Willow Creeks flow into the Republican River, which, along with the Little and Big Blue Rivers, flow south into Kansas. Flowing water was not in short supply in Nebraska, but rainfall was. Thus farmers planted along river flats hoping to eke out enough moisture to make a crop.

Accompanied by Jay Towne, a Des Moines friend, Roswell drove to Nebraska along the Lincoln Highway past Omaha to Columbus, down to the Kansas line, and over to the next county west. He then turned north to the South Dakota boundary, west one county, and back down south, repeating the pattern across eastern Nebraska as far as Grand Island, moving as much as possible through the river valleys that cut through his grid. He travelled two thousand miles in one week, stopping every fifteen or twenty miles to sell a bushel of open-pollinated corn and to tell people about hybrids. "I was vigorous and damned, damned ambitious," he said later. "I was in good health and I put in lots of hours." He started before 6 A.M. and drove until late at night, using his rapidly accumulating knowledge of the territory to break down his customers' reserve, talking about the Little Blue, Prairie Dog Creek, the sand hills, and where the rivers drained.

He observed the fields and farms as he drove, and what he saw he found both sad and exciting. Nebraska in the fall of 1936 was a dry, enervated state that had produced virtually no corn for the past three years. There were large corn cribs on every farm, but the only one that contained a substantial amount—about 500 bushels—was filled with 1935 corn, not a bushel of which, he believed, would germinate. However, the opportunity presented by this dismal scene filled him with excitement, and by the time he reached Lincoln he had already dashed off an enthusiastic note to Johnny, with more letters to follow when he got home. "I spent all of last week in Nebraska," he reported to his brother,

and the market for seed corn just bars exaggeration. . . . I am convinced that at least 500,000 bushels of seed corn will change hands in Nebraska between now and spring and it looks to me as though I can get 10% of the business and really set up a sales organization for Hi-Bred corn for next year.

He was still filled with enthusiasm in late December. "I don't know whether I wrote you fully about Nebraska or not," he wrote again to Johnny, "but I see one grand opportunity there."

Roswell immediately set to work on a plan for the distribution of his samples. He would distribute ten or twelve thousand bags of six-pound samples (each sample would plant an acre) in nine hundred townships, each consisting of six square miles, in fifty counties of Nebraska and western Iowa. "In other words," he told Johnny,

I can give away fifteen samples per township in the good ones and eight in the poor ones and get the users of Hi-Bred corn so well scattered that no man in western Iowa or eastern Nebraska can live more than three miles from a man who has had experience with it.

Before embarking on this new sales drive, he wanted all his present salesmen to have seen his processing plant, and in December he was hard at this task. He had been bringing in salesmen at the rate of four per trip and had made five round trips in the previous week, he told Johnny. "Believe me," he wrote,

I can get well acquainted with four people in a day. When the roads get bad I will likely bring some by train or by bus. It looks like I should have been born twins and I see the opportunity to put in more work than ever before.

After Christmas and throughout the new year of 1937, Roswell spent weeks at a time in western Iowa and Nebraska, looking for corn and customers, hiring salesmen and supervisors, and distributing his samples. Barney Trullinger, Viv Bell, Russ Dixon, and other early salesmen went with him or worked the territory on their own. His chief aim was to find good farmers who were willing to take the samples and sell seed corn themselves. The hiring of farmers as salesmen, like the half-the-increase program, was one of Roswell's major contributions to the industry, setting a pattern that would be followed throughout the Midwest.

He also hired supervisors for his field organization; one of the earliest was Arnold Ernst, of Auburn, Nebraska. A farmer for most of his life, in 1937 he sold buttermilk for a company based in Council Bluffs, Iowa, and had already sold some seed corn, since he had been approached earlier by Viv Bell. After a visit to Coon Rapids, he agreed to take over four or five counties in Nebraska and find salesmen. A homebody at heart and reluctant traveller—he was fed up with his present job because he had been sent out to Illinois for a time—Arnold stepped from frying pan to fire. He barely began to organize his territory in Nebraska when Roswell sent him to Oklahoma, and later to Kansas. In his first year, Arnold put 52,000 miles on his car. When he finally settled in Nebraska, he became accomplished in the use of the telephone.

Eastern Oklahoma was an early focal point for Roswell's campaign, perhaps because the family holdings there gave him a base of operations and connections with bankers and insurance companies. However, if Nebraska was dry, Oklahoma was desolate, and the going was hard indeed. John Parker, who began working for Garst and Thomas in 1933, loaded 150 bushels per load on a truck at Coon Rapids, delivered the load to the nearest north-south railhead, then drove to Durant, Oklahoma, to meet the train, unload the corn, and distribute it. The land looked withered, red, and dusty, and farming was primitive. On his first trip, Parker was asked to deliver round kernels to a salesman. Because there were as yet no planter plates for round varieties, Parker assumed that the salesman had made a mistake and brought him the more expensive medium flat kernels. "Do you know why I wanted large round?" the irritated salesman asked, "No," John replied. "Because," the salesman countered, "down here we plant it by hand."

After Oklahoma was organized, Roswell sent Arnold to Salina, in eastern Kansas, to develop a sales organization for that part of the state. Early in 1937 Roswell had discovered a directory that listed all the banks in a district, their size, and the names of their cashiers. He took the directory home – it came from the Coon Rapids bank – opened a map of Kansas, traced the rivers and their towns, and listed every bank in eastern Kansas that was in an area where corn would grow. Roswell wrote to 110 banks to announce that he was sending two seven-pound bags of seed corn and asked the bankers to distribute them to the two best farmers in their areas. Arnold Ernst made the first follow-up calls to the banks to discover what had happened to the samples. This turned out to be a slow process, made more difficult by the bank robberies that plagued the dust-bowl area and its fringe. At one bank, Arnold recalled:

I could see a man in there with a green sunvisor on, and a woman in there. And I tried to get in, but I couldn't. I'd rattle the door and he'd look up and then back down again. Finally a John Deere man from across the street came over and said, "Would you like to get into that bank? You know why you can't? This bank has been held up three times and you're not about to get in there." But he wanted to know my business and I told him, and he said, "Well, I'll get you in." He just nodded to the banker and he reached up and pulled a string on a couple of pulleys and the latch went up.

Arnold then located the farmers who had planted the corn and moved on to another bank. Later, Roswell, Arnold, and some of the Coon Rapids sales force went into eastern Kansas to make yield tests and recruit as salesmen the farmers who had good results with the hybrids.

It was through this method of spreading samples in Nebraska that Hans Larsen became a salesman/supervisor for Garst and Thomas. "I am certain," Roswell wrote several years later, "that no product has ever been marketed with such fervor as hybrid corn was marketed between the years 1933 and 1940." With the exception of Roswell, no one sold corn with greater evangelistic spirit than Hans, who could tell what he called "the story of hybrid corn" like a preacher could tell the story of Jesus. A young farmer of Danish extraction, Hans was given one sample by his banker, grew it, and agreed to sell it in his spare time. He first came to Roswell's notice at a meeting of salesmen in York and Hamilton counties, Nebraska, in the fall of 1937, at which Larsen produced the only show of enthusiasm among a group of dispirited farmers whose minds were filled with pictures of their own burned-out fields. Hans thought the new corn had performed impressively under the circumstances and said so. Asked to inspect the samples grown by the salesmen, Hans found them generally good, and reported his findings to Roswell at Coon Rapids. After a day spent looking at the plant and talking with Roswell, Larsen headed back to Nebraska to spread the word. "He was such an enthusiastic fellow," Hans said of Roswell, "that he sent you home on cloud nine, you know. And it was tough out there. We hadn't produced anything, and it wasn't easy."

"Go west, young man," Roswell had instructed Hans, who completed Roswell's work in Nebraska by moving westward through the Platte valley and its tributaries, putting out samples and recruiting a sales force. From there, Roswell sent Hans into northwest Kansas, where large crops of wheat and some corn had been raised in earlier years. By 1937, however, they had vanished into dust, even along the river valleys, and Hans found no customers. However, a chance meeting with a prominent local farmer sent him in a new direction. "If I were you," the farmer told Hans, "I would have the sun set on me in the Arkansas Valley of Colorado." Without telling Roswell, Hans followed the Arkansas River out of Kansas west towards its source in Colorado and found fertile land. He discovered that Colorado farmers were already practicing irrigation on a large scale and were willing to experiment with a new crop. Furthermore, since the state was not at that time part of the Corn Belt and consequently had not been among the territories divided between Pioneer of Des Moines and Garst and Thomas, no royalties had to be paid for seed sold there. Although it would never produce the volume of the true Corn Belt states, Colorado sales grew consistently, and Hans moved further westward into the state.

Committed to a major effort in Kansas and completely uninterested in Colorado, Roswell was furious when he learned Hans was that far west. "What the hell is he doing in Colorado?" he barked at Hans's wife over the telephone and ordered Hans back to Kansas, seeing in Hans's action not entrepreneurial enterprise but insubordination. Hans did return to Kansas and continued to try to sell amidst poverty, dust, and grasshoppers, said by Kansas farmers to be so hungry that they were eating the tips of hoes and rakes. He established a few salesmen along the Solomon River and some creek beds, but it would be twenty years—not until irrigation came to the area—before northwest Kansas would become an important corn-producing area.

Missouri, on the other hand, was one of Roswell's most promising territories from the beginning, but there he encountered opposition from the Kansas City *Star,* suspicious of hybrid corn, especially when promoted by people from outside the state. In one issue, next to a Garst and Thomas advertisement, the paper ran an article by a University of Missouri agronomist warning against Iowans who were trying to sell hybrid corn. Roswell went to the *Star* with the results of yield tests in other states but did not convince them until Bill Clemens, who organized the state for Roswell, collected letters of testimony from eminent Missouri farmers who used Hi-Bred seed. Roswell took the letters to the paper and announced that he was going to have them read as radio advertisements at Columbia, Missouri, the home of the university. The *Star* changed its attitude toward hybrid seed.

To his salesmen and supervisors, Roswell was a prodigy of energy and enthusiasm, a bubbling spring of knowledge about corn and the way to sell it, and an ebullient supplier of entertainment in an otherwise drab and difficult time. "I'll never forget when he came into the house," Hans Larsen, himself a willing convert, recalled:

He was like a breath of fresh air. A ball of enthusiasm. He came in and expounded the philosophy of hybrid corn. What it would do for agriculture, and we forgot the severity of the Depression. The room was just filled with enthusiasm. He just had the ability to do that.

There was more than a touch of the vagabond in Roswell; he loved the open road, especially when he had company and an audience. He would often turn up unexpectedly, pick up Hans or Arnold and sometimes their wives as well, and take them to Kansas or Oklahoma. When he was not talking corn he recited poetry and sang Jerome Kern melodies, "Old Man River" being the best piece in his repertoire. He frequently bought gifts for his companions and for other friends and family, usually fruit. Sometimes he carried almost no money and would borrow from his supervisors or simply tell them to pay expenses as they came along. Arnold Ernst learned to carry extra cash when he was travelling with Roswell and to report such items on his expense account. He enjoyed showing the sights to those who were less well-travelled than he was. Once he took young Pete Oliver well off the route of their trip to show him some hot springs in Missouri and that night in Kansas City took him to hear a well-known dance band.

Roswell was proud of his physical strength and vigor. At a salesmen's outing in Minnesota, an outboard motor fell from a boat into Leech Lake. Roswell grabbed a rope, dove into the water, and shifted the motor on the lake bed in order to tie the rope around it. With Hans Larsen and a customer, he closed a lever-operated gate by putting his arms around the gate and post, squeezing the gate to the post, and dropping the chain around the two with his mouth. In Nebraska Roswell and Hans faced a crazed salesman, who appeared on his front porch with a shotgun and threatened to shoot them. Roswell grabbed the man's gun as he came on the porch, took out the shells, and handed the gun back to him. His back felt very broad as he and Hans walked back to their car, he recalled, "but I never let on. I just brazened it through, and got in, and we drove off."

His sales technique was based on a combination of showmanship, a compelling presence, and the ability to talk well, an art he confessed to Arnold Ernst that he worked hard to acquire. "No matter where we went," Arnold recalled, "or no matter what was going on, Bob would get out and start talking to two or three people around there, and it wouldn't be long until a whole crowd was around Bob, because he was an interesting talker." In hotels, he occasionally attracted attention by lying down on the lobby floor and dispensing his father's aphorisms on rest. Visiting a customer at dinnertime, he might walk to the dinner table, pick up an olive or a pickle, and munch on it while he talked. At meetings, Roswell would remove his coat and hook his fingers in his suspenders and light matches by striking them on his foot. "He wasn't bashful," Arnold said, "and people would just relax." The mannerisms were merely prologue, however; when his rapport with his audience was established, the showmanship was transmuted into substance, and he could count on holding his audience with the story of hybrid corn and the promise that it held.

Although he could be breezy with his supervisors, Roswell knew the territory and expected results. "I don't think there was a river, a valley, or a creek that he didn't know about," Arnold said. "He knew the potential, and he'd put the pressure on you pretty good sometimes." In December 1939 Roswell sent a list of sales in the fifteen townships in Arnold's territory and commented on each county. Here are three of his comments:

1. Cass County—we have sold half as many customers almost as many bushels. . . . In any case there are sixteen Townships in a County that knows about hybrid corn and Pioneer with an average under 100 bushels per Township. Should 600 bushels be too much for this County? [Arnold got 800 bushels.]
2. Clay County—probably not worth the effort. However, don't you think we might get 100 bushels in there? [Arnold got only 7.]
3. Gage County—it seems to me that it is one great big opportunity. Only two Townships above 150 bushels. 24 Townships should take 1000 bushels. [Arnold got 1200.]

In the first year of Roswell's westward move, 1936–37, Nebraska went from 9 to 54 salesmen, and in 1937–38 to 160. From 1,031 bushels sold in 1935–36, the state increased its purchases to 13,000 in 1936–37. The opportunity seen in December 1936 had been rapidly exploited.

In the spring of 1937, Coon Rapids blossomed with activity and promise. In April more than 130 steel barrels of Argentine seed arrived and were broken down into samples. Garst and Thomas planted 2,700 acres of seed, and at last the weather was good. By August the Iowa corn crop was estimated at nearly 470 million bushels, well over twice as much as in 1936. The new plant seemed destined at last to operate to capacity; with such good prospects it was once again expanded. Even from Oklahoma the crop reports were "so extravagant that they just won't bear repeating," Roswell told Tom Rogers. "While we don't have facts and figures to back the assertion," Rogers wrote, heady with Roswell's optimism, "we feel justified in calling Coon Rapids the 'Seed Corn Center of the World.' "

There were more than two hundred salesmen by August 1937, and Roswell asked each of them to bring influential citizens of their communities to see Garst and Thomas and the demonstration plots of hybrid varieties. "This is spread over a ten-day period," Roswell wrote Johnny, "so we get about 100 of them in a day, and believe me this is some job. I have to keep acquainted with all the salesmen and when you get them from Missouri, Kansas, Nebraska and Iowa it becomes a feat to remember all their names and locations."

The open house at Garst and Thomas was held during the week of 9–18 August, 1937. When a group of salesmen arrived with their guests, they looked over some local fields of seed corn and toured the plant. At noon they went to the Community Building, where a committee of ladies from the Christian Church served them a dinner. During the afternoon they looked at fields near Bayard and then drove to the Pioneer experimental station at Johnston Station to view inbreds and crosses in the process of development. Rogers reported that on Wednesday 180 people sat down for lunch in the Community Building; the total number of visitors for ten days was over 1,300.

Trucks streamed into Coon Rapids bringing record yields. From Sac City, yields were reported running to 100 bushels per acre; in Calhoun County, 4-H test plots produced 99; and in Guthrie County, Garst and Thomas led in yield tests with 68 and 88 bushels. By late October 40,000 bushels of seed had been brought to the plant and processed, and the two biggest buildings in town were filled to the roof. Three hundred men worked in shifts, sacking 3,000 bushels per day, and when the season ended in late November the plant had processed almost 80,000 bushels. The previous year they had processed 15,000. "The sorting and sacking crews received their final pay check last week," Rogers wrote in December,

and for several days Coon Rapids looked like the last day of school at a college town with boys from Nebraska, Missouri, Minnesota, and various points in Iowa loading up their flivvers ready for the trip back home.

With the plant finally operating at capacity, Roswell arranged to have a movie taken of the entire process, tracing the corn from harvesting through sacking. "Have you seen Bob Garst and his plaid shirt starring in the first picture 'Happy Harvest'?" Rogers asked.

Bob is supported by a star cast, including Charley Thomas, Russ Dixon, Viv Bell and other well known moving picture stars. This picture will show at the Lyric Friday and Saturday and it's too bad the Lyric isn't going to be big enough to handle the crowd.

By February 1938 almost 65,000 bushels of this corn were sold by 347 salesmen, with 73 salesmen so newly appointed that they had not yet been heard from. By March the sales force would number 500. Roswell was delighted with the entire operation: "Believe me," he confided to Johnny,

our salesmen have worked in these new and hard-up areas, particularly in Kansas and Nebraska. . . . Think of having something like 15,000 customers who have bought a bushel each—and of the finest corn that anyone is offering anywhere.

Pioneer 322 won first place in the annual state yield contest, Pioneer hybrids won the Banner Trophy for the eighth time in the last thirteen years, and Garst and Thomas had a variety in each section of the state that had been high in its district for two or three years. "I think it's a hell of a record," he wrote of the yield-test results, "and I think the breeding department has the jump on all the competitors." Charley Thomas, who had taken over production while Roswell concentrated on sales, became a familiar sight in the fields during detasseling season, making as many as a dozen sweeps through a field to get the job done properly for the high quality inbreds supplied by Pioneer. Ralph Wheeler's talents also paid off. "I know our processing is by all odds the best in the business," Roswell concluded.

IN 1938, in spite of some dangerous late rain that made everyone nervous as the freezing season arrived, Garst and Thomas produced over 100,000 bushels, which would be sold by 855 salesmen. With a plant now too big to rely solely on a local labor force, the town was inundated with strangers for several weeks. "If you have vacant rooms," Rogers wrote, "here is a chance to make a little additional income." By September 1938 workmen were swarming to the plant, some with cars, noted Rogers, that "even bear Missouri, Kansas, Nebraska, Minnesota and Illinois license plates." Boarding houses were full and restaurants were doing a capacity business, as Garst and Thomas broke all labor records for Carroll County. Along with this influx came another open house. On one day 150 salesmen were reported to be in town, and on one Monday the Christian ladies served over three hundred meals at the Community Building.

The hybridization of the state's corn crop was well under way by 1938. In 1936, only 6,700 acres of hybrid seed had been planted in Iowa; in 1937 it involved close to 50 percent, or 18,000 acres; by 1938, it leaped to 75 percent. Along with the new corn, and fostered by its greater strength, came increasing mechanization. The Engineering Department at Iowa State reported that nearly six thousand mechanical corn pickers were used during the 1938 husking season, performing a workload that formerly would have required fifteen thousand men. In Coon Rapids, Mose Grettenberg sold fourteen McCormick-Deering corn pickers, and seventeen Farmall tractors. Two-thirds of Carroll County farms were equipped with tractors. A new age in agriculture had begun.

The seed crop was processed by 15 December. The total Iowa corn crop was below 1937's bumper yield, but it had still been a grand year. Rogers ran a picture of the Garst and Thomas drying cribs and reminisced about the season:

Then the drying cribs pictured above were going at top speed with six huge oil burning furnaces forcing hot air through the sorted ear corn, removing all unnecessary moisture. Then men tended each furnace day and night and other crews, working in shifts, worked at the drying cribs 24 hours each day. Now these furnaces are cold, the cribs quiet and deserted. The 1938 season is over but another year will see the same activity repeated. Meanwhile this section of the Garst & Thomas plant looks like a deserted village.

Even deserted, the plant gave promise of great possibilities and reminded the town that a larger event had occurred. Coon Rapids had emerged from the Depression.

Politics, Family, and Friends: 1933–41

Roswell's confident activism in the New Deal farm program enlarged his political views, bringing new friends and new possibilities. But his success created difficult choices, one of which concerned his candidacy for public office. His achievement in establishing the AAA corn-hog allotment program made him a celebrity in the state; candidates in 1936 wrote to ask for his support, and there was speculation in the newspapers about his possible congressional aspirations. He did not run because, as he explained to those who sought his help for their own campaigns, he had just begun his drive to develop new territories for Garst and Thomas and in the immediate future would be devoting himself to his business. However, for the next dozen years a political career would remain a possibility; as late as 1948 he was still considering it.

The second problem lay in his growing inability to be comfortable with either of the two major parties. He had been, and remained, a registered Republican, loyal to the progressive tradition of his uncle Warren, suspicious of the growing New Deal bureaucracy, and hopeful of finding a businessman's candidate for president. On the other hand, he was loyal to Wallace, was an early and active participant in the New Deal, was committed to Roosevelt's internationalist views, and was increasingly allied with the liberal wing within the Department of Agriculture. Not since his college years would conflicting inclinations be so apparent in his thought and feeling.

In 1939 he put into writing a personal political testament, which he mimeographed for his friends. He described himself as a born Republican, and an admirer of Hamilton, Lincoln, and Theodore Roosevelt. But, he continued, he had voted twice for Franklin Roosevelt and admired Thomas Jefferson, Grover Cleveland, and Woodrow Wilson "quite as much as the best Democrat." He went the Democrats one better when he proclaimed: "I admire Ben Franklin and neither party seems to have claimed him." Addressing the problems of recovery, he criticized the Democrats for their failure to spend enough money employing more people or providing them with modern tools. Thus he proposed an increase in income tax and some form of consumer's tax to provide the needed revenue. With this money, acquired in a very un-Republican manner, he claimed we could

build better roads and more of them—eliminate more grade crossings—put in more rural electrification lines—do more terracing to avoid further erosion—do far more reforestation. We could build more cheap tenement properties for the underprivileged city dwellers—more and better playgrounds for city children— improve and extend our flood control projects.

The heart of this vision lay in the fusion of technology and efficiency embodied in his admiration for Ben Franklin. "Think what we could have accomplished in the past ten years," he concluded, "with the seventy-five million man years we have wasted, and think what we can accomplish in the next ten years by employing this labor with as efficient machinery as we can devise."

He did not include his views on foreign affairs in this paper, but elsewhere he was unequivocating in his opposition to the Smoot-Hawley tariff. In 1941 he told former Governor Clyde Herring that the tariff had been a major contribution not only to the Depression but to the Second World War. "By and large," he confided to Herring, "I think the Republican Party has been absolutely wrong in its foreign policy during my whole mature lifetime."

As long as his progressive ideals lay within the New Deal, Roswell was prepared to work through the Democratic party for agricultural and social reform throughout the thirties and early forties. Jonathan, with whom he resumed his intellectual camaraderie, had remained in government, working for the Farm Security Administration in California supervising the migrant worker camps. In 1939 Jonathan moved to Milo Perkins's Surplus Commodities Administration to take charge of implementing the food stamp plan in all of the western states. With his business well established, Roswell plunged into the food stamp program with enthusiasm in Iowa and Nebraska, and in 1940 he was praised by Nebraska state senator Tom Lambert for his work there.

Roswell sympathized with the aims of the labor movement, with which Pat Jackson was now closely associated. In 1944 he wrote to C. B. Baldwin, a member of the Political Action Committee of the Congress of Industrial Organizations (CIO), that he lunched occasionally

with a bunch of moss-back Republicans at Des Moines, and they all agreed that PAC had been very effective in every city. They recognize your strength – and will be afraid to try anything very violently reactionary even though they would like to.

That same year he wrote Jim Patton of the Farmers Union suggesting that Patton sponsor a bill setting minimum standards of housing for farm tenants and hired men, specifically requiring running water and baths. "Iowa can afford that," he observed.

While Roswell thought and acted as a liberal on these issues, at the same time he retained his Republican ties. The "moss-back" Republicans were members of the "Round Table," a group of businessmen in Des Moines whom he met for lunch and an occasional dinner. They differed on social issues but in other respects represented values Roswell accepted, and he willingly maintained a presence in this more conservative world.

The difficulty of balancing his political views with his avowed party affiliation was clearly demonstrated during the congressional elections of 1938. Roswell favored senatorial candidate Nels Kraschel in the Democratic primary and later continued to favor him over his Republican opponent. But his support, especially in the beginning, had to be "of a quiet nature," he warned Kraschel. He reminded Pat Jackson, who was anxious for him to "fight the good fight," that he would have to change party affiliation to vote in the Democratic primary. This action, he told Jackson, "I do not think is worthwhile." When the campaign got underway, Roswell spoke on the radio in support of Kraschel, arguing that Kraschel would give Wallace and Roosevelt greater support than his opponent was willing to do, an approach based on unity in the face of the farm crisis rather than on party lines.

In 1940 the candidacy of Wendell Willkie for the Republican presidential nomination offered a return to progressivism in Republican politics. Roswell saw in Willkie a man who could capture the liberal vote, preserve the best of internationalism and economic experimentation, but at the same time turn the country toward solid, businesslike management. Twice he talked with Willkie at length and was especially interested in Willkie's move from the Democratic Party, a process Roswell was undergoing in spirit from his own Republican Party. Working through Gardner Cowles of the *Register* and John Cowles of the Minneapolis *Tribune,* both Willkie supporters, Roswell offered himself as Willkie's agricultural adviser, suggesting ways to improve his campaign style and speaking. One proposal involved Willkie's memorization of the following verse from one of the Tutt and Mr. Tutt stories in the *Saturday Evening Post:*

> Authority intoxicates,
> And makes mere sots of magistrates.
> The fumes of it invade the brain,
> And make men giddy, proud and vain.

Roswell quoted the lines frequently, even trying them on a highway patrolman who stopped him for speeding. He got a ticket anyway.

In the summer of 1940 Roswell collected Arden "Red" Bowman, his crony in political adventures and a former Coon Rapids friend who had moved to Minneapolis, and set off with him for the Republican National Convention. Writing to Jonathan afterwards, Roswell claimed that he and Red could take nearly full credit for four votes for Willkie from North Dakota, and "rated an assist" for seven from Iowa.

However, as soon as Roosevelt was nominated for a third term, and Henry Wallace was selected as his running mate, Roswell ceased his work for the Republicans and returned to "quiet" support for the Roosevelt-Wallace ticket. Writing to Doc Macklin, a former Coon Rapids veterinarian whose land he managed, Roswell put a good face on the events, claiming that his position in politics "could hardly be improved upon." He had assisted in the nomination of the best Republican candidate since Theodore Roosevelt, he told Macklin, but now that Wallace was nominated, nobody expected him to take an active part in Willkie's campaign, "because they know of my close personal friendship and close business relationships with Wallace." Because he had helped Willkie, the Democrats would not really expect him to identify himself with them and would not really need him anyway. "All anybody expects me to do," he stated, "is to go home and sell seed corn and all of them think this move is wholly justified."

In 1944, faced with another presidential election, Roswell expressed openly the strain of his dual allegiance. This time Thomas E. Dewey became the Republican candidate, and Roswell admitted his disillusion with both parties to Republican Harold Brenton, a banker and former classmate who had written to ask for a campaign contribution. The Democrats, Roswell charged, had been in office so long they had created a bureaucracy that had lost its effectiveness. However, without Willkie, Republican foreign policy alarmed him, and he was angered by the Republicans' rejection of Willkie's domestic as well as his foreign policies. But Roswell also disliked Dewey: "He doesn't know how to laugh—takes himself too damn seriously—which I think is a bad, bad, fault." In short, he had no stomach for voting at all in 1944, he told Brenton, and pronounced himself "in confusion," which to him meant uncertainty or doubt. "And when I am in confusion," he concluded, "I always go back and specialize on my hybrid seed corn business and on farming, because I am not very confused about either one of them, and it lets me sleep better.

"SHE was a good woman to work" was the epitaph Elizabeth should have on her tombstone, Roswell liked to say in his later years. He intended this as a tribute, for Roswell's obsessional preoccupation with work placed great burdens on his wife during the thirties and early forties. From the very beginning, the prospect of returning to Coon Rapids had not appeared inviting to Elizabeth, even though she appreciated Roswell's enthusiasm for hybrid corn and understood their need for financial retrenchment. Her return to the country meant giving up a life and society she enjoyed for the isolation and reduced economic and social status of a life she thought had been left behind when they moved to Des Moines.

Her social ties with Des Moines did not end abruptly or disappear entirely, although she had more difficulty maintaining these ties than did Roswell, restricted as she was to the farm for so much of the time, living a very different life from that of her city years. However, they visited friends and occasionally attended social events in Des Moines, and they entertained in return. The Wallaces visited now and then, and Henry entrusted Elizabeth with the care of some of his new hybrid chickens. They vacationed with the Brentons in Minnesota one summer, and met the Merrills, their Des Moines cousins, at Lake Okoboji each summer. However, Coon Rapids, and especially the Garsts, became the focus for her social life with Roswell. She counted Dorothy Chrystal of Coon Rapids and Eleanor Garst, the wife of Warren Garst, Jr., of Jefferson, as her closest friends. She became acquainted with such friends as Vivian Rippey and joined the clubs and discussion groups in town.

Beyond her responsibilities to her three children, husband, and farm, there was the business, which created immediate and overriding problems. In the summer of 1930, with the first seed corn crop to be detasseled, Elizabeth hit upon the idea of a summer farm camp for children to raise money and organized the operation herself. She decided she could take five children in addition to her own, hired extra help for cooking and cleaning, and sent brochures to her Des Moines acquaintances – an act that must not have been easy – announcing that the Garst farm would be a summer home for children from 5 June to 21 August. The prospective clients were offered ducks, chickens, turkeys, and lambs to feed, ponies and hay wagons to ride, and access to the community swimming pool. The screened porch, where corn would later be stored, was the sleeping area. Food would be simple but well prepared, and the water would be carefully tested. "I am a graduate of the State University of Iowa," Elizabeth wrote proudly in her brochure,

and for seven years previous to my marriage successfully taught school. Child training and care has been my chief interest for the past ten years and I have made continuous study of child psychology and parent education during that period.

At fifteen dollars per week per child, Elizabeth earned the money for detasseling and did it again in the summer of 1931. She and Bertha Thomas fed a noon meal to the detasselers each summer and fed the corn sorters during the years that operation was performed on the farm. The hours she spent in her kitchen and garden began to multiply.

Accident and illness brought additional demands in the following years. In July 1932 nine-year-old Stephen rushed out early one morning to watch a threshing rig start. He jumped off the engine just as its operator, Bill Klass, threw a can of distillate into the firebox to encourage the fire. Stephen took the full force of the resulting explosion; with his clothing ablaze, he ran for the creek. Klass tackled him, extinguished the flames by rolling him in the grass, and thereby saved his life. Roswell happened to be in town, and after a preliminary stop at the local doctor's office, he and Elizabeth rushed Stephen to Des Moines, where he was hospitalized for almost two months. He then began a long series of treatments and operations on the keloids caused by the fire. These treatments took place in Des Moines, seventy-six miles away on country roads, which Elizabeth had to travel usually on her own.

Elizabeth became unexpectedly pregnant in the fall of 1932, and in March 1933 gave birth to her fourth child (and first of a "second family"), Antonia, who was born with severely crossed eyes. That summer Roswell was away for long periods organizing the corn-hog program. Elizabeth, with an infant in tow, continued to take Stephen to Des Moines, living as frugally as possible, feeding seasonal workers, coping with her other children, and worrying about the mortgage that hung over the farm.

For Elizabeth, 1936 and 1937 were the most trying years of the Depression. The winter of 1935–36 was the coldest and most severe in memory, and she was pregnant again – this time by design – with Mary, her fifth child. Spring brought relief from a snow-bound winter on the farm, but also the loss of her close friend Dorothy Chrystal, who died from pneumonia in April 1936. Roswell promised to look after his sister's children; with four children in the house and a fifth on the way, Elizabeth took in John and Tom Chrystal for several months, while Warren and Eleanor cared for Virginia. In June, Elizabeth gave birth to Mary in Des Moines and brought her infant home to a record-breaking heat wave and drought. From 3 July to 16 July, the temperature never dropped below

100°F and continued above 90°F during the following weeks. Dust blew through the house, grasshoppers took over the fields, and Elizabeth's garden disintegrated. Antonia, wearing a patch on one eye, required periodic visits to the University Hospital in Iowa City, over two hundred miles away, which Elizabeth undertook through 1937, again with an infant in tow.

Although by the late thirties the sorters and detasselers were no longer fed on the farm, Elizabeth cooked for a steady stream of luncheon and dinner guests. In the absence of a respectable hotel in Coon Rapids, she regularly kept business associates and customers overnight or for longer periods. During these years Roswell began bringing a carful of people home for lunch on very short notice, which required Elizabeth to keep plentiful amounts of food ready to serve. Bill Clemens boarded at the farm for long periods, and in the later thirties and forties several supervisors stayed in the house to oversee the detasseling.

As these unrelenting years passed, Elizabeth found Roswell's lengthy absences increasingly trying. She resented making decisions about the children on her own and regarded the engaging and firing of hired men as burdensome. Roswell did not, in her view, provide adequate emotional support and tenderness, and she began to feel deprived and vulnerable. When he was home, he spent more time in town than she thought necessary, and at home dominated family and social occasions with corn talk, often interrupting her or telling her to be quiet. Roswell's need to "talk out" his ideas was especially hard on Elizabeth, who felt intensely her own limitations for similar social and intellectual expression. This situation bred in her a strongly competitive urge that became bound up with her search for creative outlets.

All was not drudgery and frustration, however. Roswell was not a total stranger in the house, especially after the breakthrough of 1937–38. In the winter he read a great deal, especially Mark Twain and other books Elizabeth had brought to the marriage. The couple played bridge frequently, went to Discussion Club, and travelled together throughout these years as far away as the two coasts and into the South. Although he did not show much interest in the children when they were toddlers, when they reached the age for storytelling Roswell invented Henry Horsecollar, a well-travelled Indian, he told the children, with whom he had many adventures. He was even half Indian, himself, he said, and spun out tales of action and excitement until they reached the age of disbelief.

Elizabeth was also interested in and highly supportive of Roswell's ambitions for the seed corn company and was vibrantly in tune with his New Deal efforts. She contrived to set aside time for her own interests in a peripheral way by serving on the Parent-Teachers Association and in various clubs, although she was refused a teaching post in a country school because the authorities would not hire married women. In the early thirties Roswell was active in the Farm Bureau, and Elizabeth entertained for him and attended a conference or two herself. Although Roswell could not bring himself to be a Democrat, Elizabeth could and did so actively in a town where Democrats were few and far between.

Cooking and entertaining became creative outlets for Elizabeth, and the constant flow of visitors was as much an exhilarating and welcome intrusion from the outside world as it was a burden. She shared with her husband a gregarious and hospitable personality and welcomed the interesting people he brought home. When he initiated friendships with people such as the Jacksons in Washington, Elizabeth responded positively and happily, especially since she realized that Roswell's decision neither to enter politics nor to leave Coon Rapids would limit those desired social contacts. Her garden was another source of consolation – both in its productivity and its beauty. She grew most of the vegetables she served her family and guests and transformed the rather bleak hilltop site of the farm into a luxurious ensemble of trees, lawns, and flowers. She even established a demonstration garden for hybrid corn for Roswell's salesmen and customers and became a leader in the Coon Rapids gardening club. By 1941, however, Elizabeth began to show the effects of the strains and conflicts that her life with Roswell during the past ten years had engendered.

ROSWELL was unable to enter into the interior emotional intimacies of marriage during these years. Yet he was at ease with male friends because these relationships were sustained by an unspoken intimacy and thrived on their mutual involvement in the outward business of life. When his paternal and educative instincts were accepted without challenge by those willing to learn from him, Roswell formed close relationships and supported the ambitions of those he took under his wing. Perhaps his closest relationship of this nature was with Eddie Reid, who grew up on a farm, left it for town and business, but through Roswell's influence came back to the land as a farm manager and landlord.

William Reid, Eddie's father, was a zealously religious and hardworking man, who farmed 320 acres south of Coon Rapids. Before Eddie and his brother were ten years old, they began planting, cultivating, harvesting with four-horse teams, and performing the endless rounds of chores required for pigs, horses, and corn. Little time remained except for rest. Eddie wanted to attend high school, but his father could not do without family labor. Consequently, he stayed on the farm after grade school, saw that his sisters got to high school, and began developing a "commercial touch" by taking over the *de facto* management of the farm, working on the side for extra money. He came close to being embittered. When cultivators with seats were introduced, only adults were considered strong enough to ride them, raise the blades, and manage the horses, which pushed Eddie "to the point where I hated men because they took all the easy jobs." One summer Eddie, his brother, and his father worked for more than a month helping a neighbor harvest and stack his hay. When it was time for payment, the farmer, as was customary, offered the two boys something in addition to what he paid their father. "He looked down at me," Eddie recalled,

and he said, "How much for the boy?" "Nothing," my father said. And I wanted money, you know. I thought that I would at least get a dollar or two. And George said, "Well, I think I ought to give him some money." Dad said, "No, don't give him any." When George got through fooling around with the dollar bills and got over into the silver side he picked up half a dollar, but Dad said, "No." He picked up a quarter, and Dad said, "No; none at all." And so I went home and Dad collected a little extra money from the haying, and we didn't get any.

When his father sold the farm and retired in town, Eddie, then eighteen, happily came along. His first job was at the creamery, where he first saw Roswell and listened to his talk with Jens Jensen, although he never felt it his place to speak to him. Their friendship began in 1934, while Eddie was selling tractor oil and lubricants for the Sinclair station in Coon Rapids and trying at the same time to penetrate the mysteries of the grain market, when he could afford it. Fresh from his months with New Deal economists and the corn-hog ratio, Roswell took Eddie under his wing on this matter, and Eddie's speculation began to show a small profit.

In 1936 Eddie lost the lease on his station, but he could stay in business if he built a new station with a renewed franchise. Inexperienced in financial dealings, Eddie consulted Roswell. He advised him to buy the lot for a service station, take a first mortgage as surety for the building of the station, and persuade the landowner to take a second mortgage for the cost of the lot. When this was accomplished, Roswell persuaded the Sinclair Company to grant Eddie a twelve-year lease instead of the customary five-year lease, so that he would have collateral for the building expenses. Roswell loaned Eddie the money to complete his building, and in the big year of 1937, sent customers from the Garst and Thomas open house to the filling station. The station prospered, and both mortgages were retired.

Two years later the representative of a Nebraska bank arrived in Coon Rapids to ask Roswell if he could find a buyer for 240 acres of land his company owned south of town. Because the farm was near Eddie's boyhood home, Roswell took him along to help appraise the farm. Eddie liked it and decided to buy it himself. Roswell, who had just scraped together money to enable Jonathan to buy a farm in California, made the down payment for Eddie with a postdated check and postponed the transaction by a close and time-consuming examination of the deed and survey. Eddie, farm in hand, had by now learned how to create assets without ready cash and was on his way to a successful career in property.

Eddie began to travel with Roswell occasionally, learning about hybrid corn, and, along with Roswell, took a renewed interest in the productivity of land and livestock. Their exploration of common interests acted as a catalyst; Eddie would become a sounding-board, advisor, and close collaborator when Roswell brought his energies to bear on the tired Depression land.

Reclaiming the Land: 1934–41

The first Iowa Wallace, Uncle Henry, took an active part in the great conservation movement in America initiated during the presidency of Teddy Roosevelt. Wallace excoriated those who were exploiting the national heritage, both timber barons and soil robbers, but was optimistic about the great natural wealth he saw about him. "The really good land," he predicted,

will always respond to the man who understands soils and climates and grains and grasses. It is kept in store for just that kind of fellow. . . . The good land was not made to be worn out in twenty years, or fifty, or five hundred.

Indiscriminate plowing, wind storms, and soil erosion in the twenties and thirties, combined with an already deteriorating farm economy compounded by the 1929 market collapse, brought Uncle Henry's convictions into question in a demoralized Midwest, painfully aware its natural wealth was blowing or washing away and that the nutrients in the soil were being sucked up faster than they could be replaced. The AAA provided a political and economic framework for recovery, hybrid corn and mechanization provided the foundation for a new technology; it remained for the land itself to be revived. By the later thirties Roswell had become involved in this third enterprise, leading a new generation of farm managers, learning about soils and climates and grains and grasses, and making the good land respond.

The land in question was an area in the southern tip of the Wisconsin Drift, created by the last of a series of glaciers that had cleared a roughly shaped V from the Ohio River valley to the Dakotas, Nebraska, and Kansas. This glacial action set in motion a complex process of sedimentation, mineral distribution, and growth of organic matter ultimately resulting in the vast grass-covered and forest-dotted prairies that so impressed the pioneer farmers. The Wisconsin Drift was dear to Roswell's heart and fortunes, because 20,000 years ago it had crunched to a halt in mid-Iowa, and along its boundary the town of Coon Rapids had been established. Consequently, the land north, west, and east of town was especially fertile, with a good distribution of minerals and a rich black from its high concentration of organic matter.

But the glacial age had left two difficulties for the farmer to surmount in most of the affected regions, and any development and reclamation of the land had to take these into account. The first was the presence of glacial boulders and rocks, which in the thirties were still plentiful on many a farm, although most of them had been hauled away to be used as foundations for barns or were simply piled along fence rows and covered with dirt after being broken by dynamite. These fences enclosed fields already thought to be too small for efficient farming by the late thirties; consequently, a considerable effort and expense went into the continued removal of rocks.

The second elemental problem was the presence of excess water. Much of the Wisconsin Drift had been covered with swamps and ponds; some remained and some evolved into regions of "wet prairie," but all of these areas had to be drained before they could be farmed. At the turn of the century most of Iowa was undrained, but as more people came in from Illinois and other states, the construction of drains, or tiles, became common in Iowa. This was an enterprise, it may be remembered, with which Roswell's Uncle Warren was involved during his public career. Most of the drainage systems were dug between 1905 and 1915 and consisted of pipes that were often four or five miles long, into which individual farmers connected additional systems to drain patches of wet ground. An impressively large subterranean system was created; one of the farms Roswell managed—a section of 640 acres—contained about 50,000 feet of tiling. Extensive as it was, the tiling had to be expanded, deepened, and maintained. Even this system was often inadequate in coping with excessive rain, which could be as much of a problem as the droughts that periodically devastated the countryside.

Like Uncle Henry, Roswell never lost faith in the potential productivity of this land or its essential dollar value, even in the face of the prevailing local mood of discouragement in the thirties. Roswell remembered tight-fisted farmers buying land around Coon Rapids between 1915 and 1919 for $250 per acre, a price his Uncle Warren often received for good land acquired by E. and W. Garst. During the boom of 1919–21 the price had been inflated to as much as $500 per acre but after 1921 had plunged to $100 per acre, where it remained through the mid-thirties. Roswell was convinced that the land was still worth at least the $250 of his Uncle's days, and if every penny of his own money had not been tied up in the struggle to maintain Garst and Thomas, he would have bought any good land priced at $100 per acre. Lacking the means, he did the next best thing; he influenced others to buy the land and engage him as the manager.

His entry into the management business was in good part fortuitous, beginning with a conversation in the parlor car of a Washington-Chicago train during the summer of 1933, when Roswell was engaged in "saving the world." He passed the evening of the overnight journey extolling the glories of hybrid seed corn to a Kansas member of the Corn-Hog Committee and had sold the man one bushel of corn by bedtime. The transaction was witnessed by the car's other occupant, Abe Freiler, chief of Chicago's A. Stein and Company, manufacturer of Paris garters, belts, and suspenders. Fascinated by what he heard, Freiler, who had never been known before or since to talk to a stranger on a train, asked Roswell to repeat his conversation with the man from Kansas. Roswell and Freiler met again for breakfast, and by the time they reached Chicago, Freiler had bought a bushel of seed corn. He didn't have a farm himself, he told Roswell, but his friend Irving Florsheim, of Florsheim shoes, did. "Give me a ring whenever you're in Chicago," Freiler remarked, "and we'll have lunch with Florsheim. I want him to hear about how you produce this famous corn."

Later that year Roswell made a sales run north of Coon Rapids, sold a bushel of corn to a tenant on a section in Calhoun County owned by another wealthy Chicagoan, Scott Bromwell, and discovered that Bromwell was offering this farm for sale at $100 per acre. Roswell got Bromwell's address from the tenant, drove into Lake City, and called Clyde Fletcher. "Get in your car and meet me in Boone," he told Fletcher. "We're going to drive to Chicago because I've found the cheapest farm in the United States!" They saw Bromwell, offered to buy his farm, but could produce a down payment of only $1,000. Bromwell turned them down, and they drove home.

Roswell could not get the farm and the opportunity it represented out of his mind. If he could not buy it, somebody ought to, and the Chicago association brought Freiler to mind, and Freiler's friend with a farm, Irving Florsheim. Outfitting himself with a new suit—and a pair of Florsheim shoes—Roswell drove to Chicago, presented himself unannounced in Abe Freiler's office, and asked to be introduced to Irving Florsheim. Freiler arranged lunch for the three of them at the restaurant in Union Station. Roswell repeated the story of hybrid corn for Florsheim, then moved on to the subject of inflation and the value of land as a hedge against it. ("Abe, what have I been telling you?" Florsheim said repeatedly.) Roswell then mentioned the farm that was for sale in Calhoun

County and urged Florsheim to buy it. Suspicious of this apparent windfall, Florsheim asked how he could find out if the farm was really that good. Roswell told him that Thomas Wilson of the Wilson Packing Company had seen the farm recently, though he did not buy it merely because it was not on the line between his ranch in New Mexico and his Chicago packing house. "Why don't you call him up and ask him about the farm?" Roswell suggested. Florsheim agreed and astonished Roswell by calling for a phone at the table. He reached Wilson, put the question to him, then listened for several minutes while Roswell waited anxiously. What Wilson had said, Florsheim reported, was that Florsheim should buy the farm, but only if Roswell would manage it for him. "How do I buy a farm?" Florsheim asked. "What you do," replied Roswell, "is to give me a check for $10,000 for Scott Bromwell, and pay the balance next March."

The commission on the sale provided a desperately needed windfall for the Garst farm and put Roswell into the farm management business. Florsheim and Freiler arrived in June 1934 to see the farm, and Freiler bought 240 acres himself that year. Outraged by having to submit to AAA acreage allotments, Florsheim sold his farm a year later to Freiler, who along with the Steins continued to invest in Iowa farms, as did Scott Bromwell and other Iowa landowners. By 1943 Roswell was managing fourteen farms, a total acreage of 5,614 acres. Of that total, about 3,000 acres belonged to the Freilers and Steins and 1,000 to Scott Bromwell. Much of this land had come under his management by the end of the thirties, so that although he had little land himself at the time, he could nevertheless gain experience in large-scale farming and have a ready source of money from his landlords for capital investment. His new profession also marked the beginning of a life-long personal relationship with the Freilers, Steins, and Bromwells that went far beyond the contractual arrangements among landlord, tenant, and manger.

The record of Roswell's earliest years in farm management has been preserved in his correspondence with Scott Bromwell. Bromwell's mother owned several thousand acres of land in both Illinois and Iowa, and Bromwell looked after it with the aid of professional managers. Although he sold the Calhoun County farm to Irving Florsheim, he bought three more farms nearer Coon Rapids in 1934 and 1935—a total of 1,120 acres—and asked Roswell to manage them. Roswell inherited several years of poor management, dispirited farming, and poorly kept land, which produced at best an income of about two dollars per acre. He set out first to find better tenants, and then to rejuvenate the land and its buildings.

The first year he did little about the farms and their present tenants, finding his best course was "to ease along with them and let the farms follow their usual course." In the meantime he found the kind of tenants he wanted. For one farm, whose tenant had died, he hired Anton Loefler, "a good, hard-working young Dutchman with whom I can get along and who will do exactly what I tell him to do and do it willingly." He also employed Warden Patrick and Wallace Knapp, who possessed the same qualifications as Loefler, and by 1936 he was ready to concentrate on the land and buildings.

Wallace Knapp faced the most difficult task. His farm was overgrown with cockleburs, which the former tenant intended to allow to go to seed. Before any seed corn could be planted on the Knapp farm, all burrs as well as thistles had to be removed because they were crowding out the corn of the former tenant and reducing its yield. Under Roswell's direction—and with some financial assistance from Roswell on behalf of the landlord—Knapp hauled away the rocks his plow uncovered and cleared away mounds of rubbish and rusty junk that had been accumulating for years.

Because of the drought and the resulting poor crop, Roswell chose not to spend money on the barns, corncribs, and fences on the Knapp farm, although he did "touch up" the house. The Patrick farm, however, required a more thorough renovation of the house, left dirty and dilapidated by the former tenant and manager. He also spent a substantial sum on a new corn crib, the finest in the county, Roswell wrote to Bromwell in defense of his expenditure, a corncrib that "will be there without further expense longer than our children will live." Because there was a good crop in 1937, Roswell could order repairs for the buildings on the Knapp farm, and by the end of that year he had achieved his immediate objectives—good tenants, good buildings, and well-prepared land. "I think that all things considered," Bromwell wrote in 1937, "you did a very good job on these farms and my only regret is that you don't live in Central Illinois."

During his early period of farm management Roswell held to the traditional formula for expenditure on farms, which was simply one dollar of investment per acre. His improvements exceeded that ratio and had brought about his spirited defense of the new corncrib and other buildings, as well as considerable correspondence about charging such expenses to capital investment. Bromwell was content to accept these expenses and even offered to spend more money on phosphate fertilizer; his criticisms were of Roswell's cavalier method of bookkeeping and unprofessional acts such as spending his own money instead of getting an authorization from his landlord. Apologizing for the meagerness of his reports and the delay in forwarding them, Roswell confessed to more than one landlord his indifference to tidy bookkeeping. To Bromwell he wrote:

I can only say that all of us have our qualities and our faults. I suppose my quality is that I enjoy farming, love farmland, and take a good deal of pleasure in managing farms and that my great fault is that I hate bookkeeping.

Bromwell, a kindly man, suffered these annual crises patiently, but on one occasion, with desperate tact, offered Roswell a lesson in the easiest way to keep accounts. He knew that these things were a nuisance to Roswell, Bromwell wrote, but

I have been through it with my mother and I know the easy answer to it all. No double entry bookkeeping. Just a ledger for each farm, or even one ledger for the three combined. Then just put receipts on one side and expenditures on the other and write them in as they occur or at least once a month. It really makes it a cinch!

Both Bromwell and Roswell were saved from their respective predicaments by Morrie Galloway, the office manager for Garst and Thomas, who took over the accounting records for the farms in the late thirties. It is at this point Roswell's hastily scribbled notes of expenditures begin to disappear from his correspondence.

The impact of Roswell's personality and thinking upon his landlords is best illustrated by his relations with the Stein family. Mort Schaumberg, married to a cousin of Abe Freiler, shared Roswell's temperament, visited Coon Rapids whenever he could, and like Scott Bromwell, sought Roswell's advice on the management of his Illinois farms. A volatile and enthusiastic man, Schaumberg wrote to Roswell after one of his visits to Coon Rapids that he

returned this morning after a fair night's sleep in an upper bunk and am still effervescing from the interesting and enjoyable visit from you. I guess some of my associates in the office think I am a little farm crazy because of my enthusiasm over the trip.

After another of these trips, Abe Freiler wrote of Schaumberg to Roswell, "knowing his capacity for enthusiasm and yours, I am surprised when you two got together that there wasn't an explosion of some sort." Schaumberg was anxious that his Illinois farm manager got "the real profit picture as only Roswell Garst can give it," and noted that his trips to Iowa and Roswell's letters were "making me a bit aggressive, eh what?" He also announced himself well-trained in Roswell's methods.

Sigmund Stein, the New York patriarch of the family, had also been involved by Freiler in Iowa land. He was interested in farming primarily because his son Jim was already farming in upstate New York. Thus Stein acquired holdings in Iowa in the early forties, just as Roswell's confidence and expansive letter-writing style were coming into full flower. (Roswell addressed his first letter to Stein with the salutation, "Dear Uncle Sig," because, he explained, he had only heard him referred to as Uncle Sig, "so that was the best I could do.") Sigmund Stein was especially interested in information that would benefit his son's farming methods, although he too enjoyed Roswell's flair for educating and passed around the letters to the rest of the family. "It is," he once wrote, because you always show a willingness to explain matters to me, which I am not familiar with, that I keep on writing to you whenever anything arises about which I am in doubt, but if I ask too many questions and take up too much of your time, just let me know.

Roswell was delighted with this audience and responded with a series of letters explaining the implications of the Wisconsin Drift, differences between midwestern and eastern farming techniques, and his views on the general state of farm policy. "I can make them shorter," he once wrote to Sigmund, "but don't mind writing them long, particularly when I am trying to give you a broad background." Along with other family members, both Sigmund and his son Jim became visitors to the Garst farm.

Among Roswell's Iowa landlords was Fred Lehmann, Henry Wallace's close friend and lawyer and eventually president of Pioneer of Des Moines. In a high tax bracket, Lehmann had turned to land, caring little about income from it but willing to spend money. Lehmann was bemused by the increasing income that came from his rural investment. In his droll fashion, Lehmann exemplified the change in attitude and expectation of those early farm-land investors as the profits — though still marginal with respect to their real businesses — began to roll in. "Your report has been received," Lehmann wrote in 1944, "and filed with the usual disapproval. Either I am making too much money on this place or I ought to buy the rest of the country."

With his tenants, Roswell had an equally close and personal relationship; they were his neighbors, and in several instances, life-long friends. In general, he followed the usual midwestern practice of giving the landlord half of the gross income and a rent of seven dollars per acre for pasture and hay land. The landlord furnished all grass seed; half of soybean, flax, or oat seeds; three-fifths of the fertilizer; and paid both the management fee and the insurance. The tenant provided the labor, the livestock, and the farm machinery. Since all of the farms Roswell managed also grew hybrid seed corn, both landlord and tenant received extra payments and certain guarantees, and Roswell charged the landlord only 5 percent commission instead of the standard 10 percent. Roswell also set the new pattern of payment by the landlord of a portion of both seed and fertilizer costs.

In his dealings with his tenants, Roswell exercised a benevolent paternalism and thoroughly enjoyed it. He visited with them, looked regularly at their land, planted trees around their houses, sent gifts of candy and nuts when he was travelling, gave professional and personal advice, and on one occasion, advice on courtship: "some boxes of candy, a few night letters, an occasional cable when you are abroad, and a constant flow of letters." Whenever the opportunity arose, Roswell encouraged his tenants to buy their own farms. He was successful with his own first hired man, Henry Moore, with one of the Mozena brothers, and with others. In a letter to Abe Freiler he referred to Ike Mozena and confessed:

It is a real pleasure to be able to pick up a boy whose father is on WPA—in fact two boys in the case of the Mozenas—and make substantial and successful citizens of them. I have four others who have success stories of the same kind—and the next time you come out I'll show you their farms.

With memories of the Depression ever present, and a local banker who discouraged any such investment, it was no easy task to encourage a farmer to take such a risk. Both Mozena boys were offered the chance by Roswell to buy a Freiler farm, and both had turned it down the first time. Roswell's close friend Jake Bell had also chosen to remain a tenant on a farm owned by the Connecticut General Life Insurance Company, which was still selling off its farms in the forties. When Jake, sitting at the South Side Cafe with Roswell, expressed his fears that the farm was being sold from under him, Roswell, who was commissioned by the company to make a sale, urged Jake to buy it himself and gave him three days to think it over. Jake had the five thousand dollars but was discouraged by his father, who was frightened over the possibility of another depression. Roswell accepted his decision not to buy, "but don't you ever say I sold that farm out from under you," he told his friend.

Roswell was a fervent defender of the egalitarian nature of Iowa farming, which in his view minimized social and even economic differences among landowner, tenant, and manager, even within the small town. "I expect," he wrote to Pat Jackson, "that you would come nearer seeing real democracy in Iowa than in any other place in the world—and that is particularly true of the small towns in Iowa." He was particularly critical of California, which he described as "feudal" in its organization in 1943, lacking a great middle class of agriculture. The big farmers, he charged,

own the whole countryside and have literally thousands of serfs working for them. I would guess that the average farmer in California handles ten times as many dollars as the average farmer in Iowa and employs fifteen times or twenty times as much labor, much of it hand work. The result is great quantities of Mexicans, Philippinos, Southern poor whites or negroes and in all a very distinct labor class. The whole tenancy becomes Fascist in the extreme with a good deal of undesirable relations. Certainly nothing like the beautiful democracy of the Mid-west where all are about on the same level.

His role as intermediary between tenant and landlord is clearly apparent in his correspondence with Abe Freiler, a good-hearted, witty, and articulate man, blessed with a great deal of business sense who possessed a shrewd and bemused perception not only of Roswell's talents but also of his occasional inconsistencies and his penchant for framing a discussion in his own terms. It was always important to Roswell that Abe appreciated his business acumen, and it was Abe who most often called Roswell to account over his obligations as manager to his landlord.

The most illuminating evidence of their relationship, and an example of the problem Roswell faced as buffer between landlord and tenant, may be found in the "Battle of Hendricks' Pasture," a running skirmish he and Abe carried on during the years 1943 to 1946. At issue was approximately 70 acres on the Paul Hendricks farm, which Hendricks was renting as pasture rather than using for corn. Poring over the crop charts and income per farm Roswell had provided, Abe noticed that Hendricks planted less corn than tenants on the other Freiler-Stein holdings, and he asked Roswell to maintain 400 acres in corn on every farm. Abe explained that his first responsibility was to his family:

You must bear with me on matters of this kind because these family propositions have to get pretty similar consideration and treatment to keep everybody happy, and I must tell you that these plans create the feeling that some partiality is being shown even though none is intended.

Abe's repeated requests for this adjustment brought forth a variety of explanations from Roswell in defense of Hendricks' need to maintain his 70 acres as pasture. Roswell's opening gambit was an appeal to consider the moral issues involved. If Paul Hendricks had no livestock, Roswell told Abe, he would have nothing to do from the fall freeze until April, and that would spell trouble:

He simply isn't going to sit at home with absolutely nothing to do and so he would do what all farmers do who are pure grain farmers. He would go to town and become an expert at pool – at pitch – probably at poker. He would start out by drinking a little beer and end up by drinking much whiskey. Believe it or not, that is what would happen – at least that is what generally happens to grain farmers.

"Dear Reverend," Abe replied, "your sermon of January 10th received, and I must say I was greatly impressed." But occasionally, he reminded Roswell, "you take the privilege of saying pretty near anything in order to emphasize a point, but careful analysis indicates that infrequently inaccuracy creeps in." Abe pointed out that he was not advocating that tenants should have no livestock at all, merely that some farms had more than twice as much pasture as other farms, which seemed to him wasteful and inefficient.

This time Roswell replied that the tenants were anxious to make as much money as possible. Hinting vaguely at higher values, he explained

Four of the sons of Michael and Maria Garst most closely connected with Roswell. Left to right (standing): *Admiral Perry Garst, who served in the Spanish-American War; Warren Garst, partner in the Garst Store and later governor of Iowa;* (seated) *Edward Garst, Roswell's father; Morrison Garst, salesman and land speculator, who preceded Edward in buying land in Roswell, New Mexico. (Courtesy John Chrystal)*

Samuel Goodwin, Roswell's maternal grandfather, who emigrated to America from England in 1856, bought a farm near Rockford, Illinois, and became "intensely American." He lived to the age of 91 and was a frequent visitor to Coon Rapids.

Mrs. Samuel Goodwin, whose marriage to Samuel in 1854 annoyed the Goodwin family and prompted Samuel's removal to America. Roswell, his brothers and sister spent long periods of time at her home in Rockford. (Courtesy John Chrystal)

Bertha Goodwin in 1878, then one of the first women students at Northwestern University and a roommate of Edward's sister Mary. She met Edward a year later, but did not become Bertha Garst until 1889. (Courtesy John Chrystal)

Edward Garst in his prime as a successful businessman and as a grandfatherly father to Roswell.

The Coon Rapids Women's Club, probably near the turn of the century. The leading figures of this serious-minded discussion and study group were (right side, middle row) Bertha Garst and (second from right, bottom row) Clara Garst (Warren's wife). (Courtesy John Chrystal)

The first Garst Store, occupied in the old town by Edward in 1869. He slept under the counter, paid no rent, and spent money only for meals. "My stock began to thicken from the start," he wrote later.

The Garst Store, chief symbol of progress and prosperity in Coon Rapids, about 1910. (On the right) the building was completed in 1886 (on the left), the addition by 1907.

The interior of the store about 1910: salesclerks for every department, electric lights, and a system of vacuum tubes "as used in the large city stores."

The Belle of the Coon, *still in operation during Roswell's youth and plying its way up the "rippling waters" of the Raccoon River.*

Roswell's childhood home in Coon Rapids, complete with rocking chair on the front porch, where Edward spent many hours sitting and whistling.

Edward and Bertha, probably in 1922. Bertha died in October of that year; Edward, in the fall of 1923.

The children of
Edward and Bertha
Garst: (left to right)
Dorothy, Jonathan
(standing), Goodwin,
and Roswell about
1901–1902.

Jonathan Garst in
1917, shortly after
he left Apple Farm
to enlist in the army
and serve in France.

Dorothy Garst on
Apple Farm (later
Garst farm) in 1918.
Roswell and Jona-
than had lived in the
house and farmed the
200 acres where, as
Jonathan wrote from
France in the same
year, "we have had a
lot of fun and good
experience and not
unprofitable labor."
(Courtesy John
Chrystal)

Ann Merrill and Roswell's daughter Jane at the remodeled Garst farm in 1932. To the right is the screened porch where Roswell stored his first crops of seed corn. Elizabeth was just beginning to transform the grounds around the house. (Courtesy Keith Merrill, Jr.)

The families of Roswell Garst, Warren C. Garst, Dorothy Garst Chrystal, and Rachel Garst Merrill at a reunion in Des Moines about 1935. Top (left to right): *Patricia Merrill, Warren C. Garst, Ann Merrill, Charlotte Garst, Virginia Chrystal, Tom Chrystal (below), Stephen Garst, Jane Garst, John Chrystal, Keith Merrill, Jr., Tom Garst;* middle: *Jack Chrystal, Elizabeth Garst, Mrs. Hubbard, Clara Garst, Louise Garst McBroom, Eleanor Hubbard Garst, Vina Clark, Rachel Garst Merrill;* bottom: *Roswell holding Gretchen Merrill and Antonia Garst, David Garst, Mary Garst (Warren's daughter), Nancy Garst, Rosemary Garst. (Courtesy John Chrystal, and Keith Merrill, Jr.)*

Roswell at a picnic in the thirties, characteristically attired in plaid shirt and suspenders, and stretched out in one of his favorite positions. (Courtesy Elizabeth Garst)

Elizabeth about 1940, on the better side of the Depression. (Courtesy Elizabeth Garst)

Roswell and Elizabeth in the summer of 1946. Roswell entered the postwar era in "an aggressively commercial frame of mind." (Courtesy Elizabeth Garst)

their desire for profit would and should be tempered "by an inherent appreciation of a way of life with which they are happy and satisfied." Abe could find himself in agreement with this statement about the satisfactions of rural life but did not feel that it spoke to the question of discrepancies between one section and another. Abe's notion of the issue was that which he set forth in an earlier letter. "You're a great guy for overthrowing precedent in ways and means of farming," he had written,

and I believe your flexibility in this regard has been one of the main factors in our successful results, but you have undue timidity when it comes to asking only fair and reasonable adjustments from the tenants and I think in this you are wrong, but I love you just the same.

Roswell still refused to reply directly to the charge of "timidity" or to the discrepancies between particular sections. Instead, his rebuttal stressed the excellent income both landlord and tenant enjoyed, a farm income he doubted any of Abe's Chicago friends could match. Abe again objected to the irrelevancy of this argument; the percentage of the landlord's income was not at issue, and indeed the incomes from the farms would be good if they had been half of what they were. The real issue, Abe insisted, was whether they were doing a good job with what they had. "For some reason you do not want to meet this issue head-on," he concluded, "and yet, it is my main point of complaint."

How to make the best use of the land available was indeed close to being the central issue, but the real nub was the question of who made the decision about what should be done – manager or landlord – and it was this issue that Roswell wished to sidestep. Roswell's resort to the question of income was his indirect way of asserting his own prerogatives in the matter, and he had hinted at his concept of responsibility to the landlord in an earlier letter. "I am never going to worry about small differences in the per-acre income," he maintained,

between your section, the Sig Stein section, Elizabeth Stein section, nor the farm of Al Stein. Some years one of them will always produce the best income. Some years the same farm may produce the poorest income. It will depend upon weather, crop rotation, and luck. I am just going to try to keep all of them with highly satisfactory incomes.

In effect, Roswell had drawn a line between what was negotiable between landlord and manager, and what was not. A generally uniform income from the farms was a legitimate expectation of the landlord; the disposition of a particular piece of land was not. In such an instance Roswell reserved the right to take a particular tenant into account, or any other condition which might influence the allocation of crops. The issue was not the Hendricks pasture, but Roswell's rights as manager.

The experimentation his farm management made possible during the period 1936 to 1942 changed Roswell's view of the traditional relationship between investment and income in farming. His mandate from the landlords had been to purchase land useful as a long-term stable investment that would absorb expenditures and relieve the taxes on the primary incomes of wealthy owners. Money was to be spent on the farms without particular concern for return beyond a modest and practical level, insuring the tenant a reasonable livelihood and maintaining the quality of the investment. Roswell convinced his first buyers of his belief that the land was underpriced and that asset rather than income was the most important consideration. As manager, however, Roswell continued his commitment that began during his first farming venture with Jonathan to maintain the productivity of the land itself and to improve the condition of those who actually farmed it. Roswell had subscribed to the prevailing wisdom of one dollar of investment per acre, but as he exceeded this ratio (with the consent of his landlords) and improved houses, cleared land, and drained and prepared the land to get better yields, he found the income steadily rising. Within a few years he would write Abe and his other landlords that "this farm has produced a magnificent net income in spite of rather heavy expenditures." He soon began to add "I don't really know whether I should say 'in spite of' or 'because of.' I rather suspect that the latter expression would be more accurate." Roswell credited Eddie Reid with suggesting the latter phrase as the paradoxical result of his original mandate became apparent – the more money he spent, the more the revenue increased. This early and gradual increase in investment in the late thirties, which was now exceeding ten dollars per acre, had a further unlooked for consequence by 1942. Roswell's landlords and tenants were prepared to make the great leap into heavy expenditure for fertilizer at least a decade before most farmers and landlords were willing to discard their conservative views on investment and the extent to which it could increase agricultural income.

The War Years

Bringing Fertilizer to the Corn Belt

The war years of 1941–45 do not mark a break in the continuity of Roswell's development. He was neither uprooted from Coon Rapids nor did he suffer from the death of any family member in the conflict. His business and his growing range of agricultural activity were hampered by the shortage of materials; he had to make do with fewer chocolates from Mrs. Drew's shop in Dexter, and much less gasoline from the rationing board. However, the thrust of projects such as the management of his land and the experimentation with fertilizer had already achieved a momentum that carried through the outbreak of war. These years saw a structuring of the family enterprise that determined its nature and set its course for the remainder of Roswell's life. They also mark the period in which Roswell's correspondence flourished and his intellect matured. Between 1943 and 1945 he reached his peak, both in pace and stride.

Neither did the war pass without impact on Roswell. From the beginning he was an active internationalist and in 1940 urged that the United States furnish large quantities of food and arms to the Allies and enthusiastically supported Lend-Lease to Great Britain. After Pearl Harbor he bubbled over with projects for bringing Coon Rapids into the war effort, from pressure cookers for the school lunch program to the systematic purchase of war bonds by his tenants, based on a rate of two for each acre they farmed. Among his projects was a curious national war bond promotion whose incentive was a postwar trip to see the places that were presently in the news. "Wouldn't we all like to see Java and Singapore and Coventry?" he wrote to Red Bowman in 1942. The idea did not catch on.

Food production was the area in which he saw the major opportunity for a personal contribution to the war effort, and was also the area that brought significant development in his own thinking. Between 1941 and

1943 his work with fertilizer convinced him that an enormous leap in agricultural productivity could be achieved rapidly; the outbreak of war convinced him that there was an immediate need for such abundance, which would continue when the war ended. These two propositions – the potential for American agriculture and the increasing world demand for food – formed the foundation of his future activities.

By 1941 Roswell completed the phase of building initiated during the Garst and Thomas breakthrough of 1937–38. He had organized a sales force throughout the new territories and had created an efficient farm management program. Although hybrid corn was increasing yields throughout the Corn Belt, he sought additional methods to improve seed corn production that would provide more income for his tenants, landlords, and family and meet the need for all-out production that he had anticipated since the outbreak of war in Europe in 1939. Fertilizer seemed to provide the answer, and early in 1942 he concentrated on a study of the subject.

Plants draw upon as many as a dozen nutrients for growth, but they basically require three substances: nitrogen, phosphorus, and potassium (or potash). These minerals occur in nature in abundance but often not in a form that is available for plant use. Nitrogen, for example, must be combined in a particular manner with oxygen to create a nitrate, or with hydrogen to create ammonia, in order to be "fixed" or made available to plants. This usable nitrogen is fixed naturally for plants through extraction from the air and soil by bacteria that live in nodules on the roots of legumes such as alfalfa, red and sweet clover, and soybeans. Consequently, alfalfa and clover are used in rotation farming to build up nitrogen and organic matter in the soil. However, as with phosphorus and potash, nitrogen can be synthetically produced and introduced into the soil, a process called "chemical" fertilization that differentiates it from the "natural" or "organic" process of nitrogen-fixation by legumes or the spreading of manure. Both methods rely on the same chemical and biological changes that continually take place in the soil. However, when introduced to the plant, nitrogen plays the major role in producing the cellulose plant structure of corn.

Phosphorus is found in every cell in both animals and plants and its interaction with nitrogen illustrates the careful balance needed to maintain the growth process of plants. Corn uses phosphorus at the beginning of its growth cycle and again when the plant is producing ears. Phosphorus is held so firmly in the soil in an insoluble state that it is seldom available in sufficient supply and has to be supplied synthetically. Lime helps to release it, and so does nitrogen, but in a manner that at the same time can have adverse effects. Corn can be grown on soil that is apparently deficient in phosphorus but in fact is suffering from lack of nitrogen. When the nitrogen deficiency is cured, the soil can then release phosphorus to the plant. This process is usually beneficial but has two dangerous possibilities – an abnormally high concentration of phosphorus can be released or, more likely, the plant becomes starved for phosphorus and the signs that indicate phosphorus hunger begin to appear, among them stunted growth and a purpling of the leaves.

The third element, potash, enables carbon dioxide in plants to mix with water and produce simple sugars, from which cell fibers and carbohydrates are built. Corn is a warm-weather crop, which means that it stores carbohydrates during the hottest part of the summer and grows within a relatively short period. During this period of intensive growth, photosynthesis takes place at a rapid rate; nitrates produce the cellulose plant structure, and potash completes the production of fiber and fuel. Although there are large supplies of potash in the earth, only a small percentage is available to plants because the bulk of the natural supply is locked inside rock and clay particles and requires years of weathering to be released. The "firing" of the edges of the leaves indicates potash starvation in corn.

Whether they are supplied synthetically or naturally, nitrogen, phosphorus, and potash must reach the plant through the medium of organic matter, which consists of plant residues in various stages of decomposition, and of living and dead microbial tissue. Mineral changes such as the weathering of rock and clay particles help provide available minerals, but the major changes in the availability of plant nutrients are achieved through the activity of the microbes in organic matter. This matter must decompose rapidly enough to provide nitrogen, phosphorus, and other nutrients. It should also retain an adequate supply of water and have adequate air and warmth. Organic matter is also susceptible to imbalance; anaerobic bacteria can rob the soil of oxygen if it is waterlogged or nonporous, and carbon dioxide produced by too much rotting material can displace the oxygen.

In the Midwest phosphates and potash were used in the twenties and thirties to cure specific deficiencies in parts of a cornfield, but nitrogen was not considered suitable for use on corn, even though it was used in other parts of the country for tobacco, cotton, and truck gardening. As early as 1922, Professor Sam Conor of Purdue University warned midwestern agronomists and farmers, "the nitrogen problem is the important soil fertility problem before the Corn Belt farmer, and the time has arrived when the lack of nitrogen is seriously reducing yields." Unfortunately, early research at Purdue University in 1933 suggested that synthetic nitrogen had no appreciable effect on corn yield, but in 1938 Gilbert

Walker and Harry Cook of Purdue obtained promising results with similar experiments. In that same year George Scarseth arrived at the university and organized a crash program for the use of synthetic nitrogen in corn growing. When he began, only 400,000 tons of nitrogen per year were used in the entire United States; the Corn Belt states, especially Iowa and Nebraska, were at the bottom of the league in regional use.

In the fall of 1939 the fertilizer experiments produced exciting results on a patch of poor soil in Indiana. Although the results varied, the best plot, which was dressed with a per-acre dressing of 120 pounds nitrogen, 72 pounds phosphate, and 72 pounds potash (120-72-72, the shorthand code of fertilizer application), a total of 91 bushels per acre was produced, more than twice the average yield. Two more years of experiments produced conclusive evidence of the effectiveness of balanced fertilization based upon the heavy use of nitrogen, and in 1942 the Purdue Agricultural Experiment Station published its findings. Other universities such as Missouri, Illinois, and Wisconsin were beginning to do similar work by the early forties, so that when Roswell came into the picture in 1942, research on the value of nitrogen in combination with other fertilizers for corn was well under way. Yet there had been almost no practical application on a large scale, and no substantial investment had yet been made by midwestern farmers. Professor A. J. Kleene of the University of Missouri in an article on nitrogen declared the greatest stumbling block to using synthetic fertilizer remained "hesitancy in putting money into plant nutrients to be buried in the soil."

Roswell first began working with potash in the late thirties to cure problems involving the tasseling of seed corn. Jonathan, who had worked with potash in Scotland, suggested this approach to his brother. Roswell, looking for professional advice from a source closer than California, discovered that George Hoffer of Purdue University was the leading authority on the use of potash for corn. It was apparently through Hoffer that Roswell made his first contact with the new experiments in fertilizers, but he also drove to the University of Illinois to see A. J. Lang, to Missouri to see J. W. Albrecht, and to Iowa State. He returned with offprints and advice. "The first thing I knew," he recalled in later years, "I had a whole damn bunch of people who knew what they were talking about."

Armed with this help, and with advice from the manufacturers of fertilizers, Roswell initiated his own crash program of experimentation in the spring of 1942. He tried different methods of application, different rates of application, applications of one fertilizer, and different combinations of all three on his corn, oats, clover, and flax. He was particularly impressed with the performance of nitrogen, especially on his corn in the combination 3-12-12 (3 parts nitrogen, 12 parts phosphorus and potash), which he compared with results from the use of 0-12-12.

When his first experimental hay crop was harvested and produced an increase of 1 ton per acre from an investment in fertilizer of $3.00 per acre, Roswell was so excited by this and by the progress of his other crops that he wrote all his tenants and landlords to urge a program of fertilization in 1942 and 1943 that would go well beyond the conventional ratios of expenditure per acre. The plan was also innovative in its advocacy of a blanket covering of fields rather than application on places that had specific deficiencies. The general mineral deficiencies in Iowa soil noted by the university authorities seemed to be borne out by his own experience, especially with clovers and alfalfa. Consequently, he reasoned that if the mineral content of the land were brought up to a uniform standard by fieldwide fertilization, yields per acre or per field would also increase uniformly. His plan for the Garst family farms was to apply 100 pounds muriate of potash on all fields that fall to ensure all alkali spots were corrected, plus 100 pounds phosphate and a spring-planting application in 1943 of 100 pounds 3–12–12 starter fertilizer. The cost of these applications would amount to $6.15 per acre, six times the expenditure generally thought sound in the thirties.

He did not ask his tenants to do this much in 1942. "I would only encourage you to do more than you want to do on ten or fifteen acres," he wrote. "I'll practically insist on ten or fifteen acres being done the way I feel sure is the best way." The tenants went most or all of the way, especially Ike Mozena.

The response from the landlords, who agreed to pay three-fifths of the cost, was also affirmative. "I am ready to go along with you all the way on the fertilizer," wrote Doc Macklin, the former Coon Rapids veterinarian now living in Minnesota. "Your dissertation regarding the use of fertilizer is extremely interesting," Abe Freiler replied, "and I am anxious to follow your advice." Freiler had one caveat: "The only thing I don't like about the proposition is that you leave it up to the tenant to decide whether your suggestion is to be adopted or not, and this, I think, is too lenient." Scott Bromwell finally agreed, but only after passing on the objections of his Illinois farm manager to anything but spot applications of fertilizer and receiving from Roswell a fuller explanation of the theory of uniform yields.

Meanwhile, Roswell looked at his experimental acreage as often as he could—his earliest recorded visit was three days after one crop was planted—and grew more excited by the month. On 3 June 1942 he reported to Abe Freiler that he was more thrilled with the possibilities of Iowa agriculture this year than in any other. Freiler already had fine land, fine tenants, and fine crops. "But this year," he exclaimed,

for the first time, we are really delving into fertilizers, and opening up a vision of further increases in crop yields that is so astonishing and so interesting and I believe so profitable as to be exciting.

Later in June he wrote that he had never been busier or more interested in farming than he was now. "There's a new thrill to farming every day with possibilities almost unlimited."

The fall corn crop was excellent, and the jewel among the farms was the 560 acres belonging to Elizabeth Stein and farmed by Ike Mozena, on which he and Roswell had used more fertilizer than on any other farm. The gross return was twenty-six dollars per acre, an amount well above the income from any farm he had been managing. In Coon Rapids the fertilizer age had begun.

Nonetheless, there were difficulties; the product required for the great leap forward was in very short supply in 1942. Although the war stimulated interest in higher yields, it also made the synthetic fertilizers very difficult to obtain, especially nitrogen, which was essential for the manufacture of explosives. Fortunately, Roswell's interest in fertilizer had begun before the government froze nitrogen supplies and instituted an allotment system calculated on the basis of prior level of usage. In 1942 Roswell had both used and ordered a substantial quantity of fertilizer for the plan agreed upon by tenants and landlords.

In the spring of 1942 Johnny wrote that nitrogen and phosphorus in the form of ammonium phosphate were being obtained from a company in Trail, British Columbia, and being used with great effect on truck gardens and alfalfa crops in California. Roswell immediately sent a letter addressed to "Trail Ammonium Phosphate" in British Columbia, asking for a sample of their product and a price per carload shipped to Coon Rapids. The company turned out to be Consolidated Mining and Smelting, with head offices in Montreal, and their reply eventually arrived in July. They sent samples of 16–20–0 and 11–48–0 ammonium phosphate fertilizer, which contained considerably more nitrogen than Roswell had used in that combination, but they could not yet supply a rate because they had never shipped to the Midwest. After negotiating with the Chicago, Milwaukee, and St. Paul Railroad, a rate and quantity were agreed upon — one railroad carload consisting of 20 tons of 16–20–0 and 20 tons of 11–48–0, packaged in 100-pound bags.

By the time the negotiations were completed in late August, the government froze any further orders of nitrogen for 1943, but the War Production Board, after obtaining a list of Roswell's usage to date, approved the shipment. Before the freeze, which was announced in early July, Roswell had ordered a substantial quantity of fertilizer, much of it containing nitrogen, from the Rath Packing Company of Waterloo, Iowa. By late August, there was still no government decision about allocations for 1943.

The shipment from Trail finally arrived in early December, and other growers of seed corn apparently reacted in anger. On 8 December, the

Associated Press carried a story concerning a request made to Senator Guy M. Gillette by the Associated Hybrid Producers of Hudson, Iowa, to investigate a report that one of the major hybrid seed corn companies, apparently wtih political influence, had been able to obtain an allocation of nitrogen-bearing fertilizer, while others were unable to obtain it. George M. Strayer, secretary of the association, claimed that the War Production Board had ruled that no nitrogen-bearing fertilizer would be allocated to Iowa for 1943. There is no evidence in correspondence and documents that Roswell used political influence to get his nitrogen. In fact, in the fall of 1942 he played an important role in ensuring that the entire hybrid seed corn industry received an allocation of nitrogen for 1943.

In late August, after the freeze and before the government made its decision on the 1943 allocation, John Coverdale, chief of the animal and plant food department of Rath Packing Company, reported to Roswell that he had attended a preliminary meeting on the subject with government officials. Both sides had agreed that a meeting should take place in Chicago on 15 and 16 October, and Coverdale urged Roswell to attend to battle for a nitrogen allocation for the Midwest. Roswell was sympathetic: "I don't know why the South should be favored over the mid-West" he wrote Coverdale,

and I am familiar with the fact that in the South they are using all kinds of straight nitrogen fertilizers. The only basis they can possibly use is historic and historic basis ought to have little or no economy in American agriculture now. We need food and food and more food. We have plenty of cotton.

Iowa was represented at the Chicago meeting by Coverdale, Garst, and B. S. Pickett of Iowa State College. They became part of a group of about one hundred, composed of officials from the USDA, the War Production Board, the Nitrogen Control Board, the Office of Price Administration, and farmers, hybrid seed growers, agronomists and horticulturists from all the midwestern states. Both sides made presentations, the government officials noting the uncertainty of the nitrogen supply at the moment but confident about the availability of phosphate and potash, the agriculturalists acquiescing in certain cuts in nitrogen but arguing that priority be given to hybrid seed and commercial field corn.

In his report Pickett noted, "Mr. Roswell Garst and Mr. John Coverdale were especially effective in getting consideration for starter nitrogen for hybrid field corn seed," an item, he said, "the significance of which had escaped the notice of the college representatives." Roswell argued that because of 3–12–12 (nitrogen, phosphate, potash), detasseling crews no longer had to go through the seed fields as many as a dozen times during a period of two or three weeks, because nitrogen starter fertilizer, he had just discovered that summer, brought the corn to the detasseling stage more uniformly and earlier. Detasselers could therefore start earlier and reduce the time it took to detassel corn by as much as 25 percent, a considerable saving in effort during this time of acute labor shortages. He pointed out that starter fertilizer used in the northernmost sections of the Corn Belt could speed the crop along enough to lessen the danger of a fall freeze. Supported by "very effective statistical evidence" from the Ohio growers who also used starter nitrogen, Roswell's presentation seems to have carried the day. Tom Roberts of the DeKalb Seed Company later wrote to George Strayer that "Bob Garst was present at the meeting and 'went to bat' for the hybrid seed corn industry. Due to his efforts, hybrid seed corn was included in Class "a" crops."

In February 1943 the USDA gave hybrid corn a priority and supplied the industry with about 60 percent of its 1942 quantity of nitrogen. In Iowa, amounts used per acre were not to exceed the wartime rates recommended by Iowa State, and lacking a recommendation, then whatever amount had given the best results in the past was to be used. Iowa State thus far had recommended only 2–12–6 for "late or slowly drained soils receiving little manure." As Roswell began to remark with increasing degrees of asperity, the college had not yet entered the age of nitrogen fertilizer. Consequently, he felt freed from the limitation of previous recommendations. However, there was trouble with the Nitrogen Control Board, who first insisted that the car of ammonium phosphate should constitute 74 percent of Roswell's nitrogen, which would have given him a significant shortfall of 3–12–12. But with help from John Coverdale, Roswell persuaded the board that not only had his ammonium phosphate from Trail been approved before the freeze, but that he was entitled to the full amount of the 3–12–12 which he had himself argued for so effectively at the Chicago meeting.

Approval for the starter fertilizer came in February 1943, along with signs of an early spring, and stirred in Roswell a longing to get started with his intensive program of fertilization. "The weather is fine here," he wrote to Mort Schaumberg,

all the snow is gone – and we have the feel of spring in our blood. Everybody is certainly anxious to get started farming. It's grand what a touch of spring does for a man who loves farming. It steps up my pulses about 5 strokes a minute, I suspect – makes me step a little faster and generally enjoy life better.

In the fall of 1942 the potash and phosphate were broadcast and plowed under all the Garst-managed acres, and in the spring Roswell went through his seed corn crop with two separate dressings of 3–12–12, one before plowing, and one applied to each hill when the corn was planted. He used one application on some corn and experimented with a variety of tonnage of ammonium phosphate on the flax crop. He spent time during the spring and summer of 1943 obtaining newly designed and scarce applicator attachments for his machinery, observing from his car the kind of crop his enriched soil was producing.

It was a splendid crop and by December 1943, when the corn had been sold and his accounts for the year closed, he had achieved another significant leap in per-acre income. Scott Bromwell's farms, which had attained an income in 1942 of twenty-three dollars per acre, jumped to thirty-three dollars in 1943, and comparable gains were recorded for the other farms under the Garst wing. Roswell was so pleased with Bromwell's income that he asked the Northern Trust Company, who handled Bromwell's affairs while he served in the army, how Bromwell's income compared with the many other farms Northern Trust managed. Unfortunately, no reply—if there was one—survives in the correspondence.

The success of 1943 marked a change in Roswell's view of farm income. In 1942, even after the evidence of higher productivity and income from the Iowa fields involved in the first fertilizer experiments, Roswell repeated his annual warning about expenditures to his landlords and tenants. He always kept a good portion of the annual income reserved for further investment in the land. "I think you will agree thoroughly with the idea," he had written to Bromwell in December 1942,

that during periods of large income we should make every effort to see that all buildings are put in tip-top shape so that when we eventually hit a period of low farm income, we will have anticipated every expense that could be anticipated so that you and your mother can have no particular shrinkage in your cash income.

He did not think that next year's income would be lower than the present one and ventured the observation, "with normal weather, I even anticipate that it may perhaps rise." The phrase does not have the ring of expansiveness and optimism that characterized his better known agricultural predictions a decade later. But by 1943 the confidence in a continuing increase in prosperity began to appear. In December 1943 he reported to Bromwell:

I have always told you not to expect a continuation of high income. I would not say that this year. I believe that with decent weather the income from all of the farms should be as great, if not greater, next year than this.

Roswell still worried about a repetition of the Post-World War I depression, but at this point his annual predictions of gross income tended to overshoot the mark, and he began to display a lack of interest in the more modest figures of net income that occasionally proved severely trying to Abe Freiler and Sig Stein. A letter to John Coverdale in the summer of 1943 conveyed in another way his sense of a new beginning:

Encouraging the use of fertilizer and observing the use of fertilizer, watching for new uses and studying the results has given me more enjoyment and satisfaction than any other thing I have done in years. It reminds me of the early days of the hybrid seed corn business.

The technology he was helping to create and explore offered possibilities for other changes in traditional attitudes towards Corn Belt farming. Garst Company crews plowed under corn stalks after harvest to increase the organic matter in the soil, applying large quantities of ammonium nitrate and discing it into the ground with the stalks in the expectation that the stalks would decay more rapidly and hence provide more microbial activity. Musing about this rejuvenated soil in December 1943 Roswell began to question the continuation of prescribed patterns of crop rotation. He had a feeling, he wrote to Mort Schaumberg, "that we may find that we can continue to keep a higher percentage of the farms in corn permanently by a continuous and generous fertilizer program than has ever been suspected in this country." In any case, if corn yields started to go down, as they had always when corn was planted continuously, it would be easy to shift back to clover. However, the success of fertilizer thus far, and the increased knowledge about soils now available from the universities and research stations suggested a truly revolutionary possibility in the continuous growing of corn. "Neither the tenants, nor I," he wrote to Schaumberg,

are absolutely sure what 10 years will bring. We are both hopeful that 10 years of this type of program may prove it to be so sound that we will end up with actually better land than we started with in spite of having had greatly increased incomes during the whole ten year period.

He thought it would be "an interesting thing" to watch.

Personal Relations

When Aden Owen became his secretary in 1942, Roswell was reaching his prime as a letter writer. Roswell found in Owen someone whose own talents helped him to bring his distinctive style to fruition. Owen also began the systematic collection of a working file of correspondence.

Aden Owen had learned to type at Audubon High School and had taken to the road to work for an insurance salesman, typing with a portable on his knees while his boss drove the car and dictated letters. He could type a letter faster than he could take shorthand and once proved it to his commanding officer in the Marines in 1944. He came to Garst and Thomas as a billing clerk in 1938, but after his marriage in 1942 he took over the secretary's job to earn overtime, and there was plenty of it. His work frequently started between 4:30 A.M. and 6:00 A.M. on the days Roswell came into the office to dictate letters before driving to the sales territory, to be resumed late in the evening when Roswell returned. He often worked on Sundays and generally responded when Roswell called to say that he was in a letter-writing mood. Aden typed Roswell's dictation directly, took out the letter (and a copy) for Roswell's signature, then went on to the next. There were no draft copies for correction or revision by either party.

Roswell used to tell his salesmen that he simply "talked to the typewriter," but in fact he talked primarily to Aden, partly to the person for whom the letter was intended, and sometimes to others who happened to be in the office. Roswell always liked to have an audience, but he did not require a great deal in the way of verbal response. Since his usual conversation was largely a monologue, the lack of reply from Aden was not a serious disadvantage. He had a remarkable capacity for making the same points over and over again with undiminished enthusiasm and would dictate letters containing the same subject matter to several people, changing the content or allusions slightly for each recipient. He often mentioned Aden in his letters and sometimes concluded with the announcement that he was going to call his correspondent at that moment, which he often did. Consequently, his letters were like his talk, which was described vividly by John Dos Passos:

He had a slow persuasive expository way of talking. His manner was between that of a lecturer explaining the solution of a problem at a blackboard, and a lawyer pleading with a jury. There was a disarming friendliness in his voice that had a way of dissolving objections before you brought them up.

There were, of course, sales letters, taken down by Owen and retyped on stencils, but Roswell took less pleasure in them, even though he had also mastered their technique. "He would rather write a personal letter to a salesman on a typewriter than he would put out a mimeographed one," Owen reported, with the result that his pleasure in expository talking caused Garst and Thomas to lag behind in the adoption of more sophisticated reproduction techniques for the office. Once, in the late thirties, Roswell had emulated Henry Wallace by purchasing a dictaphone and announced that henceforth he would be composing all his letters in this efficient manner. After two weeks, the dictaphone was discarded. He could no more talk to it than he could talk to a typewriter.

Roswell dictated his family correspondence and other personal letters to his secretary. The ordinary distinction between public and personal is blurred in Roswell's writing, largely because there is little in his personal or privately expressed thought that runs counter to his outward opinions and interests or suggests an inner life different from that outwardly observed. It is very likely that he had such thoughts but throughout his life he kept private a whole range of his feelings. He was not by nature an introspective man. He focused on ideas rather than feelings, and his emotional life was channelled almost exclusively into his work and agricultural interests. Consequently, both the public and the private man intermingle in the large volume of correspondence which flowered during the war years.

WITHIN the family, the event of most consequence was the establishment in May 1941 of the Garst Company, a partnership created between Jane, then 19, Stephen, 17, and David, 15. The company's purpose was the "buying, selling, owning, renting, leasing, dealing in, tending and operating farm land," and buying and selling livestock, corn, and other agricultural products. Each partner planted crops and contributed livestock plus grain and equipment purchased from their father with money he had loaned them, as well as the equity in a 480-acre farm in Carroll County and a 160-acre farm in Greene County that Roswell had given to the children. He also leased to them the 200-acre home farm, his interest in a 40-acre farm owned by Ada Garst Ballachey, and the management of a 320-acre farm owned by Doc Macklin.

The boys had started farming seriously the summer before, when Roswell sent them to help Joe Davis with the Macklin farm in Pocahontas County. "I built a shack 12 by 20," he reported to Jonathan in May of 1940,

put in a double bunk just like we had in Canada—gave them Elizabeth's old electric stove—put a barrel up in the attic and put in a shower bath and a stool and Elizabeth's old kitchen sink. The three of them are batching and cultivating 105 acres of corn and 115 acres of soybeans with one tractor and a four-row cultivator.

Steve baked pies, Roswell observed, "and I imagine will do about as well at the cooking job as we did in Canada. I think it will be a very grand experience for them this summer and they are getting the world's biggest kick out of it."

The central question in creating the company was whether it was legally possible for minors to form a partnership. Clyde Charleton, Roswell's lawyer in Des Moines, concluded that it could be done but suggested that Roswell should "emancipate" Jane, Stephen, and David, so it would be clear that any earning and property they subsequently acquired would be their property exclusively. Charleton prepared a comprehensive brief on the subject of emancipation, and Roswell entered into written agreements with each of the three children in which he divested himself of control over the property given to the Garst Company and the business affairs of the partnership.

The arrangement constituted the kind of synthesis that Roswell liked to achieve in his affairs, accomplishing at one stroke several goals. Mindful of how he benefited when he farmed his father's farm alone and learned from experience, he wanted his sons to learn in the same fashion and to use now what would be their rightful inheritance eventually. There was a practical tax advantage in removing his name from the farm property and for creating an instrument to pursue his experiments in farm management in cooperation with his sons and with the managers of the company who would take over when Stephen and Dave were in college and the army. It was a nicely balanced arrangement for Roswell. The children were genuinely independent financially but following their father's lead in his approach to farming; Roswell could remain the guiding force but was released from the practical burdens whenever other matters demanded his attention. He managed to appear less involved than he was and tried to maintain a balance between his authority and his sons' independence. "He would drive by the fields and just suggest," one of the family members observed. "But never an order about 'you get out and do this or that.' " There was discussion and argument over the techniques of farming and raising livestock along with constant evaluation and constant experimentation. When the Garst Company was formed, Stephen recalled "we were really just facing the age of mechanization that came with the hybrid corn industry." Stephen found himself in the middle of a farming revolution and very much a participant, and along with David was "the guy who actually got these ideas into use." The arguments generated by new possibilities he found "very educational, because you had to defend your position."

The new arrangement meant that Roswell also had to maintain a balancing act with his landlords in Garst Company matters. In March 1942 Eddie Reid sold his tank wagons and became manager of the Garst Company (with part of his salary a write-off of his remaining debts to Roswell). "I can give Ed the same kind of advice that I give Ike Mozena and the other tenants on farms which I manage and forget all of the details," Roswell wrote Joe Davis, "and I am sure they will be well managed." In January 1943 Roswell announced to his landlords that he was turning over the management of all their farms to the Garst Company and renegotiated a management fee to be paid henceforth to the Company. Although he appeared to dissociate himself from farm management by ceasing to collect the fees, in practice he never abandoned this pleasant responsibility. He also had to show he was keeping his hand in. Describing his "retirement" from active management to Scott Bromwell he wrote, "because Mr. Reid and I are extremely close friends, and because I thoroughly enjoyed [sic] farm management, I always accompany him on inspection trips and planning trips in the Lake City area." Silent as a mouse, no doubt.

Stephen and David started farming 1,000 acres at a time when their schoolmates who went into farming would farm one half-section at the most. The operation was unique in its extent, stretching across Greene, Carroll, and Guthrie counties, with 360 acres seventy-five miles north in Pocahontas County. The boys moved machinery back and forth through these counties, mastering by trial and error the techniques of large-scale farming, both in its extensive and intensive aspects. They also managed 300 hundred head of cattle and took on yet another large-scale operation under their father's direction, the farrowing of pigs in close confinement.

Roswell had been interested in the mass production of pigs since the summer of 1938, after the seed corn business had at last been well launched and he was able to pay more attention to farming. The college, he learned, had not yet done much experimentation with confined pigs, but he found four or five farmers who had some success with the new method. Roswell was thinking big, and he projected a three-story building to accommodate one thousand sows, who could be expected to produce two litters per year. Micko McBroom assured him that such a building could be constructed cheaply. "I have spent many an hour driving along the road painting this kind of a picture," he wrote to Jonathan in September 1938: "You get out of California and come to Coon Rapids or to Champaign. We organize the Garst Hybrid Pig Company and start producing feeder pigs in a big way." The more he wrote about it, the more attractive it became: "I actually think it's bigger than the seed corn business," he concluded, and by 1941 he questioned Paul Taylor of the University of California at Berkeley about the chances for reversing the present pattern of hog raising, in which the largest operations sustained the largest loss of pigs. With the demand for pork created by Lend-Lease in 1941, the time for such a venture seemed propitious and the Garst Company the appropriate vehicle for its development.

The most successful program Roswell had seen was that of John Hendricks, of West Liberty, Iowa, who developed a small production line in which a certain number of sows farrowed every two months. When the grown hogs were sent to market, a new litter would be placed in the regularly vacated pens, thus ensuring a year-round operation. Roswell and the boys made several trips to view the Hendricks operation, and Steve and Dave remained for over a week to watch the daily routine. By this time Roswell's project became more modest as the practical difficulties and the expense were considered in detail. Instead of a three-story cement building, he decided on a single-floor frame structure, and instead of 1,000 pigs per month giving 150 litters, he planned for 20 sows to farrow every two months. "I hate to admit it," he wrote McBroom, "but I have weakened on the size of the project."

On the home farm, the Garst Company built a 310-foot pig barn, installed a coal furnace, purchased a large quantity of protein from Rath Packing Company, and went into business. By the end of 1942 they were producing about 1,000 pigs per year; yet impressive as the total may sound, it did not approach the expectations for growth anticipated by Roswell and the boys. The hog business would not be greater than hybrid seed corn, and the Garst Company would never exceed the national average of 7 pigs per litter. The greatest difficulty in this era before antibiotics was disease, which killed many little pigs within two weeks and gave the coal furnace an unanticipated use. Strains of hybrid pigs and chickens were still erratic in behavior and performance in the early forties, and labor was scarce during the war. Consequently, when both Stephen and David entered the army in 1945, the hog business was terminated.

Another idea of Roswell's that did not materialize was the great apple orchard project. Roswell discovered that more than half of all apples eaten in Iowa were imported, even though homegrown apples were of high quality and, according to the horticultural department at Iowa State, produced as large a volume of fruit as those of any other area. In 1942 Roswell had Steve and Dave plant a small orchard on the hill above the home farm and at the close of 1943 was still enthusiastic about the possibilities of Iowa becoming the Washington state of the Midwest in apple production. "I have every belief," he wrote Jim Stein, "after several years of study, that a truly large commercial profit could be made over a period of the next seventy-five years by a decent-sized apple orchard here in Iowa." He was especially intrigued because it took eight to ten years to get an orchard into production, during which the development costs could be deducted from his income tax. He thought the rolling land south of Coon Rapids would be the place for orchards. But different events and ideas overtook this project, and the land south of town would provide different opportunities.

In addition to the value of work, Roswell took it upon himself to indoctrinate his sons with certain other verities by which he lived. Sometime during 1943, while in Des Moines with the boys, he marched them into a leading bank. "I want to show you how dumb people are," he told them, and took them to the office of the farm manager who had charge of the largest number of farms in the state. He engaged the manager in conversation about nitrogen fertilizer and the replacement of legume crops. The manager, obviously not a farmer, hardly knew what Roswell was talking about; his management skills did not include any practical knowledge about soil nutrition. Roswell took the opportunity to point this out to the president of the bank: "You don't want that dumb son of a bitch running your farms," he told him, and once outside, repeated his view to the boys. "Let that be a lesson to you," he said. "Not everyone in high position knows what he is supposed to know."

Stephen stayed in Coon Rapids as a deferred farmer until 1944, but in the fall of 1943, David, sixteen, enrolled at Stanford University for the liberal arts education recommended by his father. Roswell's letters to David, though full of advice, were different in subject and tone from his demonstrations of human folly at home. Travel was always an important educational activity for Roswell, and when David told him that he had purchased a Model T Ford, Roswell responded with this judicious advice:

I don't think buying the Model T was too bad, if you have sense enough to forget all about it when school starts except on week-ends, and then drive far far away from Stanford about once every two or three weeks. . . . Always remain curious — and don't be afraid to ask questions of the natives about how they farm — or herd sheep — or do almost anything else for that matter.

Roswell's father had been liberal with money for his children, and so was Roswell. "Your mother said you were worrying a little bit about the money you spend," he wrote.

Take this advice from your father — don't waste it — but spend amply because you'll only be in school once — and you want to see everything and do everything while you are there. You never will enjoy spending it when you are eighty and don't have any teeth.

At home he enjoyed revealing his own working past to his children. He gave some thought to running the corn picker for a day in the fall so that Steve could go pheasant hunting. "I don't think he thinks that I can run a corn picker. I milked a cow the other night and neither Mary nor Toshie believed I could milk until they saw me do it."

IN 1943 Roswell found his lost brother Goodwin. Goodwin, it may be remembered, had sold his interest in the Garst store and moved to Illinois, settling eventually in Chicago. In the thirties he divorced his wife, embraced Communism, and was last reported somewhere on the East Coast. Roswell thought he might have gone to Russia, then began to think that he was dead. But in October 1943 Roswell received a postcard from the Reverend John Newton Garst of the First Baptist Church in Schnectady, New York, informing him that Goodwin was alive and living in Philadelphia. Roswell was determined to see him again. "I am sure he was always as fond of me as I was fond of him," he wrote to the reverend, "and I am sure that he will be happy to see me once the first blush of embarrassment is past." He hoped to persuade Goodwin to move back to Iowa, "where I believe he would be more at home and more happy." In November, on his way home from Washington, Roswell found Goodwin, now an inspector at the naval shipyard at Philadelphia and remarried to a former college teacher with a master's degree from Northwestern. Roswell was very impressed with Julia. "His wife is one of the most outstanding women I have ever met," he wrote Elizabeth. "I am sure you will rate her with Eleanor Garst." The meeting apparently went well, and the two brothers were in touch occasionally until Goodwin's death in New York in 1950. He reported Goodwin fatter, and found that he had resented terribly being called "Goodie" and now called himself George. He was embarrassed about not having written, "but I told him I understood," Roswell reported, "and let it go at that." Roswell sent money to pay Goodwin's hospital bills during his last illness and to provide a vacation for Julia. At the time of Goodwin's death in 1950, she wrote Roswell a moving letter of appreciation for his continuing care for Goodwin and for herself.

Roswell's affection for his brother and his well-intentioned aim to tidy up Goodwin's life by bringing him back to Iowa reflect his general attitude toward family. The affection and warmth he felt for them was expressed in the rather narrow form of financial arrangements, preferably, as in the case of his children and grandchildren, in the gift of land. He either ignored or attempted a quick patch-up of personal problems, which he regarded as unnecessary emotional loose ends. During the early forties Elizabeth continued to have various physical ailments that seemed to be rooted in previously described strains she experienced earlier. Roswell chose to see her problem solely as one of overwork and thought that a month's vacation would correct the matter. As one of his children remarked, in Roswell's view "Garsts just didn't have problems." When they did, Roswell was always the first to look outside for both cause and remedy.

However, in 1943, his family was thriving, and there was an abundance of promise and opportunity on the Garst farm. It was not difficult for Roswell to keep his eyes firmly fixed on the bright side of things and to encompass in his enthusiastic optimism the economic and social implications raised by the new style of farming taking shape throughout the Midwest. Paul Taylor, an economist at the University of California, Berkeley, was among those who viewed with some foreboding the new agricultural technology. He corresponded with Roswell in 1940 and 1941 and paid a visit to Coon Rapids during the period in which Roswell was formulating his hog-raising project. On the question of the financial hazards of mechanization, Taylor noted the academic view that expanded and mechanized operations such as Roswell's faced hazards the smaller operator was more suited to survive.

Roswell expressed "complete opposition" to this view. He saw the new trend as inevitable and his own success more likely, simply because farming was at heart a commercial enterprise in which high investment was now the key to success. He believed that larger farming units would be vindicated socially through the greater abundance which their commercial success would bring. "You hate to see farming on a large scale," Roswell wrote Taylor in 1941. "You would love to think of farming as a way of life rather than as a commercial enterprise. At least that was my summary of our visit." But Roswell argued that something more important was at stake: "Greater efficiency," he wrote, "must give the world greater plenty." He saw the production of more pork, his preoccupation of the moment, as "tremendously important." If hogs could be produced with much less feed and much less labor, he asked Taylor, "is that a social mistake?"

Ultimately, Roswell was acting from the springs of his personality and intuition as farmer, businessman, and salesman rather than on a carefully thought-out program for social and economic change. "I am an enthusiast," he told Taylor. "I frequently get a dream and ride it."

Feed Grains Crisis

Roswell's intervention in the controversy over corn acreage during the war years brings together all the elements of his talent and personality in their mature form. His subject was the need for abundance. His tools were his knowledge of the corn-hog ratio, his ability to interpret production figures, and the persuasive capacity of his writing and talking. He was able to turn from the support of scarcity to the support of full production when it was a very unpopular thing to do and to argue for his position by reshaping the methods learned in the thirties to accommodate the new circumstances of the forties. He pursued his objective with a persistence and single-mindedness reminiscent of the selling of hybrid seed corn, extended at first into the New Deal corn-hog program and now firmly transferred to a larger arena. It was his first campaign conducted largely on paper; he never had a better one. It shows him at his best in persuasive letter writing and represents his intellectual coming of age.

In mid-May 1940, while German panzer divisions were streaking for the French coast, Roswell reported his views on American agriculture and the war to Spike Evans, the former corn-hog committeeman who was now administrator of the AAA. The newspapers speculated that since England had been cut off from Danish pork, butter and eggs, and from Dutch dairy products, the United States would probably have to make good these losses by large-scale exports of agricultural commodities. Roswell feared that a mistake had already been made in reducing corn acreage for 1940 and foresaw the possibility of a shortage of corn in 1941. "I know that we have the ever-normal granary pretty well filled up with corn," he wrote, "but I am beginning to fear that we should have a double normal granary in these kinds of times."

Evans and most of the Department of Agriculture did not share Roswell's concern about corn acreage. Not only did the United States have a bulging granary of corn and wheat, but Canada had 250 million tons of surplus wheat, and Argentina had a 300-million bushel surplus of corn. Wickard, moving in January 1940 from his post as director of the North Central Region of the AAA to become under-secretary and then secretary of agriculture, shared Evans's view. In October 1940, campaigning for the Roosevelt-Wallace ticket, he praised the ever-normal granary but was privately worried about the present domestic surplus of 500 million bushels. He believed the war in Europe pressaged a fall in exports, was happy to see a reduction in fall pig numbers, and, along with the Farm Bureau Federation, was content with the present acreage allotments and reduction goals.

Two months later, the situation changed dramatically. In December 1940 Roosevelt and his cabinet formulated a substantial program of aid for Great Britain, primarily military in nature but including the shipment of pork, lard, and other agricultural commodities. In accordance with the presidential directive, Wickard — not without misgivings — issued a call for increased production of pork and beef during the next two to three years. The American Farm Bureau and many AAA administrators were outraged at Wickard's seeming heresy against the dogma of curtailed production, and the Iowa Farm Bureau called for his immediate resignation. However, Director R. K. Bliss of the Iowa Extension Service, several Iowa State economists, and Roswell supported Wickard and the president. (Roswell had advance notice of the lend-lease program and could not resist telling Eddie Reid to buy up a quantity of lard, which they turned into a neat little profit in the new year.)

Claude Wickard took office at the beginning of a period of change and controversy in the USDA. His main task was to ensure full-scale war production of foodstuffs, a job complicated by the conservative-liberal split within the department and the farm organizations, the increasing concern of the president over inflation in a war-time economy, and the increasing fragmentation of the secretary's control over food production and prices by various new governmental agencies introduced during the course of the war. Finally, Wickard had the unenviable task of succeeding Henry Wallace and suffering from the continual comparisons made with the former secretary of agriculture.

The most militantly conservative force in the agricultural establishment was the Farm Bureau Federation, organized along with the Extension Service in the twenties to help farmers at the local level. Led by Ed O'Neal and Earl Smith, it was virtually an independent organization, representative mainly of large farmers, anxious for the highest possible market prices and campaigning vigorously to decentralize the USDA, mainly by transferring control of certain departmental functions to the Extension Service. The Farm Bureau was supported in these activities by the farm bloc in Congress, especially in the person of Representative Clarence Cannon.

The Farm Bureau was especially critical of the "socialistic" programs of the Farm Security Administration (FSA), which was the stronghold of liberalism and littleness within the USDA. Created in 1937 from Rexford Tugwell's Resettlement Administration and always a favorite with Roosevelt, the Farm Security Administration was devoted to helping the small farmer, laborer, and sharecropper, and strove to diminish the gulf between the top and bottom of the agricultural economy. The agency granted low-interest loans, administered rehabilitation programs to improve land and farming techniques, organized cooperative enterprises, and looked after migrant workers. Among those associated with the FSA were Jonathan Garst, who administered the migratory worker programs in the western states until 1939, Robert "Pete" Hudgens, C. B. Baldwin, and until 1940, Pat Jackson. Jackson continued to work on the periphery of agricultural liberalism while officially working for Phil Murray of the CIO until February 1942, when the White House asked Wickard to give Jackson a job in agriculture. In addition to the FSA staff, Milo Perkins, director of the Federal Surplus Commodities Corporation, which Johnny joined in late 1939, was in the liberal camp, as was Howard Tolley, now chief of the Bureau of Agricultural Economics. Other members of the liberal establishment were Jim Patton and Bill Thatcher of the Farmer's Union, and Roswell Garst.

The lend-lease bill was passed in March 1941 and in April Wickard followed up his general call for production with a specific program. The Commodity Credit Corporation (CCC) would purchase bacon, dried eggs, poultry, milk, and cheese and would offer prices slightly higher than the present market price. The Farm Bureau was furious over what they thought to be unnecessarily low prices set by Wickard, but the administration was firm in its intention to keep prices closely under control. From the very beginning, Wickard had to balance the farmers' desire for purchasing power in the marketplace against Roosevelt's increasing political need to keep prices stable.

While the conservative agricultural lobby pressed for continuation of production restrictions and higher prices and the president insisted upon control of inflation, the third element in war agriculture appeared, the encroachment of other agencies on Wickard's authority. The Interdepartmental Conference Committee, created by Chester Davis in 1940, was concerned over agriculture's slow mobilization and began an inventory of farm production. In 1941 its function was handed over to the Office of Production Management (OPM). The most important agency to appear in 1941 was the Office of Price Administration (OPA), headed by Leon Henderson, a body which proved to be the USDA's most powerful competitor in determining farm price policy.

As these patterns in agricultural policy emerged in 1941, Roswell grew increasingly uneasy over the lack of attention to feed-grain acreage. He heartily approved of Wickard's new production goals but did not believe they could be achieved without an increase in corn acreage. This view was not shared in 1941 by Mordecai Ezekiel, a leading USDA economist and old New Deal friend of Roswell. In February 1941 Ezekiel told Roswell that he was a year too early in his call for increased planting, since the surplus on hand would act as a hedge against any possible shortages in the coming year.

However, as in 1940, Roswell thought it essential to begin to increase the grain supply immediately and in March 1941 began a letter-writing campaign to get the 1941 spring-planting acreage increased. He enlisted Pat Jackson, Jonathan, and Milo Perkins, but by the end of the month little had been accomplished. Johnny reported that on 28 March he had ridden across Washington in a taxi with Perkins, who doubted that corn acreage expansion would be included in the Wickard program but thought that the negotiations with Great Britain over the lend-lease agreements might produce some indirect results. "I wasn't fast enough on my feet," Johnny concluded, "and I was getting out of the cab about the time he got that far. I haven't been able to get to him since, but I must say I am about ready to give up." There was no expansion of corn acreage that spring. "It was a swell campaign," Roswell wrote later, "but it wasn't effective."

That summer, Roswell studied closely the crop reports and feed estimates and took particular exception to the USDA's July 1941 report on the feed situation. On the surface, it was a comforting document; although corn disappeared more rapidly than ever because of increased livestock production, a near record feed supply was in prospect for 1941–42. The combined supplies of corn, wheat, oats, and barley increased from about 105 million tons in 1937–38 to 122 million tons in 1940–41, an increase mainly in corn. However, Roswell calculated grain disappearance beyond 1942, and, after a close study of the August crop report and a good guess on the September figures, came to a more pessimistic conclusion. In his view, the carry-over of this year's unused corn would be only 300 million bushels by October 1942, rather than the earlier prediction made by Louis Bean of over 500 million bushels (and by July 1941 the USDA was already reducing its own estimate of 1942 stocks). He also believed more hogs were being raised than the USDA realized and that by October 1942 this combination of reduced grain carry-over and increased feeding would reduce the grain reserves of 1942 by more than one-half. "We will be tooled up for, by all odds, the biggest disappearance of corn in history," he concluded.

Although Perkins and Jackson were impressed by this argument and some USDA economists were beginning to feel uneasy, Wickard reflected no such concern in September 1941, when he announced his production goals for 1942. Hogs, beef, milk, and eggs were to increase substantially in quantity, and although oats and barley were to be increased by 4.5 million acres, corn – the most efficient of all feed grains – was to be reduced by 6 million acres. Roswell believed that the program would create enough feed for 1942 but would be totally inadequate for 1943 and beyond, and he began writing again urging an increase in corn acreage. He asked Henry Wallace to consider the long-term effects of crop curtailment on the ever-normal granary "in the face of a National Emergency which looks like it might continue for several years," and wrote in a similar vein to Wickard, citing the possibility, to which Wickard had given little thought, of a war with Japan. "There's no doubt," he wrote Wickard,

that we have enough corn and enough grain to last us until we raise another crop. And isn't that a grand position to be in. But 1943 and 1944 are on the way – probably the demands for food will be even higher, and yet present plans call for using up reserves – unnecessarily using up reserves – at a time when farmers are willing and anxious to maintain or even increase them.

When the plan was formally announced in November 1941, the acreage increase finally crept up to 10 percent. But with short-term prospects for supply still vouched for by his economists, Wickard continued to try to keep the surplus to a minimum.

WITH the attack on Pearl Harbor on 7 December 1941, Wickard, Dean Albertson has written, "at least knew he had not encouraged farmers to raise too much. But before him now lay the terrifying specter of too little." Roswell was similarly disturbed, and during his annual December stock taking and meditation had written a series of critical letters to the Department of Agriculture. Fearing that they might do more harm than good, he did not send most of them, but restricted his expressions on this subject to Henry Wallace, Milo Perkins, and Pat Jackson. Because he thought Perkins, head of the Bureau of Economic Warfare, was not sufficiently familiar with midwestern agriculture to defend himself in the continuing argument over production goals, he considered an immediate trip to Washington but postponed it. Wickard, he wrote Jackson, "is grand and a good one," but Roswell thought he was too dependent on Evans and the scarcity psychology. "In times like these," he warned, "it seems to me we can hardly produce enough."

Wickard was coming to similar conclusions himself. He reorganized the USDA into eight major bureaus, and to these bureaus and their chiefs he added three men to form an eleven-man Agricultural War Board. Evans was promoted to this board with the intention of diminishing his authority, and early in 1943 he resigned to join the Federal Reserve Board. Yet all-out production for Wickard did not include any substantial increase in feed grains, so there was no progress on this front.

Prices took the limelight instead but became increasingly difficult for Wickard to use as a means of increasing production. To encourage production and ensure an adequate feed supply required an upward adjustment of prices on both ends of the corn-hog ratio, but Roosevelt, interested in stabilizing the cost-of-living index and preempting union demands for higher wages showed little concern for the niceties of agricultural economics. According to Albertson, FDR remarked repeatedly to both Wickard and Wallace,

I know New York and I know New England. I know the cotton south. But this thing you're trying to tell me about the corn belt I just don't comprehend. You talk about your corn-hog ratio. It doesn't mean a thing to me.

In February 1942 there were as yet no price ceilings on feed, but the USDA was trying strenuously to maintain as low a price as possible for feed grains, counting on the present surplus and encouraging farmers to market hogs and cattle at maximum weights. "In view of the tremendous reserves of wheat as well as corn which are on hand," Mordecai Ezekiel wrote to Roswell that month, "there would seem to be no sense to pushing the price up to a level which would in any way discourage feeding animals to the highest weights possible." Both the USDA and the OPA were concerned over the effect of a rise in corn prices on the narrow price margins in which dairy and poultry producers were operating. Consequently, they held the line on corn prices.

Roswell disagreed on the basic question of the reserves and expected the price of corn to rise in any case because of the increased feeding. "When I read each succeeding daily paper and see how hard Claude Wickard is trying to keep corn prices down," Roswell wrote to Pat Jack-

son in February 1942, "I can't help but think of the *Rubaiyat* of Omar the
Tentmaker:

> The moving finger writes, and having writ,
> Moves on; Nor all your piety nor wit
> Shall lure it back to cancel half a line,
> Nor all your tears wash out a word of it.

If Wickard had increased corn acreage by 15 percent instead of 10
percent, Roswell argued, he would have been in a position to keep corn
prices down. But, since farmers were now feeding much more grain than
usual, the resulting squeeze on stocks would rapidly push up the price. It
was too late to increase the acreage for 1942, because it would occur at
the expense of soybeans, which were also badly needed for their oil and
protein. "All that is possible now is to pray for good weather in 1942," he
wrote. "We could have been in such grand shape with really huge reserves of corn if I had made my campaign more effective last spring."

What could be done for next year? "After I wrote the letter about
Omar this morning," Roswell wrote later that same day to Jackson, "I
drank a cup of coffee – quoted all of Omar that I know – and settled back
to try to be helpful." Roswell was concerned over an abrupt swing between extremes in the corn-hog ratio. If and when the low-priced corn
was no longer available, corn would swing rapidly upwards in price to as
much as $1.10 per bushel. Farmers, unable to continue feeding their large
herds, would immediately begin liquidating, bringing a collapse in both
prices and the war production effort. He wrote Jackson, Red Bowman
(now working in Washington for the Sugar Administration), and Henry
Wallace urging that the government (1) let the price of corn work its way
up, thereby avoiding a sudden surge, and (2) develop a plan for increasing
the acreage for 1943.

DURING the spring and summer of 1942, as the Japanese pushed across
the Pacific, Roswell concentrated on his fertilizer experiments and the
struggle to obtain nitrogen. In the fall he returned to the feed grains issue
and the problem of farm prices, now included in wage and price ceilings
established by the Price Control Act of October 1942, administered by
James F. Byrnes at the Office of Economic Stabilization. He skirmished
with Ed O'Neal of the Farm Bureau, who demanded that the government
compensate farmers for their labor when computing parity payments, and
with John Kenneth Galbraith, now the chief of the OPA. When Galbraith
announced a hog price support of $13.50 per hundredweight, Roswell
wrote him an angry letter accusing the OPA of "chiselling" on the president's program by setting a price lower than the agreed upon ceiling of
$15, thereby undercutting the drive to increase hog numbers. The price

set for hogs, Galbraith replied, was finely balanced to avoid discouraging hog production and the domino effect that a higher price would probably cause. Galbraith was also trying to prevent a rise in packers' costs and was concerned that hog raising was already so attractive that farmers were not producing enough cattle and dairy stock. The margin for maneuver was becoming more limited.

While the government sat on prices, corn sales by the CCC continued to accelerate, and USDA economists were concerned about supplies for 1943. When Roswell urged Howard Tolley to require that hogs at 50 pounds above normal weights be marketed, Tolley replied that there was simply not enough feed grain for such a program. "You have been so right all along on shortages," Jackson had written to Roswell earlier in the fall, "that I think we ought to refer to you all our prophecies. I want very much to talk with you. The situation here is an unholy mess in many particulars."

Late that fall Wickard was named coordinator of the national food program. After some discussion in the Cabinet about appointing a food administrator, Wickard created two wartime administrations within the USDA, appointing Herbert "Pars" Parisius as Chief of Food Production and Roy F. Henderson as Chief of Food Distribution. ("Parisius," Roswell remarked to a friend, "doesn't even start in the race. Consumption has already outrun production.") Parisius, "one of our guys," as Jackson called him, designed a production network based primarily on the FSA; after a short and stormy tenure, he was fired by Wickard.

Roswell returned vigorously to the fight in November 1942, when Wickard announced the production goals for 1943. Once again the goals called for a continuing increase in livestock, dairy, and poultry production, and once again they held back on corn, allowing an increase in acreage only 4 percent above that of 1942. "I decided," Roswell wrote later to Wendell Willkie, "that the position taken by the Department of Agriculture in their November goals was so positively ridiculous that it could be exploded by a simple one-man campaign of a country boy." In addition to writing letters, he travelled to Washington in December "to protest that such stupidity could not stand – that it couldn't be defended." He found considerable sympathy for his message within the department but no assurance that anything could be done about the acreage restrictions. Discouraged, he returned home on 23 December to an equally discouraging letter from Russ Dixon, now working in an agricultural field service and feeling equally angry with his employers. "Russ," Roswell wrote in sympathy, "they are simply terrible." They asked for 2 percent here and 7 percent there, Roswell charged, when they could increase production by 30 percent. "The stupidity is colossal," he concluded, the lack of imagination is astonishing and the red tape is worse to get through than any barbed wire entanglements that the enemy ever erected. Frankly, what I'm trying to do is to get Jonnie to quit the Government and I think you ought to do the same.

Yet, the next day, 24 December, he was back in the fray again, urging Pat Jackson to intervene personally with Roosevelt. After a telephone call from the White House, Wickard brought Jackson back into the USDA with a brief in farm-labor relations. Jackson worked virtually independently of the department, spent a great deal of time out of the office pursuing his commitment to "the small against the big," as he once phrased it, and at the same time led the liberals in the fight for an increase in production.

Roswell's letter to Jackson on 24 December was written with Roosevelt in mind as a reader; as usual, he enclosed a sheaf of letters written throughout the previous months. He congratulated the president on his production goals, castigated the Department of Agriculture for its contrasting lack of vision, and offered his solution for inflation. "Pat," he wrote, "our only hope in maintaining present ceilings and to head off inflation is to *greatly increase production. It just has to be done.*" The prospects for action within the USDA were dim; Parisius, newly appointed to oversee production, would have little chance as long as he was "surrounded on the upper side by Secretary Wickard and on the nether side by the AAA." Only presidential intervention could save the day. Production for 1943 could even fall below that of 1942. The USDA was counting on the weather to produce another bumper crop, and the AAA was still encouraging farmers to limit their acreage. "You simply must not let it go on any longer," he concluded.

Jackson made an appointment to see Roosevelt and awaited Roswell's correspondence. YOUR LETTERS ARRIVED AT OFFICE LAST NIGHT JUST AS I WAS LEAVING TO COME HERE, he telegraphed Roswell from New York a few days later. THEY ARE MAGNIFICENT ESPECIALLY LONG ONE TO ME WHICH I WILL GET BEFORE FDR AS SOON AFTER MY RETURN THURSDAY MORNING AS POSSIBLE. Howard Tolley and Jim Maddox had prepared figures on production needs confirming Roswell's views up to the hilt, Jackson continued, which he would put before Roosevelt immediately.

Jackson's intervention brought the desired affirmative response from Roosevelt and carried the day. In early January the USDA released 100 million acres for the planting of corn in 1943. "I am delighted at the progress," Roswell wrote Jackson after reading newspaper accounts of the change in policy. "A hundred million acres of corn will be pretty fair if they can get the increase pretty well concentrated in the Central Corn Belt."

Jackson was even more buoyant than Roswell. He thought production goals would be raised significantly as a result of this pressure on Wickard. "You spark-plugged those pressures," he told Roswell. He also reported Wallace "definitely on the move" and urged Roswell to supply the vice president with ideas and facts. He believed Roswell should take the lead in a national campaign to increase food production with an article in *Collier's*. "Your standing in this whole farm program as the result of your activities in the early days of the corn-hog plan is such," he wrote, "that any national periodical must give weight to your views." Anxious to press the attack, Jackson gave a story to Ben Gilbert of the *Washington Post* that was critical of Wickard and his production goals. The secretary had had enough; shortly thereafter he fired Jackson, and in spite of pressure from the White House, refused to reinstate him.

During that first week in January, Roswell wrote Roosevelt, Harry Hopkins, and Henry Wallace, hoping to influence the president to make a statement about production in his "fireside chat" of 12 January, but during this week of apparent progress he talked again about giving up his campaign. However, to help the war effort, he continued to press for increased production, as Jackson urged, but by letter rather than by articles. "It's much better for the changes to be made by the Department without apparent pressure from the outside," he wrote Jackson. "It will work out much better if it looks like they are doing it willingly – as if they thought up the idea themselves." But he was prepared to go further if necessary in his "basic educational campaign." A long time ago, he remarked to Jackson,

I found out that "anything that is sound, can be sold." I love to sell – I believe the idea is sound. If I have to use *Collier's,* the press generally or any other means, I'm going to sell it finally. I'm going to get out all the letters that cover my desk now and then I'm going to turn right around and start out on another letter that I think is even more effective because it will be shorter. I'm going to send it everywhere too.

For that brief moment in January 1943 the battle for increased corn production looked like it might be won. However, on 12 January, the victory on acreage was virtually cancelled. The OPA, in consultation with the USDA, announced a ceiling on the price of corn of one dollar per bushel, effective for a sixty-day trial period, with the option of being made permanent on 11 March. Roswell was taken completely by surprise and responded to the announcement as "the damndest thing of all" among Wickard's decisions of the past two years, an opinion he never changed. With room for adjustment on hog prices already limited by ceilings and floors, the ceiling on corn froze the corn-hog relationship at an unworkable level. Roswell was convinced it would be impossible to maintain either this low ceiling on corn or the administration's production goals;

the low price would drive corn off the market even faster and would curtail future planting, in his opinion. It would also play hell with the vision of patriotic profit he had recently been spinning for Ike Mozena and Abe Freiler.

He immediately changed the thrust of his new campaign to an effort to remove the ceiling after the sixty-day period as part of an overall plan for meeting the feed shortage. Entitled "A Brief Outline of What Should Be Done About the Agricultural Situation," his plan made three major proposals: (1) the feed shortage should be explained fully and honestly to Congress, and Congress should be asked to use all the CCC wheat in a subsidized feeding program in which wheat would be sold at the full parity price of corn; (2) the USDA should warn Congress that it might be necessary to import and subsidize all of the Canadian reserves of wheat, oats, and barley; (3) the USDA should inform Congress that if the legislature would authorize the sale of the CCC wheat at full parity price for corn, the USDA and the OPA would remove the ceiling price from corn and establish no further ceilings on any principal feed grain in the future, except in the event of a national crop failure.

The plan was simple, courageous; it went straight to the core of the present weakness of production goals. It was also politically unrealistic and unworkable in the Washington of early 1943. From both Carl Hamilton at Agriculture and Prentiss Brown at the OPA, Roswell learned that a rise in corn prices would upset the narrow feeding margin of the dairy industry. "Another 15 cents to the price of corn as you suggest might very nearly wreck the whole dairy program," Hamilton wrote, and Brown pointed out that dairymen had already been given price increases because of rising feed costs. Hamilton, at least, was sympathetic to alerting Congress and releasing more wheat, but he could not go further on behalf of his chief, Wickard.

C. B. Baldwin of the FSA, an ally of Jackson and Garst in the production battle, passed on a letter from Roswell to Galbraith at the OPA and Maddox at Agriculture, reporting that "the price experts are ready to agree with you about 50% of the way, which probably means that you are about 100% right." However, Baldwin expected little to be done, given the scarcity psychology that he said still prevailed within the USDA. "All this," he concluded,

simply shapes down to a middle of the road point of view and is typical of a lot of decisions which are being made because of a fear of striking out in a bold, vigorous direction. It is all right for corn to go up a little but not too much. It is all right for the feed ratio to close a little but not too much. It is all right to encourage corn production by a slight rise in price but not enough to bring any substantial acreage of grass-land or oat-land into corn production. It's a fine idea to feed wheat but it's tough to battle this through Congress. Hence, the upshot of it all is that we take an easy way and hope to God that the weather will be good.

An even more important constraint on a change of policy lay outside the internal conflicts of the USDA, in the unrest among organized labor over the wage freeze. To avoid an explosion on that issue, Roosevelt insisted upon keeping all prices in line and seemed unconcerned about the corn-hog ratio.

As the deadline for the retention of the ceiling neared, Roswell sent off a final round of letters, complaining that in the process he was getting only vague replies. Jonathan wrote from California that corn was becoming unavailable in the West, and Roswell heard rumors that the elevator stocks of corn would be seized and rationing instituted. He found it especially frustrating that many officials agreed with him but could take no action. "I agree with you one thousand percent insofar as the impossibility of maintaining corn ceilings is concerned," Carl Hamilton had written privately from Wickard's office, and the Bureau of Agricultural Economics (BAE) had agreed with much that he said. "They didn't disagree seriously with anything in my logic or figures," Roswell said of the BAE:

They agreed that there wasn't enough wheat to supplement the corn. They agreed that we would have to import Canadian feed grains to feed. They didn't make any comment on rationing or on seizing – neither denying that this would be done nor confirming it.

His frustration erupted in a letter to Lachlin Currie, special assistant to the president, in which he spoke of a coming "tragedy" that would lead to "an absolute blow-up in the feed grain situation." But on 11 March, the ceiling was made permanent.

Roswell was resilient in the face of this defeat and was consoled by his own performance and the belief that things simply had to change. He had done his best to educate people, he wrote to his daughter Jane:

Both Bill Thatcher and Jim Patton reported that I had everybody in Washington pretty well worried and informed – and that they thought that even though I hadn't succeeded in getting the corn ceiling off, that I had contributed a great deal to the thoughts about the matter and that it probably would come off one of these days.

"Keep me posted on your next try at saving the country," Jane had replied.

Shortly after this episode, Roswell was offered two appointments. One involved an honorary membership on the Chicago Board of Trade, arranged through Richard Uhlmann, with whom Roswell had been in regular contact over the feed grain problem. He turned down the position, telling Uhlmann that he was just "not a committee guy." The second was the post of administrator of the food program in North Africa, where the American army was engaged with the remnants of the Afrika Korps. Roswell had earlier recommended Jonathan for the job, created by Perkins's Bureau of Economic Warfare, and now turned it down himself.

"Because for two years I have been trying to get the agricultural feed grain-livestock picture straightened out here in the United States," he wrote to Monroe Oppenheimer of the Bureau,

and because the situation is now reaching a really desperate point – and because since the appointment of Chester Davis, I am sure there will be a chance for me to be extremely helpful here, I am sure that my decision to stay in the United States was proper.

THE last phase of Roswell's struggle began in April 1943 with the appointment of Chester Davis as War Food Administrator, made by Jimmy Byrnes, who had become critical of Wickard's production program. Davis reluctantly accepted a position that gave him control of the most important USDA departments and caused Wickard to consider handing in his resignation. He did not, however, and remained in charge of the FSA, the Rural Electrification Administration (REA), and the Forest Service, resolving to continue to serve as best he could.

Soon after his arrival in Washington from St. Louis, Davis invited Roswell to Washington to meet Howard Tolley of the BAE. They were to draw up a set of recommendations to alleviate the feed shortage, whose inevitability was now generally accepted. After two weeks in Washington, during which he apparently pressed his own "Outline" as the framework for a solution, Roswell returned home to report that there had been no disagreement with his analysis, yet he had failed to get "everything that is important. . . . I failed to get it from Claude – and apparently Chester is going to follow along on Claude's bad direction." Davis pushed up the guaranteed price on hogs by fifty cents per hundredweight and obtained a rise in corn of 5 cents, which in Roswell's view left the same price ratio in effect and would not produce more corn.

Davis was simply doing what he could within the framework of accumulated constraints that had been building for two years. In April hog prices were close to sixteen dollars per hundredweight, and the OPA recommended immediate ceilings on live hogs to protect the small packers from being squeezed between prices they paid for the pork and the prices they received. Davis was trying to avoid yet another ceiling but was also under pressure to maintain a high level of hog production. Consequently, he raised the support price but warned that prices on live animals would have to drop, or ceilings would inevitably be imposed. He worked under equally severe restrictions with corn and had no chance of getting the corn ceiling removed. The president's blanket freeze order on prices was still in effect, and Davis told Roswell there was a determination "in certain quarters" that there should be no movement upward in price ceilings while the present labor dispute was in progress. It had been a major battle, he said, to get the small price rise they had achieved by moving the October price ahead to the present time. They were begin-ning to buy Canadian grains, he told Roswell, "and some of the other moves you recommend are being taken or are under consideration."

Roswell's response to this analysis apparently was yet another warn-ing on the iniquity of the present corn-hog ratio, which caused Davis, an affable but volatile man, to lose his patience. "I honestly do not see," he replied on 24 April,

how anyone could be in Washington as long and as recently as you were, and leave so completely unaware as you seem to be of the forces and their line-up. It has never been necessary for you to lecture me on the feed-livestock ratio. I did not make the price of corn a political issue. On the contrary, I came in here as you well know after all of those lines were completely established. I do not disagree with anything much in your recent letters, except the freedom with which you use the word "tragic", which, when this problem is viewed in relation to the whole world picture, is something of an overstatement. . . . Some day when I see you I will tell you something of the struggle that is going on, although I am surprised that you did not learn enough about the situation here to understand it without my spelling it out for you. I repeat, I enjoy having your letters and hope you will keep them coming.

"I can't tell you what a feeling of satisfaction your two letters gave me," was Roswell's breathtakingly brazen response. "I was afraid you didn't thoroughly understand the situation until I received them." Later, he made some concession to the political situation by suggesting that Jim Patton and Pat Jackson might be able to persuade the AFL and CIO to let the ceiling be removed, but for the most part he was simply impatient of forces that distracted attention from the logical course of action. He con-tinued to write Davis about the coming shortage of feed and its conse-quences:

You've nibbled at it about like a sucker on a fishhook, where in my opinion you should have struck at it like a big, bold black bass. In my opinion you have only nibbled—whispered where you should have shouted—intimated where you should have declared—been hesitant where you should have been bold.

It was in this spirit that Roswell made a foray into the OPA office of J. K. Galbraith in April during his two weeks in Washington. As was his fashion, Roswell walked in unannounced and told Galbraith that the corn ceiling would have to be removed. Galbraith listened, pointed out that he was employed to hold prices down, not to raise them, and that was what he intended to do. "Well, you won't last long," Roswell replied, "because the situation is going to explode." He predicted corn would be so scarce that there would not even be enough for use in the essential industries in the form of oil and starch. "How long do you think I'll last?" Galbraith asked, and Roswell named a date in the summer of 1943. The two did not meet again until several years later in Des Moines. "I know you're an economist," Roswell said on that occasion, "but I can't remember your name." "Well, I will never forget yours," Galbraith replied. "You predicted my resignation from the OPA almost to the day."

The price of corn was not the only reason for Galbraith's resignation "By the time I left OPA in 1943," he recalled, "any number of people would have wished to have taken credit for the achievement. All felt that I was robbing them of the revenues that were properly theirs." He agreed that the price of corn should have been raised but found himself in a position similar to that of Chester Davis, "stuck," he said, "in a circumstance where it was politically impossible to raise the price of corn and politically just as impossible to lower the price of hogs." The imbalance in the price of corn and hogs was about to produce the explosion Roswell had predicted.

In June the USDA pig crop survey revealed that farmers had raised far more than the department had anticipated, as Roswell had predicted, and far more than the amount of feed available. The supply of corn for the marketplace began to dry up, and corn-using industries such as steel, which needed between 5 and 10 percent of the crop in oil and flour, could not obtain these by-products. Many farmers, Roswell included, held back corn from the market as long as possible in the expectation that the ceiling price would be removed, as rumors flew in this tense atmosphere. Much of the corn that did change hands was traded on the black market, which consisted of farm-to-farm sales and purchases by small truckers. Neither of these operations could be regulated by the government. There were even barter transactions by producers trying to evade price restrictions. The USDA resorted to an organized program of personal visits to farmers by local AAA committeemen, who gave farmers shelling and trucking allowances for selling their corn through normal channels. On 28 June, unable to accomplish any significant change, Davis resigned without benefit of prediction and returned to St. Louis.

In the fall of 1943 the heavy marketing of the huge spring pig crop — 50 percent higher than anticipated — began to glut slaughter facilities throughout the Midwest as farmers unloaded their livestock as fast as possible. Hog prices dropped rapidly and by November were at minimum support levels. As Roswell had predicted, the excessively rapid disappearance of corn shifted the livestock supply too rapidly into surplus, resulting not only in the lowering of prices for the producers, but also in a breakdown of the production goals at the height of the war effort. The Office of Economic Stabilization (OES) wanted to lower the support price of hogs to discourage the slaughter but could not do so rapidly enough. Neither could they remove the ceiling on corn; thus the combination of wrong prices for both livestock and corn produced a continued feed shortage and then a livestock shortage that would last through 1946. The shortages became an embarrassing political liability to the Democrats in the elections of 1944 and 1946 and made it extremely difficult for the United States to fulfill its international obligations.

The feed shortage in November 1943 began to hurt the eastern dairy and poultry producers and became a partisan political issue for 1944 in a front-page story in the *New York Times*. "Dewey Denounces U.S. Feed Policies as Peril to State," the headline read, and the text recounted yet another of Roswell's prophecies fulfilled. Sent by New York's Governor Thomas E. Dewey on a ten-day tour of the Midwest to determine whether the feed requirements of the state could be met during the coming winter, a committee of experts returned with a negative answer. Most corn that normally moved to the East would remain on midwestern farms for the reasons described above. This circumstance prompted Dewey to declare, "The State has now exhausted every resource for the protection of its people." The statement was excessively gloomy, since New York was able to buy sufficient reserves of Canadian barley to carry dairy and poultrymen through the winter of 1943–44, and the government was purchasing wheat from Canada, Argentina, New Zealand, and Australia. But the truth was out; the CCC was forced to admit they had sold the entire domestic supply of corn.

Throughout 1943 Roswell was convinced that the corn ceiling would be lifted and he continued to press his case. There were moments of depression. "I'm sick at heart and discouraged," he wrote to Pat Jackson at the end of June. Anger at official paralysis – "I think you all lack guts" – was a continuing theme in his letters as were his moments of personal frustration expressed to Ed Pritchard at OES in October when he confessed, "I feel impotent as hell sitting out here writing letters." There was also satisfaction with his letter-writing skill in argument and persuasion. "I think the letter I am enclosing is the best I have done yet," he wrote Red Bowman that same October. "So if I were you I would file the copy of this Pritchard letter among the souvenirs to remember me by."

He enjoyed the pleasures of having been right and took particular delight in reminding his old corn-hog associates in government that he had told them so. In November he wrote William McArthur, director of the CCC, recalling that "violent" campaign in the spring of 1941 for increased corn acreage. "You told me at Des Moines that I was crazy," he wrote,

Spike Evans told me the same thing. And so the Secretary of Agriculture actually bribed farmers to curtail corn acres. . . . and I can't help reminding you and of reminding Spike and of reminding Claude Wickard that the present shortage is in quite a large way due to your mistake in the Spring of 1941.

Roswell was even more abrasive in a letter to Evans, again charging the AAA with bribery and laying most of the responsibility for the current fiasco squarely upon Evans. Evans in turn accused Roswell of making points for the coming election campaign, defended the department's policy, and concluded with a ringing defense of the AAA and all it had done for this country and England in the early days of the war. It was a sad and unnecessary exchange, prompted perhaps by Roswell's regrets at having turned down public service himself. The "bribery" motif was a distortion of the fact that a program Roswell had helped create had simply outlived its usefulness during wartime.

However, apart from this touchy area of his feelings, Roswell made no efforts to capitalize on his successful prognostication beyond enjoying the accolades from his friends and continuing to give advice. In January 1943, after he decided on a private rather than public campaign, the advertising manager for a farm magazine suggested that Roswell publish his "Outline" as an advertisement to get "full credit" for his program. "I much prefer not to get any credit by name for the program which I outlined to you," he replied, "so I certainly wouldn't be interested in using it in advertising." Early in 1944 Milo Perkins reported:

Your hell raising awhile back certainly made for a greater corn acreage than otherwise would have been the case, although nobody in God's world will ever give you credit for it. Since I agreed with you completely, I told you at the time that you were a very wise man and now that we have hind sight to help us it becomes obvious that you were a very, very wise man.

Ed Pritchard at OES already regarded the forty-six-year-old Roswell as something of an elder statesman in the field and sought his advice on the 1944 program he was drafting. "Let me hear from you," he wrote to Roswell. "Your judgment is sound and even those who won't take your advice respect your common sense."

There was another theme in Roswell's exchange of letters with Perkins in 1944—the passing of the old liberal order in agriculture. Jackson, Davis, Jonathan Garst, and most recently Baldwin were gone from the department and active government service, and Perkins's dismissal from the Bureau of Economic Warfare in February 1944 raised the casualty rate higher. In Roswell's view, the activism of enlightened businessmen and public servants that brought major changes to agriculture and to the social order in the thirties had become bogged down in bureaucracy and politics in the forties, and Perkins's departure seemed to put a seal on "progressivism." "As you know," he wrote to Perkins, who had brought food stamps and school lunches to the nation,

I urged Jonathan to do what he did a year ago—to get out of Government because I thought there would be a temporary lull in the progressive gains—because I thought we faced a period of reaction. A lot of the world will never know the grand job that you fellows all did. Probably most of the credit will never be properly placed. But the work you did in Government will survive – you laid out the road.

Roswell's mood was not pessimistic in 1943. He thought acreage limitation was already a thing of the past and predicted full employment and capacity production in agriculture, "although we may have to go through a stagnant period first." Progress may have stopped in Washington, but it continued in other places.

An earthy and almost mythic word portrait of Roswell at home on the banks of Spring Branch Creek during these years was painted by John Dos Passos in *State of the Nation,* his paean to a country whose people had the will and ability to sustain a republic of free men. Dos.Passos found much to praise in a system in which – and here is an echo of Roswell – "plentiful production of food and goods is just about a solved problem." There was a continuing American frontier in the new technology, Dos Passos argued, and with each new advance "the possibilities of our lives expand at a terrifying rate." Our people, he wrote, "are still frontiersmen." For Dos Passos, Roswell embodied a vision of the agricultural frontier.

Dos Passos and Roswell met in 1940 at a dinner party arranged in part for this purpose by Pat Jackson, a Harvard classmate of Dos Passos and a fellow campaigner in the fight to save Sacco and Vanzetti. Roswell, who knew nothing of Dos Passos's eminence as the author of the trilogy *USA,* leaned across the table during a lull in the conversation and said, "Tell me, Mr. Dos Passos, what do you do for a living?" Dos Passos answered that he was a writer; Roswell, anxious to divert attention from the laughter his remark caused, quoted Mark Twain's *Pudd'nhead Wilson* on the ways to compliment an author, chief of which was to ask to see the manuscript of his next book. As Jackson had expected, the two took to each other immediately.

At the end of October 1943 Roswell received a telegram from Dos Passos: IF I STOPPED OFF IN COON RAPIDS TOWARDS END OF THIS WEEK ON MY WAY WEST SHOULD I FIND YOU HOME? Roswell replied to Dos Passos in Chicago: I HAVE THE TIME AND DESIRE TO REALLY SHOW YOU MIDWEST AGRICULTURE. Dos Passos got the deluxe tour and wrote his wife Katy:

It's wonderful here. Nobody thinks of anything but corn – not corn liquor but hybrid corn (100 bushels to the acre) standing pale and gaunt in immense fields rising in ranks over the rolling hills. . . . The Garsts are an immense busy noisy cheerful talkative clan all very tall and rich and healthy and doing all their own work – Across the road from where they live is a sort of Ritz where 1200 hogs sows and little piglets live in considerable style. . . .

The impressions of that November visit were set forth in *State of the Nation* in 1944 ("My I enjoyed that little stop in Coon Rapids last fall," Dos Passos wrote in the copy he sent to Roswell). Dos Passos recorded a day's wanderings with Roswell around Coon Rapids, and Roswell's views on farming, fertilizer, and the corn-hog ratio. They began the day at the South Side Cafe, "a small plain lunchroom on the short main street of a small plain town on a creek in a region of broad slow lazy hills." Roswell talked of the Wisconsin Drift, a black land getting richer because "we are just starting to learn to use fertilizer on this land," of hybrid corn, and of the day when 100 bushels per acre might be the state average. They drove out of town past the seed corn factory and the great cob pile ("We burn 'em in the stoves here") while Roswell discoursed on the feed shortage about to be brought on by "the way they're messing up the corn-hog ratio in Washington." He took Dos Passos by a poorly managed farm and to one of his own tenant's farm, who made $25,000 in the past two years ("Mind you, $25,000 was his share after the landlord was paid off and all expenses paid").

On their way back, Roswell took Dos Passos past a poor farm that he believed would eventually do as well as the good one they had just seen. "As we drove back toward town," Dos Passos wrote, "my friend was saying, 'And we haven't begun to produce in this country yet.'"

Commercial and Curious

Looking Ahead

As he had promised his friends in Washington, Roswell entered the postwar world in an aggressively commercial frame of mind, determined to fulfill his personal vision of agricultural potential in a manner that also served a larger community. "As I told you," he wrote in 1946 to W. A. Albrecht, chairman of the Soils Department of the University of Missouri,

I am primarily commercial – my studies of fertilizer and its effect have been wholly based on the profit motive. The thing that interests me is that whereas you never use the dollar sign in connection with fertilizer, and whereas I always use it, we end up at roughly the same place – that it takes a complete and balanced fertilizer program to do either the thing you want – that is make better food for people and livestock – or what I want – make more money for the farm owner and the farm operator. As you say in the last sentence of your article on "Agricultural Limestone for Better Quality Foods" – surely this adds nobility to the business.

Roswell had visited Albrecht to inquire about the university's work on fertilizer and to collect relevant pamphlets and articles. He wanted to know more, he wrote from Coon Rapids, and hoped to return to Columbia to "absorb as much as possible from the things you have learned." He was not a scientist, he remarked, "just a curious farmer who likes to know the reasons behind things."

This strain of curiosity, which had led him originally to hybrid corn, continued to provide a crucial dimension to his commercial endeavors and was the trait that contributed to his business success and gave it a wider significance. He was not really a scientist; his engagement in research was dedicated primarily to the practical application of knowledge, the transfer from laboratory to field. University researchers reckoned that the usual period for such transference was about ten years. Roswell was much too impatient to wait that long, and much of his coming confronta-

tion with Iowa State centered on his desire for a much more rapid leap
into the future. A business needed a better product; a salesman needed
volume. In both there was always the consideration of time.

He was ebullient over the prospects ahead. In 1945 he saw "nothing
to be pessimistic about," and in a letter to C. A. Barber of Rockford,
Illinois, he showed himself firmly forward looking, confident that new
forces were at work. "I spent a good deal of time looking over your chart
of business booms and depressions," he wrote:

It is most interesting.
It isn't the real chart that I wanted.
It shows from 1875 to 1944, inclusive. That's interesting, but the hell of it is it is
also history.
I wish you would also kindly forward me another chart showing the same statis-
tics from 1945 to 2045.
When I receive it, I will know how to proceed.

THE years 1944–45 marked a personal milestone for Roswell. "We had a
hell of a season last summer," he wrote Pat Jackson in early 1945,

expanding our business in the face of the worst farming conditions last spring in
history, and in the face of a terrible labor shortage. We had to build a very large
drying plant and all in all it was a rough go. But, we did get it expanded—we did
raise an excellent crop—we do have it sold—we have rested up—and we are
getting ready for another round. I believe 1944 will go down with me as having
been the roughest.

In March he reported to David that for the first time in a long while he
had "the satisfied feeling of having everything in hand." He had completed
new wage negotiations, obtained a priority for a new warehouse, seen all
the farm tenants, ordered all the fertilizer and grass seed. "I even wrote to
Bottom Sigler a few minutes ago," he reported, "and when I get down to
that I am *not* pushed." If David could lead as happy and as interesting a
life as he had led for the past twenty-five years, he wrote later, "you can
mark it down as pretty successful, and I don't see any reason on earth you
can't."

In 1945 Stephen and David joined the Army, Stephen from the farm
and David from college. By 1946 Roswell was anxious to see them dis-
charged so that they could finish college and come home to work. "You
just can't imagine," he wrote David, now serving in the occupying forces
in Korea,

how many things you could be doing here that would be useful—that would not
only be useful to us, but useful to the world. . . . With the drainage program, and
the house building program, and 10,500 acres of hybrid seed planned for next

year, and ever-increasing amounts of fertilizer—we just need someone around like you who is capable of handling a crew.

He wrote to Stephen in a similar vein and to the military and selective service officials to try to obtain early release for his sons. They finally returned in late 1946, too late to begin school that fall, but in 1947 they were both at Stanford.

The girls were still at home in 1945; and Jane, finished with her wartime teaching and planning to return to college, travelled with Roswell to one of his winter sales meetings. "We went all over Nebraska from one end to the other on sales meetings," Roswell reported to David, "and she entertained the salesmen's wives, and got a big kick out of it." She also travelled to the East Coast with her father, then went West to enter Stanford in the fall of 1945, receiving advice similar to that received by David two years before—get a car and see the countryside.

In 1948 Jane married Clarence Kamps, and in the fall they moved to Coon Rapids to take their place in the Garst Company farming operation. In 1949 David married Georgianne Orenstein, whom he met at Stanford, and Stephen married Mary Garst, a daughter of Warren and Eleanor. Within a period of eighteen months the older children married and returned home to claim their patrimony. They were now raising their own families, each taking hold in the town in his own way, and the old balance between parental authority and filial independence established in the early forties when the Garst Company was founded had to be redefined. "God it's hard to say 'they' after running the Garst Company for so many years," Roswell remarked to Johnny in 1955, as he struggled to make an adjustment. In spite of problems, these years marked the beginning of a collaboration with his sons that Roswell had looked forward to. For Jane and her husband Clancy, who came to Coon Rapids on a more provisional basis, the arrangement was not a happy one, and in 1950 they moved to Clancy's home state of California.

In a letter written in November 1949 to his new daughter-in-law Mary, Roswell reviewed his stewardship of the Garst Company. The building program on all the farms the company managed was nearly complete; Jake Bell's house would be remodeled by Christmas, and John Chrystal's shortly thereafter. "I doubt if you all realize," he wrote,

that in the last 15 years I have supervised the modernization of every house on every farm that the Garst Company manages—the tiling of each one of those farms—the surface draining of those farms—and getting them into shape where they practically run automatically.

Although his feelings towards the Garst Company were valedictory, and he was acknowledging that the old order was giving way to the new, he had also fixed upon a new project. In the same month he announced he was "transferring" his affections to the Toshiami Trust, his means of providing for his daughters Antonia ("Toshia") and Mary.

The Toshiami Trust consisted of two farms in 1949. The first was the Viv Bell farm, a few miles north of town off the Glidden road and farmed by Jake Bell's brother Viv, a moon-faced man with a short and very round body to match and an endearing knack for mispronouncing the English language. He was also a first-rate farmer, a canny judge of the value of antiques, and one of the South Side Gang who followed Roswell's teaching on the new agriculture. The second property was the farm that Samuel Goodwin, Bertha Garst's father, had bought near Rockford, Illinois, the oldest of the Garst family holdings and farmed by William Motter. It was too far away to be managed by the Garst Company, but Viv's farm was not, and Roswell served notice that he was not going to disappear from the farm management business. Of the Toshiami property he wrote, "I'm going to build up my interest – and exercise my mentality, giving you all the advice I know how."

The post-war years also marked the beginning of a period of close collaboration between Roswell and Jonathan, carried on largely by correspondence, since Johnny continued to live in California. But there were visits, also, and in January of 1949, Roswell noted:

Jonathan was back for a week and the house rang with loud voices – laughter – and serious talk about the intricacies of new agriculture from all angles. I simply re-affirm what I have always known – he's the smart member of the Garst family. He knows more things for sure than anyone I know.

Jonathan was indeed an original, inquiring thinker and was brilliant, witty, and provocative in his writing and conversation, serving Roswell as a consistent purveyor of ideas and information. However, the image of Johnny as the idea man and of Roswell as practical journeyman, which Roswell himself often fostered, is misleading. Johnny came into most of Roswell's major projects after they were launched; and while he had much to contribute, their collaboration was very much one of cross-fertilization. Jonathan moved from idea to idea more rapidly than Roswell, and, even more than his brother, had the instincts and training of the academic researcher. Johnny liked to apply his knowledge in a practical way, too, but Roswell was more effective in the follow-through and was creative in building upon his experiences in a way that Johnny was not. The nature of their relationship was expressed in a letter by Roswell to Farm Quarterly editor Grant Cannon, which described the Garst brothers' correspondence. "It doesn't make much difference what the subject is," he wrote of his correspondence with Johnny, "it goes back and forth about as rapidly as conversation." He gave an example of their present interest in nitrogen and urea:

I send copies of that letter to Jonathan and to all of the universities. Jonathan sends it to the Beltsville station and I send it to DuPont and Barrett and then we throw it back and forth via mail. . . . We have not lived closer than 1,200 miles from each other in 25 years—and yet the correspondence has been extremely steady. Sometimes it's only once every two weeks during a busy season. Then it will be every day for two weeks at a time.

Jonathan's correspondence bears its own particular style, but there are similarities to Roswell's writing in the choice of apt phrases and in the lucid exposition of technical agricultural matters. His letters tend to be more abstract at times than Roswell's and are more diverse in subject matter. They occasionally borrowed from each other, and in their work on nitrogen—both letters and articles—it is often difficult to distinguish the separate contributions of the two.

Jonathan was never the businessman Roswell was, even though he seemed to think he should be. Ideas were his passion, and money and crops regularly disappeared through his inattention to detail and sudden interest in something new that attracted his attention. Roswell continued his financial assistance to Jonathan not only for love but also in the way a university gives grants for research. Roswell could share with Johnny the same kind of excitement he shared with George Hoffer and George Scarseth, except that with Johnny it was more expensive.

Finding Enough Fertilizer

Convinced of the promise of fertilizer by his own experiments in 1942 and 1943 and by the research in progress at the colleges, Roswell continued his own field trials and began a campaign to persuade others of its efficacy for the Midwest. In July 1945 he wrote Johnny that he was spending all of his time showing Garst and Thomas seed growers fertilized and unfertilized seed fields and was educating them on the fertilization of oats as well. Seeded with clover, oats provided a greatly improved level of fertility in the rotational system of oats and corn. Nitrogen made the most dramatic difference with corn, but a combination of nitrogen and phosphorus produced results in oats that were astonishingly good, and he reported this fact to the experimental station at Beltsville, Maryland. "I have had one group coming down this morning, and another this afternoon," he commented to Johnny:

I have already had people here from the University of Nebraska, from Missouri University, from Iowa State College, from several of the leading fertilizer companies, and from some of the farm papers. Of course, it will be a long, slow job, because the productive facilities of fertilizer companies will not grow rapidly. . . . People have always been afraid to use [nitrogen] before on purpose in this area — they won't come to it too fast.

One of his new tricks in showing his demonstration fields was to drive a speeding carload of visitors directly into one of his well-fertilized stands of oats or clover. He also wrote a huge 'N' with nitrogen on a grass hillside.

During the war, Roswell urged John Patterson of the Spencer Chemical Company of Pittsburg, Kansas, to go into the fertilizer business when his wartime contract to produce nitrates for ammunition expired, and in 1946 he talked the company into supporting one of his best-remembered promotional schemes for the dissemination of fertilizer. The promotion was the gift of a ton of ammonium nitrate to every salesman of Garst and Thomas who sold 100 bushels more of seed in 1946 than he had in 1945. It resulted in the distribution of 1,000 tons of fertilizer in areas where it had never been used, or perhaps even seen before. Again, Roswell used banks in Nebraska for the dissemination of samples of ammonium nitrate.

In Roswell's view, the best immediate means for producing enough nitrogen to meet anticipated domestic and foreign demands was the conversion of government munitions plants to the fixation of nitrogen for ammonium nitrate, a solution he proposed to Secretary of Commerce Henry Wallace in the summer of 1945. But once again he found himself in conflict with the USDA, this time over the projected use of fertilizer. In October 1945, writing in the journal of the Department of Commerce on "Ammonium Nitrate — from War to Peace," C. Kenneth Horner reported that the Department of Agriculture had recommended the use of 1,100,000 tons of nitrogen per year by American farmers. The USDA believed that farmers would actually use only about 750,000 tons; therefore they recommended that the government's ammonia-producing capacity should be reduced to only 40 percent of its wartime level to supplement private production. "A greater export trade in nitrogenous products would be to our advantage," Horner wrote, "but this outlet does not appear likely to account for a very substantial share of total production."

Shortly thereafter, late in 1945, the ordnance plants owned outright by the government ceased production and were declared surplus. It was not until the spring of 1946 that Roswell found out — perhaps tipped off by Jonathan — that the capacity to produce 1,500,000 tons of ammonium nitrate was lying unused. "I guess the only one in the United States that did not stop production was the plant at Pittsburg," he wrote Glenn Buck, editor of the *Nebraska Farmer*. "Because it was running," he told Buck, "I foolishly presumed that all the rest of them were running. . . . I think you ought to just raise hell." He wrote other editors, Congressmen, and Al

Loveland of the AAA, who advised his superiors in the USDA that Iowa alone could use the 1,500,000 tons of nitrogen, 400,000 tons above the recommended national total. Jonathan went to Washington to urge that the plants be reopened, and Wallace, at Roswell's urging, got in touch with John Snyder, Director of War Mobilization and Reconversion. It appeared, Wallace reported, that the plants were going to be put back into use, but in May 1946 Wallace was not certain whether they were going to manufacture fertilizer or explosives. ("I wish you would tell me where I can buy a couple hundred pounds of the nitrogen-phosphorus combination," he added in a letter to Roswell. "I should like to try it out in my sister's garden here in Washington." Roswell sent him the 200 pounds.)

The plants were going to produce fertilizer, but not because of the efforts of Roswell, Jonathan, Henry Wallace, or the USDA. They were reactivated because Generals MacArthur and McNarney warned the War Department that the occupied zones could become ungovernable if the severe food shortage in Asia and Western Europe continued. As Secretary of War Robert Patterson reported to Wallace, the War Department could not obtain "any substantial amount" of nitrogen fertilizer and was told by the Fertilizer Committee of the Combined Food Board that the world shortage of nitrogen was so severe that during the next year it would have nothing to allocate to the occupied areas. To avert a second year of famine, the War Department decided to reactivate sixteen ordnance plants and requisition 60,000 metric tons from the civilian supply, which they agreed to replace when their own plants went into production. The reactivation would increase nitrogen-producing capacity in the United States by more than 60 percent, but even that would only be enough to alleviate the overseas demand and would cause an immediate shortage in available domestic supplies.

The USDA estimated that the nitrogen plants could produce fertilizer enough to produce 10 to 12 million additional bushels of wheat, enough to feed more than twenty million people, and continued to ignore even the evidence of shortage so dramatically highlighted by the War Department. In response to a query by Wallace, the USDA predicted a world surplus of nitrogen, and a memorandum prepared by his own staff in the Department of Commerce assured Wallace that "we need have little apprehension over the future of the nitrogenous fertilizer supply of the United States." Wallace relayed this information to Roswell. "I don't care about the rest of the people around Washington," Roswell replied, "but I think it would be fun to have *you* remember the predictions I made to you in late July of 1946 which follow." He predicted a severe shortage of ammonium nitrate in the spring of 1947 because of the necessity of exporting to occupied territories. He believed that by 1948, if the exports diminished, there might be an ample supply for "an uneducated market," and that some efforts at sales would have to be made. "But by 1949," he predicted,

the whole countryside will be educated and the demand will be far beyond comprehension. There will be every pressure that an over-demand can place upon an under supply. Included in this pressure will be terrific pressure on Congress for additional plants. They won't be available in sufficient quantity before 1955, no matter how rapidly they are being built.

In addition to showing fertilized plots to carloads of visitors, Roswell extended his calendar of speaking engagements. His audiences ranged from vocational agricultural students at high schools throughout the region to the farmers' clubs of Kansas City and Chicago, the National Farm Institute in Des Moines, and the Iowa Farm Managers Association at Ames, Iowa. He was often away for two or three nights a week in the Coon Rapids area. He did not charge a fee, viewing his efforts as the creation of an educated market.

At the meeting of the Iowa Farm Managers Association, Roswell pressed home his offensive against the college for what he considered their extremely slow pace in fertilizer experiments and adoptions. He invited the soils specialists in the Iowa State Agronomy Department to the meeting, announced in his speech that they should all be fired for their failure to recommend the use of more fertilizer, and concluded with a triumphant vindication of commercialism in the service of agriculture. Bruce "Bugs" Firkins, a former classmate and now a faculty member, suggested that Roswell did not have to worry about the commercial aspect of fertilizer because his Chicago landlords could afford to put far more money into fertilizer than an Iowa farmer. "I'm commercial as hell!" Roswell answered. "I get more than twice as much money back as the fertilizer cost. What the hell is lacking in commercialism in that?"

In fact, the college was coming along. The head of the Agronomy Department, W. H. Pierre, came to see Roswell's work in 1946, as others had come in 1945, and fertilizer research was intensified at the college. By 1947 Roswell could write to George Hoffer that "the college at Ames, which formerly was pretty terrible in its recommendations—or at least it was so in my opinion—have come out with startlingly good recommendations finally."

Firkins's concern over the cost of fertilizer was reflected in the continued resistance to the use of chemicals, but there was another reason for reticence in the case of nitrogen—its destructive side effects. Apart from simple misinformation about its use, there were difficulties such as excessive accumulation of nitrates when the nitrogen was not properly applied, shortages of other minerals, and the dangers of handling nitrogen under pressure. Along with the universities, Roswell evolved a successful technique for application that eliminated the excessive formation of nitrate salts (a condition that also occurred naturally), urged farmers to use a balance of fertilizers to offset any deficiencies, and kept in touch with the latest research on side effects of nitrogen. In 1947 both Roswell and Jonathan were upset over a munitions explosion in Texas City, and Roswell contacted his scientific sources to find out about the chances for explosions of nitrogen in bulk. The Department of Agriculture had already produced a bulletin entitled "Explosibility and Fire Hazard of Ammonium Nitrate Fertilizer," among other things an acknowledgment that American farming was entering a new phase in its technological development. The new solutions were bringing with them new problems.

The fertilizer companies were delighted with Roswell's educational campaign. As early as 1943 Roswell had probed the possibility of selling fertilizer for either Spencer Chemical or Consolidated Mining and Smelting, but nothing came from these overtures. Roswell was committed to the widespread use of fertilizer whether he was a direct beneficiary of sales or not, so that the fertilizer companies had in effect a first-class volunteer. What he did get from the companies as the price of his advocacy of fertilizer was the commodity itself, still scarce throughout the late forties, as he had predicted. He paid the standard price for the commodity but, as he wrote to George Hoffer, he would "lay down on fertilizer companies to supply the amounts and kinds of fertilizers that I need to do a really good job of fertilizing our seed fields and the fields of the neighbors of the men who produce seed for us." In 1949, writing to John Patterson of Spencer Chemical, he reminded Spencer, "I still work for you about half-time on a 'for-free' basis—only if I catch you cheating me on the amount of Ammonium Nitrate I need, I'll quit work." The Garst Company eventually went into the fertilizer business independently, to fill a void in the local distribution of chemicals.

By 1947 Roswell stopped laying out fertilized and unfertilized strips to demonstrate the virtues of fertilizer, "because it has become an old sort of thing in this community." By that time an entirely new opportunity had presented itself in the form of corncobs as cattle feed.

Cobs for Cattle

Roswell had been trying for years to find some way of using the mountain of corncobs that accumulated each fall during the processing of hybrid seed corn. In 1943 he learned the Navy wanted cobs for cleaning carbon from airplane engines and wrote the USDA to find out about this and other possible uses for his waste product, questioning Iowa State as well. Corncobs seemed to be good only for burning in stoves or as bedding for cattle in the feedlot. However, in 1946 a man from California turned up one day and offered to buy the entire mountain of cobs in Coon Rapids. His purpose, he told Roswell, was to send the cobs by railroad to California, grind them up, and sell them as cattle feed there. Astonished that anyone thought cobs had feeding value, he asked at Iowa State if it was legal to sell the cobs as feed in California. The answer was affirmative, because the state of California accepted the results of experiments conducted at the Ohio Agricultural Experiment Station in Wooster, Ohio. The sale of the cobs to the gentleman from California fell through because of high shipping costs, but that was an affair of little consequence. Roswell was already on the scent of bigger game, the experiments themselves and the men who were conducting them.

In Ohio, Roswell found closely related experiments being carried on concurrently at two locations. The first project, of immediate interest to Roswell, was the feeding of corncobs to cattle as a partial substitute for the traditional ration of corn, either shelled or on the cob. It had been carried on at Wooster under the direction of Paul Gerlaugh, a Pennsylvania Dutchman without a Ph.D. but endowed with an inquiring mind and a charismatic personality. Aided by Wise Burroughs and L. E. Kunkle, Gerlaugh had been giving a variety of feed mixtures to several hundred cattle over the past six years. He and his colleagues concluded that ground corncobs had a feeding value of between one-half and two-thirds as much, pound for pound, as shelled corn, up to one-third of the total ration. The other two-thirds of the feed consisted of shelled or ground ear corn and a substantial amount of protein in such forms as linseed or cottonseed cake, soya bean meal, or urea (a synthetic protein).

While this work was in progress, Wise Burroughs, based ninety miles south of Wooster at a veterinary research center, was also pursuing studies in the digestability of urea and corncobs and doing more open-ended research into the nature and function of the four stomachs of cattle. Burroughs came to Ohio in 1939, fresh out of graduate school to the only job he was offered, intending to pursue physiological research on amino acids. However, at the USDA substation near Columbus he was assigned to the laboratory of A. F. Schalk, a pioneer in rumen physiology, and soon got to know of Gerlaugh's work at Wooster. The connections between the veterinary group and its work at Columbus and the feedlot research at the main experiment station at Wooster altered Burroughs's scholarly direction. Largely influenced by Gerlaugh, Burroughs began research on the rumen and the succeeding series of stomachs in cattle.

Although it was common knowledge that ruminants such as cattle, sheep, and buffalo could digest cellulose because of their rumen, or first stomach, the processes of ruminant digestion had not yet been studied closely. The war gave further impetus to such study by creating a scarcity

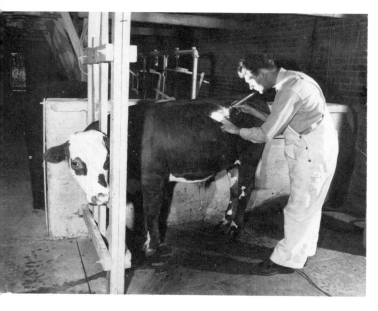

Wise Burroughs in 1948 peering into the stomachs of Christopher Columbus, where he found a new world of bacteria, a discovery that revolutionized the feeding of livestock. (Photograph by Joe Munroe)

Charley Thomas, Roswell's partner and chief of seed production, in 1955. In earlier years, he took detasseling crews through a field as many as 12 times to ensure the quality of the final cross. On the wall is an autographed picture of Henry A. Wallace. (Photograph by Joe Munroe)

Some of the "Southside Gang" in the early fifties. Standing: *Dennis Brannan;* seated (left to right): *Eddie Reid, David Garst, Stephen Garst, Roswell. "If you were away from the coffee table at the Southside Cafe for a few months," Jonathan Garst wrote, "you hardly knew what they were talking about when you got back." On the wall is a picture of the seed corn plant. (Photograph by Eric Hartmann, Magnum Photos, New York)*

Aden Owen, Roswell's secretary for many years, and chief of printing and mailing. At sales meetings Roswell liked to have Aden hold up his fingers to show how they had been "worn down" from typing letters. (Photograph by Joe Munroe)

Ralph Wheeler, the self-taught mechanical engineer who designed the original equipment for the seed plant. "I never made a mistake that wouldn't work at least the rest of the season," he liked to say. (Courtesy Evelyn Wheeler)

Roswell in 1963 using his artificial voice box to talk to his old friend Jake Bell, also one of the "Southside Gang." (Photograph by Joe Munroe)

Jonathan Garst early in the seventies, not long before his death.

Planting seed corn in 1975 with a 12-row planter. The electrical apparatus on the tractor hood controls the quantity of seed dropped and has printed on it a "population density table." Alternating groups of "male" and "female" rows are planted. (Photograph by Joe Munroe)

Tom Chrystal harvesting seed corn planted for Garst and Thomas in 1959. (Photograph by Joe Munroe)

A detasseling crew in 1954 moving through "female" rows on a nearly invisible detasseling rig, whose prototype was designed by Ralph Wheeler. The driver sits on an elevated frame, flanked by two ramps, each holding 3 detasselers. This field has 6-row stands of "female" pollinated by 2-row stands of "male" corn. Each field is isolated against pollination from other fields by strips of different crops, usually soybeans. (Photograph by Joe Munroe)

The Original
GARST and THOMAS
Plant

The original Garst and Thomas seed corn plant built in 1934, from an advertising brochure of the late thirties.

The seed corn plant in 1953. The original building may be seen here as the nucleus of a much expanded facility. (Photograph by Joe Munroe)

A truck being unloaded in 1953 by means of the hydraulic unloading ramp. (Photograph by Joe Munroe)

Trucks with seed corn varieties from all over the western corn belt waiting to discharge their loads in the fall of 1953 into an underground bin. Varieties are called in after germination tests and according to a carefully organized plan. (Photograph by Joe Munroe)

An employee bagging one of the varieties that has finished its journey through the plant in 1953. (Photograph by Joe Munroe)

Women engaged in the initial sorting process in the plant in 1953, culling defective ears as they pass by on a conveyor belt designed by Ralph Wheeler. (Photograph by Joe Munroe)

The mountain of ground corncobs left over in 1952 at the end of the processing season. Until 1946, the mountain was believed to be a useless byproduct. (Photograph by Joe Munroe)

By 1952, when this picture was taken, ground corncobs were being fed on a large scale to Garst Company cattle in the highly mechanized fashion shown above. (Photograph by Joe Munroe)

During the fifties and sixties, all other available cellulose was also collected for feeding. Here a "stalker" moves through a harvested seed corn field in 1975, grinding up stalks and leaves to be deposited in trench silos as silage. (Photograph by Joe Munroe)

A forage harvester in 1963 cutting and chopping giant forage sorghum imported to Coon Rapids from Rumania. Such "whole-plant" harvesting of both corn and sorghum provided the cellulose for the large commercial feedlots that were springing up in the Central Plains states. (Photograph by Joe Munroe)

Trench silos similar to this one pictured in 1954 were cut into high ground on farms and filled with cellulose. (Photograph by Joe Munroe)

During the sixties and seventies the Midwest was becoming "home on the range" for cows and cowboys. Here, in 1975, a cowboy and some vehicles move cattle south of Coon Rapids from range to feedlot. (Photograph by Joe Munroe)

of protein, and part of Burroughs's work involved urea, a cheap synthetic protein developed originally in Germany but being manufactured and tested in the United States at that time by DuPont. By 1945 Burroughs had developed an artificial rumen, which allowed him to conduct forty or fifty experiments simultaneously, but his best publicized work concerned a four-month-old Hereford steer named Christopher Columbus. With the approval of the American Society for the Prevention of Cruelty to Animals (ASPCA), Burroughs directed that a window be inserted into Christopher's rumen by the vets at the substation so that it could be observed at any time by himself or his assistant, Lorraine Gall. In the winter 1948 issue of *Farm Quarterly* there is a captivating picture of Burroughs, his head topped by an unruly shock of black hair, his slight, thin frame enveloped in great white overalls, holding a flashlight and peering intently into Christopher's rumen, finding processes at work that would revolutionize the feeding of cattle.

Burroughs and Gall found an enormous number of bacteria in the rumen of cattle, about 90 billion per gram of rumen content, an area about the size of the eraser on a pencil. Observing them for the first time with a high-powered telescope, they discovered that these bacteria could attack and consume fibers of cellulose of any kind – straw, corn, cobs, corn stalks, and grass, which were thought to be of almost no feeding value except for their utility as roughage in the digestion process. Burroughs and Gall found that these bacteria were performing two tasks: (1) breaking down the roughage and converting it into a form that the cow could use as food, and (2) converting it into the most important constituents of the animals' diet. For example, some of the cellulose was converted into Vitamin B, and the nitrogen in hay was converted by the rumen into proteins that could be digested later on in the other stomachs. They also confirmed that the bacteria could convert urea into protein. The fundamental pattern of digestion for the ruminant consisted of the break up and conversion of the contents of the rumen by bacteria, followed by actual digestion by the enzymes of the fourth stomach and intestines. By 1948 the *Farm Quarterly* could report that "it looks as if we have just scratched the surface in our feeding practices."

In 1946 Roswell was excited by the practical possibilities of the applied research in the feedlots at Wooster. He also wrote about cellulose and urea to Jonathan, who supplied him with yet another source of information on these subjects. After a visit to Ohio, he drove to the University of Wisconsin to visit Dr. Gus Bohstedt, head of the Animal Husbandry Department. Jonathan attended high school and the university with Bohstedt and was aware that Bohstedt had a grant from DuPont to carry on research in urea as a source of protein. Bohstedt had also been feeding various forms of cellulose, using urea for only part of the protein because it was believed that urea contained no amino acids. By the fall of 1946, Roswell was ready to put this knowledge to work, but there was another practical difficulty to solve. If he were limited to corncobs for one-third of the roughage, he would have to purchase an enormous amount of shelled corn or ground ear corn to use up his mountain of cobs. He wrote Gerlaugh to ask what would happen if the cattle were fed on a higher proportion of corncobs; Gerlaugh replied that he didn't know and didn't have a cob pile he could use to find out. "You've got a cob pile," he replied to Roswell, "why don't *you* find out?"

Roswell was not yet ready to take such a step and decided to ask Iowa State to experiment. Consequently, Roswell, Charley Thomas, and Maurice Campbell, a former county agent now employed by Garst and Thomas in their production department, approached the Animal Husbandry Department with an offer to pay for an experiment involving the feeding of corncobs. Dubious about the value of cobs as feed and disinclined to use their research facilities on such a project, the college authorities told the Coon Rapids delegation much the same thing as had Gerlaugh. "You've got the cobs, if you think there is an advantage in feeding them, *you* try it." Infuriated by this cold shoulder from the Animal Husbandry Department (and still critical of the Soils Department for its caution over nitrogen fertilizer), Roswell was pushed into action. He got a feeding formula from Gerlaugh, purchased thirty steers, put six each in five pens, and placed Maurice Campbell in charge of the experiment, which began in the winter of 1946–47.

The steers' diet ranged from shelled corn in the first pen, through increasing amounts of cobs mixed with corn in the next three pens, and finally to corncobs only in the fifth pen. In every pen, the steers were also fed a premixed ration of soybean oil meal, cane molasses, urea, cod liver oil and irradiated yeast, and two pounds of hay per day. The cobs came from Garst and Thomas, the urea from DuPont, and the molasses—a palatable and fast-acting carbohydrate—from the government, because it was still rationed. Arthur Becker, the Washington associate of Phil Maguire, procured the molasses, noting at the time that "the USDA does not think very highly of ground corncobs for feed. If your experimental feeding is successful we can probably change their views."

Corn was scarce and high priced in 1946–47, so the relative costs of the feed combinations were as closely observed as the relative rate of gain during the winter of the first experiment. When the cattle were ready for market, the figures showed that the cob-fed cattle had gained 1.34 pounds per day, the lowest gain of the five lots, but for a cost of only nineteen cents per pound. The cattle fed entirely on shelled corn gained 2.14 pounds per day, but at a cost of almost twenty-seven cents per pound. The rate of gain for the cob-fed animals was good enough to produce marketable cattle at a dramatic saving in cost. Roswell sold the cattle for twenty-eight cents per pound and made more than one hundred dollars per head. He knew then that he would be feeding cobs.

In November 1947 Roswell mounted a second experiment on a much larger scale. He bought five hundred head of cattle, put them in a feedlot during Christmas week, and began feeding them on 20 pounds of ground corncobs per day, 31 pounds of soybean oil meal, 21 pounds of blackstrap molasses, and 4 ounces of urea. In winter conditions, with a muddy feedlot and no shelter, the animals gained 1.35 pounds per day, or 135 pounds per head in one hundred days, at a cost of about twenty-two cents per head. A few of these cattle went blind as a result. Roswell, through Bohstedt, discovered that they suffered from a deficiency of Vitamin A, which was correctable by the feeding of bright hay. "It now begins to look," he wrote, "as though cobs are worth approximately two-thirds as much as shelled corn, pound for pound, up to 100% of the concentrated feed, if they are fed in combination with heavier than normal protein and are fed to ruminants."

After another round of visits with Gerlaugh and Bohstedt, Roswell decided to do a summer demonstration of cob feeding, confident that in good weather he could achieve a gain of 1.75 pounds instead of only 1.35. In May 1948 he purchased nineteen steers, fed them Bohstedt's "Wisconsin Formula" for protein plus cobs, and weighed them once a month. They were indeed gaining almost 2 pounds per day. In September Gerlaugh came by to have a look, and, according to Roswell in a letter to the editor of *Farm Quarterly*, "expressed amazement at how well our cattle are doing." Later that month the annual Garst and Thomas open house took place, and the 3,500 visitors got their first look at cob-fed cattle.

There was another audience intended for this demonstration, the Animal Husbandry Department of Iowa State College. In the summer of 1948 Roswell sent a vitriolic letter to H. H. Kildee, director of the Agricultural Experiment Station at Ames, accusing the college of conducting experiments actually designed to discredit Gerlaugh and in the fall wrote the president of the college demanding that they send representatives to see his feedlot at Coon Rapids. The penalty for their nonappearance would be an attack by Roswell on the college in the *Des Moines Register.* He sent the letter on a Friday, and over the weekend, sure of a telephone reply by Monday, began working out a scenario for a confrontation ending in triumphant vindication of his feeding program.

Although he was challenging the college as their most successful nongraduate, the part of him in awe of the learning it represented was feeling less than self-confident. On Sunday, cooped up in the house by heavy rain, he grew increasingly nervous about the coming visit. Elizabeth had recently bought a set of the *Encyclopedia Britannica,* an act of cultural improvement that had annoyed Roswell. However, he decided to look up corncobs to find something to help convince the college and himself of their value as feed. There was also the matter of his own curiosity, which he described a year later:

For a year and a half I had been trying to explain to groups of farmers why corncobs could be successfully fed to cattle. I couldn't explain it because I had not understood it myself. It was perfectly apparent that the cattle would eat the cobs and get fat on them when a properly balanced diet was used.

He tried corncobs but found no entry and decided to look up carbohydrates. He found that there were three carbohydrates – sugar, starch, and cellulose. He looked up cellulose and found it to be composed of carbon, hydrogen, and oxygen, expressed in the formula $C^6H^{10}0^5$. He looked up starch and discovered that the formula was the same; the difference between cellulose and starch (or between the cellulose in corncobs and the starch in corn) was simply the way in which the respective chains of molecules were constructed. "So then," he continued,

I got to thinking about what other cellulose we might be feeding in a general way. I knew they fed peanut hulls in peanut districts – that oat hulls had been successfully fed – that cottonseed hulls had been successfully fed – that silage had been effectively fed. But it took me two hours before I finally thought of the most common of all celluloses – grass – pasture!

Green grass is a combination of cellulose and protein, the kind of grass buffalo fattened upon and which cattle in the West still do. Dry grass is cellulose with insufficient protein, and cattle that winter on dry grass virtually starve to death. The example of grass made Roswell realize that he had known about cellulose and protein all the time but had lacked the vocabulary to express it.

What was new to him were the associations connected with the word "cellulose," which had formerly connoted for him something of little worth. But cellulose was of great value when fed in combination with protein. As he would explain it later, all he was doing was combining cellulose and protein in the form of corncobs and urea to provide an imitation pasture. There was no need for starch in the form of corn in a steer's diet; the vast majority of ruminants on earth had never tasted starch. With the increasing availability of high protein feeds such as soybean meal and urea, cellulose could now be utilized as never before in the feeding of cattle.

Roswell condensed his new synthesis into a single, well-rehearsed sentence and with it opened his performance for the college delegation. "It has long been known," he told his visitors, "that cellulose is excellent feed for ruminants, if it is fed in combination with protein – and only if fed in combination with protein." When a member of the party expressed doubt about this axiom, Roswell, always fast on his feet, replied he had been taught that as a student at Iowa State. The form the axiom took then was that timothy hay cut late in the season was poor cattle feed, but alfalfa hay cut early, while it still had protein, was excellent food. He omitted to point out that the implications of this teaching had only become apparent to him a few days before. There followed an inspection of the cattle and a search for corn in the feedlot, a tour whose success was capped by the fortuitous arrival of a cattle buyer, who thought Roswell's herd would grade "choice."

Back at the house, Roswell launched into his finale. "What do you want me to tell people," he asked:

Do you want me to tell them that you came over and saw and believed it or that you came over and saw it and didn't believe it? They all say, "what does Iowa State College say?" I'll tell them anything that you prescribe. But it better be pretty good.

Roswell suggested they report that they were highly impressed with the demonstration, asked his permission to repeat the experiment in their own feedlots, and would report its results at Cattle Feeder's Day in the spring of 1949. They agreed to do so, departed that afternoon, and left Roswell a happy man, his curiosity satisfied, his confrontation with the college a success, a formerly useless byproduct turned to efficient use, and agreeable prospects for profit and fun.

"Revolution on The Farm"

In the spring of 1948 Roswell hit upon a way to combine his commercial ambitions for Garst and Thomas with his interests in agricultural innovation. In April he wrote Jim Bradley of Pioneer Des Moines to propose a new selling campaign, which would simply assume the superiority of Pioneer seed and concentrate instead on providing useful information for farmers – mainly bulletins on subjects that interested Roswell. "Aden Owen and I are all involved in a new way to sell the 400,000 bushels of corn," he told Abe Freiler, and described his plans to draw up three bulletins,

one of them on the feeding of corncobs – one on surface drainage – one of them on drying grain and hay so that they can be harvested on the tough side and stored. Then we propose to go over the radio and through the farm papers, etc. – and not talk about Pioneer at all—just talk about things that would be of benefit to the farmers—we're going to just beller and bawl trying to be of the greatest help possible to the greatest number of farmers possible.

He hoped to get discussions started throughout the Garst and Thomas territory during June and July, then sell corn during the regular sales season. "It's exciting times," he concluded. In a later letter to Bradley he announced a fourth bulletin on fertilizer and outlined the role he saw for himself as a popular purveyor of the latest work in agricultural research:

In each and every case quotations from experiment station bulletins could be used—the practical applications could be stated—the whole thing could be brought down to a simple, easy-to-read scale—and in each case the bulletins could be of really big value.

Of the bulletins that he wrote, "There's Gold in that Cob Pile" and "It Needs Seedin'" were the two most widely distributed and most influential. These two were printed, while the bulletins on drainage and drying were simply mimeographed. However, in addition to the bulletins, Roswell instituted a tradition of sales letters that contained information on current and experimental projects and projections of markets and demand.

The "Gold" bulletin was his first effort in 1948 and was succeeded by a smaller follow-up pamphlet to attract people to the summer feeding project of 1948. Although cob feeding would not take hold among small farmers, the 75,000 copies of the bulletin that were distributed laid the groundwork for the acceptance of cellulose in other forms, and in later bulletins on the subject Roswell included cornstalks and silage. "It Needs Seedin', " which pointed out the advantages of fertilizer, was his greatest success, running to 175,000 copies to meet the demand it created. By April 1949 the printing was exhausted, and Roswell wrote, "we are having difficulty getting enough to even supply our own salesmen's demands."

Roswell's experimental and commercial successes of the immediate postwar years were brought to national notice in 1948 by John Dos Passos in an article for *Life* magazine entitled "Revolution on the Farm." Ever since his tour through the Midwest in 1943, Dos Passos had become increasingly interested in the vitality of middle America. In 1945, writing to Roswell to ask for a job for a 17-year-old youth, he remarked that "ever since I visited your farm and seedcorn plant it has seemed to me that it would be a darn good place for a young fellow to spend the summer working—morally, educationally and in every way," and contrasted the "moribund East" with "Iowa enterprise."

Roswell did not have a job available but took the opportunity to urge Dos Passos to come out and do a story on fertilizer. Dos Passos demurred for the present; the agricultural articles, he said, would have to wait until he had acquired a little practical experience on his own farm in Virginia. "I may get that in the next couple of years," he replied,

if I can ever get that farm set up down in Virginia that I've been in on for years now. When you next come East let me know a couple of weeks ahead of time so that we can stake out an evening. I'd love to know what you think of our general situation in the world. It worries me to beat hell, to be frank.

In the fall of 1947 Dos Passos was seriously injured in an automobile accident, and his wife Katy was killed. He accepted an invitation from Roswell and Elizabeth to spend part of his convalescence in Coon Rapids. His wife, he confided, "would have loved the rolling cornfields and you," and he thought that sitting around the coffee shop in Coon Rapids might be a good way of picking up some advice on his own fledgling operation.

Dos Passos came to Coon Rapids early in November and stayed for several weeks. On rainy days Roswell came to the office and Dos Passos worked in a back bedroom on *Chosen Country,* but when the weather was good the two went out "to see the country and the people and Iowa agriculture." On his last day Roswell took Dos Passos to a hog sale. "He didn't know," Roswell wrote, "whether they were supposed to be red or white – and he was afraid to look at the auctioneer for fear the auctioneer would claim he was winking, and sell him a hog – but we all had a grand time." Dos Passos walked a great deal – much to the astonishment of the countryfolk, went to Discussion Club with Elizabeth, and immersed himself in Roswell's enthusiasm for corncobs, urea, and fertilizer.

The plan for a magazine article was apparently settled during the visit. After Dos Passos left, Roswell arranged to have fertilized plots laid out for pictures, and in January 1948 he urged Dos Passos to persevere in his negotiations with *Life* magazine. "I have been urging the importance of such an article on you now for several years," he admonished Dos Passos, "and this time I don't want you to fail me." In June *Life* photographer Carl Eisenstadt turned up, followed shortly by Dos Passos, and "Revolution on the Farm" appeared on 23 August 1948.

Dos Passos sent Roswell a draft of his article in late July and invited corrections. Roswell replied by day letter suggesting corrections, among them a request to change the word "throne" to "box seat" in the South Side Cafe that would "sound less regal and more like the fun I enjoy there," Roswell explained. He also offered a paragraph in praise of detasselers. Dos Passos promised to make the specific deletions and get in "what extra remarks I can." "I had a wonderful time out on the Wisconsin Drift," he concluded, "and I hope you enjoyed the show. Wasn't Eisenstadt a card?"

Writing in a style similar to *State of the Nation,* Dos Passos described his arrival by train at Coon Rapids, and framed his article with a question put to Roswell: "What I want to find out, Bob, is what kind of things you people who grow our food are doing to keep up with the increasing needs of this country and the world?" What followed was a distillation of his conversation and travels with Roswell during the weeks of his stay on the Garst farm and the subsequent visit with Eisenstadt during the harvest season—the talk at the South Side Cafe, the burgeoning technology of Corn Belt farming, the optimism of Roswell, Hans Larsen, and others, and the beauty of the undulating rows of tall corn. Roswell got his change to "box seat," and the detasselers were done justice, although not quite as Roswell had dictated. Roswell talked of the revolution in farming, the possibilities for higher yields with less labor, and the links between improvements in farming techniques. "Makes me feel we haven't begun yet," Roswell concluded. "Does that answer your question?"

A story in a magazine with such a huge circulation was an extraordinary coup in Roswell's campaign for recognition of the farming revolution, and, as Abe Freiler put it, "the biggest thing that ever happened to Garst and Thomas." Freiler noted that a single black and white advertising page in *Life* cost $16,000; space on the editorial pages "could hardly be measured" in value. Its larger educational purpose could be measured partially in the correspondence the article generated, estimated by Roswell at three or four hundred letters. They contained questions about all the operations of the Garst farm, some of them from overseas. "Aden and I did a good job on answering them all before we quit," Roswell told Dos Passos. He also derived great satisfaction, as Freiler put it—and with a touch of awe—"from the unprecedented recognition that will come to you through this powerful medium of circulation."

C H A P T E R   S I X

Creating the Years of Abundance

Breakthrough with Cellulose

By 1949 the revolution in American agriculture was well launched, Roswell's sons were home to help, and his educational campaigns were bearing fruit. Even the weather had improved, and in the fall of 1950 Roswell expressed his feeling of well-being to the weather bureau in Des Moines:

Because your predictions were so accurate this fall—and because the weather was so darned beautiful during October—and because we harvested a high moisture seed crop with no damage whatever—and because we kept bothering you all season with our questions—I am ordering a five-pound box of candy from Mrs. Drew's Candy Kitchen sent to your office with our compliments.

He was 51 years old in 1949, "a large ruddy man," as Dos Passos had described him recently,

with large gray eyes set rather far apart in a large blunt-nosed face that seems to be always coming at you like the prow of a ship. He's usually in his shirtsleeves. Suspenders hold up his large loosefitting pants. He's a showman and a lecturer but never from any pulpit; he's always watching the man he's talking to, ready to pounce on any useful notion that comes to the surface. . . . Raising crops is what he eats sleeps and breathes. Raising crops and selling seedcorn. His conviction is catching.

TRUE to their word, the delegation from Iowa State returned to Ames in the fall of 1948 to mount the cob-feeding experiment on their home ground. In May 1949 Roswell was invited to Cattle Feeder's Day to view the results of the experiment and talk about his own experiences in feed-

ing cobs. The results of the Iowa State program were similar to his own
and the day went well, on the surface at least. Privately Roswell was
outraged at what he believed to be the college's general lack of enthusiasm about cob feeding in spite of very good results. "I'm mad enough at
the great Iowa State College to die," he wrote to Gerlaugh in June 1949. "I
don't know much, but I know that they are being just as unfair to cobs as
possible, and the crowd at their Feeder's Day meeting really questioned
them enough to be embarrassing." He was also annoyed at their recently
published bulletin on the subject; by August, after a series of written and
verbal exchanges with the head of the Animal Husbandry Department, he
began to feel somewhat mollified. Culbertson, as Roswell reported to the
editor of the *Nebraska Farmer*, was now "perfectly willing" to make a
statement that cobs gave roughly the same results as corn silage in the
feedlot, and Rex Beresford of the college was publicizing his own favorable findings on the value of cobs.

It was a period of fundamental change for Iowa State College. The
older generation of teachers, some of whom were Roswell's instructors,
had now all retired, and such anachronistic courses as the care and judg-
ing of draft horses could be quietly dropped from the curriculum. In 1948
Floyd Andre, who was serving with the USDA in Washington on a committee that reviewed and funded research projects, was named dean of
the Division of Agriculture. Andre had examined Burroughs's work in
Ohio, and in 1950 brought Burroughs to Iowa State, urged on by Damon
Catron of the Swine Department and by Roswell. Burroughs began the
first ruminant nutrition research division at the college, working until
1953 in the chemistry building because until then there were no laboratories in the animal science department.

For Roswell, the appearance of Andre and of Burroughs marked a
new stage in his relationship with the college. He had in his own backyard
the man whose work most interested him in 1949 and 1950 and could now
get in his car and drive the sixty-five miles to Ames to see Burroughs
whenever he wished. In October 1949 Andre came to Coon Rapids to see
Roswell's operation, and in a letter to Andre after the visit, Roswell
struck what would be the keynote in his future relations with the college.
He was currently pleased with the fertilizer bulletins the college
published and was glad that they were beginning to work with cellulose
and urea. He pledged his own cooperation on any project that might
benefit from his help. But, he concluded, "I suspect I always will remain
critical—and vocally critical—of any lack of enthusiasm for new knowledge."

Other sources of information were also opening up. Gerlaugh at Ohio
State University and a group of researchers at Oklahoma State College
were exploring the molasses-urea combination, and W. M. Beeson, head

of the Animal Husbandry Department at Purdue, had conducted experiments with cobs and other cellulose products mixed with protein since the late forties. Roswell drove to Indiana to see Beeson and later used the Purdue Formula for protein in his own subsequent feeding programs. Cornell University, at Ithaca, New York, was working on urea; Bohstedt was still active and so was the DuPont organization.

Both Roswell and Jonathan tried to get more research started and coordinated. The chief of the nitrogen research facility for DuPont, F. G. Keenan, reported to Roswell that Jonathan had visited him in 1949, and "certainly did a good job of building a fire under us to do something about the major problem of cellulose utilization for feeding." Throughout this period Roswell wrote to colleges and experiment stations urging a coordinated program of research on cellulose and urea and extended his campaign to Washington. "I am telling you," he confided to Pat Jackson in 1949,

that this thing is the biggest discovery since hybrid seed corn and actually comparable to it in the effect on food supplies. In fact, I'm not so sure that it isn't even more important because celluloses are wasted all over the world—and hybrid seed corn only affects about 100 million acres.

Urged by Roswell, Jackson approached Louis Bean (then serving as an economic advisor in the USDA) to invite him to Coon Rapids to see the new feeding methods. Roswell wrote directly to Bean, arguing that only in Coon Rapids "has anyone actually tried to make a really big demonstration of the practical application of the combinations of information that are jointly available from the several stations." Bean came in the spring of 1950 and reported his impressions to Charles Brannan, the secretary of agriculture. Brannan in turn promised Roswell a comprehensive effort by the USDA to coordinate research on cellulose and urea.

The next significant research breakthrough concerned urea, until 1950 considered valuable for only about one-third of the protein requirement for feed because of an amino acid deficiency. However, researchers at Cornell University discovered that all of the essential amino acids could be synthesized by a ruminant from the nitrogen in urea alone. In May 1950 Roswell—perhaps not yet aware of the Cornell results—concluded a feeding program in which he provided 75 percent of the protein in the form of urea to twenty cattle, and achieved a gain of 2.2 pounds per day. Both Burroughs and Roswell thought that the urea was successful because of its combination with molasses. The bacteria in the rumen were fed a fast carbohydrate—molasses—and at the same time a fast protein—urea—a combination that seemed to allow the cattle to convert the protein more efficiently by providing a continual supply of quick energy. By November 1951 he excluded soybean meal from the feed ration of a small experimental feedlot and substituted urea as the sole protein. "We just broke all the rules," he wrote to Milo Perkins, "broke them completely — and it worked fine." From that time, urea mixed with molasses and fed with supplemental vitamins became the sole protein fed with cellulose for Garst cattle.

Roswell and Jonathan were also making headway with the farm press. The *Farm Quarterly* published its article on Burroughs in 1948, with considerable space devoted to Roswell as the man making most use of Burroughs's work; "Cow Feed from the Air" by Jonathan and his son Perry appeared in the same journal in 1950. There were also accounts of Roswell's work on fertilizer and crop drying in the DuPont Newsletter and the newsletter of the American Society of Agronomy. Roswell received a steady stream of inquiries on both fertilizer and cattle feeding, including one from Dos Passos. "We are feeding four steers as an experiment this winter," he wrote; "If it's not a secret would you jot down your formula?"

The journalistic climax of his efforts to introduce the feeding of cobs came in a cover story in the *Farm Quarterly* in the spring of 1952 entitled "How Crazy Can a Man Get?" by Charles Koch. He described Roswell's feeding operation, the conversation at the South Side Cafe, and quoted Roswell's latest set-piece pronouncement: " 'Legumes will be as obsolete as a dinosaur,' Garst will laugh and say. 'Out here they have absolutely no place in agriculture when synthetic nitrogen is available.' " Of his success, Roswell observed, "All it takes is know-how, guts and capital."

Roswell had only one correction to make on the proofs of this article. "I deny that I 'roar'," he complained. "I may speak loudly, but it's generally with a laugh." And he was upset over the statement on the front cover that 4,200 cattle on his farm were being fed for a profit of $244,000. "The amount is so embarrassingly large that it is not good publicity," he protested, but he could not hide his own satisfaction over the numbers. "Actually," he continued, "I looked the cattle over yesterday morning and I don't think the figure will be too inaccurate."

There were also the inevitable letters. "I have spent all day answering letters to subscribers of the *Farm Quarterly*," he wrote in March 1952:

The flood of letters has just started and my experience is that it will tend to run its course in a month. It is no hardship on me — in fact I like to be helpful to people who are interested and I try to do a nice job on each one of them.

Articles in the Des Moines and Omaha newspapers and editorials in the *Nebraska Farmer* followed, as did a television appearance by Roswell on Omaha's WOW. In February 1952 Roswell reported to Abe Freiler that more than a thousand had visited the farm in the last two months. It had been "the finest experience possible" for Stephen and David to show them around, and it was helping to sell corn.

However, a month later, just as the *Farm Quarterly* article appeared, Roswell wrote Freiler to admit he had failed to convince small farmers that they should feed their own cobs to their own cattle on their own farms. "I have tried my toughest," he wrote,

and so have Steve and Dave. But we have finally concluded that most of them will not do so. . . . I have been deeply concerned and deeply confused about this whole cob feeding project, and I don't like to write or visit when I am confused.

There had been another failure the previous year. In February 1951 Roswell told Gus Bohstedt that "under Jonathan's guidance" he was going to try to create an artificial rumen in a tank so that pigs could eat cellulose. The idea was to introduce yeast spores into a corncob, molasses, and urea mixture and let the yeast convert the cellulose into something that pigs could digest. Roswell's excitement ran through March of that year, then abruptly disappeared. Success with hogs had once again eluded him.

IF he was disappointed and discouraged over the response to the feeding of cobs, he was at the same time optimistic over other combinations of cellulose and protein. Cornstalks were more readily available to every farmer, as were nonleguminous grass pastures fertilized with nitrogen. Once again his experience with grass finally convinced Roswell that legumes were as obsolete as dinosaurs, and by 1951 he formulated his conception of the grass-nitrogen culture that would provide sustenance for vast numbers of cattle in the Midwest and on the Garst farms. If it couldn't be hogs, it would have to be cattle.

In the case of grass, it was Roswell's newly acquired land south of town that provided the necessary experience. Unlike the rolling land north of town, intensively farmed and benefiting from the natural fertility of the Wisconsin Drift, the land to the south of Coon Rapids is hilly and wooded. Here the Raccoon River pushes its way between high, steep banks and heavy stands of timber, which grow right to the edge of the river bank and extend for large areas into the surrounding hills. It is a picturesque country, in which are preserved a pioneer's log cabin, an original barn or two, and at least one piece of original, unploughed prairie. From the top of the hills there are surprising views of wilderness and along the river picnic spots and beaver dams.

In 1950 the countryside was dotted with derelict or—if still inhabited—delapidated farmhouses, eloquent evidence of the losing struggle for survival still waged by a diminishing number of farmers south of town. The timber had made the land attractive to the earliest settlers, but the hillsides and winding draws were now scarred by erosion, creased with gullies down which the southern land, not favored by the glaciers

and already deficient in fertility, washed away, producing muddy, impassable roads in the fall and spring. In the winter, snow buried the roads, and
the hill farmers were isolated from town for a good part of the year. Eddie
Reid's old farm bordered this country and the country schoolhouse he
attended, renamed "the Eddie Reid shrine" by Stephen, still stood,
another of the few remaining monuments to an age that was rapidly but
painfully disappearing.

The first Garst purchase south of town was the old Whalley farm,
eroded, untiled, low yielding, and no longer inhabited. The Garst Company cleared, tiled, fertilized heavily, and produced a yield of corn twice
as high as would normally be expected on land worth about sixty dollars
per acre. There was pasture land in abundance in this region as well, and
as more land was acquired Roswell planted nonleguminous brome grass
to supplement the indigenous and equally nonleguminous bluegrass and,
just to see what would happen, alfalfa. He and his sons put increasing
numbers of cattle on the heavily fertilized pasture and installed automatic
urea feeders. When the grass dried, they fed ground corncobs.

It was the differing result from feeding cattle on leguminous and
nonleguminous grass that intrigued Roswell. North of town, the pastures
were mostly clover or alfalfa and all leguminous; south of town they were
mostly bluegrass and brome, both nonleguminous. The cattle south of
town did better; when given a choice, "they ate the brome and laid on the
alfalfa," Roswell reported to Beeson at Purdue. Furthermore, he observed
that the best cattle from Wisconsin came from the bluegrass pastures of
Mineral Point, the best cattle from Kansas City came from the bluegrass
of the Flint Hills, and the best cattle in the lots of Omaha and Sioux City
were also fed on nonleguminous grasses.

Roswell went to Ames to discuss these observations with Wise Burroughs, now settled in his makeshift laboratory at Iowa State. From studies carried on in Ohio in the forties, Burroughs had concluded approximately 45 percent of cellulose in legumes was digested by cattle, while
about 75 percent of cellulose in nonleguminous grasses was digested.
Burroughs's studies in 1950 and 1951 confirmed these earlier results and
demonstrated further that cornstalks were at least as digestible as corncobs, and, as with nonleguminous grasses, more efficiently used by cattle
than legumes.

His own observations and the data supplied by Burroughs began to
convince Roswell that the "legumes dogma," as he called it, was wrong,
both with respect to enrichment of the soil and the feeding of cellulose. "I
have just been thinking out loud," he wrote to Beeson in 1951,

as I write you this letter. I just don't know the answers! But I'm suspicious – very
suspicious – that much of the dogma about legumes is not true. Maybe we are

going to come to the grass type of agriculture and get our nitrogen from the air synthetically. Maybe we'll use the grasses plus Ammonium Nitrate for plant food and grasses plus urea for animal food. And, maybe – just maybe – that is the way we will have to go, to feed an extra 25 million people by 1960, and an extra 60 million people by 1970.

In addition to grass, Roswell began experiments in feeding cornstalks instead of corncobs, urged implement companies to develop stalk-chopping machines, and followed closely the work at Iowa State and Missouri on the nitrogen levels that could be introduced into cellulose without inducing nitrate poisoning in cattle.

In the early fifties the Garst Company extended their investments in corn and pastureland south of town, planting grass and fertilizing it, building dams in the gullies to stop erosion and provide water for cattle. They chopped cornstalks for feed and bought more cattle. In the process they transformed the southern hills into a prosperous combination of good land and recreational area, renovating farmhouses and stocking the new ponds with fish. By 1954 Roswell could describe to the editors of *Successful Farming* the new opportunity available to all Corn Belt farmers. "Any corn belt farmer," he wrote,

can now decide whether he wants to carry twice or three times as many cattle as he has been carrying without changing the number of acres he has planted to any of his present crop and without shortening present feed supplies that he has available for livestock other than cattle.

Instead of twenty head, the midwestern farmer could now carry forty or sixty – or several thousand if he had large acreage – by feeding them the waste products of his corn and enhancing the value of his existing pasture by well-fertilized grasses. This time farmers acted, and a significant shift eastward began in the distribution of cattle from the Great Plains and Rocky Mountain pastures to the feedlots of Nebraska, Kansas, and Iowa, a process spurred during the later fifties by the new irrigating methods in Kansas and Nebraska. Most of the western Corn Belt farmers who turned to the cellulose-nitrogen culture had read Roswell's bulletins, seen his operation, or had heard him talk.

This era provided another memorable performance by Roswell for the academic community, this time a speech delivered before the American Society of Agronomy, which held its annual meeting in November 1952 in Cincinnati, Ohio. Scarseth, Hoffer, and Walter Colvin of Allied Chemical arranged Roswell's appearance by persuading the appropriate committee that a talk by an Iowa farmer about his experiences with fertilizer would be a welcome change from the usual specialist talks. The speech has come to be known in family folklore as "the horse story," a set-piece essay that Roswell had written in April 1952. The opportunity to deliver it before the agronomists offered special satisfaction for Roswell: "I'll bet you there was not one guy who did not have a Ph.D. but me, and I didn't even have a bachelor's degree."

Horse breeding, he told his audience in Cincinnati, had been an honorable profession for twenty-five hundred years, at least since the time of Alexander the Great. "We did a marvelous job with horses," he said:

We produced riding horses, and running horses, and jumping horses, and draft horses, and horses that were bred grey, black and white. We had high color horses for the Indians, pintos and shetland ponies for the kids.

But Henry Ford eliminated horses as a source of energy on the farm, and they disappeared rapidly from the farm economy.

Similarly, ever since Pliny the Elder noted crops that followed legumes yielded more, we began to do a marvelous job with legumes. We had red clover, white clover, sweet clover and annual clover, white blossom and yellow blossom sweet clover, and alfalfa. But when Haber learned to take nitrogen from the air and fix it into a usable form for plants, legumes became as obsolete as horses and, he thought, would disappear within the next twenty years just as rapidly as horses had disappeared. "You could have heard a pin drop on a carpet," Roswell recalled:

It horrified every man above the age of 45 years. If you were older than that you were mad enough to kill me, because that was all they had ever been taught, and they didn't know how to start over again. And every young guy in the place knew I was right.

The talk did make an impact. Malcolm McVickar, the secretary of an umbrella organization on fertilizer, supplied requests for transcriptions of the tape made of the speech, and intended to reproduce the talk in the Proceedings of the National Joint Committee on Fertilizer Application. "I know I don't need to tell you that you made a big hit," he wrote Roswell. "I have been on the road almost continuously since the Cincinnati meeting and everywhere I go I hear comments of Garst." Another friend of Roswell's wrote that he had heard about the talk and described it as "a smash hit." McVickar, he reported, told him "it was the best thing he had heard in years."

For many years, Warren Garst, Roswell's banker cousin in Jefferson, Iowa, had been promoting the new agriculture in his own quiet way and had given a talk at the National Fertilizer Association convention in Miami on bankers and the fertilizer industry at the same time Roswell had been talking in Cincinnati. "Your cousin also covered himself with glory in Miami," McVickar wrote. "Several people came out of that meeting and remarked that the Garst family was ripping the universe apart."

Breakthrough with Nitrogen

The immediate background to the breakthrough in the production and use of nitrogen lies in a decision in 1949 to curtail production of feed grains for the following year. On 31 December 1949 Secretary Brannan announced a cut in corn acreage of 20 percent based on a highly optimistic report of supplies by the BAE in its November pamphlet on *The Feed Situation.* Roswell's reading of the figures for the past five years was different, and he began a campaign to lift the acreage restrictions. He believed that in the past two years in particular American farmers had not accumulated as much of a corn reserve as the USDA figures showed, and that in 1950 the United States would begin another serious depletion of present reserves.

Roswell had less support from his friends on this issue than in 1941. Theodore Schultz of the University of Chicago agreed that acreage allotments ought to be lifted, but not because of shortages. "The danger of a shortage in the immediate future," Schultz wrote Roswell, "is a low probability"; with high purchasing power in the country, only an intelligent storage policy was needed to accumulate stocks during the present boom. Richard Uhlmann of the Chicago Board of Trade found logic in Roswell's position but thought he was overstating the case for imminent shortages.

Roswell himself vacillated in his own estimates of the seriousness of the situation in late 1949 and early 1950. He saw Brannan and other USDA officials and was assured that if the reserves disappeared at an unexpected rate, exports could be reduced to fill the domestic gap. Roswell was somewhat mollified by this hedge but thought that reserves would still be cut in half, which, he told Harold Brenton, was "slicing it thin enough – certainly thinner than I would have sliced it." Home from Washington, Roswell tried to look at the bright side. The USDA was trying hard to maintain a balance between surplus and scarcity, and if they left the soybean acreage unrestricted and with a good support price, he would agree that their program was sound. But his underlying feeling was one of disquiet. "In the face of the fact that every single thing you read in the papers talks about surplus corn," he wrote Brenton, "I do not believe that such a thing exists – I think it is only a pleasant reserve. I think it's a reserve that ought to be maintained."

In June 1950 the Korean War began, and by the fall of 1950 Roswell felt much more certain of his ground. He had in hand the figures on corn disappearance that he would use in a *Farm Quarterly* article and an admission from the USDA that the disappearance was running at a much higher rate than the BAE had predicted, along with the expection that the war would create even greater strains on the diminishing reserves. He wrote long letters to Brannan and Orris Wells calling for an end to crop restrictions and a swift response to the needs of war. "Ever since the President's proclamation of the Emergency," he told Brannan in December 1950, "I have been looking for a bold and dramatic clarion call from you for all-out production in the year 1951—so far without success." There was some consolation from Uhlmann at least. "A year ago at this time you were about the only person who was really right on the potential consumption of corn," Uhlmann wrote. "I am free to admit that I thought you were a little bit high in your views."

In January 1951 news of concern within the USDA came in the form of a telephone call from Phil Maguire. "I certainly was flabbergasted at your call tonight," Roswell wrote on 23 January,

because it is the first indication I have seen that the Department of Agriculture was the least bit worried about corn supplies. Then, all of a sudden, you phoned me that they are twice as badly scared as I am—and I have been the original guy who foresaw the shortage. All I can say is, "that it beats hell."

Maguire told Roswell that the department was about to prohibit the use of corn in beverages as one way of saving supplies, which provoked responses from Roswell of "utterly stupid" and "criminally negligent"; he was back in form. "Who are they to say that I should have 151 pounds of meat per year and no beverage," he asked Maguire, "instead of having 149 pounds of meat and a cool drink once in a while?—To Hell with them!"

By March 1951 acreage restrictions on corn had been removed, and in April Brannan spoke in Des Moines asking farmers to plant more corn that year. Roswell was delighted. In March, right after the "intention to plant" bulletin issued by the USDA, Roswell wrote Hans Larsen, "I am excited, only this time I am more excited than usual." He planned to work as hard as he could through salesmen, farm papers, and the radio to get farmers to plant more, although it was probably too late to get a substantial increase.

At the same time Brannan began a concerted effort to increase the production of fertilizer, a decision to which Roswell contributed and which Jonathan did much to implement. The occasion of Roswell's intervention occurred in the spring of 1951, during a trip to Washington and other points with Elizabeth and the Bells. Bringing Jake along to watch the show, Roswell dropped in on Brannan for a chat and found the secretary deeply concerned about the feed shortage and the means to increase production. Roswell urged Brannan to increase nitrogen-fixing capacity in the country and told him that Jonathan was the man for the job. Brannan listened and that afternoon telephoned Roswell at the Mayflower Hotel to get Johnny's address and telephone number. Shortly thereafter, Jonathan became "Assistant to the Secretary for Fertilizer Facilities Expansion for Mobilization," charged with issuing certificates of necessity—

including tax advantages—for the building of new nitrogen plants throughout the country.

Jonathan, whose twenty-year-old younger son Andrew had just died from spinal meningitis, threw himself into his new task to "drown his sorrows," Roswell thought. And Brannan told Roswell in July 1951 that Jonathan was "doing a grand job in a very, very tough field." In June two major nitrogen plants were ready to go into operation with urea as their first priority. Phosphate would remain in the same supply as in 1950 and nitrogen would be increased by 22 percent for 1951; potash would be 24 percent more available. Brannan toured the Corn Belt, included in his itinerary a stop at Coon Rapids, and worked through the summer to promote increased yields. "We have, in effect," he observed in one of his speeches that year, "just crossed the threshold of a 'fertilizer era' in American agriculture."

Interest in fertilizer, and especially nitrogen, reached a significant stage in the farm press and in research stations. In August 1951 John Strohm, associate editor of the *Country Gentleman,* read about Roswell's program to combat the feed shortage in a letter passed on to him by a Garst and Thomas salesman. Strohm wrote for information, including Roswell's bulletins, and published a short piece on the subject. Finally in 1952, again relying heavily on Roswell, Strohm wrote a major article on nitrogen, considered by George Scarseth to have been one of the milestones in the fertilizer era. In the spring of 1952, also under Roswell's tutelage, Fred Knoop wrote an article entitled "New Tricks in Corn" for the *Farm Quarterly* that emphasized the possibilities of growing corn after corn instead of using the traditional rotation of corn and oats. Knoop talked with George Scarseth, now with the American Farm Research Association and with Walter Colvin, a former agronomist and currently head of Allied Chemical's Barrett Division in Ohio. From these sources, marshalled for him by Roswell, Knoop found out about innovations in liquid nitrogen, applicators, and the combinations of nitrogen, phosphorus, and potash that were creating a soil rich enough to sustain the continuous planting of corn. "Out in central Iowa," he wrote, "there are a group of farmers like Ed Reid of Coon Rapids who have found out that [continuous corn] is not only possible but also more profitable."

In research stations, one step towards this new concept came from a reexamination of the effects of crop rotation. By 1949 Roger Bray of the University of Illinois, where at the turn of the century Hopkins formalized the concept of rotation, demonstrated that all rotations—including those with legumes—were depleting the organic matter of the soil. By 1960, H. Jenny at the University of Missouri would be able to measure the loss at about one-half of the native organic matter in midwestern soil, a loss primarily attributable to nitrogen-consuming corn. One solution was to abandon the planting of corn, advocated by some but economically impossible. The other solution lay in the increased use of nitrogen fertilizer.

In 1950 George Scarseth attended a meeting of the Soil Conservation Society of America to deliver a paper entitled "Building Soils with Deep-Rooted Legumes." At the moment of delivery he put aside his written text, and instead posed two questions to his audience, questions he and Roswell had mused over as early as 1943. "Can corn be grown by such methods as will make it a soil-improving crop rather than a soil-destroying crop?" he asked first, and then, "Can land be improved with continuous corn?" Scarseth argued affirmatively on both questions, citing his own experience and the work of Sigurd Melsted at the University of Illinois. Both farmers and researchers were finding nitrogen the solution to the problem, because nitrogen created far more organic residue in the root system of corn than legumes or manure could provide. When a few cornstalks were plowed under to supplement the decomposing residues already in the soil, organic content increased. Unfertilized, the corn plant was a soil destroyer; properly fertilized, the same plant was a soil builder.

Although he had become a leading practitioner of continuous corn, Roswell had a moment of doubt in 1952. In April he discovered that in his enthusiasm for nitrogen he had seriously depleted the phosphorus and potash levels on his own land. Taking no chances, he followed George Hoffer's recommendation of heavy fertilizer application *and* a period of rotation that included clover. In October 1952, with an excellent crop in hand and just before his Cincinnati speech, he could again feel confident about his views on legumes. "I still think you're an old fogie," he wrote Hoffer, "even with the sweet clover." He concluded that the balance of fertilizer had been the only problem and reaffirmed his belief "that balance of fertilizer is just as much of importance as the amount." He was already looking toward new pastures, and as early as 1950 he told Keenan at DuPont, "I am promoting *your* product – not because I feel you fellows need any help, but because I think the world needs some help."

Agricultural Prospect

Roswell's view of the implications of these years of breakthrough appeared in a 1951 article for the *Farm Quarterly* entitled "The Agricultural Prospect Before Us." Its content and the circumstances of its inception reflect the intellectual superstructure that he built upon the activism of his postwar years.

The immediate sources for Roswell's decision to speculate on the future of American agriculture were twofold. The first and most important was an article by economist Sumner Schlicter entitled "How Big in

1980?" appearing in the *Atlantic Monthly* in November 1949. The second was a book by John Dos Passos entitled *The Prospect Before Us,* which Roswell read in the summer of 1950.

In his article, Schlicter forecast an American economy for 1980 that was very big indeed, with an output of goods and services of 500 billion dollars – more than twice that of 1948 and produced by a population of 175 million at increasingly efficient levels per man-hour. Schlicter's projection was virtually a manifesto for expanded production, which would in turn bring shorter but more productive working hours, more intensive and vigorous competition, the development of substitutes for scarce raw materials, and an increasing advance in technology that would produce not only industrial advances but also "revolutionary changes in agriculture." In the next 30 years, Schlicter predicted, the United States would produce about 70 percent more than it had produced in the entire preceding 150 years, an increase that might not even be enough for the destiny he foresaw for America in those optimistic postwar years. His figures, and his view of America's potential influence in the world, touched a responsive chord in Roswell. The rate of production, Schlicter argued,

would certainly not be too much for a country which has undertaken to maintain the peace of the world, to help war-stricken countries adjust themselves to the post-war world, to help industrially backward countries develop their resources, to provide incomes for millions of its own citizens on the basis of need.

The second immediate source was Dos Passos's *The Prospect Before Us.* It reflected his fears of the totalitarian regimes of Eastern Europe and South America, his disillusionment with socialism in England, and his hopes for American enterprise. It was a roving look at the state of the world, based this time on a lecture-seminar group of representative Americans. The *Life* article, with some alteration, appeared again, with midwestern farming presented as the world's best agricultural hope. "Our task," Dos Passos concluded,

is to shape the Republic to fit corporate industry and to shape productive institutions to fit the aims of the Republic. To get a notion of the penalty for failure, all we have to do is to visit the ruins of Berlin or to imagine the lives men live in Prague or Bucharest or Moscow.

Roswell took the book on a circuit of sales meetings and told Dos Passos he had read it "from kiver to kiver" and wanted to use the title for a piece of his own. He sent Dos Passos a copy of Schlicter's article and a copy of a recent letter to Jonathan and Stephen that "gives you the basic type of thinking that I expect to pursue." Schlicter had written on the economic prospect, Dos Passos had written on the social and political prospect; Roswell was going to do the same for agriculture. "I think I'm in better shape than any one to do one on the agricultural prospect," he said, and was even considering expanding it into a book.

The letter to Jonathan and Stephen was written early in November 1950 and had as its starting point Roswell's analysis of population growth in the United States. In 1930 there were 122 million people, in 1940 the figure had risen to 130 million, and in 1950 it stood at approximately 150 million. If the United States continued to grow at the rate of 2.5 million people per year, it would have Schlicter's 175 million by 1960 and would be closer to 200 million by 1980. The rate of gain was increasing, extending ever more sharply upward when represented in a graph. The shortage of grain, which ought to have been even more acute as a result of this increased rate of gain in Roswell's view, had been temporarily alleviated by the disappearance of 20 million horses and mules since 1930, the use of hybrid corn to increase yields, and the increase in production of eggs, poultry, and pork. However, these means of increasing food production were levelling off. "In short," he wrote to Jonathan and Stephen,

in the last twenty years we have accomplished the easy job of keeping up with the moderate part of the population curve. But, as I pointed out, the population curve is steepening—and the curve representing most of the other known factors is flattening. So the gap is starting to widen.

After writing to Jonathan and Stephen and others, Roswell went to Washington in late November 1950 for research on population and feed grain figures at the Bureau of the Census and the USDA. He found nothing that suggested to him his projections were incorrect and little evidence of similar speculation along the lines he was following. "They seem to just write history in the Bureau of Agricultural Economics," he complained, "they do not try to predict the future—that is, they don't try hard enough."

The literary result was an article for the *Farm Quarterly* that Roswell entitled "The Agricultural Prospect Before Us." Grant Cannon, the journal's editor, wanted to change the title to "The Surplus Is Gone," but with his heart set on following Schlicter and Dos Passos—and not at all convinced that there was as yet a surplus anyway—Roswell protested and finally achieved a compromise. Both titles appeared, with Cannon's in slightly larger print. "I told them that I didn't care which one they used as the major title," Roswell explained later, "but I certainly wanted mine at least included." Cannon wrote a more dramatic lead paragraph, compressed the article somewhat, but left the bulk of it as Roswell had written.

The article progressed in the same general fashion as the letter to Jonathan and Stephen but included figures on the decreasing carryover of corn reserves during the past three years. When he came to the question of increased production, Roswell listed eight "jacks" to achieve this aim: more fertilizer, feeding cellulose, improving farm machinery, applying hybridization to poultry and livestock, contour plowing, improved drainage and irrigation, better rotation and erosion control, and artificial drying. The first step in meeting the anticipated demand for food, Roswell concluded, "calls for an understanding that it is not temporary or short-lived." It was a permanent challenge that would become more difficult to meet during the 1970s than during the 1960s, and more difficult in the 1960s than in the present decade. The Korean war was making it more urgent but was not the root cause of scarcity—the fundamental demand for more food came from population growth.

Before and after the article was published, Roswell made his own energetic contribution to its distribution. At the time of printing he ordered 100,000 copies of the article for distribution through his own channels and in addition reproduced another 100,000 copies of his own condensation of the article, getting his own back on Cannon by entitling the latter piece simply "The Agricultural Prospect Before Us." He sent a long list of recipients for this issue of the *Farm Quarterly*, had Garst and Thomas advertise it over the radio, and provided suggestions to the magazine's advertising department. He balked only when an overzealous member of that department suggested that Garst and Thomas salesmen hawk subscriptions to the magazine. "We are certainly grateful to you," a senior editor wrote to him, "for the promotion you are doing on the issue."

Roswell was happy when he anticipated the benefits that might accrue to Garst and Thomas sales, especially since the article would reach the newsstands just before the spring selling season. In December 1950 he sent a draft of the condensed article to his own advertising manager, Bill Hill. "Don't be showing this to anyone," he cautioned Hill,

but just think of the effect of getting one of those things to each one of the 100,000 customers the day before he comes in after his corn. If it doesn't step up deliveries one bushel for every four customers, I'll be a little bit shocked and surprised. That's why I'm privately dreaming big dreams—why I am so steamed up.

We may deduce from these remarks that Roswell's commercial drive was undiminished in 1951. However, in the population study he embarked upon lay the seed of a wider application of his curiosity.

AT the very beginning of the postwar years another seed had been sown but thus far had found no opportunity to grow. In September 1946 Henry Wallace made a speech critical of the already developing cold war mentality which, in the view of President Truman, undermined American foreign policy and threatened to undercut the American position in negotiations being conducted in Europe. Wallace lost his cabinet post at commerce over the affair.

As a result of Wallace's speech and its dramatic consequences, newspapers throughout the country published an earlier letter he had written to the president in July 1946:

It is of the greatest importance that we should discuss with the Russians in a friendly way their long-range economic problems and the future of our co-operation in matters of trade. The reconstruction program of the USSR and the plans for the full development of the Soviet Union offer tremendous opportunities for American goods and American technicians. . . . War with Russia would bring catastrophe to all mankind, and therefore we must find a way of living in peace.

Although his own political conservatism made him critical of Wallace's later participation in a third party, Roswell was deeply moved both by Wallace's speech and the letter and wrote Wallace to congratulate him on his contribution to the cause of peace. The event became one of Wallace's most enduring legacies to Roswell.

Beginning the East-West Dialogue

Background: Living with the Surplus

The agricultural breakthrough created in a remarkably short time a formidable domestic surplus. "I will be kidded," Roswell confided to Pat Jackson,

about predicting that from now on we were not going to have any surpluses – but I did not know at that time that the Government was going to subsidize the building of nitrogen plants by the fast tax write-off which did subsequently happen and which did terrifically expand nitrogen production through the method of tax incentive.

However, Roswell was not as upset as the new administration was over the size of the surplus. He continued to advocate a large reserve and believed that in reducing stocks (which even he conceded might be occasionally necessary) the government ought to use the surplus to create more protein at home and as an instrument of aid and diplomacy abroad. To these aims he began devoting much of his time in 1953.

That same year Congress debated Public Law 480, designed to sell the mounting surplus abroad, which passed in July 1954 and initiated the Food for Peace program. The law's intent was "to make maximum efficient use of surplus agricultural commodities in furtherance of the foreign policy of the United States," but in an age of strident anti-Communism its provisions had been circumscribed by Martin Dies to apply to "friendly nations" only. Indeed, even the domestic agricultural program of Ezra Taft Benson, Eisenhower's secretary of agriculture, was ideologically pure. Criticizing his predecessor's planning concepts, Benson wrote that "this philosophy that the government knows how to operate farms better than the farmers themselves is more than an academic theory. It is almost exactly the concept by which the Communist economies operate over nearly half of the earth." The "socialized" agriculture of the Brannan plan was anathema; Benson's guiding purpose would be "to strengthen the individual integrity, freedom, and the very moral fiber of each citizen." The language was stirring, but the point of view did not encourage pragmatism as an approach to the problem of a growing surplus and a diminishing farm income.

It was also a year of increasing polarization between Eastern Europe and the West, the excesses of Joseph McCarthy, and the escalating arms race. In 1950 McCarthy had made his stunning accusation that hundreds of Communists were working in the State Department, and by 1953 the new Republican administration attacked the Truman-Kennan policy of containment of Russia, advertised its hopes of rolling back Communism in Eastern Europe, and declared a policy of massive nuclear retaliation in the event of any aggression by the Soviet Union. The death of Stalin in 1953 had thus far produced only a power struggle in Russia, with no concrete evidence of a significant change in Stalinist policy.

Working out his own approach to Wallace's hopes in 1946 for a lessening of East-West tension, Roswell began a campaign to use America's agricultural surpluses as a weapon for peace by including Iron Curtain countries as potential buyers of the surplus. "I think," he wrote Representative Clifford R. Hope of Kansas,

if wheat and cotton and food were really given their rightful emphasis in place of armament production, we could not curtail them. I just can't get away from the fact that two billion dollars worth of food and fourteen billion dollars worth of armaments is better than sixteen billion dollars worth of armaments. I have yet to find a single person who doesn't believe this to be true! I am going to keep it as my theme song."

That same summer of 1953, Roswell went to Washington to talk with Benson about his concern for the surpluses yet to come. Benson was not personally available, so Roswell warned Don Paarlberg, the secretary's economic assistant, that an explosion was occurring in agricultural techniques that would make any previous surplus "look insignificant as compared with the surpluses that were going to accumulate." Paarlberg did not foresee any such explosion and reminded Roswell that no food could or would be sold to Eastern Europe. Roswell returned home to his work with cellulose and fertilizer.

The following year Public Law 480 was passed, as well as the Agricultural Act of 1954. The former made foreign food aid programs a permanent part of U.S. policy, within the limitations described, and made it easier for soft-currency nations to acquire some of the surplus with their own money. The latter program instituted a sliding level of price supports, under which the level of price support would decline as supplies of any particular commodity increased. It was Benson's major means of controlling the growing surpluses, but it did not work. Prices declined, but commodities did not diminish in quantity; the technological revolution was undermining the traditional restraint on production of low prices.

During December and January 1954–55 Roswell gave the domestic aspects of the farm problem further thought and transmitted his conclusions to John Kenneth Galbraith in February 1955. "What disturbs me," Roswell wrote, "is that while the population is gaining at the rate of something like 1.7% a year, I suspect that agricultural production is gaining at least twice that rapidly on a five-year basis." He saw "no hope at all" in the present domestic farm program, and little likelihood of an increase in exports very rapidly. Consequently, the only alternative would be to encourage a high protein diet. This could be done, he thought, by giving compensatory payments for the producers of meat and dairy products so that the surpluses might be eaten up. "We just have to go to a high protein diet if American agriculture is going to survive," he concluded and asked to see Galbraith in April.

Galbraith was interested in a meeting and in Roswell's proposals. "I was delighted with your letter," he replied:

I have been thinking along much the same lines in the last few months and, indeed, just lectured the Department of Agriculture on these lines. Presently we are subsidizing cereals or, at a minimum, giving them price protection. How much more sensible it would be to subsidize the less efficient but also more agreeable proteins!

During talks with Galbraith, John Davis (director of the program in agriculture and business at Harvard), and John D. Black, Roswell worked out the details of his compensatory payments plan and started to sell it. According to Roswell, the Harvard group believed the present program would have to collapse of its own weight before something new could be tried. Roswell thought differently and said so to Red Bowman:

Now, Red, not any one of the three can be, by the longest stretch of the imagination, referred to as "opportunists." And, if you and I have one thing that we might be called, it is "opportunist." An opportunist is simply a fellow that does things at an opportune moment – sees an opportunity ahead of the crowd – acts on what he sees. So I think we are a better judge of timing than they are.

Arden "Red" Bowman had grown up in Coon Rapids, worked there until the thirties, then moved to Minneapolis to work in the grain business. After a tour of duty in Washington during World War II as sugar administrator, he returned to Minneapolis and became friendly with Mayor Hubert H. Humphrey. An inveterate politician, Red constantly urged Roswell to run for office and was his closest political crony. Roswell

and Elizabeth were staying with Red and Tillie in 1948 the day that
Humphrey was named "Man of the Year." That night Humphrey and a
group of his university advisers breezed into the Bowmans; Humphrey,
ebullient and excited, held forth until 4 A.M., striding up and down the
room talking, laughing, and exuding vitality. "Sit down, Hubert," Red
admonished occasionally, "You're not in the pulpit now!" Beginning that
evening, Roswell became an acquaintance and admirer of Humphrey.

While he waited for Red to get in touch with Senator Humphrey,
Roswell once again promoted the international side of his program to
Herbert Hoover, Jr., in the State Department, and again to Agriculture. "I
keep reading in the Press," he explained, "that one great difficulty in
Russia is food." He noted Khrushchev's speech of February 1955 asking
for an Iowa Corn Belt in Russia, guessed that it would take five years
before the Russian program would bear fruit, and for the meantime proposed that the United States expand its pork production by 20 percent
and sell it to Eastern Europe. He also suggested the possibility of some
"solid, long-time trading"; the U.S. should import, for example,
manganese from the Russians as we had done in the past. "I think in food
we have a potent weapon to use for peace," he concluded, "and particularly when the fellow on the other side of the table, whether he be a
Russian or a Chinaman, is hungry." He had been talking to Jonathan and
some of his phraseology on this issue was beginning to come from his
brother.

In June 1955 came word from Humphrey. Their "mutual friend" Red
Bowman, he wrote, had given the senator copies of two of Roswell's
letters and a memo on the farm price support situation. Humphrey welcomed any information Roswell could give and urged him to be a witness
before the Senate Committee on Agriculture, now conducting hearings on
price supports and formulating a new program. The present program,
Humphrey said, "is unworkable and merely aggravating the
situation. . . . Give me the benefit of your advice and counsel."

Roswell responded with a long letter of two parts, in which he made
his proposal on price supports and set forth his views on food for peace.
His proposal differed from earlier proposals and the present program in
advocating a drop from 90 percent to 75 percent of parity on feed grains
but at the same time offering higher supports on protein products by
means of compensatory payments. Acreage restrictions would be maintained, and feed crops would be shifted from corn, oats, and sorghum to
hay or grass so that cattle numbers could be raised. "I suspect that we are
going to go to 125 or 150 million head of cattle under any kind of program
in the next ten years," he had written at the same time to Jim Naughton,
"and that is going to mean beef prices will need nominal support."

It was to Paarlberg that Roswell wrote one of his finest letters in

1955, taking as his major text the coming surpluses and charging the USDA with complacency over the problem. "It is," he told Paarlberg,

as if agriculture has a cold – and that if agriculture went to bed and covered up its head in a few days the cold would disappear. . . . Actually, the situation is desperate. . . . It's like the beginning of a plague – or it's like a small fire in a big structure. The difficulties are not about over. . . the difficulties are just beginning.

The present program of fluctuating price supports was only negligibly different from the old program of 90 percent support, and neither program was any longer viable. "In a rapidly changing world," he said, "for anyone to take a fixed position and keep it for a ten-year period is for him to court disaster. The individual might not change – the world changes."

There were, he concluded, a number of things to be done, and done at the same time. We needed to export more food and ensure greater consumption at home by lowering the price to consumers of protein and dairy products and compensating the farmers. There were domestic markets as yet untapped. The school lunch program could be enlarged, the food stamp plan could be revived to ensure more protein for the disadvantaged, and inmates in federal institutions could have improved diets. There seemed be to no one solution to the problem. "I think we are going to have to use every tool and every bit of imagination we possess to solve the problem," Roswell wrote, "and not break farmers in the process." The list turned out to be an accurate forecast of the measures that would finally be used.

That winter the proposals for compensatory payments and exports to Eastern Europe were taken up by Humphrey when the Senate Agriculture Committee met during the winter of 1955–56 to draft a new bill. "You have been more than generous," Humphrey told Roswell in December 1955, "and the more I read what you have to say, the more convinced I become that you are right." He planned to go over the material with some agricultural economists in Washington and would discuss it with every member of the Senate Committee on Agriculture. "What you propose," he wrote,

is so sensible that I can't quite understand why I haven't grabbed hold of it long ago. I guess we get so confounded busy down here we don't have time to do constructive thinking. We literally fight for a few moments to write a letter, much less to plan and meditate.

A subsidy to increase consumption of the end product had been the concept Brannan had been trying to promote several years ago, Humphrey believed, but the Brannan Plan had become embroiled in political argument and had not been considered on its merits.

However, Humphrey did not succeed in promoting compensatory or, as he called them, production payments. He failed by one vote (8–7) of getting such a measure approved by the committee, and failed also to get a premium incentive payment for light-weight hogs and cattle. "These Republicans have done such a smear job on Charles Brannan and the whole production payment idea," he wrote, "that even our Democrats shy away from it."

There was also no change in the restriction on selling food to Eastern Europe, even though events in 1955 moved Eisenhower to propose trade with the Iron Curtain countries and to release certain items from the list of strategic materials. Humphrey characterized the moves as "a feeble gesture" toward trade with the Eastern European nations and complained that no testimony had been given by any ranking administration official. "In fact," he told Roswell in February 1956, "they ducked and shied away from it almost to the total exclusion of any comment. . . . You are absolutely right when you say they are afraid."

Throughout 1955 and 1956 Soviet policy underwent significant change, the Eisenhower-Dulles position on East-West relations was modified, and trade with Eastern Europe became a fact. Furthermore, Iowa agriculture was in the vanguard of this change, just as Roswell had hoped, but in a manner totally unexpected.

First Agricultural Exchange: 1955

The rise to power of Nikita Khrushchev changed the political climate of 1955 and provided Roswell an opportunity to put into practice what he had been preaching.

Khrushchev entered Russian political life in the early 1920s as a student at the Donets Mining Technical School in the Don Basin. He had already helped get the mines in his area back to work after the civil war and had seen his first wife die of hunger and exhaustion during those cruel years in Russia. After two years of active party work in the school, he graduated in 1925 and took the job as party secretary in a district in that same area. By 1932 he worked his way to Moscow as deputy to Lazar Kaganovich, secretary of the Central Committee of the All-Union party, and took charge of the construction of the Moscow underground, whose miles were measured in the blood of a considerable number of its workers. In 1937 he was dispatched to Kiev to rule as the chief party official in the Ukraine. When World War II began for Russia in 1941, he became a political commissar, survived Stalingrad and Stalin, and after victory returned to Kiev to supervise the rebuilding of the city and the Ukrainian economy. In spite of a severe drought in 1945 and consequent famine, Khrushchev managed the economic recovery of the Ukraine sufficiently well to please Stalin, who brought him back to Moscow in 1949 to direct all Soviet agriculture.

Although he was not trained as an agriculturalist, Khrushchev had learned enough in the Ukraine to make agriculture his path to power. It was in several respects an unpromising choice. Stalin was obsessed with industrial development and would not invest in agriculture; the enforced collectivization of 1927–28 had brought about death or exile for the entire landholding and managerial class – the "kulaks" – in agriculture and silenced any potential Roswell Garsts. Food production, especially livestock, limped along at levels below that of the days before collectivization; the collectives themselves were a hodgepodge of farms of all sizes, short of good labor and machinery. To change any of these conditions required great energy, organizational ability, authority, and courage. Khrushchev had these qualifications, as well as a breathtaking – and dangerous – zest for grandstanding gestures and adventurism. There was also, within that explosive and ambitious personality, a degree of commitment to responsible leadership that made his accession to power a significant and hopeful event.

Before World War II, Russian agriculture suffered a chronic state of low production. Average yields, according to an analysis by Roy and Zhores Medvedev, did not increase from 1913 to 1953 largely because of the lack of fertilizer and were never more than one-third of the yields of other European countries. The "Kholkozes," or collective farms organized around villages, and the "Sovkhozes," or state farms, supplied feed grain and wheat, but the small private plots allowed to peasants for raising small quantities of livestock and garden produce by 1940 were producing one-third of the meat, milk, and butter and 93 percent of the eggs available to the populace. These small holdings, in relation to their size by far the most efficient, were heavily taxed and by the end of the forties were themselves in danger of collapse as production units.

To a perilous margin of adequate production came the devastation of the war. Of the 20 million lives lost during 1941–45, 15 million casualties had been village residents, most of the agricultural work force. The continuing agricultural crisis drove many of the few millions who returned or remained in the villages to seek work in the cities, which also took first priority in reconstruction. Edwin Crankshaw, who travelled in Russia shortly after the war, has described the effects of the fighting and the scorched-earth policy instituted by the Germans in their retreat. From his railway carriage, Crankshaw noted,

for hundreds of miles, for thousands, there was not a standing or a living object to be seen. Every town was flat, every city. There were no barns. There was no machinery. There were no stations, no water-towers. . . . In the fields, unkempt, nobody but women, children, very old men could be seen, and these worked only with hand tools. . . . The whole country, apart from the tremendous new war industries in the east, was derelict and at a standstill. The Ukraine was ravaged, burned, and blasted too.

In the Ukraine, Khrushchev's first major agricultural reform had been a change from small collectives of workers supported by a Machine Tractor Station to "brigades" of workers cultivating larger units. He had also prevented Kaganovich, acting under the advice of Trofim Lysenko, the Soviet geneticist, from replacing the traditional planting of winter wheat in the Ukraine by a spring variety that Lysenko believed could be "environmentally" adapted to the Russian breadbasket. In 1949–50 Khrushchev in Moscow amalgamated all the Russian collectives—some of which were still as small as 200 acres—into larger units of land and increased the size of the work brigades. His long-term aim was the creation of agro towns, large new settlements that would replace the small villages and house an agricultural labor force able to work the land in the way that industrial workers labored in factories.

When he became first secretary of the party, Khrushchev was able to make further improvements in a country making great strides in postwar recovery, but was still saddled with the repressive and uncaring policies of Stalin. In the summer of 1953, after Stalin's death, Khrushchev enacted in law a sharp reduction of taxes on household plots and certain types of household properties, replacing the old system as well by a more equitable tax based on the size of household. In September 1953 he reduced taxes even further, encouraged nonagricultural workers to keep livestock and garden plots, and later eliminated entirely the tax on cows and pigs. These reforms produced a great increase in livestock and poultry, provided a crucial boost in morale for the peasants, and averted an immediate crisis which, of all the leaders in the Soviet Union, only Khrushchev seems to have perceived. According to the Medvedevs, he was the only senior official who visited the countryside for a firsthand view, and by then he had acquired a national reputation as an agricultural authority.

However, greater measures yet were needed, which at first followed the same lines. In the September 1953 Party Plenum, Khrushchev publicly exposed deficiencies in Soviet agriculture, arranged for collectives to receive a much greater return from the state for their products, initiated a plan for increased production of fertilizer, arranged credits for the construction of dairy farms, and increased agricultural wages. In late 1953 and early 1954 Khrushchev launched his most spectacular programs—the opening of the untilled virgin lands in Khazakstan and the shift to corn as the major feed grain in the traditional farming areas.

In 1954 thousands of young volunteers moved into the vast areas of Khazakstan and southwest Siberia to break 6 million acres of land in that first year, and 32 million acres by 1955. The first year of production was small but good on the new soil, and 1955 brought a bumper crop, just in time to help Khrushchev reach a commanding position in the power struggle that followed Stalin's death. Although his victory over Malenkov was not assured until 1957, by 1955 Khrushchev had emerged as his country's leader after a brief period of collective government.

The harvest reaped in the new lands was intended as a temporary measure while the traditional farming areas underwent a change to a corn culture for livestock and a general improvement in the level of agricultural technology. In his introduction of this new crop, Khrushchev was encouraged and abetted by the anti-Lysenko wing of the agricultural establishment, headed by N. I. Vavilov, who looked to the development of hybrid corn by the United States in the thirties as a lesson for Russia and a means to restore classical genetics to Russian science.

Khrushchev introduced his plan for an increase in corn acreage in September 1953, several months before the Virgin Lands Program was announced, but very little of this new crop was planted, and mostly on an experimental basis. When 1954 produced only a small increase in corn, Khrushchev launched a personal campaign to urge that corn be grown in large quantities. He toured the Ukraine and the Crimea, told his audiences of the beneficial effects that accrued from the forcible introduction of potatoes into Russia in the eighteenth century, and by 1955 achieved a harvest of 18 million hectares. A corn research institute was established in the Ukraine; a corn pavilion appeared at the permanent Agricultural Exhibit in Moscow; a journal entitled *Corn* was founded, and in Moscow there was even a store called "corn."

The new direction Khrushchev intended for the Russian economy was made firm during the Plenary Session of the Central Committee, which met in Moscow during 25 to 31 January 1955. In his report Khrushchev signalled the change in emphasis from the Stalinist period by a mere passing reference to heavy industry which was relegated to serve as a base for the development of light industry, consumer goods, and above all, agriculture. Increasing agricultural production was the first priority, especially grain for animal fodder, and Khrushchev suggested three ways to achieve this goal: increase the harvests on arable land, continue to expand the virgin lands, and increase substantially the growing of corn.

Khrushchev then turned his attention to a lengthy analysis of the feed-grain yield in the United States, attributing its increase to the success of hybrid corn. He quoted figures on corn production in the United States over the preceding fifteen years, and compared Soviet and American acreage. In 1953, he reported, nearly 30 million hectares of corn had been grown in the United States, but in Russia only 3.5 million. What was required, he said, was an increase in Soviet acreage by not less than 28 million hectares by 1960, an Iowa Corn Belt for Russia. Consequently, he called upon the Ministry of Agriculture and the Ministry of Collective Farms to develop hybrid seed corn and to set up experimental stations and research institutes that could be converted entirely to hybrid seed corn within the next two or three years.

Khrushchev's recommendations were adopted as a party resolution that was published in full on 2 February 1955 under the heading "Concerning the Increase of Production of Animal Produce." His speech was published the next day in *Pravda, Izvestia,* and in the journal *Agriculture.* Khrushchev's favorable comments on U.S. agriculture and his evident wish to make use of Western technology made his remarks big news in America, and on 11 February the newly emerging Soviet leader granted an interview to three American journalists. In this interview, reported also in Russia, Khrushchev suggested that agriculture might be a basis for better relations with the United States.

An important figure behind the scenes in the shift to the production of hybrid corn was Ilya Emilianov, a Soviet geneticist, at that time the newly appointed vice-chairman of the Bureau of Scientific-Technical International Cooperation. After degrees at the Moscow agricultural academy, Emilianov, a pupil of N. I. Vavilov, joined the Ministry of Agriculture in 1944 and was sent to the United States for three years to procure food for the Soviet army. It was then that he began studying the hybridization of corn. Emilianov later told Roswell that Khrushchev hoped for an American response to his speech, as the interview with American newsmen suggested, and that Emilianov himself played a leading role in urging Khrushchev to go to corn as Russia's principal feed grain.

Behind this maneuvering lay the continuing controversy over Lysenko, who advocated environmental modification as the means for plant breeding rather than Mendelian genetics. Certainly Lysenko's fall from power played an important part in the events of 1955, but Khrushchev remained sympathetic to Lysenko and ambivalent in his attitude toward Lysenko's work. According to Emilianov, even the Khrushchev visit to Iowa in 1959 was in part related to the need for Khrushchev to say that he had seen for himself the American success with hybridization.

On 9 February, the Khrushchev speech was reported in headlines in the *Des Moines Register,* followed by a lead story by Harrison Salisbury on the rise of Khrushchev. On 10 February Lauren Soth, chief of the editorial page of the *Register,* replied to the Khrushchev speech with an editorial entitled "If the Russians Want More Meat. . . ." In this editorial Soth noted that Khrushchev, "who seems to be the real boss of the Soviet Union now," had signalled his rise to power by an attack on the management of the Soviet economy, particularly against agriculture, and had taken the "rare line" of praising the United States. In advocating the development of a feed-livestock agriculture based on corn, he was "talking sense," Soth said. "We have no diplomatic authority of any kind," he continued,

but we hereby extend an invitation to any delegation Khrushchev wants to select to come to Iowa to get the lowdown on raising high quality cattle, hogs, sheep and chickens. We promise to hide none of our "secrets." We will take the visiting delegation to Iowa's great agricultural experiment station at Ames, to some of the leading farmers in Iowa, to our livestock breeders, soil conservation experts and seed companies. Let the Russians see how we do it.

Soth suggested that a delegation of Iowa farmers, agronomists, livestock specialists, and other technical authorities go to Russia, if invited. More knowledge on both sides would benefit everybody, Soth suggested, might move the Soviet leaders away from the conviction that the United States wanted war, and "might even persuade them that there is a happier future in developing a high level of living than in this paralyzing race for more and more armaments." He did not think that the Russians would do it or that even our own government would be willing to cooperate in such "an adventure in human understanding." But, he concluded, "it *would* make sense."

In retrospect, Soth has remarked of his editorial that "it was a rather obvious thing to do after hearing the speech." There may be truth in his appraisal, but his response required independence and courage, considering the climate of opinion in the United States in early 1955. The extent of the confrontation mentality that had developed was graphically revealed by a news item published in the *Register* two days after the Soth editorial. A Gallup poll had shown that six out of ten Americans thought the West would have to go to war with Russia eventually; conversely, only one in four thought we could continue to live peacefully with the Soviet Union. Soth continued to editorialize on the subject, and for years was the recipient of hostile letters from those angry with his initiative.

The idea began to gather momentum in the United States as the *Register* persisted in its proposal. Shortly after the first editorial, Fletcher Knebel of the *Register* Washington staff asked President Eisenhower at a press conference if he thought that an exchange of agricultural delegations with the Russians would be a good thing. Eisenhower replied affirmatively and talked rather expansively on the subject. Both the *Christian Science Monitor* and the *New York Times* echoed the idea approvingly, and officials in the State Department and Agriculture were—like it or not—obliged to take the idea seriously.

Roswell approved wholeheartedly of Soth's proposal, and, visiting

Washington in March, told Phil Maguire, Arthur Becker, and Pat Jackson that he would visit the Russian embassy to offer to send some samples of hybrid seed corn to Russia in order to have some growing when the American delegation arrived. All three spoke up to dissuade him, pointing out that the embassy was watched, the phone tapped, and his attempt to make personal contact likely to get him into trouble. Roswell called Richard Wilson, also on the *Register*'s Washington bureau, to ask if he would take the message to the embassy. Wilson was dubious, said he would check with Des Moines, and phoned back to say that the paper felt it had gone sufficiently out on a limb already; it was not prepared to make direct contact with the Russian embassy.

In Russia, the journal *Agriculture* responded first by announcing Russian agriculturalists' readiness to send such a delegation, an item immediately picked up by American papers. On 3 March, *Pravda* printed a remarkably straightforward account of the favorable response of the *New York Times* to the proposal and the latest words from Soth on the possibilities of exchange. The article noted the *Times* of 2 March had published an extract from the editorial in the *Register,* in which Soth had expressed the *Register*'s pleasure that the Russians wished to send a delegation and hoped that the State Department would not respond with a hasty refusal, which would denote only fear on America's part. Negotiations between the two governments began.

Arrangements for the exchange were concluded by early summer. In America, the Land-Grant College Division of the Department of Agriculture was finally designated to select the delegation that would travel to Russia in the summer. Of the twelve members, five, including Soth, were from Iowa, and consisted of several farmers, an agronomist, and Dean Vincent Lambert of the University of Nebraska. The party flew to Moscow in June and travelled through the Ukraine, the Don Basin, visited Stalingrad, moved on to Tashkent and to the Ural Mountains, dividing into two groups for travel in Siberia. Soth and his companions found people spontaneously warm and welcoming, their agriculturalists open to new ideas and change and determined to be self-sufficient in grain. Soth discovered how far north and how dry much of the Russian farming area was, and he found a cumbersome management system, poor supply service, poor transportation, and inefficient use of labor. There was much to be done, as Khrushchev had said.

While the Americans were in Russia, the Russians came to America, and the political overtones of the visit produced some awkwardness for both the State Department and the Department of Agriculture. Concern for hostile attitudes toward a group of Russians touring the country and the problem of governmental identification with the group made officials nervous. According to John Strohm, the agricultural journalist chosen to escort the party, the Department of Agriculture thought State should sponsor the visit, and State thought that Agriculture should be the official hosts. Finally, Earl Butz, assistant secretary of agriculture, suggested that the Department of Agriculture take on the assignment but arrange to have a private citizen escort the group, thereby distancing the Russians from the government. Strohm, a friend of Butz and a visitor himself to the Soviet Union in 1947, agreed to be chief guide.

The question of what the Russians should see also presented problems. Strohm took them directly to Des Moines rather than to Washington for formal briefings, a decision that got the tour off to a good working start. He consulted with officials at Iowa State College and the Farm Bureau to make up a list of farms and facilities to be visited. According to Strohm, it was decided to show a variety of sizes of farms, from 160 through 640 acres. However, sensitive to the presence of a large contingent of press and TV reporters and photographers, and to the public view of the small farmer as the backbone of American democracy – a view assiduously promoted by the farm associations – the smaller acreages predominated. The Americans in fact took a more political view of the trip than the Russians, who came primarily seeking necessary information.

Roswell blamed the State Department for this approach, but Strohm denied that any such directive was given him. Rather, as his account of the visit suggests, the attitude was really a consensus of the organizers of the tour and of the farm community itself. In Roswell's correspondence there is a copy of a speech made to the Russian delegation on 18 July, 1955 by E. Howard Hill, president of the Iowa Farm Bureau Federation, in which Hill emphasized that the Russians would be seeing small family farms, noting categorically that they would not see "our largest or our fanciest farms." He said that Iowa farmers would be interested in trade but said nothing about Russians learning American farming techniques. Roswell, at that time in the well-publicized vanguard of the latest techniques of cattle-feeding and hybridization, both of which the Russians had mainly come to see, had not been put on the list.

Roswell got to the Russians through luck and by being the kind of opportunist he had described to Red Bowman. His chance came when the Russian delegation was housed overnight in Jefferson, twenty-six miles away from Coon Rapids, the night before they were to travel to Iowa State. Two members of the delegation, Alexander Tulupnikov, an English-speaking economist, and Boris Savelev, an agronomist, were staying with Warren and Eleanor Garst that Saturday night. After alerting Roswell, Warren invited his daughter Mary and son-in-law Stephen to dinner that night. During the course of the evening Stephen described the Garst farming operation in detail to Tulupnikov and suggested a visit the

next morning. Tulupnikov and Savelev agreed and came down with Warren and Eleanor for an early breakfast at the farm and a quick tour of the
farming operation. Tulupnikov, a short, bushy-browed, humorous man,
was excited by what he saw and said he would describe Coon Rapids
farming to the head of the delegation, Vladimir Matskevitch, the Deputy
Minister of Agriculture. ("I discovered Roswell Garst," Tulupnikov liked
to say afterwards.) The party had to rush back to Jefferson to make an
obligatory appearance in church. "I will go," Tulupnikov had volunteered,
to show, he said later, "that Communists went to church." His hosts,
Warren and Eleanor, not churchgoers, were obliged to attend, also. Politics makes strange pewfellows.

On the afternoon of that same Sunday, a Russian representative
called to invite Roswell to a party that evening in Ames, given by the
Russians for all their American hosts. When Roswell, Mary, and Tom
Chrystal arrived at the Sheldon-Munn Hotel, Tulupnikov was waiting for
Roswell at the door and directed him to Matskevitch. Through his interpreter, Matskevitch told Roswell that his was the first farm of any size
any of his delegation had seen, and that Tulupnikov's report had made
him anxious to see it. Could Roswell persuade the College to take him
there? Roswell tried, but the authorities would not budge on a change in
itinerary. "Do you know how to insist?" Roswell asked Matskevitch.
Matskevitch allowed that he did, and Roswell instructed him to insist on
the following morning that he be taken to Coon Rapids, even if the rest of
the delegation went on to their next stop in Spencer.

On Monday morning the delegation departed for the north, even
though Matskevitch had asked to go to the Garst farm. True to his word,
he had his car stopped, got out, and refused to go anywhere except to
Coon Rapids. It was arranged that the rest of the delegation would continue, but Matskevitch and two others would be driven by Don Murphy of
Wallaces' Farmer to Coon Rapids. Matskevitch spent most of the day with
Roswell, learning about feeding cellulose and protein, inspecting the hybrid seed corn plant, and learning about drought-resistant hybrids and
grain sorghums. Roswell also showed him his current pet project, farm
buildings constructed out of cottonwood, a lightweight and inexpensive
lumber, an idea, however, which did not take hold either in America or
Russia. However, the 2,600-acre farming and managerial operation was
something that at least approached the scale of farming in the USSR, and
the feeding techniques were like nothing Matskevitch had ever seen. He
invited Roswell and Murphy to Russia for the agricultural show in November, then departed to rejoin his delegation in northern Iowa.

Roswell did not immediately accept the invitation. Events had moved
too fast even for him, and he wanted some time to consider the implications and possibilities that might arise from such a visit. In addition to the

easing of cold war tensions Roswell hoped for in such an opportunity, there were practical questions of sales of seed corn, appropriate growing areas and varieties, and the attitude of the State Department towards a personal initiative.

Roswell had not talked with Matskevitch about the purchase of seed corn from Garst and Thomas or Pioneer because the opportunity had not presented itself at their first meeting. "I simply impressed them," he wrote to Arthur Becker,

with the fact that hybrid seed corn was the real basis of corn belt production . . . and then I impressed them with the fact that I think a closer association between the Russians and the United States is a big step toward the easing of world tension – which I sincerely believe to be true – and that they could get lots of good information from us here at Coon Rapids. I think that's all a pretty good start.

To Senator Burke Hickenlooper of Iowa he wrote that "instead of having a World War III in the foreseeable future, I think it is much more likely that we will have a contest of economics – which I think is much more desirable from every standpoint."

Shortly after the invitation was issued, Roswell travelled to Washington to ask State Department officials if they would approve his intention to sell seed and disseminate information about American agricultural practices. Because of the climate of unease and suspicion surrounding even the official exchange, Maguire and Becker advised Roswell to take a low-key approach and to tell State that it was up to them to decide whether or not it was in the best interests of the United States to disseminate agricultural information to Russia. However, Roswell was prepared to argue – and did – that if his request was granted, he should be free to tell them everything he knew about agriculture and to sell equipment and seed if they asked for it. "It would be ridiculous to tell them about how rapidly we could plant corn," he pointed out, "and then say 'we won't sell you a corn planter.' " Officials at the Eastern European desk of the State Department heard Roswell present his case and assured Roswell they would take the matter up "at the highest levels." This was presumably a reference to Secretary of State John Foster Dulles, who was with Eisenhower in Geneva at the first Summit meeting with Khrushchev. Significant moves were also being made at those "highest levels."

Before going to Washington, Roswell wrote his two most revered sources, Henry Wallace and Jonathan, to find out about corn growing in Eastern Europe. From Wallace he received information about the maturity of Russian corn – it was comparable to corn grown in southern Minnesota – and a warning to be very careful about rainfall and temperature in various parts of Russia. He also called Roswell's attention to Hungary

and Rumania as potentially better areas for corn growing than Russia.
From Jonathan, Roswell asked for and received a set of tables showing
temperature and moisture for several areas of Eastern Europe and Russia
in comparison with American cities and a map showing corn-growing
areas in which again Hungary and Rumania were filled with the black
spots of corn acreage. When they returned, Roswell visited Dean Lambert of the University of Nebraska and Lauren Soth. "I think the real
opportunity," he wrote to Arthur Becker in late July, "is to break open not
only Russia but Rumania and Bulgaria and probably some areas in Aus-
tria and Hungary," and he decided to include the Balkans on his itinerary.

Wallace had put Roswell in touch with Dr. Louis Michael, Wallace's
former teacher at Iowa State, an expert on Eastern European corn, and
for many years the agricultural attaché in Belgrade. Michael was at that
time eighty years old but still active in Washington and employed to
estimate and keep a watch on the production potential of the Balkans for
the CIA, according to Roswell. Michael gave him further technical advice, told him to talk only about corn, warned him not to be too curious
about industrial installations or to talk politics, and to give Michael a
report on what he had seen. Michael also outlined the history of pre-
Communist Rumania, describing how the "boyars" – large landowners –
were exiled when the monarchy collapsed. Roswell remarked that this
would have left Rumanian agriculture without any talent, so perhaps they
should have left a few in the country. Michael replied that if they had left
just one boyar it would have been too many; the boyars, he charged, paid
fifteen cents a day to their men, ten cents to their women laborers, and
spent most of their time gambling their profits away in the watering
places of Europe. Michael's hatred of the boyars made a deep impression
on Roswell and helped to form the approach he would take to the present
regimes in Rumania and Hungary.

Two weeks after his first meeting with the State Department,
Roswell was summoned to Washington to hear the decision from "the
highest levels." According to Roswell, the department did not believe he
would have much success with either selling or teaching but agreed to the
trip as an exercise in opening lines of communication with the Soviet
Union, now that official talks had taken place in Geneva. They also
agreed to grant export licenses if Roswell actually managed to sell anything and stamped his passport to allow entry to Hungary, Rumania, and
Czechoslovakia, although the consensus was that those countries would
refuse entry. Unable to find any English-speaking officials at the Rumanian legation, Roswell decided to wait until he reached Moscow before
trying to get visas for the satellite countries.

Roswell was accompanied on this second Washington trip by Geza
Schutz, a long-time friend, Hungarian born, and most recently a labor

negotiator, whom he had chosen to take with him to Eastern Europe. Murphy had been unable to go, a plan to take a geneticist had fallen through, and Matskevitch had tactfully but firmly refused to invite either Elizabeth or one of his sons. A man who always liked to take a crony on his corn-selling expeditions in the old days, Roswell hit upon Schutz as a person with the right personality and the linguistic qualifications to help him now that he would be on the road again. "I have enough sense," he wrote Schutz in his invitation,

to know that to be a good salesman, the linguist has to be able to interpret enthusiasm and the good humor and a desire to be helpful—but these things are not always done by word—frequently the inflection even in English is more important than the word.

There were other old feelings stirring in Roswell at the prospect of this undertaking: the evangelical enthusiasm he had written of to Schutz, the "if it's sound, it will sell" echo from his earliest salesman mentors, and the notion of patriotism and profit that had so appealed to him during the feed-grain controversy of World War II. "He who serves best profits most," Roswell reminded Schutz.

I used to hear the preachers say that when I was at church as a kid. I thought they meant you profited most in inner satisfaction. However, a good long experience has taught me that you not only profit in inner satisfaction which is of course true, but that you also profit in a commercial way.

He thought the adage would bear fruit once again in the sale of hybrids to Eastern Europe. The purchaser, he reminded Schutz, would realize 1000 percent of his investment by the fall of the same year, as many farmers had when they converted to hybrid corn from open-pollinated varieties in the thirties and forties.

But Russia in 1955 was not Nebraska in 1936, and the uncertainties of this venture were different from the purely financial risks he had taken twenty years ago. When Fred Lehmann asked Roswell what the State Department thought about the trip, Roswell replied that about half believed the Russians were interested in accommodation and half considered them hypocritical in their intentions. Lehmann thought it made little difference which view was true; the hypocrite, he said, would be fooling himself first, and a move toward accommodation would set change in motion anyway. Lehmann's remark reminded Roswell of some lines from the song "Only Make-Believe" from Jerome Kern's *Showboat:* "We could make believe I love you / We could make believe that you love me / Cause to tell the truth, I do." Geza played the tune on pianos or accordions during their journey, and it became another "theme song." Underneath its bravado lay a considerable degree of anxiety.

First Trip to Eastern Europe: 1955

Roswell and Geza flew to New York on 20 September 1955 and then to England, spending two days at the agricultural experiment station at Rothamsted, one of Jonathan's favorite haunts, then on to Moscow on 25 September. Roswell submitted a long letter to Matskevitch for translation and submission to the appropriate experts and began with Geza a two-day visit to the permanent agricultural exposition, followed by visits to an experimental station near Moscow, a collective farm (kholkhoz), and the University of Moscow. The last two days in Moscow were spent at the Ministry of Agriculture, during which Roswell gave morning and afternoon lectures followed by question periods to groups of experts on hybrid corn genetics and production, fertilizer, livestock, and poultry. By the end of these sessions, Geza had learned enough to be able to fill in later in the trip when even Roswell began to flag.

Matskevitch, now minister of agriculture, told Roswell that his government wished to buy American hybrids but did not know how much to buy or which varieties. In consultation with Roswell, who had brought along Jonathan's "spotted" map of corn areas in Russia, he worked out an itinerary of areas most promising, concentrated almost entirely in the Ukraine. Roswell was asked to make an inspection tour, recommend a corn-livestock program, and choose the varieties of hybrids that should be planted.

From Moscow the party flew to Kiev, visited the agricultural college and some nearby farms, moved on to the Kharkov region, and worked their way further south toward the agricultural areas around the Black Sea. On this leg of the journey a typical day for Roswell included a visit to an experiment station, kholkhoz, sovkhoz or tractor station in the morning and another in the afternoon. The leaders of each establishment began with a report, including statements on their progress and goals. Roswell would congratulate them on their progress, describe corn farming in the United States, outline the development and virtues of hybrid corn, and how its use could help them. After this exchange, which took approximately one and one-half hours, the party would go into the fields to inspect the crops, livestock, and machinery, and view their feeding methods. Afterwards, there would be a large meal, with wine and toasts, even if they had eaten only two hours before.

The Russian toasts were to cooperation, peace, and "the spirit of Geneva." Roswell replied in kind:

I would point out that if it was sensible to trade information on the peaceful uses of the atom as was done by all countries at Geneva recently, then it was equally sensible for the world to trade information about how to produce more food—

especially meat, eggs and milk – and that meat, eggs and milk were best produced through the use of corn . . . and that Dr. Schutz and I were primarily corn people and that I would therefore propose a toast "peace through corn."

Roswell said that this was his standard toast for three weeks, if he only needed to make one. "I would vary it a little bit," he said, "if I was forced into two."

In the evenings there was more eating and drinking, and both Roswell and Geza found it a struggle to stay afloat in the sea of liquor consumed during evening banquets and toasting. After less trying evenings, Roswell would read or sleep, while Geza and the interpreter played chess and discussed Marx. Geza's presence as a guest who had not been officially invited stretched the complex protocol of the visit in curious ways. One day in a park Roswell asked Geza to buy an ice cream cone for all the party. The Russians would not allow him to pay – except for his own ice cream. He was not invited, they explained.

Except for his forays into Marxist theory, which made Roswell uneasy, Geza proved to be an invaluable companion. He had a Ph.D. in economics, had studied in the United States and abroad, spoke several languages, and was an accomplished musician. Roswell wrote of him:

He could play the Russian folk songs, the Rumanian folk songs, the Hungarian folk songs on an accordion, a piano or a violin and they all love music. He knew their history – he was without doubt exactly cut out as the best possible companion for me. He furnished the culture and I furnished the agriculture.

Along with Louis Michael, Schutz helped Roswell approach Eastern European history, especially agriculture, with a sympathy for the struggles of its peasantry and with a knowledge of the problems Russia faced in the years since the Revolution. Geza's dissertation for the University of Geneva had been a study of the condition of workers and peasants in Central Europe from 1890 to 1914, a condition which had generally been abysmal. Roswell approached Communism as an attempt to deal with that legacy and was prepared to look optimistically for signs of progress in the condition of the peasantry.

In his daily speeches, Roswell made it a point never to begin with unfavorable comparisons between Eastern and Western progress in agriculture; instead, he composed what he called a "preface." He did not begin the preface with 1890, but with 1917, noting that Russia had thirty-eight years to undertake the building of a new society, but not, he emphasized, an uninterrupted thirty-eight years. It had taken at least ten years to increase literacy to acceptable levels and reorganize the country, after the years of civil war following World War I and culminating in the devastation of World War II. Consequently, Russia had only about eighteen years of uninterrupted opportunity. Given these difficulties, the country had made extraordinary progress, which was not comparable with the virtually uninterrupted development of the United States. After this preface, he believed he could talk about deficiencies in Russian agriculture and what might be learned from America without arousing hostility.

The party moved on to Dnepropetrovsk, then to Odessa. At Odessa, Roswell was interrupted during his morning speech, called outside the hall, and informed that Khrushchev, at his summer residence in the Crimea, wanted to see him, and him alone. Geza was not invited. Accompanied by Matskevitch, Mikhail Spivak, secretary of agriculture for the Ukraine, and his interpreter Marina Rytova, Roswell flew to Yalta. It was a two-hour drive to the old Czarist summer residence used by Soviet heads of state. At the house were Anastas Mikoyan, the minister for trade, Ilya Emilianov, and one or two important managers of collective farms.

Roswell spent the bulk of the afternoon with Khrushchev and Mikoyan, who were joined later by Matskevitch and the others. Roswell once again delivered his set pieces on the production of corn, livestock, and chickens and engaged in a lengthy discussion of the possibilities of East-West trade. As he had argued in the United States to Humphrey and others, Roswell stated his view that Russian agricultural production was ten to fifteen years behind its population, while American production was ten to fifteen years ahead. Consequently, Russia should buy substantial amounts of surplus American farm products and gradually reduce the amount as their own agricultural output grew. He promoted his idea that the Russians should buy 20 million hogs.

When the question of what the Soviet Union could export to the United States arose, Mikoyan suggested first paper pulp, then minerals, metals, caviar, and wine. Roswell suggested manganese, to which Mikoyan and Khrushchev were favorably disposed if they could receive food and fiber in return. By the end of the afternoon, Roswell was convinced that they were seriously interested in trade with the West over the long term. Moreover, they were ready to start the more immediate business of buying seed corn the following morning. Khrushchev wanted to get inbreds and single crosses for production in Russia and told Roswell that he wanted to send over engineers to study the drying, grading, treating, and bagging of corn. He was anxious to begin the production of seed corn as soon as possible.

About 5:30 P.M. Khrushchev called for a break in serious conversation and ordered drinks served before dinner. Roswell asked Khrushchev why Russia seemed to know so little about American agriculture. They had easy access to all the farming journals and bulletins of the Department of Agriculture and could have learned everything Roswell told them that afternoon. On the other hand, the secret of the atomic bomb had been carefully guarded but was stolen in three weeks. Khrushchev laughed when he heard this comment translated and raised two fingers: "It only took us two weeks," he said, and replied to Roswell's question with a variation on his potato story. The potato, he explained, had been fenced in by the aristocracy when it was first introduced and was therefore stolen immediately. "You locked up the atomic bomb, so we had to steal it," Khrushchev said. "When you offered us all this information about agriculture for nothing, we thought that might be what it was worth – nothing!" Then, Roswell recounted, he "roared with laughter."

At approximately 7 P.M. the party sat down to a dinner that was supervised by Nina Khrushcheva, who joined the table with her daughter Rada. It was the most bountiful meal yet served and lasted for almost three hours, including drinking time. (Asked what went on after dinner, Roswell replied, "My God, there wasn't any after-dinner!") There were different wines for every course: Mikoyan, a Georgian, argued with Khrushchev over the superiority of Georgian wine, while Khrushchev extolled Ukrainian vintages. Nina Khrushcheva, Roswell noted, kept a discreet eye on Khrushchev's consumption. When he wasn't looking, she had the servants pour only small portions of the new wines into his glass.

The next morning, Khrushchev, Mikoyan, and Matskevitch began negotiating with Roswell for seed corn. Roswell suggested that they plant at least 3 percent of their corn acreage in American hybrids as a demonstration of their potential. Khrushchev asked Matskevitch if that sounded right, Matskevitch concurred, and Khrushchev approved Roswell's figure. On the issue of kernel sizes, things did not go so easily. Roswell's extra supplies consisted mainly of medium-round kernels from the tips of the corn, which were just as good as the flat varieties but still not favored by Iowa farmers. Khrushchev wanted the larger round size, but Roswell was adamant. He could not give the Russians large kernels, he told Khrushchev, because his own customers would feel ill used, and they were his long-term clientele. The sole way to defend his financial and political position at home, he explained, was to sell the smaller kernels abroad. Since the Russians should and would be producing their own hybrid corn within a relatively short time and would be getting a good price on the small kernels they took, they would be losing nothing. Khrushchev gave in and agreed to take medium round and no medium flat.

After discussions about the appropriate varieties, the Russians ordered 5,000 tons in three categories – early maturing, extra early maturing, and medium maturing – as well as some parent stock. Roswell suggested they send a delegation to Coon Rapids to conclude the agreement after they had seen the corn and after Roswell knew exactly what he had available. Roswell suggested a geneticist, an engineer, and a livestock expert, and urged them to come next month, before winter set in. Khrushchev agreed.

In late morning Roswell, his interpreter, and two escorts drove along the coast to Yalta to catch a flight back to Odessa. They stopped along the way for a swim in the mild October sea, stripped to their underwear, and plunged in. Roswell, still a powerful swimmer, struck out from the shore "just like I was going to swim across the Black Sea." He heard shouts from the shore and saw his party waving at him. Thinking that there might be sharks, he returned. There were no sharks: not knowledgeable about Roswell's capacities as a swimmer, they feared for him, and, they candidly admitted, for themselves. "Please don't do that, Mr. Garst," one of them said. "Think what would happen to us if anything happened to you!"

From Odessa, Roswell and Geza journeyed west to Moldavia into territory that had once belonged to Rumania. They stopped in Kishinev, rebuilt after the war, a city surrounded by black, fertile land similar to Iowa. Word of Roswell's meeting with Khrushchev had been published in Moscow, and it was at Kishinev that Daniel Schorr of "CBS News" telephoned Roswell for an account of the meeting. Roswell produced the first news for Western correspondents of Khrushchev's wife and daughter.

At Kishinev, after some difficulty in finding a railway timetable, Roswell and Geza parted with their Russian hosts and entrained for Bucharest, uncertain once again of the nature of their reception. It turned out to be impressive. They were met at the station in Bucharest by a delegation that included the president of the Chamber of Commerce, who held cabinet rank; Virgil Gligor, the deputy minister of agriculture; Silviu Brucan, a newspaper editor and member of Parliament; and Grigor Obrejanu, a leading geneticist. Roswell and Geza were taken to the government guest house for a rest, then feted until midnight at another long dinner. The Rumanians outlined an itinerary of twelve days, which Roswell managed to reduce to eight so he could visit Hungary and be home in time to receive the Russian delegation and any others he might still collect.

After a day spent touring Bucharest, Roswell and Geza were driven to a railway station built for King Carol's personal use, walked on 150 feet of leftover red carpet produced for the occasion, and boarded a private train that provided their accommodations and transportation for most of their visit. They spent several days touring corn fields, experiment stations, collective farms, and state farms. At that time, collectivized farms accounted for only 26 percent of the farmland in Rumania, the remainder consisting of small peasant holdings of 5 to 15 acres each, but comprised of plots that might be in several different places. "They don't know how to handle that one and neither do I," Roswell wrote. They visited a tractor factory, spent two days in the Transylvanian Alps, and journeyed down to Constanta on the Danube Delta, where they went duck hunting. The remaining time was spent in Bucharest.

Roswell found corn yields in Rumania "not too bad," but they were certainly in need of, and anxious to obtain, hybrid seed. Their greatest problem was lack of equipment. "Their lack of mechanization is simply beyond description," he wrote later. Eleven million of 17 million people worked on farms, there were only twenty thousand tractors in the country, and an enormous population of horses and oxen. More than half of their wagon boxes were still constructed from woven willow branches, which meant they could not even scoop corn out of the wagons during harvest but had to shift it all by hand. They watered their livestock from wells that had been dug hundreds of years ago by the Turks, from which, by extracting a three-gallon bucket of water suspended from a pole and rope attachment, one man could water fifty or sixty head of livestock per day. It would have taken thirty men so employed to water the Garst cattle, and when Roswell described his watering tanks with automatic floats and heaters for year-round use, his listeners were incredulous.

Roswell felt more at ease in Rumania than in Russia. The country was much smaller, with a farming area about the same size as Iowa, and its problems and possibilities were on a scale that seemed more manageable. The uncertainties of the journey were beginning to fade, he was more relaxed, and he could deal directly with the English-speaking Brucan, with whom he quickly established a lasting rapport. As in Russia, however, he was touched by the Rumanians' desire to improve their circumstances, their pride in what little improvement had taken place, even if it was only a few trucks, more electricity here and there, or a little more farm produce. "Their present situation is pretty terrible by our standards," he wrote, "but infinitely better than their past."

He had learned more about Rumania than any of the other Eastern European countries from Michael and Schutz, and in his preface he touched upon the long period of Turkish domination from the midfifteenth century until 1858, a grinding feudal system, the rise of fascism in the twentieth century, and the Nazi takeover immediately before World War II. During the war, Americans bombed the Ploesti oil fields, Germans laid waste to the country during their retreat, and Russians were intent on maintaining an influence in the postwar period.

Nor had there yet been any progress in relations with the West, especially with the United States. Westerners were regarded as self-seeking imperialists, Rumanians with dual American citizenship were refused exit visas and in some cases arrested, the American legation was severely restricted in its movements in Rumania (the U.S. State Department responded in kind), and American claims for casualties suffered during the Ploesti raid rankled in official minds. When Roswell visited the American legation for his mail and inquired about visas for travel to America, he encountered equally hostile feelings toward the Rumanians. They were astonished he had been allowed to travel so freely, surprised he should be arranging the visit of a delegation, and doubtful that the State Department would even allow visas for travel in the United States. At best, it would take a long time, he was informed. It was disquieting news.

Roswell then attended a meeting of the full Rumanian cabinet to give his final report. They needed not only hybrid corn, he told them, but machinery, and badly. He thought it probably took them twenty times more man-hours to raise a bushel of corn than it did the United States and urged that they spend $500,000, half on hybrid corn, half on machinery. The corn would increase the yield by 35 percent, and the machinery would demonstrate dramatically the enormous savings they could make in man-hours. Although the idea was appealing, a cabinet member replied, they simply could not afford the investment. Roswell took out a cigarette and held it up in front of him. "In the United States," he said, "a cigarette like that costs three cents."

There are 17 million Rumanians, and 17 million times three cents is $510,000. And I don't want anybody in this cabinet to tell me that you can't afford to spend the price of one cigarette per person to learn how to raise crops with less labor.

The ministers conferred for a few minutes, then told Roswell that he was right. They would find $500,000 and make the purchases, but they needed his help. Roswell advised them to send a delegation consisting of Brucan, Gligor, and Obrejanu. In addition to hybrid corn, they should buy ten complete sets of the best available corn production machinery – tractors, discs, rotary hoes, planters with fertilizer attachments, cultivators – everything, in short, that the Garsts used at Coon Rapids, so that they could have 100-hectare, or half-section demonstration farms in ten different regions of Rumania. He estimated that it would cost about $25,000 per complete set and promised them help in making the farms thrive.

During the meeting Roswell initiated a political discussion for the first time, moving beyond Michael's injunction to talk only about corn. Both Roswell and Geza – who was not excluded from this meeting – urged the Rumanians to allow people with dual citizenship to leave the country and to rescind the travel restrictions on American diplomats. Roswell spoke very plainly on this latter issue. If the Americans saw the whole of Rumania, they would see mostly peasants; if the Rumanians could travel in the United States, they would see much more. "I explained to them," he wrote, "that they were just damn fools because America was so much bigger and there were so many things to see." He urged them to see himself and Geza as "icebreakers," to look more to the West and take advantage of both systems – to become another Switzerland.

Roswell's appreciation of Brucan had grown during their short acquaintance; his pride in Rumania, his droll wit, and his pragmatic desire for Western help for Rumania made a great impression. Roswell's interest in having him come to America was further enhanced by information from the American legation that Brucan was an influential man. Short, round faced, with an endearing – and at times enigmatic – smile, Brucan looked rather like the Roswell Garst of the early thirties. He had read philosophy at the university, been a member of the anti-Fascist underground during the war, and emerged as a member of the first generation of administrators, technocrats, and intellectuals of the new socialist order in Eastern Europe. He was deputy editor of the newspaper *Scintera* and was an articulate, affable, and active man. At the conclusion of their stay, Roswell and Geza (with Brucan along), were received by the prime minister, Georghi Georghiu-Dej. Roswell saw an opportunity to further advance the icebreaking process. The prime minister made a brief speech, remarking that Rumania wanted to improve its relations with the United States. Roswell listened, then, "in his blunt way," as Brucan described the moment, replied to Georghiu-Dej, "if you really want better relations, why do you have an ambassador in the United States who can't speak English, and an interpreter who can't do much better? Why don't you send Brucan as ambassador. He speaks excellent English." The prime minister agreed to consider the matter.

From Bucharest, Roswell and Geza travelled by train to Budapest, to be received by another welcoming committee of high-ranking officials, who urged them to stay longer than Roswell felt they could. Consequently, they stayed only four days but took different routes so that they could see what would ordinarily have taken eight days.

Roswell spent a full day at the Agricultural Research Institute at Martonvasar, located about forty miles southwest of Budapest, on the route to the resort area of Lake Balaton. Here he met Dr. Sandor Rajke (pronounced rýe-key), the newly appointed head of the institute, which operated under the auspices of the Hungarian Academy of Sciences. The son of a kulak, a landowner whose holdings were nationalized during the postwar collectivization of Hungary, Rajke was born and raised on a farm in southeast Hungary near the Rumanian border. During World War II he was a university student and exempt from call up into the Hungarian army, which in 1944 was falling back with the Germans in front of the Red Army. Shortly after he returned to his village to be with his family, Russian armor rolled through early one morning, and he was pressed into service to organize farming in his district. Still within earshot of the Russian guns, Rajke and his men began working 5,000 acres with a total mechanized force of one tractor and two steamers, each a pair of steam engines placed on either side of a field and drawing a plow back and forth between them. He returned to the university in 1945 to complete his undergraduate work and in May of that year rode on the roof of an overcrowded railway coach to western Hungary to begin his first teaching job in genetics and plant breeding.

In 1948 he returned to Budapest, joining the staff of the Ministry of Agriculture, moving to the office of the prime minister and becoming involved in the creation of a research institute at Martonvasar. It was to be a plant research center, Rajke has written, "where theory and practice would be combined, where basic and applied research in plant biology, genetics, physiology, breeding and seed production would form a harmonious, new type of amalgamation." The main thrust of the research was to move along the path of Soviet agrobiology, in the Lysenko tradition.

Martonvasar came into being on 8 June 1949 and in October Rajke left for Russia to study for his Ph.D. at Moscow University. There he met the woman who became his second wife, a distinguished geneticist in her own right, whose German origins caused her a frighteningly close brush with internment in a labor camp during the Stalin era. Rajke was forced to return to Hungary in 1951 by the Stalinist Rakosi regime, survived a Hungarian reign of terror during 1952–53, finished his Ph.D. in Moscow, and in July 1955 came to Martonvasar.

In October 1955, when Roswell came to Hungary, Rajke had just been appointed director for the institute. The amalgamation of research had not proven to be as harmonious in practice as it had in theory. After ten years of existence, Rajke has written recently "the institute resembled nothing so much as an Eastern bazaar, dealing in virtually everything." Ferenc Erdei, Rajke's friend and minister of agriculture, tried to persuade Rajke to work on corn, but Rajke was mainly interested in wheat genetics and under Endre Pap's direction thought that the institute had the field of corn research sufficiently well covered. However, Rajke agreed with Erdei that a concentration of effort was needed, and he was trying to decide the form it should take when Roswell arrived.

A bluff, extroverted Magyar, Rajke was remarkably similar in temperament to Roswell, and the two hit it off immediately, in spite of Rajke's inability as yet to speak English. Rajke was on the verge of a free-wheeling, unorthodox, and controversial career, confident of his abilities, single-minded in his devotion to Martonvasar, a patriot, and a humanist. Roswell was impressed by Rajke's ability and enthusiasm, and Rajke, equally impressed by Roswell, wrote down his impressions of Roswell's quick visit for Erdei and began to consider Roswell's recommendations for the development of a hybrid seed corn industry in Hungary. A few weeks later he was invited to come to Coon Rapids, the only member of the Hungarian delegation specifically requested by Roswell.

"BY the time I got to Rumania," Roswell recalled later, "I knew I wasn't there just to sell seed corn." The commercial feat in opening up this enormous new territory satisfied the salesman in him and would continue to do so. The pleasures of the commercial touch never ceased to attract him. However, the warmth of his reception, the great desire of his new customers to improve themselves, his own capacity for helping, and above all the opportunity to establish an East-West relationship – at least in agriculture – all touched on deeper satisfactions and opened up more that was new than merely a sales territory.

Perhaps for the first time, Roswell had some doubts about the potential for change he had so vigorously pursued. For a while he chewed over the problem of America's national self-interest in the matter. Should Eastern Europe be liberated from their low standard of living or kept at survival level? Roswell decided on the former. The logic of the situation was that there would be no political revolution in either case and that coexistence was the most realistic hope. He also held with Jonathan's hypothesis on hunger and the arms race. "We cannot afford to have one-third of the world possess the atomic bomb and the hydrogen bomb and nothing else – and be hungry at the same time." Ultimately, he decided, it was a matter of "decency alone." Poor diets ought to be improved on whatever part of the map they occurred.

There were many who took exception to this point of view. In December 1955 Marguerite Higgins of the *New York Herald-Tribune* wrote an article on the naive businessmen who were foolishly rushing to do business with the Communists, and at the same time Roswell was receiving critical mail. He fashioned a standard response to his critics:

You may be right – you may be wrong. I may be right – I may be wrong. It is the difference of opinion that makes us a great nation. All I know how to do is to follow my own best judgment.

The diplomatic line was closer to Roswell's view. The foreign ministers followed up the July summit with another meeting on the German question in late October, and on 3 November Secretary of Commerce Sinclair Weeks announced that certain controls on private commercial trade with the Soviet bloc would be eased, "to carry out further the objective urged by President Eisenhower at Geneva in July 'to create conditions which will encourage nations to increase the exchange of peaceful goods throughout the world.'"

For Roswell personally, the underlying and most consistently impelling emotion was excitement. "I wouldn't have missed it for anything," Roswell exclaimed in his family letter, and as the delegations began to arrive he became even more enthusiastic. It was a feeling shared by his European counterparts. Victor Lischienko, a Russian official who was an agricultural student in 1955, recalled how elated he and his fellows were at the prospect of getting information from America, feelings echoed by the Hungarian and Rumanian delegations. The excitement had its roots in the sense of possibilities that Roswell captured in a letter to Secretary Benson in December 1955. "We thought of ourselves as Marco Polos when we were in Russia," he wrote, "they think of themselves as descendants of Columbus – discovering the United States for the second time."

Whose Iron Curtain?

Geza flew from Budapest to Geneva to report on his journey with Roswell to members of the American delegation at the Foreign Ministers' Conference. Disquieted by what he had heard at the American legations in Bucharest and Budapest, Roswell flew directly to Washington to arrange visas for the groups he had invited to the United States, hoping they would arrive before the winter snow. When he left Iowa in late September, visits by Eastern Europeans to America were based on the principle of reciprocity contained in the original exchange of farm delegations, an arrangement geared to slow and cautious movement. The extraordinary and unexpected success of his own visit required Roswell to persuade a reluctant State Department bureaucracy to change its policy and change it quickly.

Much to Roswell's annoyance, the problem of the delay in granting visas and the issue of reciprocity made the front page of the *New York Times* and other papers on 11 November 1955. "A Midwest seed industry representative," Harrison Salisbury wrote that day, "charged the State Department Friday with 'deliberate, misleading distortion' of facts concerning a proposed visit to the United States of Russian seed experts." The seed representative was Geza Schutz, who decided to mount a public attack on the State Department's delay in holding up the visas of ten Soviet delegates who applied to come to the United States at Roswell's invitation. The State Department said that such visits could only occur on "a fully reciprocal basis in an 'orderly' fashion" and that they would take months to arrange.

Schutz maintained that the department had been fully informed about the possibility of such a visit beforehand and had given its tacit support to the arrangements. The visit of the Russians "was entirely at American instigation and initiative," and was intended to conclude contracts provisionally agreed upon in Russia. The visit was therefore reciprocal, Geza was in effect arguing, but on a personal rather than governmental basis. The State Department's expectation that Roswell would not sell anything had been mistaken, and they were now faced with the political consequences of his success.

Initially, Salisbury's State Department sources saw the situation in terms of Cold War gamesmanship. State Department aides "frankly admitted," according to Salisbury, that the Russians "had grabbed the ball on the 'cultural exchange' front," apparently because they knew just what they wanted, while American policy was still "in a state of uncertainty." They believed that the Russians were aware that the United States had not worked out the principles of cultural exchange and saw the visa applications as an attempt to embarrass the country by making proposals that "would be found difficult to accept and equally difficult to refuse." Roswell's visit seemed to have been officially nonexistent. The same officials told Salisbury that there was no American agricultural group ready to go to Russia on an "exchange basis." The gap between the fact of Roswell's experience and the dogma of the Cold War was made strikingly clear.

In addition to this uncertainty about reciprocity, Roswell faced opposition on other specific aspects of the invitations. His most dramatic confrontation came over the invitation extended to Silviu Brucan. The State Department objected to Brucan because he was not an agriculturalist but rather an influential newspaperman and leading spokesman for a government that was still considered outspokenly anti-American. In short, the State Department objected to Brucan for some of the reasons Roswell had put forward for inviting him. When Roswell first appeared in the State Department's Eastern European Affairs Office, he got a flat "no" to the visa for Brucan and was asked to submit another name in his place. Roswell was furious. "You *are* going to let him come," he replied. "No, we are not," countered the State Department spokesman, thumping the table with his fist. "You *are* going to let him come," Roswell insisted, "and I'll tell you why." He would write an article for the *Saturday Evening Post* entitled, "Whose Iron Curtain?" if they refused; and, he continued, "you don't dare let me write that kind of an article." Roswell said he was going to wire Brucan not to unpack his bags, and he expected the State Department to countermand their refusal to issue the visa:

I'll be back up here tomorrow morning to find out which way it is. If you don't [issue the visa] I'm going to write the article for the *Saturday Evening Post,* and if you don't think I have guts enough to do it just try me!

It took more than overnight, but the vehemence of Roswell's argument— Maguire said he had never heard anyone use such strong language in the halls of the State Department before—had a salutary effect. Approximately a week later, Brucan was reinstated as a member of the delegation.

The size of the delegation, which numbered ten, created a problem for Roswell as well as for the State Department, and he was quite prepared to compromise on this issue. As Khrushchev had said, the Russians were in a hurry for a great deal of technical knowledge and consequently wanted to send a variety of experts, but Roswell did not think it would be practical for him to deal with so many people. He suggested that the Soviets be allowed to send five now and five later; the final figure was simply five.

Although the State Department had by now accepted in principle the visit of the delegations, the Department of Commerce created another hitch by holding up the export licenses for anything the delegations might buy, while it considered whether such agricultural equipment and commodities had strategic value for the Russians. The fallacy in the Commerce Department, Roswell complained later, was that

someone in some of the departments that Commerce advised with apparently thought that we had a monopoly on farm machinery – that we had a monopoly on hybrid seed corn and the hybrid seed corn know-how – that we had practically a monopoly on brains. It just so happens that we do not have monopolies on any of the above.

He pointed out that France, Italy, Yugoslavia, Hungary, and Mexico had hybrid corn, and the West Germans, Czechs, and even the Russians were making farm machinery. America was not the only source for technology in these fields, so that there was no question, in Roswell's view, of ultimately being able to deny information to the East. It was better to reap the advantages of providing these things in the United States rather than sending the Eastern Europeans to other markets. Roswell telephoned these arguments to his Washington negotiator, and also pointed out Eisenhower's message to Congress asking for surplus commodities to be sold to the East. The licenses were finally granted.

There were further small points to settle along the way, even while the delegations were in America. The Rumanians did not get their visas until they provided housing for an additional staff member at the American embassy in Bucharest, and the State Department's list of restricted areas included a number of colleges Roswell wished the delegations to visit. Roswell worked these matters out along the way, but once, in a moment of frustration, asked State to send him a list of their restricted areas so that he wouldn't inadvertently venture into one if, for example, the delegation wanted to know something about turkeys.

The first of the delegations to arrive that fall were the Russians, a serious and rather somber group of specialists, but led by Ilya Emilianov. Unprepossessing in appearance ("mousey," one observer called him) and not at all flamboyant in manner, he nevertheless demonstrated then and later as agricultural attaché in Washington his ability to influence the views of others and the decisions they would make. "I think you should make the following points," he would advise before a meeting, and in such a way operated effectively from the sidelines. The Russians looked at the operation in Coon Rapids, received the plans for the seed corn plant, and travelled extensively in other areas of the Corn Belt, sometimes with and sometimes without Roswell.

The arrival of the Russian delegation brought into Roswell's life Valerie Tereshtenko, who was to prove an invaluable interpreter, business assistant, and friend in all his future dealings with the Russians. In the fall of 1955, Tereshtenko, a Russian-born emigré, was teaching economics and banking at Columbia University and consulting part time for a New York investment house. His name had been given to Phil Maguire as someone knowledgeable in agricultural economics. Tereshtenko had accompanied a representative from the Department of Agriculture to Russia during the 1947 drought and famine and had met Khrushchev in the Ukraine. Maguire telephoned Tereshtenko and asked him to apply for two weeks' leave from Columbia to work for Roswell. He met Roswell and the party of five Russians in New York a few days later and accompanied the party to Coon Rapids.

The technology of American hybrid seed corn production was relatively new to the Russian delegation but completely unknown to Tereshtenko. He did not know what the sorting and grading machines in the plant were doing, either in English or in Russian. That night, he told Roswell that he didn't think he could do the job. However, with no one else available on short notice, or perhaps at all, Roswell decided to give Tereshtenko an intensive briefing on the plant, with the understanding that Tereshtenko would then explain it to the Russians as best he could and let the Russians worry about technical words. The plan worked, and Tereshtenko, who was able to pick up a technical vocabulary from the Russians when he himself was stuck, extended his two weeks' leave into two months of travel with the Russian delegation.

While the Russians were travelling in the United States, the Rumanian delegation arrived in New York. Its members were three of those who had met Roswell's train in Bucharest: Brucan; Virgil Gligor, assistant minister of agriculture and a livestock expert; and Grigor Obrejanu, assistant director for the Rumanian Agricultural Research Institute. Their final difficulty in entering the United States involved a film on Rumanian agriculture they brought, which passed through customs only after Geza telephoned the State Department. Roswell arranged a press conference for the delegation at the Waldorf-Astoria Hotel, then whisked them off to Coon Rapids.

After being outfitted for the Iowa winter at the Garst Store, the delegation was initiated into the rituals of the Roswellian tour. They visited Garst and Thomas, drove through fields and pastures ("He used his car like a horse," Brucan remarked), ate breakfast at the South Side Cafe while Roswell held court, heard about cellulose and urea, and enjoyed the experience immensely. They were intrigued by the absence of workmen at the feed lots and came back several times in freezing weather to watch the automatic watering tank, with which Roswell had impressed them so much in Rumania. "The Rumanians were really the most open and interesting of the groups," one Coon Rapids observer noted:

They would see something like an automatic waterer and they just couldn't believe how the water got to that place. They were delightful and they weren't ashamed of being ignorant.

Like all the Eastern European delegations, the Rumanians were impressed that Roswell, Elizabeth, and the children all worked. The image of the absentee capitalist landlord, living in luxury on the proceeds of his wage slaves, was a preconception they all freely admitted having brought with them. They were completely unprepared for the midwestern lifestyle.

During their stay in the United States, they travelled with Roswell to Chicago and Minneapolis, visited the John Deere and International Harvester plants, and ordered equipment. Roswell did the ordering and the bargaining for the ten sets of equipment they bought, and, when International Harvester declined to send a service representative with their equipment because their branches in Eastern Europe had been nationalized, arranged for the actual sale to take place through the Grettenberg Implement Company of Coon Rapids. The Grettenbergs agreed to send a mechanic to Rumania to service the machines and teach the Rumanians how to maintain them. Finally, Jonathan Garst and Geza Schutz escorted them around California, paying particular attention to the delta of the Sacramento River, which resembled the Danube delta farming region, and also took them to the University of California agricultural research station at Davis.

Before the Rumanians left the country, the Hungarians arrived. In addition to Rajke, the delegation consisted of J. Keseru, another wartime university student, now at twenty-nine the director of the largest state farm in Hungary, and Mikos Csillag, head of the department of heavy machinery in the Ministry of Agriculture. Csillag, a brother-in-law of the Hungarian leader Matyas Rakosi, was not an agriculturalist, but rather was what Rajke called the "political" of the delegation, watchful of the behavior of his companions. In Paris, Rajke arranged to meet Keseru and Csillag at the Gare du Nord one afternoon to catch the train to London, from whence they travelled by ship to the United States. Rajke stopped at the Louvre after visiting a friend, and almost missed his rendezvous. He rushed to the station in a taxi and was confronted by a white-faced Csillag, who thought he had defected.

Keseru's main impression of his visit was of the contrast between the kind of agriculture he had learned at the university and currently practiced, and the agriculture of continuous corn, high technology, efficient labor, and advanced feeding methods. "We had to rethink all of our knowledge," he recalled. "We were not only shocked by the technology, but the efficiency and economy of the Iowa farming methods. We thought we would try to perfect a revolution of this kind." Keseru found Roswell enthusiastic, single-minded, and "fanatical" in his aims for agriculture and recalled an occasion on which they brought out some of their best Hungarian wine to present to the Garsts at Christmas:

Mr. Garst was speaking to Mr. Csillag about maize. We opened the wine and poured it into small glasses to toast. We expected that when he tasted it that we would then tell him how nice it was. We were disappointed because in fact he had no reaction at all. He just went on talking to Mr. Csillag about maize.

For Rajke, the prospect of a concentration on wheat and corn by his research institute began to emerge at Coon Rapids. Roswell advised him that in addition to a plant at Martonvasar, he should install plants and research facilities in each of the regions of Hungary as well to assure the most efficient breeding of the corn for each area. Rajke decided to take Roswell's advice. "It is no exaggeration to say," he has written recently,

that the discussions held under Bob Garst's leadership at the Garst Farm and on at least a dozen other Iowa farms, at the seed processing plant of the Garst and Thomas Hybrid Corn Company, with Jimmy Wallace at the Pioneer Hi-Bred Corn Company headquarters, with Bill Brown at the Pioneer research laboratories and with Professor Sprague at Iowa State University, together with the debates in the family circle, stretching into the night, on what we had seen and heard, had a decisive influence on my career.

Between 5 December 1955 and 5 February 1956 Roswell concluded contracts for substantial amounts of seed corn and parent stock for Russia, Rumania, and Hungary; presided over the sale of farm equipment and of three complete seed corn plants purchased by the Russians; and gave freely and exhaustively of his knowledge. The business aims of his trip to

Eastern Europe and the consequent visit of the delegations were grati-
fyingly fulfilled. He profited and served and demonstrated to a doubting
officialdom that he could find a market where none seemed to exist.

Roswell's success with his delegations brought him into conflict with
yet another governmental agency, the Federal Bureau of Investigation
(FBI). During the weeks of their visit, a dossier on Roswell's activities
was rapidly growing, and would eventually reach 205 pages, of which 180
have been released under the Freedom of Information Act. Unfortunately,
virtually all of those available are either completely or largely blacked out
under the exemptions granted by the act. What remains demonstrates
that Roswell's relations with the agency during these years fluctuated
from cooperative to stormy.

The FBI picked up news of his impending trip to Russia from newspaper clippings but did not contemplate "additional investigation regarding Garst or Maguire" at that time. However, the controversy over the
admission of the Rumanians and the other delegations was closely followed by the Washington Field Office, including a report of Roswell's
"two-hour lecture on the intricacy of the hybrid corn seed business" that
he had delivered to the State Department. After the visas were granted,
Roswell was approached directly by the Omaha Field Office. He was
initially cooperative, reporting among other things that he had not been
approached "for intelligence purposes." He promised to let them know if
that happened.

However, while he was in Chicago with the Rumanian delegation,
Roswell marched into the FBI Field Office to accuse the bureau of holding up a cable the Rumanian legation wished to send to Bucharest and of
placing the Rumanian delegation under surveillance. The bureau dismissed these as "unfounded allegations" and the field operatives were
instructed to have "no further contact with Garst" without "specific" bureau authority. A similar confrontation in Chicago was alluded to in
another document, this time over the Russian delegation. "Difficulty was
encountered," the memorandum stated, "due to Garst's outspoken manner."

Various forms of surveillance continued. For a 1957 visit, Omaha,
Minneapolis, and Chicago were instructed to "cover the activities of the
delegation," and the firms visited by Roswell on behalf of the Rumanians
that year were visited afterward by bureau operatives. Having elected to
avoid the possibility of further confrontation with Roswell, the bureau
sidestepped him by cultivating a source within Garst and Thomas to
report the comings and goings of the Eastern Europeans.

On one occasion, when an agent was in Coon Rapids speaking to his contact, Roswell entered the building. "Mr. Garst," the agent reported with obvious relief, "exhibited a friendly attitude," then engaged in a lengthy discourse for the agent of his farming operations and the "interests of foreign countries in learning modern farming techniques used by Mr. Garst." Roswell explained what the delegations were doing, and even threw in Khrushchev's potato story. The agent seemed to find it an instructive afternoon.

Roswell does not seem to have come under personal suspicion. After a review of his files in 1959, the bureau saw "no indication in our files of any subversive activities, membership in communist front groups or the Communist Party, and it is quite apparent that his main interest in Russia and the satellites is in the sale of his product to these countries." By 1960, they were again in direct contact with him and, over the telephone at least, found that he "appeared friendly and cooperative."

Months of Progress, Days of Disappointment: 1956

Silviu Brucan returned to Rumania in January 1956. By March he was on his way back to the United States as ambassador, having been appointed by Georghiu-Dej, who decided to take Roswell's advice. Brucan and his government set about repairing relations between the two countries: the Rumanians issued exit visas to ten people with dual citizenship and were studying further cases; they invited the new United States minister in Bucharest to visit factories and other points of interest; and they invited a number of nonagriculturalists, including writers, musicians, and athletes, to visit Rumania.

The most newsworthy initiative in the United States was the Rumanian offer to negotiate a settlement of United States claims for war damages over the WW II Ploesti raid and property nationalized by the Rumanian government, an initiative first broached by the Rumanians in early April 1956 and made public on 1 May in a news story by Dana Adams Schmidt of the *New York Times*. In the story, linked to the presentation by Brucan of his credentials to President Eisenhower, Schmidt commented on these recent developments in United States-Rumanian relations and reported at length remarks by both Eisenhower and Brucan at their meeting.

Eisenhower's "cordial tone" in his remarks to Brucan, the article said, suggested that the U.S. response to the Rumanian note might be favorable and that the American government on its part would consider releasing Rumanian gold bullion that had been frozen by the United States as partial compensation for the nationalization of American property and war damages. Brucan remarked that his government and people cherished "a sentiment of friendship for the American people," and were "whole-heartedly ready" to participate in an improvement of relations.

The president responded in kind, noting that America had "constantly supported" measures for improving relations.

Roswell was delighted with the story and immediately wrote to Brucan to congratulate him. "This is real progress," he wrote,

progress which I hope and expect will continue. . . . So I am proud this morning— proud in feeling that I have been helpful—and happy that I have been helpful— and that the Garst Family has been in a position to be helpful and to continue to be helpful from now on.

Agricultural help was being continued by further exchanges. Another Rumanian delegation was to come to Coon Rapids to watch the fertilizing and planting operations, which Roswell had also arranged to have filmed, and it had been agreed with the Rumanians in December that Stephen and David, along with their wives, would visit Rumania during planting and harvesting to train and supervise Rumanian technicians and workers in the growing and harvesting of hybrid seed that was purchased at Coon Rapids. They would be taking along Harold Smouse of the Grettenberg Implement Company, who would perform a similar mission with the machinery that was now on its way to Rumania. In February 1956 Brucan replied:

We have chosen the fields that will be sown to this corn, the mechanics who will operate the machines, the place where Mr. Smouse will instruct the mechanics, as well as the men who are going to conduct this important experiment. We have also selected the interpreters for Mr. Smouse, Steve, and Dave.

Brucan invited Roswell and Elizabeth to return to Rumania sometime during this period, as well as Geza Schutz, and proposed another hunting party on the Danube Delta. ("We suppose," Brucan remarked, "you will have to receive your wives' permission for this hunting-party, which may prove a more difficult matter than to obtain an export license from the State Department.")

During April, when the governmental initiatives were getting underway, David, his wife Jo, and Harold Smouse were already in Rumania, engaged in the work outlined by Brucan and acting in a quasi-diplomatic role as well. The Rumanian papers reported in late April:

Mr. [David] Garst and Mr. Smouse have met Rumanian agricultural specialists and have visited state farms and agricultural colleges in different parts of the country. They have visited industrial enterprises and cultural establishments as well, and have had the opportunity of seeing some aspects of the economic and cultural life of the Rumanian People's Republic.

A later report centered on the activities of David's wife Jo, who made official visits to schools and displays of handcrafts and accompanied David on some of his rounds.

Imposing a high-level technology even on a small scale proved difficult from the beginning. The plan for ten experimental farms proved overly ambitious for an unexpected reason. The farms, all collectives, were much too big for a standard complement of machinery for even a large American operation. Consequently, it was decided to divide the equipment among only three state farms; at Fundulea, the largest and soon to be the site of the major research station suggested by Roswell; at Dragalina; and at Justin Georgescu. Harold Smouse, who stayed in the country from April through November, moved from farm to farm during the spring planting, instructing groups of mechanics and keeping the machines going. The International Harvester "IH" symbol on the back of his jacket made him an immediately recognizable figure in the fields, and he was almost constantly on call to repair machinery. Tools were scarce and often disappeared into the pockets and kits of his eager pupils. Smouse is famous in Coon Rapids for his telegram to Grettenberg Implement Company: "Not for my sake, but for God's sake, send more pliers!"

When the planting was finished, and after an emotional farewell, David and Jo departed, to be replaced by Stephen and Mary. In a long letter at the end of August, Stephen described their problems and their progress. He discovered that the average yield of Rumanian corn was from twenty-five to thirty bushels, with a forty-bushel yield causing as much excitement as ninety bushels would at home. The corn had a poor root system, commercial fertilizer had been used up to now only on wheat, ears and stalks were small, and root worm a serious enemy. In the experimental fields of hybrid corn, only a single variety had been planted in each area, and even at the experimental stations no more than half the varieties had been planted in one place. This meant that it would take longer to find out how each variety performed in the various regions of the country. However, in the plains around Bucharest, the variety planted, 301, was so far "doing a good job," Stephen reported.

There were also problems in finding enough wagons for the harvest, the spray rigs and spray for root worm had not arrived in time, and the silage was to be put into deep pits "designed," Stephen wrote, "by the devil to break men's backs." Some of the machines didn't work well because none of the fields had been levelled, roads were inadequate or nonexistent, and the fertilizer available was in powder form, which caused it to plug up the spreaders.

In spite of these problems, Stephen was optimistic. On one farm, overseen personally by Buccor Schiopu (the minister for state farms), Stephen saw a fertilized field that he thought would make seventy bushels. Schiopu himself, Stephen wrote, "reminds me a little bit of you. He is willing to plunge on his own." Schiopu was eager to experiment with fertilizer and could evaluate Rumanian agriculture with such capitalist values as time, efficiency, and quantity. This was particularly true in the production of chickens and eggs, and Stephen urged his hosts to send a representative to the United States to study the production of chickens for meat and for laying eggs. "There is a terrific amount of activity going on in the country," he explained:

Everywhere, they are building roads, water systems, machine shops, putting in gas lines, and I think are well on their way. Rumania has quite a potential— agriculture can be doubled in production fairly easily, especially when one compares it with a country such as Mexico. They are going to finally achieve a fair degree of prosperity with or without our help. I would rather end up helping them and end up being their friend than to remain a stumbling block as we have in the past and end up having them being unfriendly.

Schiopu, Stephen added, asked almost daily when Roswell and Jonathan were going to come to Rumania, and he particularly needed help in organizing fertilizer production. "It looks to me like you have another trip in order, whether you really want to or not."

There was also time for entertainment. "Last night," Stephen reported,

Mary and I had our 7th wedding anniversary. Mary received enough flowers to make it look like a funeral home. We had a big party in the evening and ended dancing to our own private 8-piece orchestra, on our own little terrace. Suica, wine, beer, dancing, cognac, and eight courses of dinner lasted til 3 A.M. Mary is still recovering.

THE Russians planted the largest amount of Pioneer seed in the spring of 1956, and Mikhail Spivak, the Ukrainian minister of agriculture, described to Jack Raymond of the *New York Times* the great increase in hybrid seeds. The Ukraine was experimenting with twenty varieties of seed bought in the United States and within two years intended to go entirely to hybrids. The day before the interview, Trofim Lysenko resigned as head of the All-Union Academy of Agricultural Science. Spivak, according to Raymond, "was inclined to be tolerant" toward him, and said that Lysenko was not opposed to hybrid corn planting but only sought to limit it to research purposes.

As well as seed corn, agricultural information was also flowing into Russia from the West. When Emilianov and his delegation left the United States in the late fall of 1955, Amtorg, the New York-based Russian trade organization, engaged Valerie Tereshtenko to screen and transmit useful pamphlets and articles on a variety of agricultural topics to Russia for translation. Tereshtenko spent several months in early 1956 selecting more than seven hundred documents, which he passed on to Amtorg. The work of Paul Manglesdorf at Harvard was already known in Russia, but among works newly translated in 1955 was *Corn and Corn Growing,* by Henry Wallace and Earl Bressman. Emilianov, who had published on the subject for some time, founded the journal *Kukuruza* (corn), and A. S. Shevchenko, Khrushchev's principal agricultural advisor, was preparing a book on corn. Another member of Emilianov's delegation, Shmanenkov, was preparing a book on the American feed industry.

Before Shmanenkov's work appeared, two other accounts from the 1955 experience in America appeared in 1955 and 1956. The first was the account of the initial Russian delegation in the summer of 1955, *Report on the Visit to the USA and Canada of the Soviet Agricultural Delegation,* published in Moscow that same year. The bulk of the book described in detail each farm or industry visited by the delegation and contained a large number of drawings of equipment and facilities. It also described the organization of Iowa State University, the county agent and research station system, and the state and federal connection with American agriculture, noting the lack of a national planting "syllabus" and the degree of local autonomy. According to the delegation, the lessons to be drawn for collective and state farms were the raising of productivity, the lessening of unit production costs through uniform practices and mechanization, the importance of taking into account the cost of labor, and the use of labor-saving devices. Apart from the technical material, there appeared in the introduction and conclusion such matters as a quotation from the original editorial in the *Des Moines Register,* the intention on the Soviet side in recent years to establish closer links in agricultural matters, and the "spirit of Geneva" evoked by the summit meeting in the summer of 1955.

The other work was a pamphlet written by Roswell in August 1956, translated by Tereshtenko, with a preface on Roswell written by Emilianov. Approximately 25,000 copies were printed in Russian, and later in Rumanian. Roswell entitled his work *Food Unlimited . . . and Good Food,* which Tereshtenko translated as *Maize . . . a Reliable Source of Abundance.* In his own introduction, subtitled "An Outline of Corn Production and Corn Usage," Roswell listed six conditions necessary for the most efficient production of corn: hybrid seed, fertilization, irrigation (where necessary), mechanization, the use of insecticides, and the use of herbicides. The last two — insecticides and herbicides — did not receive separate chapters but were discussed within the text. The chapter on hybridization was printed in the November/December 1956 issue of *Corn.*

The pamphlet was an extended bulletin of the type Roswell did so well, a simple, lucid exposition of the basic principles of modern farming practice in the midwestern United States. He wrote five chapters — on

hybridization, fertilization, irrigation, mechanization (in which he included insecticides and herbicides), the uses of corn, and the uses of the
whole plant for cattle. The last chapter on the whole plant was one that
Khrushchev liked particularly, Tereshtenko reported to Roswell in 1958.
The little book stressed the interdependence of the new technologies that
had been developed in agriculture. "No one thing raises a maximum crop
with minimum labor," Roswell explained.

It takes a combination of good practices and the yields will be no better than the
weakest link in the chain. . . . It is the coordination of doing a good job on *all* of
the things that lets most people, most areas, most countries double corn production with less and less hours of man labor.

Both the book and pamphlet appear to have had wide distribution among
the agricultural hierarchy. Perhaps more importantly, they reflect the
ideas that were being talked about and circulated informally within the
agricultural establishments in Russia, Rumania, and Hungary, and which
now had the imprimatur of official approval.

During the Emilianov visit, Roswell's return to the Soviet Union had
been informally discussed. In September 1956 Georgi N. Zaroubin, Soviet
ambassador in Washington, issued a formal invitation to Roswell; to Bill
Brown, the chief geneticist at Pioneer; and to Jack Mathys, head of the
Garden and Packet Division of Northrup, King, and Company of Minneapolis from whom the Russians purchased sweet corn and a company
that had traded with Eastern Europe before the war. Roswell and Mathys
also brought their wives and were accompanied by Valerie Tereshtenko.
Roswell wrote to Matskevitch that he thought it was "very worthwhile to
encourage Mrs. Mathys and Mrs. Garst to come along with us this Fall so
that they too could realize the probability and hope of increasingly
friendly relations." (Elizabeth maintained that she had been invited only
because Jack Mathys had first invited his wife to accompany him.) They
planned to arrive in Russia in early October and stay until 17 October, so
that they could then spend three days each in Rumania, Hungary, Czechoslovakia, and Poland. Their intent in the first three countries was to see
the corn in the fields at several different locations.

In Russia the party followed a route very similar to that taken by
Roswell during the previous year, looking this time at the 5,000 tons of
hybrid corn dispersed throughout the southern farming areas.

They found the Russian corn program was well launched. "One of the
most amazing things to me," Bill Brown wrote home in mid-October,

has been the extent to which the Russians have developed their own hybrid corn
industry . . . this year they have in production 9,000 hectares of parent single
cross seed. . . . I saw one seed corn plant under construction. It is as large as, or

larger than Coon Rapids and is expected to be finished in December. We were told that in addition three other smaller plants were in about the same stage of construction.

During the trip, Roswell displayed his traditional public style, and Elizabeth came into her own as an ambassador of good will. During a visit to the botanical gardens in Sukhumi, a town in the Georgian Republic, Roswell decided to stretch out on the grass. Matskevitch, personally responsible for Roswell's well-being and afraid that he might get pneumonia in the wet grass, urged him to get up. "Explain my rules to him, Valerie," Roswell instructed Tereshtenko, who recited Edward Garst's aphorism, "never stand up when you can sit, never sit when you can lie down." Elizabeth, in a more serious vein, spoke to Mrs. Matskevitch at a dinner party on the common aspirations of women the world over for their children, and caused Mrs. Matskevitch to burst into tears. "I think we had better toast the women," Matskevitch gallantly responded.

Early in October Khrushchev was staying at his villa in Sochi on the eastern shore of the Black Sea entertaining Marshal Tito and Erno Gero, who had taken control of the Hungarian Communist Party that summer after the fall of Rakosi. It is not known whether Khrushchev intended to summon Roswell again, but in any case, events in Poland would have overtaken any such plan.

Since his accession to power in 1955, Khrushchev had made a series of decisions that had produced ferment and expectation within Eastern Europe. In addition to his more Westward-looking policy and agricultural reforms, Khrushchev implied in a visit to Tito that the satellite nations might enjoy greater self-determination, and in February 1956 at the Party Congress he exposed the crimes of Stalin and set in motion the dismantling of the Gulag Archipelago. The possibilities for the establishment of more liberal regimes as a result of de-Stalinization sent waves of hope through the satellite community and tremors of fear through its old-line Stalinist leaders. Poland, restless and mutinous since the early fifties, became the first test of the amount of freedom that Khrushchev was prepared to tolerate. When the Garst party left Russia, Khrushchev was occupied with the question of intervention in Poland.

In Rumania Roswell found his family name "a household word," as one Rumanian put it, and relations between the American legation and the Rumanian government vastly improved. The corn Roswell sold and that his sons and Harold Smouse helped to raise looked good, especially variety 301. At a Rumanian function in Bucharest's old Athenee Palace Hotel, Roswell favored his audience with "Old Man River," and at a party sponsored by the American embassy, when his turn came to speak, he got up and sang "Oh What a Beautiful Morning." The corn on the Bucharest plain was perhaps not quite as high as an elephant's eye, but things were certainly going Roswell's way.

Roswell had by now ascended from optimism into euphoria, both over the prospects for his corn and for the pace of developing relations with the Eastern bloc. In Bucharest, his feelings produced an expansiveness of behavior at the Rumanian banquet, which was described by Robert Thayer of the American legation. Much to Thayer's discomfort, Roswell brought up in public the issues being negotiated by both sides, launching into "a long tirade," as Thayer described it, on Rumania's refusal to allow U.S. citizens to return home. Among his "fantastic" remarks, Roswell stated that if the Rumanians sent back the three hundred citizens, he was sure Thayer would be willing to make an arrangement on Rumania's financial claims against the United States. A mere $20 million made little difference to the American government, but three hundred citizens did. Thayer interposed a strong objection to "bartering" human beings for financial considerations, but it "made no impression" on Garst, who continued "in the above vein" for most of the evening. "He even went so far," Thayer concluded, his diplomatic sensibilities by now exceedingly frayed, "as to announce in a loud voice that what Rumania needed was capital in order to purchase road grading machinery and that the United States should see that she got it."

FROM Bucharest, the party travelled by private train to Budapest, there to be received by Sandor Rajke and other officials. They continued their trip by car to Martonvasar, the 7,000-acre experimental farm and research station located on the former estate of the dukes of Brunswick, onetime patrons of Beethoven. In 1956 the eighteenth century manor house served as the headquarters for the station that also contained the Rajke apartment and overlooked a small lake, where concerts were held on an island in the summer. It was, and still is, an idyllic setting, although further populated today with a research laboratory, and, a few kilometers away, a large corn and wheat processing plant. At Martonvasar, Roswell sat down with Rajke before a map of Hungary and plotted the locations of the thirteen regional seed plants, all of which are in operation today. The party returned to Budapest on 23 October, the eve of the Hungarian uprising.

In Hungary, the attack on Stalin and other speeches made at the Twentieth Congress in February 1956, according to Miklos Molnar, "hit Hungarian life like a stone falling into a wasp's nest." In universities, factories, and offices, people discussed the implications of anti-Stalinism and nationalism for Hungary, still ruled by Matyas Rakosi, a Stalinist hard-liner. The Petofi Circle, devoted to free political discussion, was established by the Federation of Working Youth in the spring of 1956, and Hungarian party leaders during this time were ordered by Moscow to read the secret speech of Khrushchev at party assemblies. Intellectual ferment grew throughout the summer, dissent against the Rakosi regime was expressed at meetings, and by the fall, even in the newspapers. The revolt in late June at Poznan, in Poland, had frightened Rakosi, who attempted to arrest four hundred members of the opposition. However, Mikoyan arrived in Budapest in July to forbid the arrests and to declare that Russia was withdrawing its support from Rakosi, who resigned on 21 July. Unfortunately, he was replaced by Erno Gero, another Stalinist, who carried on a program of ruthless suppression despite the virtual disintegration of the Hungarian Communist Party. Replacing one figurehead with another was simply not enough when fundamental changes now seemed possible.

The main thrusts of rising expectations were the desire to reform the existing party apparatus in Hungary and to become independent of Russia. Although there was a substantial body of opinion anxious to reassert the Western tradition of Hungarian life, none of the groups involved offered a plan to renounce socialism and return to capitalism. In the beginning, at least, the dissidents looked for reformation in party politics and greater independence in choosing national policies, for change rather than revolution, for realignment rather than apostasy. According to Molnar, who was a participant in these months of excitement, there was no ideology or clear model for change put forward; rather, the country was united by its aspiration for freedom. The political leader who became the focus for these newly released feelings was Imry Nagy, a moderate party member, who seems to have had this role quite suddenly thrust upon him.

By October 1956 de-Stalinization had lost its momentum in Hungary but not in Poland, and it was that country the Hungarian students in particular looked to as a model for their own hopes for change. Vladislaw Gomulka and his more nationalistic wing of the Polish Communist Party had outmaneuvered the Stalinist wing, and by the time of the meeting of the Polish Central Committee on 19 October, Khrushchev was alarmed enough by this turn of events to intervene. Khrushchev, Kaganovich, Mikoyan, and Molotov turned up unannounced at this meeting in Warsaw but found a majority of the Central Committee and the government determined on a more liberal policy. On 21 October, Gomulka was elected first secretary, Khrushchev acceded, and Soviet troops returned to their bases.

Demonstrations of support for the Poles by students and other Hungarian groups materialized between 16 and 22 October, culminating in Budapest on 22 October when 5,000 people approved a fourteen-point program that included the withdrawal of all Soviet troops from Hungary and noninterventionist treaties with both Russia and Yugoslavia. On 23 October the Petofi Circle forced the government to withdraw a ban on a proposed march that day, and just before 2 P.M. a procession led by thousands of students began to work its way to the center of the city. The procession marched along a two-mile route, across the inner boulevard of Pest on the left bank, across the Danube via the Marguerite Bridge, which also spans the southern tip of Marguerite Island, and proceeded to Bem Square on the Buda side of the river. By now there were about 300,000 people on the streets, and part of the procession went back across the bridge to Kossuth Square, the crowd chanting slogans such as "We want a Hungarian government," and "Russians go home." The march had turned into a revolution. More people gathered at Parliament House that evening in Kossuth Square, others marched about in the main streets, and shots were fired about 9 P.M.

The Garst party arrived in Budapest late in the afternoon and that evening made their way to the opera through crowds of marching and milling demonstrators. Their Hungarian interpreter, although obviously agitated, dismissed the extraordinary scene as "nothing special," according to Tereshtenko, but during the performance he went outside several times. Afterward they moved through the crowds to their car and were driven through dark back streets to the Grand Hotel on Marguerite Island, where they had been staying. About 2 A.M. Tereshtenko and Brown were awakened by the sound of automatic weapons. Brown jumped out of bed and went to the window. "Get back," Tereshtenko ordered. "I have more experience in these matters—when you hear machinegun fire, you stay *away* from windows!" "I hear shooting," Elizabeth called to Roswell at about the same time. "You're dreaming," he replied. "Go back to sleep."

By morning the inhabitants of the Grand Hotel discovered, along with the rest of Budapest, that an armed uprising was in progress. The fighting began at the radio station, then spread toward the factories and the depots containing arms and ammunition. Russian tanks moved into Budapest late that night but at the moment could only patrol the main boulevards and the bridges. From the Grand Hotel, a tank on each end of Marguerite Bridge was visible.

For the next ten days the guests of the hotel remained idle and isolated as battles and negotiations ebbed and flowed on the mainland. The hotel became an assembly point for foreign visitors stranded by the fighting, who found themselves guests of the government on the island, with instructions to stay put. "Don't worry," the manager observed early on, "it's just a misunderstanding." Roswell and Elizabeth played a great deal of bridge and socialized with the international community. For the first few days gunfire could be heard sporadically from the factory district down the river.

On 28 October a truce was concluded between the rebels and the combined Hungarian special police units and Russian forces, and by 29 October the Russian tanks were on their way out of the city. On approximately November 3 the Poles produced an old coaling ship that would take the international party up the Danube to Czechoslovakia. The ship could not berth at the island, so the 150 refugees straggled down the river to a wharf, followed by a baggage truck with Elizabeth in the cab and Roswell perched on the baggage.

The wharf was already crowded with people who had brought letters to be delivered out of the country; the Garsts had a final visit from Mr. Fono, an ex-aristocrat and expert on garden seeds, who told Roswell that the only happy time in Hungary's history had been the reign of Suleiman the Magnificent. Roswell passed out gum and Life Savers to the children on the boat, took a searing drink of moonshine liquor offered by an old peasant, and with the rest of the party settled down as best he could on the grimy collier. On this occasion he did not sing "Old Man River."

The boat got underway in the evening, chugged its way north, turned west as it reached the Czechoslovak frontier, and ran out of coal about 2 A.M. It moored of necessity at a steep bank, adjacent to an open field, and the party sat on the collier awaiting the arrival of Czech customs officials. They arrived, climbed down the bank on a makeshift ladder, and began a lengthy conversation with Tereshtenko, who spoke Czech. "Damn it, Valerie," Roswell exclaimed finally in exasperation. "You tell them we want to get off this boat!" Eventually they made the steep ascent and walked to an improvised interrogation point, which consisted of a few tables illuminated by a string of lights. The Czechs interviewed every family, with Tereshtenko translating as well as he could in some common language. "I'm a refugee from Iowa," Elizabeth said when her turn came. They were taken by truck to the local railroad station, fed soup by the Red Cross, and sent to Prague.

At the American embassy in Prague Roswell discovered that Nagy's new government had proclaimed its neutrality and withdrawn from the Warsaw Pact, thereby bringing upon itself the full force of Russian arms. On 4 November the Russian tanks returned to Budapest and were bloodily dispatching the fierce but vastly outgunned resistance. Although ready to accept some degree of accommodation, as he had in Poland, Khrushchev decided that Hungary had gone too far. Furthermore, on 31 October the Anglo-French invasion of Suez was launched, and Prague was full of talk of a third world war. Long lines of people tried to buy foodstuffs in anticipation of shortages and siege. Czechoslovakia closed her border to Hungary, and all of Eastern Europe was uneasy.

With the promise of Rumania dissipated by the tragic events in Budapest, tired and dispirited by the ignominious departure up the Danube and the talk of war, Roswell was ready to go home. Tereshtenko urged him to explore the possibilities in Czechoslovakia, continue to Warsaw, and then on to Moscow to conclude the agreement for next year's corn deliveries. Roswell did visit the Department of Agriculture in Prague, but, very much out of the mood to go East, sent Tereshtenko on to Warsaw and Moscow. Tereshtenko had little success in Warsaw and in Moscow received a wire from Roswell, now home, telling him not to sign any agreement for the sale of corn. Roswell had declared a personal moratorium on East-West relations.

CHAPTER EIGHT

Starting Again

Aftermath of Hungary

"I am terribly disheartened about the recent turn of events," Roswell wrote in early January 1957 to Gabriel Reiner, a travel agent just leaving for an exploratory tour of Russia and the satellite countries.

In the summer of 1955 when Matskevitch came over I thought I saw the first opening that might lead to a more peaceful world. That feeling grew with me all through the winter of '55–'56 – and all through the year 1956 until Budapest. It seems to me it is becoming worse daily since Budapest – and I do not see much likelihood in its reversing for quite a long period. It makes me heartsick of course – and I hope ever so much that I am wrong.

Roswell had come to believe in a rapid movement from communism to socialism in the East in line with Jonathan's theory that the state would continue to control the large industries but would relinquish the smaller industries and services to private hands and increase their efficiency and their freedom. Now he saw no hope for any kind of relaxation "in the foreseeable future." Euphoria had given way to depression. He was, he wrote to Reiner,

presently afraid to invite Russians to come to the United States because of fear of incidents. And I have a good deal less fear along these lines than most Americans. I am afraid to sell even as innocent a product as seed corn to the Russians for fear the material would not be loaded on ships without incidents and bad publicity. The bitterness against the Russians is even greater than it was before Matskevitch came to the United States.

To Tereshtenko he confided his belief that this feeling was justified. In view of the Russians' mockery of their October 1956 declaration about rights for the satellites, he wrote, and until they decided once again to take the issue seriously, "I have no desire to renew the pleasant relationship I did have with the men in government in the USSR." He would

215

continue to pursue contacts with the Russian "colonies," but not with Russia herself.

However, by March depression had in turn given way to activism and to a decision to resume relations with Russia as well as with the satellites. Although he initially contemplated another trip to the East, he settled on a different approach. He wrote Leon Pearson that he would

just stay at home and visit with and *display* and *demonstrate* to them what they can do – and how to do it most efficiently – teach them how to avoid all of the mistakes we did make in our surge forward. I believe it can be better done here at Coon Rapids than anywhere else in the United States.

Starting in February, Roswell began negotiations with the Polish embassy for the visit to Coon Rapids of a delegation and in March had Tereshtenko get in touch with the Czechoslovakian government to encourage a visit. With the Danube valley farming area in mind, Roswell organized a small display of irrigation at Coon Rapids, even though it was not practiced there. He also attempted to arrange for a visit by a Bulgarian delegation.

Bulgaria presented difficulties because relations between this small Balkan state and the United States were still at the stage they had been with Rumania in 1955. Roswell had met Peter Voutov, the Bulgarian ambassador, had liked him, and had invited him to Coon Rapids. Voutov said he would like to come, but was restricted to a twenty-five-mile radius of New York City. Roswell managed to send corn and grain sorghum seed to Bulgaria in April and was informed that the seed would be sown in experimental institutes in three different districts of Bulgaria. In May and June the Czech and Polish ambassadors visited Coon Rapids, and in late summer a delegation appeared from Warsaw.

There remained, as Roswell put it, "the curious problem of what to do about Hungary." Because of a slight drought in Hungary and Rumania in 1956, the American hybrids showed themselves at their best and produced well beyond the 35 percent increase over other varieties. Consequently, on the morning of the Hungarian revolution, Ferenc Erdei, the minister of agriculture, told Roswell that he wished to order 1,000 tons for 1957. Nothing was heard from the Hungarians until February 1957, when they repeated their order. Roswell vacillated. He went to the State Department, discussed the matter with them, and decided not to sell the corn. After a talk with a refugee geneticist, he thought he would sell, but only if encouraged to do so by the State Department. Maguire advised him that the State Department was still feeling "tough" about Hungary but would probably be less so after the UN debate on 10 September and advised Roswell to do nothing until that time.

Roswell was ambivalent about Russia. In June he told Tereshtenko, "I have, frankly, been in confusion and hoping that the confusion would end, but it hasn't entirely ended." However, he thought that the political situation had improved sufficiently to consider selling corn to Russia next year, "if conditions remain as they are now—or improve only slightly." But he was not at all sure that Pioneer of Des Moines would be willing to do so "unless they improve quite a lot." He wrote a letter to the Russian ambassador, thought about it for a week, then threw it away. Finally, he decided to reestablish relations in a quiet way,

to just be quietly helpful and courteous and decent—to do business with them just as I would do it with my domestic customers—to be helpful in showing them how to raise the biggest corn crop possible—and to show them how to use that corn with the greatest efficiency.

His inclination to do business with the Eastern Europeans once again was fortified by news reaching him in the fall of 1957. In September Harrison Salisbury, travelling for the *New York Times* in Eastern Europe, wrote from Bucharest that "United States Secret Agent 301 has sowed the seeds of a made-in-America revolution in Rumania." The secret agent was the Pioneer 301 that Stephen had seen prospering on the Bucharest plain and Salisbury saw as "by no means limited in its consequences to crops or agriculture." Its success, and Roswell's, Salisbury learned, were at the root of the new rapprochement in American-Rumanian relations. The "American revolution" in Rumania, Salisbury was told, was a direct consequence of selling hybrids to Russia first, thereby creating official acceptance of the use of Western technology. "I cannot tell you," Salisbury wrote to Roswell after he had returned home,

how many times I had to promise to convey to you the greetings of these good people to you and to repeat to you their persistent demand, reiterated over and over again, that you come again and visit them, the sooner and longer the better.

Gabriel Reiner of Cosmos Travel visited Rumania in October and brought similar news. "I met with their Prime Minister Stoica Chiou," Reiner wrote to Roswell. "We talked quite a bit about you, and it seems, without question, your name is fixed in their history, regardless of politics, in honor of your great contribution."

Roswell received news from Russia in October from Valerie Tereshtenko, travelling in the Krasnodar region with George Finley, whose company, Finco, had sold the seed plants to Russia and Rumania. "The memory of your visit," Tereshtenko wrote,

is as vivid as if you were there yesterday. Everybody spoke highly of you, regretted that you did not come this time, and sent you his or her best regards—from Mr. Zenkov who travelled with us last year to Georgia to the girls who served that unforgettable "lunch" after your lecture to 50 assembled specialists.

At home, there was more good news in the report of the National Planning Association, which confirmed that Khrushchev was still committed to carrying out his intention of improving the diet of the Soviet people. If the drive was "carried out vigorously with a serious effort to reach the Khrushchev goal," the report said, "the Russians will have to divert resources away from heavy industry and military preparation towards agriculture. . . . This is a 'butter instead of guns' policy and, if really carried out, should be applauded everywhere."

Spurred by these gratifying reports, Roswell approached Charley Thomas and Pioneer in December and January of the new year 1958 about selling corn to Russia. He noted the profit the two companies had made from the sale of 365,000 bushels of seed corn, 770 bushels of parent stock, and 1,360 bushels of grain sorghum, but spent much of the letter putting their business in the context of East-West relations. Pioneer was not entirely convinced, nor was Charley Thomas, but they agreed to go along if Roswell felt it to be that important.

Roswell himself was not entirely convinced. On 7 January he cabled Tereshtenko in Moscow to draw up contracts; on 10 January he cabled him to stop the sales. It was primarily the reaction at Garst and Thomas that caused his hesitation; if his action divided the company, he wrote Fred Lehmann, he "just figured it wasn't worth it." However, he did not think the decision on 10 January was "necessarily permanent." Indeed, it only lasted for four days. On 14 January he cabled Tereshtenko to proceed.

IN Moscow, Tereshtenko was having more problems than Roswell's changes of mind. He arrived in Moscow on 17 December to begin negotiations for sales and for the visit to Coon Rapids of a delegation but found Emilianov away on holiday, and Matskevitch, now in the Central State Planning Administration, a very difficult man to see. When he finally reached Matskevitch he was told that nothing could be done without Emilianov, so it was not until February, after the telegrams from Roswell, that Tereshtenko could make any progress. Emilianov returned to attend an All-Union conference on corn production in February, over which Matskevitch was presiding. Unable to reach anybody by telephone, Tereshtenko concocted a cable in which he said he was conveying Roswell's greetings to all the participants in the conference, whose work he followed with great interest. In view of the recent agreement on cultural, technical, and educational exchanges reached by the United States and the Soviet Union, Roswell, Tereshtenko said, hoped for further contacts with Soviet agriculture. "Three hours later," Tereshtenko wrote,

"I received a call from the ministry, and the whole business went into motion." As soon as the conference ended, Tereshtenko, Emilianov, and Matskevitch got together and it was agreed to send a delegation to Coon Rapids.

In May the delegation was organized. Matskevitch told Tereshtenko that Khrushchev kept reminding him that Roswell, on his visit to the chairman in the Crimea, had promised to demonstrate his methods of field work. Khrushchev was anxious to pursue this invitation and blamed Matskevitch for the failure to follow up. Consequently, in addition to Emilianov and an interpreter, two "field workers," Alexander Gitalov and Vassily Shuydko, would spend the entire summer and part of the harvesting season in Coon Rapids. Gitalov was the head of a tractor brigade of the Ukrainian Machine Tractor Station, a man with a great reputation for efficiency and a personal friend of Matskevitch. Shuydko was an engineer in charge of a similar station in the Krasnodar region. The delegation arrived in Coon Rapids in June; the Russian link once again existed.

On 13 June 1958 Roswell celebrated his sixtieth birthday by taking the afternoon off, but not because he was tired. He felt, he said, "like a firehorse waiting for the whistle to blow – or a coon hound in the fall."

His feelings derived partly from the anticipation of a big year for Garst and Thomas, partly from the arrival of the Russians. As Khrushchev desired, Roswell put Gitalov and Shuydko to work immediately. They planted grain sorghum, cultivated crops, chopped hay, and fed cattle. His own aim, he said, was to demonstrate to them that "while one man could not farm 100 hectares, six men could farm 800 hectares with ease."

Gitalov, Shuydko, and Emilianov stayed through October, living with John Chrystal, who became their official host and companion. When they were not working or observing in Coon Rapids, they travelled to state universities and to other farming operations and carried on negotiations for the purchase of cattle. They assiduously pursued their mandate from Khrushchev to gain practical experience.

During 1958 Roswell renewed his Eastern European travels, primarily in Yugoslavia, and regained the momentum that had slipped away after the events of October 1956. In December Roswell sent the Khrushchevs a telegram containing a New Year's greeting, and received a reply from the Soviet embassy on 26 December. "I am requested to inform you," the ambassador wrote, "that N. S. Khrushchev received your telegram for which he would like to thank you: on his part he sends you the best wishes for the coming New Year from his family and himself."

Conversation with Khrushchev

Roswell opened the new year by entertaining a delegation from
Bulgaria in January of 1959. Tereshtenko brought them along, but only
after Roswell and Phil Maguire had arranged visas. The United States
had no formal relations as yet with Bulgaria. During this visit, Anastas
Mikoyan arrived in Washington and Roswell left immediately to see him.
The next day Tereshtenko brought the Bulgarians to Washington, where
they attended a reception given by Mikoyan. Roswell achieved a further
minor thaw in the Cold War by introducing the Bulgarians to the American officials present.

Roswell was anxious to see Mikoyan for two reasons. The first concerned a misunderstanding with the 1958 delegation over farm machinery
that was being ordered. Roswell told them that one man could farm a
large acreage, but only if he did it on a cooperative basis with other
farmers, so that they could divide the work. The delegation was unable to
explain this satisfactorily at home, and confusion and suspicion had arisen
over the order. "Your bureaucracy is as bad as ours," Roswell complained
while explaining the situation. "Fellow Bolshevik!" Mikoyan exclaimed
and reached across the table to shake his hand.

Roswell wished to see Khrushchev again, and Mikoyan agreed to
arrange it. Roswell and Elizabeth were taking a Mediterranean holiday in
February and March that would take them as far as Lebanon. It was
agreed that the Garsts would stop in Rome to receive a message from the
chairman and interrupt their scheduled journey to fly to Moscow.

Back in Coon Rapids, Roswell wrote to Khrushchev to confirm the
general arrangement and explain why he wished to talk directly with the
Soviet leader. He was "extremely disappointed" because his recommendations made last summer (and reviewed in the letter) had not been accepted in their entirety. He did not want to be connected with the failure
that was "sure to come from the partial acceptance of broad recommendations." He had told Mikoyan, he continued, that he no longer wished to
entertain guests who received advice but did not act.

I am perfectly willing to contribute my time and my energy and my thoughts to
the helping of you in your promotion of greater agricultural productivity in the
Soviet Union if you are going to accept that advice and act upon it. But I am
impatient with the fact that your government, after studying my recommendations, divided my recommendations by ten, whereas I thought they should have
been multiplied by ten.

Men who had small ideas were described by his father as people who
would take two bites at a cherry, he said, and he had been taught to look
down on such people. It was very tough talk, indeed.

In addition, Roswell wanted to speak to Khrushchev about "getting this armaments race stopped." It was "the most important single thing" facing the world today, requiring the improvement of relations between the United States and the USSR so that the world could cease wasting its industrial capacity "preparing for a war that nobody wants—nobody expects—a war that no one could survive."

With this blunt preface in the mail, the Garsts set off on their holiday, found a message from Khrushchev awaiting them in Rome, and flew from there to Moscow. Vladimir Matskevitch met them in Moscow, escorted them to Krasnodar to observe one of the new seed corn plants, then through the Caucasus to Sochi on the Black Sea. After a day's wait in town while the chairman finished talks with Prime Minister Harold Macmillan, Matskevitch, Ilya Emilianov, interpreter Marina Rytova, who had been in Coon Rapids in 1958, and the Garsts spent a day at the premier's dacha with the Khrushchevs. For the most part, it was a relaxed and intimate visit. In his memoirs, Khrushchev recalled that Roswell and his wife, "a lovely woman," had visited him and that "we spent a few relaxed hours on the balcony of our state dacha on the shore of the blue waters of the Black Sea." Elizabeth found Khrushchev affable and humorous and Nina Khrushcheva, who was now learning English, charming and impressive. The chairman, Roswell, Emilianov, and Matskevitch talked mostly Russian agriculture in the warm afternoon sun.

The only change in Khrushchev's temper came after Roswell moved into a discourse on the arms race. The chairman, Roswell remarked, was a poor horse trader; he had to spend 20 percent of his gross national product to keep up with the arms race; the United States had to spend only 10 percent. "Why the hell don't you quit the arms race?" Roswell concluded. "How would you like to be surrounded by air bases?" Khrushchev replied in a suddenly angry voice and recited a list of U.S. military installations in Turkey and Western Europe. Roswell countered with the opinion that America was not going to war, nor was Russia; they should be competing in foodstuffs rather than arms. "You ought to laugh about those bases," Roswell said. Khrushchev, however, was not amused.

By the time of this second Black Sea meeting, Khrushchev's appraisal of Roswell as a knowledgeable and helpful Western connection was fully confirmed and formed the core of their relationship. There were also other considerations that made the two men easy in each other's company. They preferred the slower rhythms of conversation, laced with anecdotes and proverbs, carried on at length, and out of which their intensity and energy might occasionally erupt (Khrushchev was irritated at Vienna in 1961 with Kennedy's brusque and efficient manner). They shared a similar kind of humor and set considerable value on it. Khrushchev was genu-

inely interested in agriculture and enjoyed talking about it. He also enjoyed foreigners and perhaps found some release in conversation with
sympathetic outsiders. Both were aggressive and argumentative when
they disagreed; neither was put off by the appearance of these traits in
the other. Rather, in such exchanges they perhaps sensed a more fundamental congruence. They both possessed an overriding desire to achieve
rapid and comprehensive change; they were both campaigners. At their
first meeting Roswell was convinced of Khrushchev's determination to
change the direction of Soviet agriculture. In his memoirs, Khrushchev
repeated an anecdote about Roswell in which he saw and admired a
similar drive. On his tours of Soviet farms, Khrushchev had been told,
Roswell would get very angry if he saw someone doing something "stupid." "I was told," Khrushchev recounted,

that one day he dropped in at a state farm during corn planting. He saw that the
farmers were sowing the corn without simultaneously fertilizing the soil. He
pounced on somebody, saying, "What do you think you're doing? Don't you know
you need fertilizer here?" The chairman of the collective farm explained that
mineral fertilizer had already been put in the soil. Garst brought himself up short,
his eyes flashing under his thick brows. Who knows what he would have done if
he'd been in charge?

Roswell's direct appeals to Khrushchev to halt the arms race are
above all a testament to the strength of his own convictions on the subject
and to "having good guts." He persistently called upon Khrushchev to
divert money from arms to agriculture, accompanied by practical suggestions on how such money should be spent. In the sixties there is evidence
that Roswell's public linkage of the two issues was useful to Khrushchev
in marshalling support for these policies. It was very much the way in
which Roswell hoped that he might be helpful.

At the conclusion of their visit, Elizabeth invited the Khrushchevs to
visit them in Coon Rapids if they should come to America. Khrushchev
replied that if he did make the journey, he would certainly do so.

Khrushchev told the Garsts that relations between the United States
and Bulgaria had been regularized, so that they could now make a visit to
that country. They travelled by train from Hungary, visiting collective
farms and conferring with Bulgarian agricultural officials. At one farm a
group of women who were planting tomatoes when the Garst party arrived interrupted their labor to collect a bouquet of daffodils and presented them to Elizabeth with good wishes from the workers of Bulgaria
to the workers of America. They returned home in mid-April.

IN 1959 the USDA estimated corn production in the Soviet Union for
1958 at 600 million bushels, more than double the 1957 harvest and well

above the previous high in 1956. The average for 1950–54 had been about 190 million bushels. Khrushchev's corn campaign was thus far a success, and he had pressed home his advantage at a Central Committee meeting on agriculture in February 1959. The "antiparty" group of Malenkov, Kaganovich, Molotov, Bulganin, and Shepilov were castigated for having opposed his agricultural policies; American methods, especially those of Roswell Garst, were very much at the center of the proceedings. "We must send some people to Mr. Garst in the USA," Khrushchev said during the meeting. "We have had very good relations with him." Khrushchev also referred to the letter Roswell had sent as a preface to his recent visit and from which the recommendations were extracted for public presentation. "In the letter which he wrote us," Khrushchev said, "there are examples of good agricultural practices."

At another session of the five-day meeting, Alexander Gitalov reported on his experiences on the Garst farm. "Does he have a good setup?" Khrushchev asked. "Yes, very good," Gitalov replied. "At Garst's I worked as a tractor driver and fed 800 head of stock." "You see," Khrushchev quipped, "he worked for the Americans" and got a laugh out of the committee. Later, Khrushchev recalled Roswell's invitation to send workmen to his farm:

Comrade Gitalov did go there to work and he learned a lot from Mr. Garst. We are indebted to him. We Communists are always reproached for allegedly just criticizing the capitalists. But, as you can see, we thank a capitalist farmer for useful information.

In closing the meeting, Khrushchev renewed his call for competition with the United States, comparing it to a horse race:

If this metaphor is applied to our competition with the USA in the field of agriculture, what should our horse be? Obviously, there's no better horse to choose than corn. Corn's the horse we need.

Khrushchev in Coon Rapids

On 6 August Roswell was informed that the Soviet leader had expressed a desire to visit Coon Rapids during his forthcoming visit to the United States. Roswell's connection with Khrushchev suddenly became international news.

Much of August was devoted to the demands of this new level of recognition, as journalists began telephoning and appearing. Roswell gave happily of his time for interviews with American and foreign newsmen and prepared statements for Radio Moscow, *Izvestia,* and a Russian trade journal. By 28 August the State Department received 471 requests for accreditation by journalists who wished to cover Khrushchev on the farm, "still a month ahead of the story," Roswell enthused. "I think the

very name 'Coon Rapids' intrigues everyone," he wrote to Ed Boss of the
Hotel Fort Des Moines, who was debating whether to serve Khrushchev
choice or prime grade beef on the evening of his arrival in Des Moines.
The implications of this deluge of coverage were not further remarked
upon.

His mail increased in volume to the extent that he had to compose a
form reply. In the form letter he described his relationship with Khrushchev and his desire for a continuing improvement in the East-West
dialogue. Most of the correspondence expressed hopes similar to
Roswell's. About 20 percent, according to Roswell's estimate, contained
bitter condemnations of him. Roswell personally answered another kind
of letter—what he called "cases of compassion," pleas to him to act on
behalf of relatives who wished to leave Eastern Europe. Roswell compiled a list of thirty-one requests, sent letters to the respective embassies,
took up the matter personally with Khrushchev, and continued to pursue
them after the visit. He was successful with at least four.

Roswell had his own ideas about the shape the Khrushchev visit
should take and corresponded with everyone involved in the arrangements. Early on he asked for twenty-four hours and invited both Eisenhower and Nixon, thereby making the farm the focal point for the entire
visit. When an overnight stay in Des Moines and a day-long visit to the
farm and to Iowa State were decided upon, Roswell put forward another
suggestion privately to Khrushchev—that the chairman should tiptoe out
of his hotel in Des Moines at 6 A.M. without the official entourage and
come with Roswell to Coon Rapids for a quiet viewing of the farm and a
chat. Khrushchev was much amused by this piece of innocence. "If I tried
to run off secretly with Garst when he came to fetch me," he wrote in his
memoirs, "it might appear that I'd been kidnapped, like a bride in the
Caucasus."

A few days before the visit the vanguard of the media arrived, and as
James Reston reported in the New York *Times,* everything but the hogs
was wired for sound. In town, a telephone communications center was
established for both the press and the official entourage; on the farm, the
wire services commandeered barns and erected aerials, while television
crews sited cameras at potentially strategic points around the house and
farmyard. The space beyond the front lawn of the house was a maze of
cables, power units, and other technical paraphernalia; reporters were
turning up regularly to view the interior of the house. On the eve of the
visit, Roswell decided not to make a pooling arrangement for the press,
but rather to let them all come.

THE day itself, Wednesday, 23 September, dawned bright and calm. The
farmhouse, resting comfortably on a knoll just off the highway that

Silviu Brucan, a member of the first Rumanian agricultural delegation, with Roswell in Coon Rapids in 1956. Brucan later served his country as ambassador to the United States and afterwards to the United Nations. (Photograph by Ken Scarpino)

The Garsts with Chairman Khrushchev at Sochi in the spring of 1959. Khrushchev, already well acquainted with Roswell, recalled the visit as "a few relaxed hours at the Soviet state dacha overlooking the Black Sea." Left to right: *interpreter Marina Rytova, Elizabeth Garst, Ilya Emilianov, Chairman Khrushchev, Vladimir Matskevitch (Minister of Agriculture), and Roswell.*

(Above) *Khrushchev amid the crush at the Garst farm in 1959, walking up to the house. He is near the CBS van; his white hat may be seen below the cameraman standing on the van. (Photograph by Joe Munroe)*

Roswell, looking unhappy, escorting Khrushchev around the farm buildings, using a walkie-talkie attached to a bull horn in an attempt to be heard by reporters. Directly behind him is Henry Cabot Lodge, Khrushchev's escort for the American journey. (Photograph by Joe Munroe)

Roswell throwing silage to clear reporters off a trench silo. This was the most widely reproduced photo of the visit. (Wide World Photos, Inc.)

The Garsts and the Khrushchevs, back at the Garst farm and walking in a more tranquil mood to the luncheon tent. Coming out the front door is Phil Maguire, Roswell's Washington attorney. (Photograph by Joe Munroe)

Adlai Stevenson, Garst, and Khrushchev sharing a joke with Henry Cabot Lodge, who is not pictured. (Photograph by Joe Munroe)

Roswell and John Chrystal in Russia in 1963.

With the Khrushchevs in 1963 at their dacha outside Moscow. In this picture, autographed by Khrushchev, are (left to right) *interpreter Marina Rytova, Chairman Khrushchev, his daughter Rada, Roswell, son-in-law Adzhubei, Nina Khrushcheva, John Chrystal, and another Khrushchev daughter.*

Another autographed picture of Khrushchev and Garst at the country dacha in 1963. They talked and occasionally argued on a whole range of subjects, "a general conversation you might have with anybody," John Chrystal reported.

Dear Mrs Garst!

Thank you for the books and other things that I've got from your husband in my house.

I send some foto-album of Moscow and Leningrad. I hope You had no time to take such ones when you were here.

Best wishes to You
and the whole family.

Excuse my bad English.
I'm forgetting the language
every month and every
day. 63 = is the age!
    Be happy!
        Nina Khrushcheva
Moscow
15/V. 1963.

A letter written during the 1963 visit by Nina Khrushcheva for Elizabeth, brought back by Roswell. (Courtesy Elizabeth Garst)

Elizabeth and Roswell in front of their farm home, 1959.
(Photograph by Joe Munroe)

touches Coon Rapids to the south, looked prosperously midwestern, indicating its uniqueness only by a wrought-iron "g" proprietorially affixed to its white wooden front. The trees, bushes, and flowers of Elizabeth's garden encompassed the grounds with beauty, impervious to the depredations of the previous week. Beyond the house and stretching up the hill lay a feed mill, assorted other buildings, and a feedlot filled with cattle fattening on cellulose and urea. The farm was encircled by National Guardsmen, whose numbers lined the drive to the highway and stretched eastward—over seven hundred of them—along the seventy-six miles to Des Moines. Roswell and Elizabeth had spent the night in Des Moines and were on the highway with the Khrushchev party.

As the sun burned off the morning dew, onlookers began to gather at the farm. Reporters poked around, finding access to the house easy, and camera crews made preliminary sitings. An occasional vehicle moved up the farm road, the sun began to disappear behind clouds, and the calm of the morning dissipated suddenly with the sighting of the official party. The lead cars turned left onto the wooden bridge over Spring Branch Creek, followed by seven busloads of the press. Nina Khrushcheva and her daughter Rada accompanied Elizabeth into the house, while the main party set off to view the feeding operation on the farm. Newsmen swarmed around the party, officially led by United Nations Ambassador Henry Cabot Lodge, covering the farm like a visitation of locusts. "There were hordes of people following us," Khrushchev later recalled,

a whole army of journalists—journalists in all directions as far as the eye could see. It reminded me of what Prokop, the game-keeper on our shooting preserve in the Ukraine, used to say to me when I asked him how the hunting looked. "Well, Comrade Prokop, any ducks today?" "Ducks everywhere, Comrade Khrushchev," he'd answer in Ukrainian. "Ducks as far as the eyes can see—more ducks than shit."

Roswell grew increasingly annoyed as reporters and photographers obstructed views of buildings, livestock, and feed. He shouted at them and at one point ordered a horseman to mount a charge. The most publicized incident occurred a few miles away from the home farm at a trench silo scooped out of a hillside for the storage of silage. As Roswell tried to explain its construction to Khrushchev, photographers and newsmen swirled around him. "If you fellows don't move out of the way, I'm going to kick you out of the way," he threatened, and executed a wide, half-kicking movement that caught his friend Harrison Salisbury of the *New York Times*. "Even if your name is Harrison Salisbury!" he added. Both Salisbury and Khrushchev laughed. (Years later, accepting an invitation to visit Coon Rapids again, Salisbury wrote that he would love to come; "I'm sure I'll get a big kick out of it.") It was here that Roswell launched his silage-throwing offensive and ensured for posterity his reputation as "colorful."

In spite of the crowds and the skirmishing, the purposes of the visit were being accomplished. Khrushchev saw the operation and carried on conversation and repartee with his host. "You know," Roswell said to the chairman at one point, "we two farmers could soon settle the problems of the world faster than diplomats." "Oh, excuse me," he added when he looked around to see Henry Cabot Lodge standing nearby. At lunch under a tent on the north lawn, Khrushchev, Garst, and Roswell's guest Adlai Stevenson sat together at the table and talked at length on a range of world problems from health to trade, from armaments inspection to the ability of the two countries to shift to peacetime economies. At an impromptu press conference after lunch, Stevenson was very hopeful over the negotiations that were to open later that week with President Eisenhower at Camp David. When asked if there was any "give" in the Russian position on arms limitation, Stevenson replied, "maybe it is not so much a matter of 'give' as of education." Another reporter asked Khrushchev whether Garst had put him into a good mood for the Camp David conference. "He's been creating that mood ever since we met in the Crimea," Khrushchev replied.

After lunch Elizabeth took Nina Khrushcheva on a brief tour of the farm, pointing out the silage as "sauerkraut for cattle," and the Garsts and Khrushchevs gathered on the front lawn for pictures. The Khrushchev entourage moved on to Iowa State University, and in the fading afternoon light Roswell concluded his performance with a television interview conducted by Morgan Beatty of NBC.

THE printed response of the press to the day's events varied considerably, both in emphasis and interpretation. A few reporters, their feelings ruffled by Roswell's aggressive gestures, centered their reporting on this clash in their lead stories as well as in features, portraying Roswell as the villain of the piece and implying that his actions constituted a threat to the freedom of the press. One reporter referred to his "palatial" home in a context that suggested it was a fortress of unrepentant capitalism (a home that Khrushchev thought remarkably unpretentious). Later in the week *Life* magazine labeled the affair "A Cornball Act Down On The Farm," focused on the activities of a portly gate-crasher, and missed or ignored the opportunity to link this visit to Coon Rapids with their own article written eleven years earlier by John Dos Passos on the farming revolution, which in effect explained why Khrushchev had come in 1959.

James Reston chose to look critically at the role of the press, noting in the *Times* there were so many reporters covering the story that they changed the story. They were no longer the witnesses of history, he wrote, "but principal characters in the drama," smothering the story and each other:

Never in the history of journalism have so many resourceful scribblers kept each other from following a big story closely, or written so much on a character they couldn't hear and often couldn't see. There were so many of them around today they changed everything at the Garst Farm but the smell.

The *Des Moines Register* and the *New York Times* gave better balanced accounts of the day. Salisbury, who knew Roswell well enough to judge that there was as much showmanship as anger in his performance, retired to an empty feedlot that afternoon and wrote a story that led with Stevenson's remark on "give" in the forthcoming negotiations. Although his story included a description of Roswell's pugnacious behavior, the context was firmly that of the larger dimensions of the visit. Morgan Beatty, who had prepared himself well on the background of Roswell's activities, conducted his television interview in a manner that allowed Roswell to expound his views on arms and agriculture.

The visit brought another flood of mail, most of it sympathetic. Roswell was praised for cutting the diplomatic fog, for presenting "the real America," and for demonstrating American hospitality. His treatment of the press was generally regarded as salutary, and several people contrasted Roswell's friendly behavior to Khrushchev with the belligerency of the mayor of Los Angeles. His warmth, honesty, and sincerity were generally remarked upon, as well as his effective if unorthodox diplomacy. There was, in short, in this small sample, evidence for the beginning of a climate of acceptance for the attitudes Roswell represented.

But there were also letters of disapproval, a number of them from Garst and Thomas customers. One person wrote that he had bought eighty bushels of corn but was now cancelling his order and suggested that if Roswell liked the Russians so much, he should go live with them. "I don't want to live with them—never have, of course," Roswell replied. "Neither do I particularly want to die with them. With hydrogen and atomic bombs, I really think we have that choice—living with them or dying with them on this earth."

KHRUSHCHEV's remarks raised high hopes for progress in the new atmosphere. In the October issue of *Foreign Affairs* he discussed the prospects for disarmament and trade and concluded that we faced a choice between peaceful coexistence or "the most destructive war in history." In reply to Roswell's holiday greetings in December, he expressed his desire for a further development of understanding and cooperation. "In this respect we in Moscow, as you, Mr. Garst," he wrote, "expect much from the forthcoming visit to the Soviet Union by President Eisenhower. He will be a welcome guest here."

The Sixties

Agriculture on the New Frontier: 1960–63

The Khrushchev visit gave Roswell wider public recognition as an agricultural innovator and established his bona fides both as a commentator on relations with the Eastern bloc and as an authority on what should be done to improve the agriculture of the underdeveloped nations. He was in increasing demand as a speaker and found easier access to a wider group of influential people. As he moved to take advantage of these new opportunities, his optimism was renewed by the portents for change he saw at the beginning of the new decade.

In February 1960 he began to pay close attention to the presidential campaign and in particular to the candidacy of Hubert Humphrey. Although still a registered Republican, Roswell had voted for Stevenson "with enthusiasm" in the last two elections and in general continued to find his own political and agricultural objectives bound up with the Democratic party. His friends in high places—especially Humphrey, Stevenson, and Galbraith—with whom he saw eye-to-eye on issues that mattered most to him—were Democrats, and his own controversies with the USDA during the Eisenhower years enhanced his potential for influencing a Democratic administration. Humphrey, then, was his first choice for president, Stevenson his second, and John F. Kennedy, whom he did not know, a provisional third. Even though he was "not sure" about the senator from Massachusetts, he thought he would be better than Richard Nixon. In Roswell's view, whoever was nominated in 1960 should campaign against the conduct of both the USDA and the State Department during the Eisenhower years and should pledge the cooperation of the two offices in any future administration. If not nominated, Stevenson should be secretary of state and Humphrey should be secretary of agriculture. "At the moment," Roswell wrote to Humphrey,

no agricultural program can be good that does not use and in a rather big way —
Food for Peace. We have an accumulation due to the previous stupidity of the
Department of Agriculture and the Department of State that will sink us if we
don't use a large part of the accumulated surplus as an instrument of diplomacy.

Roswell pressed this view in letters and speeches throughout the
spring of 1960, arguing that Benson failed to understand and control the
productive leap of the fifties and neither John Foster Dulles nor Benson
was interested in the Food for Peace program that Humphrey had so
assiduously promoted. When Humphrey was finally beaten in the bitter
West Virginia primary, Roswell decided to place his hopes in Kennedy
and in August wrote to the senator in a similar vein. American agriculture, he noted, was no longer a sectional problem or even a national
problem; it was now part of the international problem.

Because of this new international context, it was no longer necessary
to appoint a midwesterner as secretary of agriculture. Roswell's new candidate for the job, he told Kennedy, was J. K. Galbraith, even though he
doubted that Galbraith would be interested. At least Galbraith would be
able to find a good secretary, Roswell argued, and in the process signal
the shift to internationalism in agricultural policy. ("I do not want to be
Secretary of Agriculture," Galbraith wrote later to Roswell, "but I would
like whoever is to listen to you.") Roswell moved well beyond a simple
dumping program for American surplus. By the time our own surplus was
disposed of in immediate aid to countries like India, the poorer countries
should themselves be well on the way to self-sufficiency, largely through
educational programs initiated by the United States and international
agencies.

Kennedy's reply was heartening. The senator would indeed want his
secretary of agriculture to work with Adlai Stevenson and others in making agriculture an instrument of diplomacy. "I am convinced," Kennedy
wrote to Roswell,

that we can use more of our agricultural abundance than the Eisenhower administration has done in combatting famine abroad and in underwriting economic development. This our farm plank says, and this I firmly believe. We can and will
use our agricultural surpluses above conventional domestic needs as an instrument of foreign policy.

On the choice of a secretary of agriculture, Kennedy wrote that he
thought symbols were important and that the Midwest was the symbol of
American agriculture. Consequently, he still wanted a midwesterner.
"Can you help me find such a man?" he concluded.

When the results on that long morning after the election of 1960 finally confirmed a narrow victory for Kennedy, Roswell, along with a party that had been out in the cold for eight years, was elated. He immediately wrote to Humphrey to inquire if in fact a new agricultural order was in the making and received a gratifying reply. Humphrey reported Kennedy in genuine agreement with the idea of close cooperation between State and Agriculture, and to that end he created the post of Food for Peace Administrator as a White House appointment within the purview of the State Department and with the stipulation that the administrator's staff be drawn from Agriculture. The intention of this arrangement was to permit the administrator, George McGovern, to act as a bridge between State and Agriculture. Invested with the authority of the White House, he would be in a position to ensure the cooperation of the two departments. Humphrey reported further that he had been passing on Roswell's ideas to the new secretary of agriculture, Orville Freeman, and hoped to arrange a meeting between the two. "You make life exciting," Humphrey said. "Come see me."

It was in an expansive and jubilant mood that Roswell, Elizabeth, and other family members set off for the inauguration in January 1961. Roswell arrived the Sunday before to complete his traditional round of visiting and promotion. He had a two-hour lunch with McGovern, Phil Maguire, Pat Jackson, and Louis Bean, finding McGovern "bright," "nice," but too gentle. "He is no Milo Perkins—nor Jonathan Garst." He also lunched with Freeman, who was interested in Roswell's plan to convert grain into protein and was full of technical questions about packing and refrigerating meat in large quantities. Central and South America were the focus for further meetings with Bourke Hickenlooper, now chairman of the Senate Foreign Relations Subcommittee on Latin America, and with the revered Perkins and Pete Hudgens, two of Roswell's heroes from New Deal days.

The remainder of the visit was mostly just fun, as Democrats old and new poured in from all over the country to reclaim the White House, undeterred by a record snowfall that required many celebrants to exercise that vigor whose triumph they had come to celebrate. Roswell and Elizabeth attended the reception Sam Rayburn organized for Lyndon Johnson, at which two lines of handshakers moved in opposite directions across the ballroom of the Statler Hotel ("Where the hell did this other line come from?" Johnson complained), and caught a hastily improvised bus service to one of the five Inaugural Balls. They spent the following morning watching the frosty inaugural ceremony on television at the Maguires, and, as a coda to a heady week, drove to John Dos Passos's Chesapeake Bay home to visit and discuss the promising state of the nation. The new administration and the sixties were well launched.

ROSWELL'S personal goal in the international sphere was to extend the export of American agricultural techniques throughout the underdeveloped world. Filled with confidence over the success of his efforts in Eastern Europe and working closely now with his brother Jonathan, Roswell turned his attention to India, China, and more especially Central and South America. However, success did not immediately follow, as cultural differences, political considerations, and other complexities changed the straight road of midwestern progress into a labyrinthine profusion of paths, some of which led nowhere.

The immediate question for Roswell in 1961 concerned the kind of role he should play. In May McGovern offered him a place on the American Food for Peace Council, a position Roswell turned down. "I don't want to be on any Food for Peace Committee along with a hundred other guys," Roswell told Phil Maguire, "because as you know, I am not a committee guy." At the same time, Humphrey was working not only to obtain a hearing for Roswell's ideas but also for some kind of appointment for him. In June Humphrey asked the International Cooperation Administration (ICA) to call in Roswell as a consultant on his plan to produce broiler chickens abroad. "Insist that somebody do something on these matters," Humphrey had written to Herbert Waters. A reply from McGeorge Bundy informed Humphrey that someone was doing something about the plan in the person of Jonathan Garst, now a consultant in Brazil. There was no mention of a job offer to Roswell.

The "chicken plan" had been one of Roswell's favorite projects for several years. The idea was to provide a feed mill and a broiler chicken factory in every large port in as many poor countries as possible. Chicken was not objectionable to any major religion and could be sold live to provide a cheap and acceptable form of protein. In the late 1950s, when Roswell first proposed the idea, the single problem was a scarcity of soybean meal for feed, which now was being alleviated by Secretary Freeman at the urging of Humphrey. Bundy and the ICA were also interested in the idea. However, the project was not implemented as Roswell envisioned it and seems to have been lost somewhere in the corridors of Agriculture or State.

India was now a country of great concern to Roswell, in large part because of his brother. In 1959 and 1960 Johnny had grown especially interested in India's enormous potential for production. "India is not overpopulated," he liked to say, "just underfertilized." In the fifties Roswell was interested in selling seed corn to India, but under Jonathan's tutelage, his plans for the country shifted to a more general program of increased yields through fertilization combined with the use of rice-straw as cellulose for feed. Roswell's path to this goal began during the ride with Khrushchev and Lodge from Des Moines to Coon Rapids. The conversation focused on the underdeveloped countries, and Roswell quoted Jonathan's aphorism about India. Lodge offered to arrange a meeting with Ambassador V. K. Menon, which later took place in New York. Through Lodge, Jonathan met people in a position to help with the project, including B. K. Nehru. (Nehru's wife was Hungarian and already knew of Roswell because of his success in getting the family of a close friend out of Hungary after the revolution.)

By 1961 there was a large file of Roswell's correspondence on India, but no concrete proposals involving the participation of either Jonathan or Roswell. The appointment of Galbraith as ambassador to India provided a spark of hope that something might turn up for the Garsts, but by now Johnny had given up on the country and would shortly be back in Brazil at work for the ICA. Roswell labored on throughout 1962 and 1963 on behalf of the fertilizer plan but received only sobering instruction on the problems of change from Welles Hangen, NBC Bureau Chief in Delhi, whom Roswell had helped to get reaccredited in Moscow after the Hungarian uprising. Responding to Roswell's impatience with the pace of change, Hangen noted a "disheartening combination" of bureaucratic "muddling," lack of incentives, and "actual disincentives" to produce. Indians did not value Western efficiency, were not disposed to change ancient patterns of tillage, and were adding more millions in population than tons of fertilizer. Roswell was outraged by the lack of agricultural attachés in Washington; Hangen was less optimistic about the bureaucratic funneling of such information in any case. "Have you any idea of the enormous abyss in ideas, attitudes, way of life and everything else between the Indian official – *any* official – and the people who actually make their living from the Indian soil?" he asked. There were some bright spots, Hangen thought, notably in the Peace Corps work and in the Ohio State agricultural advisers at Ludhiana University, but change was going to be a slow process. In 1962 Roswell still considered going over himself but did not do so.

ROSWELL had high hopes for establishing agricultural contact with China, in spite of the confrontation with Nationalist Taiwan over Quemoy and Matsu islands and the presence of the U.S. Seventh Fleet off the China coast. In 1959, shortly after the Khrushchev visit, he attended a convocation at Simpson College, Iowa, and met Brooks Hays, a former legislator who at the time was on the board of directors of the Tennessee Valley Authority. Roswell suggested to Hays that the two of them apply for visas to visit Communist China to initiate some sort of agricultural mission. Hays relayed the idea to Christian Herter, then secretary of state, who advised Hays to drop the idea. Herter told Hays that it might be viewed simply as a publicity stunt; Hays thought the real reason was that Herter was turning down all requests for visits to China, even from members of Congress. In 1961 Hays entered the Kennedy administration as assistant secretary of state with hopes—similar to Roswell's—for a new policy of accommodation with the mainland government. However, even cultural exchanges were not yet possible, Hays reported to Roswell, because of the "tough and unyielding" attitude of the Chinese. Hays gave as an example the fate of one of Roswell's suggestions, an exchange of newsmen. At the 102d ambassadorial level meeting in Warsaw, the Chinese delegation refused to consider this proposal unless the United States withdrew its forces from Taiwan and the Straits and ceased to support the Nationalist government. The Kennedy administration considered these demands totally unacceptable in the context of the present confrontation over Quemoy and Matsu; the Chinese, already engaged in a secret confrontation with Moscow, were not disposed to adopt peaceful coexistence as policy. There would certainly be no trip to China for Roswell.

In 1961 Jonathan was back in Brazil, writing a series of letters to Roswell in which he criticized the U.S. foreign aid program as "about the most useless thing ever devised by man." He accused the ICA of being "a two-year tourist agency" and charged that most of the people connected with it should be fired, suggesting that short-term commercial projects were a better way of helping poorer countries. He urged Roswell to organize a corporation called "Agricultural Revolution Associates," which in turn would set up a large-scale model farm in Brazil. From El Salvador Johnny wrote in a slightly more optimistic tone. Although it sometimes seemed to him that the the situation in Central and South America was "hopeless" and that everything seemed "to stand still," he had decided that "it isn't that bad. I figure they are bound to catch up in agriculture." While in El Salvador Johnny made several proposals that he said the Americans had approved but would not act upon. He had better hopes, he reported, for the Salvadoreans themselves.

Jonathan had also told Roswell that we should be sending salesmen to the underdeveloped countries instead of Ph.D.s. It was a slogan Roswell was happy to adopt and provided a focus for his increasing complaints about the American foreign aid programs, complaints fueled in part by genuine problems and in part by his own frustration thus far in finding a role for himself. His letters in the spring of 1962 are full of his inimitable brand of "violent" denunciation, expressed in a language similar to that previously reserved for the agricultural colleges. "I see all kinds of college professors," he told Welles Hangen, "being sent out by the State Department who would starve to death if they were farming—to help other farmers learn how to farm—when they themselves only know the theory of farming." To Pat Jackson he wrote of the contrast between the desire of the Eastern European countries for high agricultural technology and the apparent lack of interest by the underdeveloped nations. He had always kept his relationship with the Communist governments commercial; "maybe," he told Jackson, "the commercialism has something to do with it." He would rather place his hopes on the farmers Johnny was working with in Brazil than with a government agency. "Those guys were *doers*," he told Jackson. "They will put on demonstrations that are really worthwhile."

A program for demonstrations of the the effectiveness of fertilizer and other modern practices was the fruit of these two years of ferment and frustration. The seeds of its inception lay in Roswell's discussions with Jonathan, the information from Hangen and others, his own experience in Eastern Europe, and ultimately, as he used to say, from his thirty years' of experience in teaching people how to produce more and better food with less labor. In contrast to Jonathan, who was trying to convince the Brazilian authorities to set up a model farm on the scale of the operation at Coon Rapids, Roswell concluded that the best way to educate the illiterate rural farmer was "by massive numbers of small demonstrations" in as many countries as possible. He was also less contemptuous than Jonathan of government bureaucracy and believed that he would be more effective if he were sponsored by the Agency for International Development or the Food and Agriculture Organization of the United Nations. He was not prepared to put himself entirely in the hands of such an agency, however, but envisioned spending a few months each year at the job over a period of several years.

In setting forth the particulars of his project, he drew upon the success of his programs of distributing samples of hybrid seed and later of fertilizer in the new western territories of Garst and Thomas in the thirties and forties. He proposed giving each farmer in the experiment enough seed, fertilizer, and other chemicals in small packets to be spread over a one-fortieth-acre plot. He believed that the cost to each farmer would be approximately one dollar, and would increase the yield on the plot from 12 bushels to 80. He also looked back to the thirties in estimating that the farmer could repay the cost of his original packet by half the increase from his one-fortieth acre. He hoped to spend the early months of 1964 in touring Central and South American countries to see how fast the local governments would be willing to move and also to promote demonstrations on the feeding of molasses and urea. By the following summer the packets could be shipped, so that at the end of a year the whole program would be well under way. Within two years, he believed there would be enough enthusiasm generated "to let us double corn yields within another two or three years."

Such was the plan he had formed by 1963, and thus he described it to

Phil Maguire in December of that year, a month after the assassination of John F. Kennedy. He asked Maguire to pass it on to the appropriate authorities and to advertise Roswell Garst as "an Iowa farmer who wants a job."

Bringing Cattle to the Corn Belt

Roswell's major domestic enthusiasm at the beginning of the sixties was a campaign to increase in significant number the production of cattle in the Corn Belt during the new decade. "I have been having fun this winter," he wrote in early 1960 to Walt Colvin, his friend in the chemical industry,

And as usual, you and your darned Nitrogen Division ought to benefit from my fun. I have given talks all the way from the Dawson County Cattle Feeders' Day at Lexington, Neb., to the Farm Forum up in Minneapolis to the annual meeting of the Grain and Feed Dealers at Kansas City–and a good many outposts in between.

Roswell told these audiences in the north central and western Corn Belt that the country now had 100 million head of cattle. Although this was the greatest number in history, livestock remained high priced, which demonstrated that there were certainly not too many. Rather, he continued, with the population growing rapidly we would have to learn how to feed 125 million cattle by 1970 just to keep up. In fact, we should really be increasing the cattle population even more, so that there could be an increase in per capita consumption of beef. "This takes a little doing but not much," he concluded.

Once again Roswell placed himself in the vanguard of a major new development of the midwestern farming revolution: the establishment of a regional cow-calf industry to make use of the new feed resources now available and adapted to the new markets created by a westward-moving population. The story, in which Roswell had already played an earlier role, has its roots in the fifties and falls into two parts. The first includes the introduction of corn to western Kansas and Nebraska and the subsequent rise of commercial feedlots in the Central Plains states; the second is the story of the introduction of large cattle herds to feed on the corn plants and fertilized pastures of the traditional central Corn Belt.

In the early fifties, Kansas was not as corny as nurse Nellie Forbush had supposed in Rodgers and Hammerstein's *South Pacific*. Until that time, corn was grown only in the northeast corner of the state, an area bounded roughly by Highway 81, which wound its way from Columbus,

Nebraska, to Wichita, Kansas, entering the state just north of Belleville, not far east of the geographical center of the United States. To the west, through the geographical center and along the Solomon River—whose dusty valley Hans Larsen traversed twenty-five years earlier—and along the Arkansas River of southwest Kansas and south to Oklahoma lay the grain sorghum belt. At that time grain sorghum was the only commercial feed grain that could stand the hot, dry climate of the shallow river valleys and the sandy soils of Kansas flatlands and hills. Garst and Thomas entered into the grain sorghum business in the fifties; and after a false start with a sorghum plant in Coon Rapids, they transferred the operation to Garden City, Kansas, on the Arkansas River. It was essential that the company produce sorghum in order to be in the corn business in this area; salesmen-farmers had to be able to sell sorghum as well as corn in order to survive, because corn was merely secondary to the livelihood of most of them and of their customers.

The balance between the two crops began to shift shortly after David Garst took over the leading sales role for Garst and Thomas in 1956. Although he began hiring salesmen in Kansas primarily to sell sorghum, he was very much interested in the potential for corn. He discovered that this was also true of his newly hired district sales manager, Don Williams, a latter-day corn evangelist from Halstead, a small town north of Wichita on the Little Arkansas River. Williams had already grown corn as well as sorghum, was highly experienced in newly developed methods of irrigation, and was knowledgeable about water distribution, largely as the result of his leadership in litigation between Halstead and Wichita over the precious water supply in that part of Kansas. Williams in turn made a point of hiring other irrigators as salesmen.

Williams firmly believed that with irrigation, corn, a better feed crop than sorghum, could be grown just as successfully in the dry West and was anxious to begin a full-scale selling and teaching program for corn. David Garst, sharing rather uneasily the sales direction for Garst and Thomas with his father, was an enthusiast himself and just as anxious to find a project that would establish his own credentials in the field. It was a risky and rather daunting project. Sorghum farmers did not have corn planters or proper heads for their combines, and the agricultural colleges believed that the heat, dryness, and insects made western Kansas unsuitable for corn. In order to make the project work, farmers would have to make the most efficient use possible of all available agricultural technology.

David Garst and Don Williams began by organizing a series of corn clinics throughout the state, inviting Hans Larsen to help them. Roswell also appeared occasionally. Each of the three would speak for twenty minutes: David on hybrid varieties, Don Williams on irrigation, Hans

Larsen on planting techniques and fertilization. They also changed positions from time to time and filled in what one of the others might have missed. Their main concern was that farmers did not "cheat," that is, that they followed the planting instructions precisely and did not try to reduce their investment by using less than the prescribed amounts of chemicals. Hans Larsen would take his chalk in hand and draw a line across the center of the blackboard: "Up here is for the men," he would say, "down here is for the boys. I don't believe there is a boy in the crowd but I'm just going to put this line across here and tell you what you should do. And this," he would say, pointing to the lower half of the blackboard, "is for the people who will cheat a little."

It turned out to be a textbook operation. With so much investment at stake, nobody cheated. Everyone used the recommended seed varieties, planted them according to instruction, fertilized, irrigated, used insecticides and herbicides, as well as the new planter shoe devised by Williams. The first year's result was a yield of 125 bushels per acre, a record in itself and a standard of performance that would increase over the years.

Irrigation proved to be the key to the operation, not only for stabilizing and controlling the required moisture but also because it opened up vast acres that could not have been planted before. A particular kind of irrigation was required for the sandy soil of the Central Plains, a method that had already been developed in Nebraska and patented in 1952 — center-pivot sprinkler irrigation.

The Valmont system of sprinkler irrigation was designed primarily for the sandy soils in western Nebraska that were unsuitable for ordinary furrow irrigation. Water that flows into a furrow does not spread into the crops in sandy soil; it simply drops straight into the ground below the furrow. With a sprinkler, however, a farmer could distribute water evenly throughout the field. Other sprinkler systems had been in use in various parts of the country for years, but because they had to be moved by hand they were too labor intensive for the size of Corn Belt farming. The Valmont system, on the other hand, was self-propelled, making use of the water itself to move the system in a wide circle every seven days. Anyone who flies across Nebraska or Kansas can see the new circular configurations that have imposed themselves on the old surveyor's square miles.

A Nebraska farmer and cattle-feeder, Bill Curry, was the first person to use the new system on a truly extensive scale. Curry was an early and enthusiastic reader of Roswell's first pamphlet on fertilizer, "It Needs Seedin'," obtained a franchise to distribute nitrogen fertilizer in Nebraska, and used his profits to invest in irrigation and cattle. He fed his livestock in the approved Garst manner, locating his feedlots in between irrigated circles on his fields. The idea spread to western Kansas when

Don Williams brought a young salesman, Dean Gigot, to see Currry's great circles of irrigated land. Gigot, his four brothers, and his father started selling the systems in Kansas and using them on their own rapidly expanding farming operation. They eventually acquired fifty systems, enough to irrigate 50 square miles of corn and to produce crops well above the 125-bushel average. During the sixties the 5,000 acres of corn that had been grown in Kansas increased to 500,000 acres, of which two-thirds was supplied by Garst and Thomas. Over half the total acreage in Kansas is irrigated; in western Nebraska, which also increased its production significantly, more than half of the corn is also irrigated.

The end for which this new flowering of agricultural technology was intended was the production of cattle feed for a home-based, cow-calf and feeder industry. "You are all big producers of livestock," Hans Larsen had told his customers at the corn clinics,

but you need to take them the last mile. There is no need to take your calves into Illinois and Iowa where they have an excellent economy because they have fed your cattle for the last 50 years and have made a good deal of money doing it. Why don't *you* make it right here?

Two more technological developments were necessary before the herds of the Central Plains could be fattened on the spot. The first was the adaptation of the trench silo—heretofore used only for silage—for the storage of high moisture corn that was harvested early while it still contained 30 to 35 percent moisture. By harvesting early, farmers could avoid field loss and the expense of using dryers, and by using trench silos they could avoid the expense of conventional storage facilities necessary for dried corn. High moisture corn could only be fed to cattle, but by concentrating on the feeding of livestock, farmers could save up to 30 percent of their production costs. The final technological breakthrough was the invention of a cheap grinding process, which could be performed near the trench silos.

When the Gigots and other farmers had harvested and stored their corn in trenches, they either bought cattle or sold their corn to cattle feeders, who in turn brought their herds to the corn and began establishing large commercial feedlots. In the sixties the idea spread from Kansas and Nebraska to Oklahoma, Texas, Arizona, California, and the Dakotas. By the seventies approximately two thousand large feedlots were fattening 60 percent of the nation's cattle, most of them in areas that in the early fifties had not enough feed to come close to maintaining such a population. This significant alteration of the economic structure of the Central Plains was the result of a complex web of existing and new agricultural development and salesmanship.

SINCE the late forties, Roswell had never ceased to be interested in promoting the feeding of cattle in the Midwest. During the late fifties, throughout the period of his most intense involvement in his Eastern European ventures, he continued to call attention to the population explosion in the United States and the consequent potential for increasing cattle herds now that greater quantities of feed were available. He paid close attention to the cattle population as well and urged continuing growth. From 1949 to 1960 the number of beef brood cows in Iowa alone doubled from 500,000 to 1 million; by 1970, Roswell was predicting in 1960, the state ought to have 2.5 million. Furthermore, in his view the national figure should increase by 20 million, so that in 1970 the nation would have a cattle population of 120 million. In 1959, shortly after the Khrushchev visit, he was outraged by the assertion of an agricultural credit official in Kansas that there was no need to increase the beef population. "We don't have too many cattle," Roswell had snapped, "we just have too little knowledge."

Roswell's renewed effort in this matter in the early sixties was rooted in the direction that the Garst farming operation was taking, which was quite simply to capitalize on the enormous amount of cellulose feed the seed corn business produced as a by-product of its operation by getting into the cattle business in a big way. In 1958 Roswell put it succinctly to a researcher at the University of California at Davis, to whom he had written for information:

Because of our immense cob pile and the fact that we sell the bulk of our grain as seed and because we have some very beautiful pastures, we are not interested in getting into the *fattening* business half as much as we are interested in getting into the *growing* business. Furthermore, we have had very long and very large experience in the growing of cattle. We have a beautiful setup for that purpose. The whole thing fits together in a way that pleases me.

These remarks reflected not only the special situation of the Garsts, but a significant change taking place throughout the traditional Corn Belt. Until this time, cattle were almost exclusively produced on the ranges of the West and Southwest, brought to the Midwest to be fattened on the more plentiful feed available, marketed in the Midwest, and shipped mainly to the population centers of the East. With the population center rapidly moving West, the markets and the movement of beef were more dispersed and generally shifting westward with the population. The Corn Belt was now in the center of the market, not on its western fringe. Furthermore, the rapid growth of the commercial feedlots in the Central Plains states had two effects on the traditional corn-growing areas. The feedlots demonstrated dramatically that the new feeding techniques could sustain large numbers of cattle and profitably so; the feedlots also created significant competition for the acquisition of cattle from the western ranges. Consequently, it began to cost more for an Iowa or Illinois farmer to bring feeder cattle in from the West. All of these factors – the population shift, the competition of the feedlots, the availability of feed on midwestern farms and pastures – made a homegrown cow-calf operation a very attractive proposition. As a businessman, Roswell wanted to capitalize on this new set of circumstances; as an educator, he wanted his family's operation to be a model for what he believed every midwestern grain farmer could achieve in some degree.

It was also a time of changing relationships within the Garst family. Roswell was depending more and more on Stephen and David to follow through on his domestic projects, a burden they were both willing to shoulder. They had chosen the family agricultural enterprises as the focus for their own careers; it remained for them to divide up the territory and achieve a working relationship with each other and with their father. In 1956 David had moved from the Garst Company (in which he remained a partner) into Garst and Thomas and discovered his own sales ability. Consequently, he became Roswell's heir as chief of sales. Stephen's flair was for farming and finance: he was playing an increasingly important role in shaping the family's corporate structure, and as chief farmer it was he who organized the cow-calf and bull-breeding business in the sixties. When Roswell referred to the Garst cattle operation, he was really speaking of the Garst Company, of which Stephen was the manager. Roswell was still the grand strategist of the family farm and cattle operation; Stephen was his chief-of-staff and principal tactician. It was a competitive and complicated set of relationships but an arrangement that worked. Roswell, whose penchant it was to ignore the rougher edges of the family structure, found this new arrangement satisfying.

The sixties brought satisfaction for him in another long-standing but changing set of relationships – his connections with the universities. He entered into a period of fruitful association with Iowa State and other agricultural schools, largely because much of their work in animal science and nutrition was running on lines parallel with Roswell's interests. Wise Burroughs was extending his research into cellulose and urea; S. A. "Bud" Ewing, formerly of Oklahoma State and now at Ames, was surveying and defining the new trends in beef production in the Corn Belt; and Louis Thompson was looking at American agriculture in the context of national and global population trends. Since 1956 Burroughs, Ewing, and other staff members at Iowa State had produced a series of pamphlets on the feeding of ground corncobs and chopped cornstalks to livestock, and on the production of feeder calves on corn land. By 1962 Roswell was recommending these bulletins in his articles for farm journals and quoting them in Garst and Thomas bulletins on similar subjects. It was a period in which the most influential educative forces in the western and north central Corn Belt were moving their constituency together towards fulfillment of the promise heralded in the breakthrough in agricultural research that had occurred in the forties and fifties.

However, his contentment with the manner in which the colleges pursued their aims even when Roswell approved of them never seemed to last long, and Roswell's ruminations during the winter of 1961–62 about pressing ahead with his campaign for increasing beef production would bring him once again into a degree of contention with Iowa State. In March 1962 Roswell wrote to his old friends George Hoffer, George Scarseth, and Walt Colvin that he proposed to dedicate the next eight years of his life to doubling the number of cows in the Corn Belt. The renewed campaign was to center upon an attack on the putting up of hay as winter fodder for livestock, a practice decreasing somewhat as the whole corn plant was being used more effectively, but not decreasing at a rate fast enough to suit Roswell. "After good contemplation," he wrote to Colvin, "I have decided that the place to start and drive the hardest is by *slandering hay!*" Because oats were the traditional nurse crop for alfalfa, they too would have to go. "Oats," he wrote later to his daughters, "were just a bad habit really."

As he used to describe the process himself, Roswell's method of establishing a line of action was to review his past successes, consider the present state of knowledge and the implications of that knowledge, assimilate these two sets of data, and devote himself single-mindedly to the conclusion he believed correct and inevitable. If it looked as though it would not be inevitable when Roswell thought it ought to be, or not inevitable fast enough, he took it upon himself to speed up the process. To be around him when he was engaged in this process could be alternately exciting, entertaining, boring, and frustrating, an amalgam of emotions that varied in proportion to the length of exposure, the nature of the listener's relation to him, as well as the degree of involvement and interest of the listener in the topic at hand. Talk was the supreme method by which Roswell distilled his ideas, and he possessed an extraordinary capacity for repeating himself with unflagging enthusiasm, selecting and discarding ideas and formulating his persuasive phrases. It was not always easy for the family to remain unflagging when the same topic was presented at breakfast, lunch, dinner, and in between.

In the present instance, Roswell concluded that hay was simply obsolete. Just as ten years ago he told the agronomists that legumes were obsolete, an expensive and inefficient way to fix nitrogen in the soil, so now, with that earlier battle won, it was time to demonstrate that hay was also expensive and inefficient as cattle feed. The growing of hay was "just as ridiculous as the leguminous soil building practices we used to use," he insisted. Unfortunately, he would continue, people still thought of hay in terms of protein content and still thought of the fixation of nitrogen in pastures as "perfectly logical thoughts." This was not true, he argued; the "logical thoughts" in cattle feeding were now the use of cellulose and urea in feedlots, combined with nonleguminous grass pastures heavily fertilized. These were the twin supports of his program for a vastly expanded Corn Belt cattle industry, and from these two articles of faith he believed that all economic blessings would flow.

In the spring and summer of 1962 Roswell augmented his speaking, talking, and letter writing with a series of articles for farm journals. *Successful Farming* published an article by him entitled "Bob Garst's New Crusade" ("It was not my title," Roswell later wrote, "but I accept the charge."); *Wallaces' Farmer* and *Nebraska Farmer* also published his work. A highlight of his speaking campaign was an address delivered to the American Association of Agricultural Editors, presented that summer in Des Moines. His themes were the competition of the commercial feedlots, the best sources of feed, the work of Iowa State University, and the folly of putting up hay.

Roswell was sometimes abrasive and aggressive in public pronouncements, but often simply amusing and persuasive. A paragraph from the *Wallaces' Farmer* article is identical to a passage from his talks on the subject and is a good example of the Roswellian light touch, incorporating as well a new phrase — "the despotism of custom" — which he had discovered in a quotation from the English philosopher John Stuart Mill:

For several years, I have been laughingly — although I think truthfully — telling people that if they put up hay for beef cattle, they fall into one of three classifications. Either they are so rich that they just don't care to be frugal. Or they believe that the exercise they get from haying is more beneficial to their health than fishing (which I deny). Or third, they are influenced by the despotism of custom. (Their grandfathers put up hay, their fathers put up hay, their neighbors put up hay, it is the custom to put up hay — and they are afraid to break the custom).

Roswell also argued for the use of the entire corn plant in the feeding of cattle. To use only the shelled corn was to use only 60 percent of the potential feed units available from a cornfield; the cob and stalk provided another 40 percent. "No farmer, no country, and no state," Roswell wrote, "is so rich they can afford to waste 40 percent of what they have produced." To this end, Roswell spent several years lobbying the implement companies to produce a stalk chopper so that the whole plant could be more easily converted into feed. One such machine had been on the market, but it was not designed for the high yields now common in the Corn Belt. By the end of the decade, Roswell's efforts in this respect were rewarded. Making hay obsolete proved a more difficult task.

As the planting season gave way to the growing season, Roswell's own pace customarily picked up. The articles and letters flowed, and his inspection tours around the countryside increased. He loved the growing season and never missed at least one daily ride – and usually more – by himself or with Eddie Reid, or with the steady flow of visitors. Driving north of town over the Wisconsin Drift soil, south over the newer cornfields and fertilized pastures, he looked closely for signs of fertilizer deficiency, admiring the corn when it looked well – which it usually did – and the cattle when they looked healthy – which they usually did – and the pastures when they were lush with brome grass – which they usually were. In the late summer he would happily submerge himself almost exclusively in Garst and Thomas affairs, as the time approached for the seed corn plant to begin processing the harvest of corn that would soon pour in from growers throughout the western Corn Belt.

However, in the fall of 1962 Roswell's pace began to falter. The seed corn plant was in full swing in mid-September; trucks and visitors were arriving in great numbers. Ordinarily, Roswell would have been in top form during this climactic moment of the agricultural year, but now he simply felt tired and spent hours lying on his couch in the living room. This lack of energy was something new; he had been ill with a gallstone in 1959–60 but had not been slowed down for long, and before that had virtually never been ill. Many years earlier, he had once had what he referred to as "stoppage of the bowels" and had spent several days in bed. The doctor was called, made his examination, and came downstairs to tell the family that Roswell would "surely be missed." Elizabeth was frantic for a few moments, until it became apparent that the doctor had merely been musing on the fate that must befall all mortals. Roswell had quickly recovered.

This time, however, Roswell developed a sore throat and laryngitis and was examined by a doctor who assured him that the one thing he did not have was cancer of the throat. Roswell had not even considered that possibility, and the doctor's intended reassurance upset him sufficiently enough for him to arrange a visit to the Mayo Clinic in Rochester, Minnesota, during the first week in October. He arrived on a Tuesday; on Wednesday surgeons found a small malignancy between the vocal chords and the upper end of the vocal box. The larynx would have to be removed.

Roswell could not be admitted to the hospital until Monday, so he flew back to Des Moines on Friday, picked up his car, and returned to Coon Rapids for a day before driving to Rochester with Elizabeth on Saturday. On Friday afternoon he wrote to his sales supervisors to inform them of the diagnosis. The cancer had been caught early, so that there was every reason to expect a complete recovery without recurrence, but in two days he was going to lose his natural speaking voice forever. "They say that learning to talk over again is largely dependent upon desire," he wrote to his supervisors. "Of course, as you know, I have desired to talk for every waking hour of 40 years—so I presume I will be a pretty good student."

Roswell had also written that he had been shocked less by the news than he now thought he should have been. But there had been little time to think about the prospect; he was on the road again almost immediately to Rochester. On Sunday night he called all his children to tell them that this was the last time they would be hearing the old voice, and on Monday his larynx was removed.

The struggle to learn to talk again began in earnest in November 1962. The doctors told him that he would be able to be understood within two or three weeks, be proficient in three months, and accomplished in six months. He was visited in his hospital room by people who had also had laryngectomies and spoke with the esophageal technique, who assured him that he would speak again. He had support and encouragement from Elizabeth, all the family, and friends. "I think about you again and again," wrote Henry Wallace, who had been one of the visitors that fall in Coon Rapids, "as you fight the battle of establishing new nerve channels of communication. You have rendered a great service to the world and you are going to render a great service. I wish you joy and vigor and pertinacity in your current problem."

Week after week Roswell sat at home trying to master the technique of esophageal speech. The idea was to swallow as large a quantity of air as possible, then belch it upward, and shape it into speech by using the area of the throat above the missing vocal box. Air was sucked in through the hole that was made in the throat by the operation (the hole ended Roswell's swimming; the pool was eventually filled in and annexed by Elizabeth for her garden). Roswell drank carbonated soft drinks to help with the belching, but he made no progress. There is a knack to the process of esophageal speech, which some people pick up very quickly; getting the knack does not mean that they blossom into speech immediately, but it gives them the capacity to improve rapidly. Roswell could not pick up the technique: over four months after his operation, in late February 1963, he wrote to Phil Maguire that he was finding esophageal speech "slower than hell and very discouraging." He was still working at it, but he expressed only "fair" confidence that he would make it.

In fact, he never spoke at all, unless he is given credit for one "possible." Alarmed at his failure to improve and his growing tendency to simply sit in involuntary silence, neither writing on his tablet nor reading, Elizabeth insisted that he have another drink of his carbonated beverage and continue practicing. Roswell pushed the drink away and emitted a sound which Elizabeth took to be "no!" She was elated and told her bridge club in the afternoon that Roswell had spoken. However, the sound was never repeated, and Roswell continued to exist with his vitality locked up inside. Unable to dictate, the volume of his correspondence dropped significantly; he found writing physically difficult and inhibiting, probably because of a touch of the family dyslexia. For his family and friends it was an unsettling and depressing experience to be in the same room with Roswell and find that he no longer filled it with his voice and sheer presence. What it felt like for him can only be guessed at; even to Elizabeth he did not unburden his feelings beyond the kind of hints conveyed to people such as Phil Maguire.

However, Roswell's condition became virtually as well-known as he was, and in March 1963, not long after the letter to Maguire, a man in Des Moines who had had a laryngectomy invited him to try an artificial voice made by the Bell Telephone Company. He found his correspondent using a machine about the size of a small flashlight that contained a battery and a vibrating diaphragm. Roswell placed the machine against his throat, pressed the switch, and talked as he would normally. What came out was a broadcast in monotone, but a broadcast that was clear, easy to produce, and allowed Roswell to talk as long as he wished without having to pause for breath (in that respect an improvement upon the natural limitations imposed on the human voice). Roswell went immediately to Bell Telephone, and for $27.50 got his old life back again.

Roswell happily set out to make the most of this extraordinary reprieve and soon made himself an accomplished communicator with his new machine. He quickly learned to resist the temptation to drone on and on without stopping and generally kept to the natural pauses of ordinary speech. However, since his monotone prevented him from using the ordinary tools of pitch and emphasis, he was able to compensate for this lack to a considerable degree by stopping at climactic moments in a sentence or longer narration by removing the box from his neck to rest for a moment, thereby creating anticipation in his listeners as they waited for him to bring the arm up again, put the machine to his neck, and complete his thought. He was also very quick to take the initiative in conversations with people who had never encountered this method of speech, putting them at ease, and, more importantly, getting them to listen. He was very good at putting children at ease by buzzing the machine first in the air, then on their arm. The "child buzz" was brief and benevolent; the "Elizabeth buzz," which he employed to interrupt his wife, was long and strident. It elevated an established and offensive practice to a new height of barbarity.

There were some situations in which he was vulnerable. In a noisy restaurant he could hardly be heard; in a less populated one he broadcast to every table. He was very careful never to speak during a funeral service. At the first one he attended with his new voice he leaned over to offer his condolences to the bereaved and heard his voice echoing throughout the church, unnerving himself and the entire congregation with a passable imitation of the Last Trumpet. However, the new voice uncannily projected enough of the original low-pitched, incisive, and dominating voice of old to make the listener sometimes forget that this one was mechanical. The essential Roswell was heard again, with but one exception; he could no longer laugh, as he used to do frequently and zestfully. The most he could manage now was a kind of wheeze. His listeners had to do the laughing for him.

Roswell was angry with the Mayo Clinic for failing to start him out on the machine, but he was grateful enough to become a benefactor and to take his turn counselling other laryngectomy patients. He had occasional minor difficulties resulting from the operation but did not have a recurrence of the cancer. He seemed to have slowed down in a general way, but that rather modulated change in his life-style may have been due to processes not directly connected with the operation. He was sixty-four when it was performed, and the bout of lassitude he suffered prior to it was not necessarily related to the onset of his very small malignancy. However, he had been a lucky man, and he knew it. What might have been an ending had turned out to be simply an interlude.

ROSWELL'S activities in the livestock business gradually regained their momentum. In 1964 he produced another major Garst and Thomas bulletin entitled *1964 Agricultural Prospects and Opportunities,* which summarized the Garst experience with feed and cattle and gave considerable space to the work of Burroughs and Ewing at Iowa State University. He spoke rather circumspectly about hay, quoting university authorities on its expense as a feed, but pushed hard for the use of the whole corn plant. It was essential, he argued, for farmers to raise their own cattle; it was costing too much to import them in the traditional manner.

In the midsixties Roswell shifted his attention to promoting the use of fertilized pasture and instituted his favorite teaching device, the demonstration plot. The amount of pasture land was increasing rapidly in the Corn Belt as a direct result of the Diverted Acres Program instituted to control the surpluses created by higher yields. Farmers were paid a premium to divert corn acres to conserved land or pasture, the only proviso being that acres diverted to pasture in a given year could not be grazed until 1 September of that year. Since 1961 the Garsts had taken one field in particular north of town out of production each year and pastured it each fall. By 1965 the grass in the field was showing the short growth and sickly yellow color that signal nitrogen deficiency. In April 1966 Roswell fertilized four strips in the field with amounts varying from 50 to 300 pounds per acre. The grass in the fertilized strips was easily visible from the roadside and spectacularly so from the air. Because it was virtually impossible to see quantitative differences between the various fertilized strips, 1 square yard of each strip was cut each year and weighed along with a control patch of nonfertilized pasture. The samples demonstrated an increase of from one and one-half to five times as much grass produced with fertilization. After three years of trials, it was decided that an annual application of 150 pounds of nitrogen would more than double the yield of brome and other grasses. Furthermore, the cattle put to graze the strips ate first in the section in which cornstalks had been left, then moved to the most highly fertilized strips, and lastly made their way to the unfertilized part of the field.

Roswell made the most of his demonstration. In 1968 he published a Garst and Thomas pamphlet entitled *It is Profitable to Fertilize Pastures,* the text of which was centered upon the experiment and its results. Each year that the pastures were fertilized, Roswell invited a wide variety of visitors to Coon Rapids, among them farmers, salesmen, county extension directors, representatives from chemical companies, and in 1968 representatives from Iowa State University. All were impressed, but the university representatives pointed out that the vast majority of farmers would not plant brome grass in their new pasture; they would plant clover and alfalfa for hay, which would choke on additional fertilization.

These comments crystallized a two-fold problem that Roswell faced in his campaign against hay, which had reached a new pitch in 1968. Many farmers were far behind him in their degree of innovation and investment; the university was committed not only to new concepts in feeding techniques but also to dealing with Iowa farming as it actually was. Roswell, who complained that the university and the extension department were "drifting with – rather than leading – Iowa agriculture," believed that on the basis of their own research the university authorities should be joining him in slandering hay. The university was sympathetic to his aspirations for Iowa agriculture but not prepared to go that far. In 1968 Floyd Andre, Bud Ewing, and Marvin Anderson wrote him that "while we do not choose to state categorically that hay is obsolete, we agree that hay making presents problems both from the standpoint of harvesting efficiency and labor." They were not prepared to go further because "on some farms hay is still a useful alternative in providing winter roughage." The university did not feel that it could be single-minded in Roswell's way; rather, they conducted long-term experiments of great variety, including the use of alfalfa as the basic pasturing for cattle but supplemented by the use of cornstalks and cobs with added protein and vitamins. This method was a fairly simple extension of present farming practice, a method that constituted a practical improvement for the average farmer rather than a sweeping innovation. In the university's view, there was room for both and indeed an obligation on the part of the extension service to provide a variety of alternatives for the Iowa farmer.

However, there was one point on which the university and Roswell could agree: alfalfa hay (at eighteen dollars per ton in 1960) was more expensive than corn silage or cobs (ten dollars per ton in 1960). Because of alfalfa's nutrient value, it was not more expensive to feed up to four or five pounds of alfalfa per head per day, but beyond that amount it was, a situation that provided the economic rationale for the university's recommendation of cheaper feeds with supplements. Roswell's approach to the nutritionists of the Department of Animal Science was to ask them to make as strong a statement as they were able on the expense of hay beyond a certain point and to state as well that alfalfa was certainly not necessary as feed. He achieved both of these aims, and in his 1968 bulletin on fertilized pastures he was able to attribute the above statements to the Department of Animal Science of Iowa State University.

Roswell's patience in "teasing" these conclusions from the university reflects his respect for the work being done at Iowa State in the sixties and represents a change in attitude from his sweeping condemnations of the forties. However, the old belligerence could still surface, as it did during this same period in his correspondence with Sydney James of the Department of Economics. James wrote that he was conducting a survey of beef raising in Iowa and hoped to find out why more farmers did not use the cellulose and urea method pioneered in Coon Rapids. Would Roswell lend his assistance to the project? Roswell replied with a rambling historical essay designed to demonstrate that the failure of farmers to do so lay solely with the Iowa State Department of Economics. Cooperation was not offered.

AT the close of the decade, Bud Ewing put together some figures from his continuing study of beef production in the United States. From 1958 to 1965 the Central Plains states of Nebraska, Kansas, Texas, Oklahoma, and the Dakotas had shown the highest rate of increase with 44 percent, followed closely by 43 percent in the Corn Belt states. The national herd was increasing at a rate of 1.4 million per year; Iowa's beef herd had increased by 64 percent in the last eight years, and now stood at 4.6 million head. These statistics were reflected in Coon Rapids by more palpable signs of change. There was now as much pastureland as cornland in the state – 10 million acres of each – a changing proportion to be seen in the proliferation of pastures in the rolling hills south of town and even in the heavily planted corn land to the north. Feedlots proliferated and cattle dotted the hillsides, filling the big trucks that moved them throughout the state and over to the packing plant in Denison. The Garst operation was reaching toward five thousand head, with a separate bull-breeding operation of several hundred, all of which required feedlots, trench silos, and eventually a sale barn. The cattle brought cowboys, some with college educations and all of them with horses. The barns at the home farm were filled with saddles, and pastures that fed working plough horses fifty years ago now fed working saddle horses. The Garst children now preferred summer jobs on horseback spotting "hot" cows ready for artificial insemination and performed the insemination as well. Cattle talk was as common as corn talk in the evenings. This new overlay of cow-town ambience gave credence to remarks made in 1969 by W. M. Beeson of Purdue, one of Roswell's earliest sources of information twenty years before. The records at universities and on cow-calf farms, he wrote, demonstrated that feeder calves could be produced more cheaply on Corn Belt farms than on the western range. "In the next two decades," he prophesied, "the Corn Belt will become the 'Home on the Range'."

Russia Again: 1960–64

Khrushchev's visit to Coon Rapids established a reputation for Roswell in the West; in the East it underlined the chairman's intent to acquire for Russian agriculture the technological expertise of the West and affirmed publicly that his principal Western adviser was to be Roswell Garst. Another Russian tour and critique of Soviet agriculture was planned for Roswell in 1960, but his first major health problem prevented the journey. A gall bladder operation, postponed because of the Khrushchev visit in 1959, could not be delayed further and would require a period of convalescence. Roswell was also beginning to feel the fatigue that would reach its climax in 1962 and was for the first time daunted by the effort required for an Eastern European tour so soon after the activity of the last two years. Consequently, he decided to send his nephew, John Chrystal, in his place. The arrangements were made through the offices of his travel-agent acquaintance, Gabriel Reiner, who was in Moscow early in 1960 exploring the possibilities for tourism.

John Chrystal was thirty-five years old in 1960. He farmed with his brother Tom in Greene County, northeast of Coon Rapids, until the winter of 1958–59, when he joined the staff of the Iowa Savings Bank at Roswell's invitation, ostensibly for a short period of work. He had already served his apprenticeship in the Russian story, having housed and been generally responsible for the education of the Alexander Gitalov delegation in the summer of 1958. He knew agriculture well, demonstrated his knowledge to the Russians, and was taking hold in the bank. John's days in the Garst household after his mother's death in 1936 had sown the seeds for a close relationship with Roswell, who had promised his sister that he would look after her children. Chrystal's ability and availability made him the appropriate choice as Roswell's aide in his international activities, and, along with his work in the bank, gave him the opportunity to define his own role in the family, just as Stephen and David had done.

Excited by the opportunity and apprehensive over the task of substituting for Roswell, John, who had never been east of Chicago, arrived in Moscow on 1 June to begin a two-month tour of Russian agricultural regions. The schedule was strenuous: almost daily travelling, with days beginning at 6:30 A.M. or 7:00 A.M. and often not ending until after a long evening banquet, a routine broken only by a week in the Black Sea resort of Sochi. John was taken to at least two farms each day, or a farm and an agricultural plant of some sort, with a stop at an agricultural college at least once a week. He viewed corn, pigs, orchards, ducks, machinery, answered questions, gave speeches, and responded as enthusiastically as possible to everything he was shown. At one huge pig farm he encountered five hundred be-medalled female attendants stationed at every fourth pen, and reckoned that he had also personally inspected two thousand pigs by the end of the afternoon. On another occasion he was taken to an equally extensive orchard of mixed fruits, where, his feet sinking in the soft dirt, he trudged through row after row past equally impressive numbers of attendants, all female, this time standing behind hundreds of small tables filled with cherries, plums, and other fruits, all of which he resolutely admired.

As the weeks passed, and Chrystal was handed across provincial boundaries from one delegation to another—a ceremony that often took place on bridges—his knowledge and stamina won him increasing respect, earning him the dubious distinction of increasingly elaborate banquets and receptions. He became more than simply a substitute for Roswell and was catered to accordingly. What he lacked was news, and he suffered the summer in ignorance of the political processes at home, in which Roswell was involved. A high point of his trip was a visit to the farm of his Coon Rapids guest Alexander Gitalov, where he held seminars and was enthusiastically defended by his host when he described American farming practices some of his audience found hard to believe. The last overland leg of his visit was a flight to the new lands to see wheat farming, a journey pressed upon him even though he made no claim to expertise about wheat farming. On the return journey he was taken to the giant new dam on the Dneiper River, walked through the turbine rooms, and afterwards was taken on a launch upriver to picnic on an island. The picnic was served by waiters, eaten with silver cutlery on china spread on a linen tablecloth on the ground.

On his return to Moscow, John met with a group of officials he took to be the Executive Committee of the Ministry of Agriculture, made recommendations based on what he had seen during his tour, and answered more questions. From Russia he went to Hungary and Rumania for brief visits, then home on 1 September. His visit was a personal success and maintained the continuity of relationships between Coon Rapids and the Russian agricultural establishment, virtually from top to bottom.

WHILE John Chrystal was enjoying a warm reception in the hinterlands of Russia, there began in that summer of 1960 a bad patch in America's — and Roswell's — relations with the Soviet Union, occasioned first by the U-2 crisis of May 1960 and aggravated further by the confrontation over Berlin in the fall of 1961.

On 1 May 1960, two weeks before the four-power summit conference met in Paris to discuss the problem of a divided Germany, an American U-2 reconnaissance plane was shot down in Russian airspace. The Russians had known of these flights for several years, although they had never yet been able to intercept one. But now they were able to produce both pilot and plane to refute the American denial that this was a spying mission. Khrushchev's immediate reaction was relatively mild; he said he would accept a statement from Eisenhower that the president had known nothing about the flights. However, on his way to the Paris summit, Khrushchev decided to demand an apology from the United States, a halt to all future flights, and the punishment of those responsible for sending the mission. Eisenhower refused to affect ignorance of the flights, was willing to suspend them for the immediate future but would not commit himself to a permanent suspension, and flatly refused the other demands. Khrushchev denounced Eisenhower, cancelled the president's invitation to visit Moscow, and suggested that a further summit meeting be postponed for six months — in effect, until there was another president — and left Paris with East-West relations back in their posture of the fifties. Fearful that the Soviets might turn their rights in Berlin over to the unrecognized East German government, the United States put its armed forces on world-wide alert. In the event, Khrushchev did not carry through either his threat to sign a separate treaty with East Germany or to change his official commitment to peaceful coexistence. However, there could be no hope of progress until a new president came to office early in 1961. The chance for a rapid breakthrough in East-West relations was suddenly erased.

As in 1956, Roswell was riding high on an optimism verging on euphoria over the prospects for East-West accommodation. He had been, he believed, very much a part of the process by his contributions to the establishment of an atmosphere for negotiation and was convinced that peaceful coexistence was about to become a reality. Consequently, he felt personally betrayed by the actions of the principals on both sides. He was furious at Eisenhower for his refusal to disassociate himself from knowledge of the flights ("The son-of-a-bitch told the truth!" he exclaimed in the heat of his first reaction) and was upset over the president's intimation that flights would eventually continue. He was also angry at Khrushchev for his brutal attack on Eisenhower and his deliberate scuttling of the Paris summit. He was sought out by the press as a confidant of Khrushchev, told them he thought that the chairman had insulted the president, and found himself answered by Khrushchev in the chairman's defense of his actions. Although he could understand Garst's feelings, the Soviet leader said,

> I would say to Mr. Garst: Suppose someone at night stole your corn. You want to take him to court, but the thief tells you, "I like your corn, I have stolen it before and propose to steal it again."
> What if a Soviet plane flew over your farm and then the Soviets said they had to fly over your country to maintain their security? You would be indignant because you are an honest man. So you see, Mr. Garst, if after that I sent my visiting card to the President, I would have deceived not only my own people but all honest people in the world.

Sympathetic with Khrushchev's complaints about overflights, but not wishing to be drawn into the argument on either side, Roswell limited his public remarks to generalizations on the "sadness" of the present situation, an opinion he was able to convey to Khrushchev in October via Gabriel Reiner. "Mr. Khrushchev did agree that it is a sad situation now," Reiner replied after his return from Moscow, "and he also agrees with you that we should not despair for the future as a way will most likely be found out of the present unpleasant state of affairs." The chairman hoped Roswell would be visiting the Soviet Union again before long.

Although he continued to believe that it had been "a sad mistake to have the U-2 over Russia" and was critical of Khrushchev's excessive response, his natural resilience asserted itself. "It takes longer than I thought it would take to get some sensible approach toward disarmament," he admitted to Reiner, but he would press on when the opportunity next arose to present his views on the arms race. He stuck by his well-turned phrase: "It is global insanity—and nothing else—for the world to spend 100 billion dollars a year preparing for a war that no one wants—no one expects—a war that no one could survive."

However, a year later, September 1961, when Russian and American tanks faced each other in Berlin and the Wall went up, Roswell's hopes reached their nadir. In a letter to Jonathan he amended his "global insanity" statement: "I haven't ever been worried about a war breaking out until lately—but I am rather worried now." He was "amazed" that Khrushchev had started nuclear testing again, found him "uncompromising," and "turning out to be almost as impossible as Hitler was." Roswell told Johnny that he had "pretty good hopes" five years ago, but "little hope now that the darned thing is going to get straightened out." All he could do now was to lose himself in selling corn and trying to teach more people how to raise more food with less labor. But even that seemed "damned futile." To Gabriel Reiner he reported himself in "deep confusion."

In the spring of 1962 Roswell was invited by *U.S. News and World Report* to present his view on Russian agriculture which, as was his aim when he sent a copy of his statement to the Russian embassy, provided the means to renew his dialogue with Khrushchev. As a response to reports that Khrushchev's farming revolution was not going at all well, the magazine's interview with Roswell appeared in its 2 April edition entitled "The Real Story of Khrushchev's Farm Failure." "How bad, really, is the Russian farm problem?" the editors asked, and for an answer went to "the American regarded as closest" to the Russian effort.

In Roswell's view, the problem was not as bad as people thought it was. Although Russia began a program of capital investment in agriculture in 1955, the amount was far too small and was underestimated by Khrushchev. There were also the geographical disadvantages of the short and dry growing season; the lack of machinery; and the need for many more fertilizer plants, adequate roads, and transportation. In his preface Roswell agreed that the Russians were having difficulties, but that they were less catastrophic than they seemed. Roswell believed that Khrushchev had set impossibly high goals, especially with his boast that he would surpass the United States in agricultural production. Khrushchev wanted too much too soon; his immediate goal should be to lay the groundwork for a balanced program of investment, tailored to the limitations of Russian geography. The arms race, he concluded, should also be taken into account. "The logic of the situation," Roswell said "is that he ought to want to cool off the armaments race, so he would have more capital to put into agriculture and a lot of other things the Russian people want badly." The Americans could more easily afford an arms race; in Russia, he observed, "spending for armaments comes right out of the people's hides."

A response to the article was not long in coming. Gardner Cowles of *Look* magazine, a friend of Roswell's from the Wendell Willkie days, visited Khrushchev in Moscow shortly after the publication of the interview, and on 25 April, Cowles, now back home, published his own conversation with the Soviet leader. Khrushchev told Cowles that he had read the Garst interview and agreed with its analysis of Soviet agricultural ills. He would like to visit Garst, he told Cowles, but of course that was impossible, even if he were to wear a false beard and moustache, he said, and call himself Mr. Ivanovitch. Further confirmation of Khrushchev's continuing interest in Garst came from Lauren Soth of the *Register,* who saw Khrushchev in July and reported that the chairman said he wanted to see Roswell sometime during the year. "He told me," Soth wrote to Roswell, "that he got great satisfaction out of talking with you about agricultural matters."

Roswell was never uninterested in talking agriculture with anyone, but in 1962, with his educational interests now directed towards the underdeveloped nations, Roswell was primarily concerned with initiating a dialogue with the chairman about the arms race. He hoped that Khrushchev's undoubted confidence in his agricultural opinions might be transferred to the problems of inspection of nuclear facilities and a reduction in the arms budget of both countries. Heartened by the reports from Cowles and Soth, Roswell wrote to Moscow offering to come and was immediately invited for October 1962.

In September Roswell entertained a Russian delegation sponsored by the State Department and the USDA, to be reciprocated by a visit to Moscow by Secretary of Agriculture Freeman. Still journalist-shy after 1959, Roswell allowed only pool coverage of the delegation's visit. "One experience with too many photographers and too many correspondents at the time of the Khrushchev visit is enough," he wrote. In that same month Roswell's health began to fail again, and in October he was in the hospital recovering from his laryngectomy. A trip to Russia that fall was out of the question.

As it turned out, Khrushchev was also otherwise engaged in October. The missiles he was installing in Cuba to cancel out America's numerical superiority in nuclear weapons were discovered by yet another U-2 reconnaissance aircraft, and after thirteen days of the most dangerous confrontation yet to occur between the superpowers, he ordered them withdrawn. Roswell and the rest of the world breathed more easily and fervently hoped the Soviet leader had finally learned that the risk of such adventures was too high.

During these events the agricultural promotion in Moscow, which was apparently to have revolved around Roswell, was carried on anyway. On 24 October, the day two Russian ships and a submarine were approaching the Kennedy blockade of Cuba and the Western world awaited the hourly news reports, *Izvestia* published "An Open Letter to Mr. Garst" from Alexander Gitalov. He noted he now harvested the same amount of corn as he had when working on the Garst farm and was doing it at a slightly lower cost. He asked Roswell what the yield was now in Coon Rapids. (Valerie Tereshtenko thought it "a nice letter"; Western journalists reported it as belligerent in tone; Roswell pointed out privately that American yields were still higher.) On 27 October the Moscow newspaper *Agricultural Life* published the text of Roswell's speech on the need for increased cattle herds he had given in Des Moines to the Association of Agricultural Editors which, according to Tereshtenko, "was widely discussed by all agricultural specialists in Kiev."

In November at the Congress of the Communist Party, Roswell's name came up on at least two occasions, the most interesting of which occurred when Gitalov gave the report on the accomplishments of his farm. His report produced the following exchange with Khrushchev:

K: Alexander Vasilievich Gitalov, you should write him [Garst] about this and say that you were his pupil for one year and now exceed the economic indices of Mr. Garst. Write him about the results which you achieved on your farm and how much more corn you got in comparison with what he receives on his farm. [Applause].
G: Very well, Nikita Sergeevich, I shall write to him.
K: Generally speaking, Mr. Garst is a sensible man. He is a capitalist, but he is for competition with us on an honest foundation. We should utilize his experience in the growing of corn and learn from him. His experience is great.
G: In 1958 I worked at Garst's. . . .
K: [Interrupts] Not all the delegates know that Comrade Gitalov went, in 1958, to the USA to Garst's farm. Garst himself suggested this to me. "Mr. Khrushchev," he said, "send me your people. I shall teach them so that one man could take care of 100 hectares of corn." Well, Comrade Gitalov went to Garst. Comrade Gitalov, who else worked with you at Garst's?
G: Comrade Shuydko from the Krasnodar region.
K: They went and for the whole summer worked at Garst's. And one should say that they worked with use, benefitted greatly, and acquired good experience from him.

Khrushchev's intervention at this point in the proceedings illustrates his continuing esteem for Roswell and the extent to which he was prepared to invoke Roswell's reputation within the Soviet Union and in the West to help shore up his own agricultural programs. In fact, in 1962 Russian agriculture was in difficulty. Heavy rains caused great losses in corn and wheat, a situation aggravated by their lack of roads and other problems endemic to Soviet farming. These problems were compounded rather than improved by Khrushchev's well-intentioned but poorly conceived and executed campaigns to increase agricultural output. His obsession with surpassing the West, which may also be seen in the exchange with Gitalov, combined with what Roy and Zhores Medvedev have called "the absence of any cautious restraint" in his corn and meat programs, in the restructuring of the agricultural bureaucracy, and in the unwieldy scale of his projects in the virgin lands were all beginning to put a severe strain on an agricultural establishment struggling to use Western technology effectively, but increasingly stretched too thin between excessively high goals and inadequate resources.

In the spring of 1963, with his mechanical voice literally in hand, Roswell once again took up his Russian enterprise where he had left it, at the planning stage for a visit to the Soviet Union, and for the same reason. "I want to make one more hard attempt," he told Phil Maguire in April 1963, "to get Chairman Khrushchev to be more flexible and cooperative in doing away with further nuclear testing—and in getting a *lowering* of the arms burden on both of our two countries."

As usual, Roswell paved the way for his journey by consultations in Washington. He wanted approbation of his general course of action—he was less of a maverick in these matters than he sometimes intimated— and he wanted some bargaining leverage concerning further Soviet investment in American equipment. To the secretary of commerce Roswell outlined his plans to urge further Soviet investment and asked Commerce to be willing to approve export licenses for farm machinery and road-building equipment. To Llewelyn Thompson, the ambassador to Russia, and to officials at the Eastern European desks in State, and to White House assistants he presented his hopes for a discussion of the arms race with Khrushchev. The consensus in diplomatic circles was that aid to Russian agriculture should be encouraged, especially now that the resolution of the missile crisis offered an opportunity for more stabilized relations with Moscow. Although Roswell's personal initiative in asking Khrushchev to begin discussions on a nuclear testing ban did not rate a high chance of success, he was encouraged to speak his mind on the issue. He was also given a message by Chester Bowles to deliver on behalf of the administration. According to Roswell, Bowles requested him to tell Khrushchev that President Kennedy could not go to Congress and suggest a treaty with less than seven inspections. Bowles also asked Roswell to stress the mutual advantages of a step away from nuclear testing. Roswell, hopeful that Khrushchev's testing of Kennedy's resolve had ended with Cuba, set off for Moscow with considerable optimism.

His reception in Russia was extraordinary. "Travelling with Uncle Bob through Eastern Europe," John Chrystal wrote to his cousins, "is . . . what I imagine it is like to travel with the Queen of England in the outlying parts of her Empire." The name "Garst" opened all doors, John reported. All they had to do was get in and out of cars and talk. The outward signs of their regal status in that stubbornly privilege-conscious society were dramatically demonstrated on two occasions: they were driven through the pedestrians-only precinct outside the Palace of Congresses in the Kremlin to a performance of the Bolshoi Ballet; the nonstop Aeroflot flight from Moscow to Budapest was ordered to land at Kiev to carry them on to Hungary.

Roswell and John were met at the airport by Ilya Emilianov, the agricultural attaché in Washington; Vladimir Matskevitch, minister of agriculture, both veterans of Coon Rapids; and A. S. Shevchenko, Khrushchev's personal agricultural adviser and in John's and Roswell's opinion "the practicing head of agriculture in the USSR." After a brief stop at their hotel, the party plunged into its usual taxing routine. Early in the trip they met the minister of chemistry who, when Roswell offered to press Khrushchev for more funds for agricultural chemistry, said "Don't!" because he already had more than he knew how to spend efficiently. They met with the minister of roads, who painted a more somber picture of his difficulties in dealing with the dirt tracks constituting most of the road system, which were rendered useless even by a normal rainfall. John soon noted with satisfaction that Roswell's mechanical voice did not make communication difficult, even with people who spoke little English, and that Roswell's vigor seemed fully restored. "They kept the physical requirements of the trip high," John said, but Roswell was up to the pace.

The climactic event of the Moscow leg of their journey was the meeting with Khrushchev, which had been arranged for 10 May. At 3 P.M. Roswell and John were driven to the Kremlin for a two-hour session in Khrushchev's office. Roswell and Nikita Sergeevich talked and occasionally argued about a wide range of subjects, "a general conversation you might have with anybody," John reported. They talked agriculture, of course, not only Russian but also Roswell's new interest, Central and South America, as well as ways of getting peasants to accept new ideas, a subject that prompted Khrushchev to reminisce about his own early years of poverty. At one point, during an exchange about Russian agriculture, Khrushchev and his aide Shevchenko had a long, heated, and untranslated argument about the Russian geneticist Lysenko.

Roswell had two further topics that he pressed throughout the day, the first a case of compassion, the second the arms race. The compassionate case concerned the brothers of a friend of Roswell's from Omaha. When Roswell asked that they be given exit permits to come to the United States, Khrushchev brushed the matter off as something that did not directly concern him. Roswell continued to bring up the matter, much to Khrushchev's annoyance, persisting until the premier said he would see if something could be done. The next day, an official turned up to collect details concerning the brothers. However, Roswell and John learned later that the men had asked to go to Israel rather than the United States and had been denied permits.

Roswell talked at some length on the economic burdens of the arms race, emphasizing the disproportionate amount of money Russia and the United States were spending compared with other Western nations. On the issue of inspection of nuclear facilities, Roswell passed on his message about Kennedy and the U.S. Congress. Khrushchev replied that he and Kennedy were playing the same game, which was to get as much as they could out of their respective bureaucracies. "I have got all I can get," Khrushchev said; if Kennedy had got all he could get, then Khrushchev did not know what else could be done. "Go back and tell Kennedy," he told Roswell, "that when he leaves the presidency he'll still be a rich man. When I leave this job, I'll just have one pair of trousers." Roswell did not find Khrushchev at all conciliatory on the subject: shortly after his return, Roswell wrote that he and John had pressed Khrushchev on the advantages of a testing treaty "as strongly as we knew how, apparently with little effect."

John found Khrushchev knowledgeable about agriculture, amiable during most parts of their conversation, but also "a politician to the core," who talked with gestures and at length on political topics, a practice that annoyed Roswell sufficiently for him to give Khrushchev the "Elizabeth buzz" with his mechanical voice. The intrusion was "effective but startling," John reported, "and I think hardly in order for use with heads of state."

At 5 P.M. Khrushchev, Garst, and Chrystal left the Kremlin by car, unescorted, and drove to the Khrushchev town house on the bank of the Moscow River near the heights on which the University of Moscow stands, there to pick up Nina Khrushcheva; her unmarried daughter, who was a lawyer; and her son, an engineer. They stopped for a brief walk around the grounds, during which Roswell presented Madame Khrushcheva a gift from Elizabeth, and she in turn drew John aside to inquire about Roswell's health. From there they journeyed to the Khrushchev country dacha, John travelling in a small car with the son and daughter.

The dacha nestled in roughly a half-section of land (360 acres) planted largely in apple trees, whose groves stretched down to the Moscow River, about twenty miles from their earlier stop. The visit began with a walk in the mild spring evening from the front gate of the estate down to the river, along its banks, and back again, a circuit of almost two miles. At one point, Khrushchev asked if Roswell were tired. "You're older, keep walking," Roswell replied. Back at the house, they were greeted by Khrushchev's daughter Rada and her husband Adzhubei, who had visited the Garst farm in 1959. The house itself had a covered patio on which the party ate, a large dining room, a pool room, a sun room filled with gifts from visiting dignitaries, a study, and one downstairs bedroom and bath.

The supper, prepared by Nina Khrushcheva, her daughter, and two maids, consisted of a vegetable salad, caviar, tomatoes, fried potatoes, fish, and duck. "Who do you think shot the ducks?" Khrushchev asked and answered, "Castro." "What is Mr. Castro like?" Roswell asked. "A nice young man," Khrushchev replied, "who is still a little wet behind the ears." Dinner was served informally, and the conversation was "spirited," according to John Chrystal, "covering every topic you can imagine." There were drinks for those who wanted them, but Nina Khrushcheva kept an eye on her husband's consumption, and once put her hand over his glass when he was about to pour himself more.

About 9:30 P.M. Roswell and John left and were walked by the entire family through the apple trees to the front gate, where farewells were exchanged, and the two visitors returned to Moscow. John found Khrushchev an engaging, pleasant man who was very fond of his family. "If you could forget or explain away Hungary or the previous liquidations," John concluded, "you could not find a more delightful man."

From Moscow they took an overnight train to Kiev, there to be met by the ranking officials of the Ukraine and to be reunited with Valerie Tereshtenko, comfortably established in an apartment on Mechnikova Street and much in demand as a lecturer on American management techniques. They journeyed into the countryside for several days to visit farms and to renew old acquaintances. Wherever he went, Roswell was greeted with a warmth and affection that sprang not from the favor of Khrushchev but from the past eight years of his own efforts to improve the farms of the Ukraine. He was shown the best of them and was encouraged by what he observed; his message to them was "you don't need me anymore." Roswell did not let down as a performer. Visiting the inevitable duck farm and called upon to respond to what he had seen, Roswell asked the chairman of the collective if he had had any success with Khaki Camel ducks. John thought he had invented a new breed on the spot, but it turned out that Roswell remembered that he and Johnny had raised a few Khaki Camels on the farm in 1915.

In Budapest, after the unscheduled flight from Kiev, there were more dignitaries and more old friends to meet them. Chief among the latter were Mr. Fono, who had seen Roswell off on the coal boat during the revolution and had flown back from London for the present occasion, and Sandor Rajke, who flew in from Rome while they were still at the airport. In Budapest they stayed once again at the Grand Hotel on Marguerite Island, where Roswell and Elizabeth had played bridge under the unsettling protection of Russian tanks. They met government officials, travelled to Rajke's Institute at Martonvasar, drove to Lake Balaton to sample wine, and returned to Budapest with three wicker hampers of gift bottles.

In response to a request by Roswell, the ministry of agriculture sent a man to wrap the hampers for travel. "He spoke no English," John recalled, "and arrived at our hotel with a ball of twine, a knife, and wrapping paper; completed his job and was driven away."

The Hungarian newspapers gave extensive coverage to Roswell's visit, and in the flush of his success, he "dropped in at the legation for a chat," as Leopold Gotzinger, second secretary, reported, and repeated his optimistic view of Eastern European progress. "In his call at the Legation," Gotzinger remarked, "Garst displayed above all tremendous pride in his friendship with bloc leaders, and especially with Khrushchev." He "waved off" the claims of the American press that Eastern European agriculture was in a crisis.

In Bucharest they were met by more former visitors to Coon Rapids, and from their base at the government guest house made a series of visits to farming establishments. "They show great effect from their association with Coon Rapids," John noted. "It seemed to us that they had been the most willing to borrow from us and thus had profited most." At Fundulea, the research station founded shortly after Roswell's first visit to Rumania and largely at his suggestion, Roswell entertained and instructed. John Chrystal recorded the following anecdote:

One man kept saying a machine was too wasteful that lost seven per cent of the corn grain in harvest. Roswell spotted him from the questions and accused him of being an economist. He told the crowd an American with a cornpicker could pick 45 times as much corn as a Rumanian by hand. Roswell said the way to convince this man was to make him pick corn himself for a day and learn that waste of human energy was worse than a small grain loss of machine harvest. The man confessed to being as accused, an economist.

On an overnight trip to Transylvania they visited a tractor factory producing for export as well as for a domestic market, a poultry plant with 1.5 million broilers and layers, a 500-cow dairy farm equipped with Western European machinery, and a greenhouse producing vegetables also for export.

On their last day in Rumania the party drove about ten miles from Bucharest to the lakeside residence of Vice President Magarush for drinks with a number of guests. Then they embarked in well-appointed motor launches for the journey to a lakeside restaurant in which they were the only diners. "We ate for a while," John recorded, "then everyone jumped up and in walked the president, Georghi Georghiu-Dej, his economic planner, and the ministers of chemicals and petroleum. Our little translator almost fainted, his first language other than Rumanian being Swedish, and English second." After a long discussion about agriculture with the president, they travelled again by boat to see a palace and were taken by automobile to Georghiu-Dej's summer home. They sat on the patio talking agriculture until 10 P.M., returning to Bucharest for a late visit with Silviu Brucan. "The next day," John wrote, "we left for home after what I would call a triumphal march through Eastern Europe."

Both Roswell and John left confident that within five to ten years the countries they had visited would achieve an increased production "within the limits of their climates," enough to satisfy their domestic needs and in some instances to export, a prediction that was fulfilled in the case of Hungary and Rumania. In an interview with Donald Janson of the *New York Times* Roswell emphasized his valedictory feelings towards Eastern Europe and his new interest in Central and South America, India, and Asia. "Soviet agriculture has made 50 times as much progress in recent years as these areas have," he told Janson, and it was to other parts of the world that he now proposed to turn his attention.

That summer there was progress of a kind that surprised but certainly pleased Roswell. In June 1963 it was announced that "high-level" talks were to be held in Moscow on a nuclear-test treaty and arms reduction. It sounded like a significant step away from the years of confrontation and, as it turned out, marked the beginning of a policy change by Khrushchev that blossomed into detente. "I take a little quiet pride out of the announcement," Roswell wrote to Phil Maguire. He allowed himself the delicious thought that his conversation with the chairman might have "contributed a little" to the decision to enter into negotiations. "Anyhow," he concluded, "I have the pride of having tried to contribute."

ALTHOUGH his interest was shifting to Latin America, Roswell took pains to follow through on the suggestions he made to Khrushchev and on queries made by the chairman and other Russian agriculturalists. He arranged to show a delegation the Garst and Thomas sorghum operation in Kansas, investigated the feasibility of exporting fertilizer plants, and, after further consultation with Washington, assured Khrushchev that American road-building equipment would be made available if Khrushchev would but order it. He also wrote more on agricultural topics for the Russians. The performance of these chores was sweetened for Roswell by the signing of the partial test-ban treaty in August 1963. Khrushchev, he believed, was serious about putting more money into agriculture and was willing at least to trim his defense budget to accomplish this end.

For his part, Khrushchev took steps to maintain the new burst of momentum in agricultural planning, of which Roswell's visit seems to have been part, an activity spurred by the worsening situation of the Russian farm economy. A drought in the late summer of 1963 caught the Soviet Union without adequate reserves of grain, and for the first time they were forced to purchase wheat from the West. In December 1963 a plenary session of the Central Committee agreed on a new budget that provided increases for the farming sector, and a later meeting in February 1964 was entirely devoted to agriculture. Khrushchev continued to invoke Roswell's prestige in the USSR by publishing various writings by his American friend. At the time of the December deliberations by the Central Committee, two letters from Roswell to Khrushchev were published in *Country Life,* both on agricultural matters and including Roswell's congratulations on the signing of the test-ban treaty.

The next publication occurred because of a specific request by the chairman, made through his agricultural aide Shevchenko. In January 1964 Shevchenko wrote to thank Roswell on behalf of the chairman for the recently published letters. "Maybe Nikita Sergeevich himself will write you a letter," Shevchenko predicted, "but now he is very busy with urgent affairs." Shevchenko sent copies of the *Country Life* publications, noting that "specialists and practical farmers are interested in your articles and letters. That's why we considered it possible to publish . . . part of your letters. . . . From our talk in Kiev I understood you meant it would be possible." Shevchenko, on behalf of the chairman, requested one more letter timed to coincide with the Central Committee meeting in February, when "the problems of intensification of agriculture through wide applications of fertilizers and mechanization" would be discussed. "We would appreciate very much," Shevchenko continued, "if you could write for [the] Soviet press, as soon as possible, a big detailed article about your experience in farming, about your farm and general trends in farm management in the US." The topic was broad, but Shevchenko was confident that "you are a man of great knowledge, big practical experience and, no doubt, you will find what to say to our agricultural people."

Shevchenko's letter was an accurate indicator of the general line Khrushchev took in the February meeting. The largest agricultural expenditure was to consist of a "sharp increase in the production of fertilizers, herbicides as well as irrigation projects," as Shevchenko put it, with a continuing emphasis on the production of machinery. Roswell's suggestion of road building would not be pursued because of the "huge investments" in chemistry, Shevchenko said, which left no funds available for large-scale road construction.

In fulfilling this request, Roswell wrote the traditional preface comparing American and Russian opportunities for progress and then briefly discussed the four areas of progress in American agriculture responsible for its present level of efficiency that should be emulated by Russia. The first area, the use of hybrid seed corn, had already been mastered in Eastern Europe; the second, mechanization, was one in which the Eastern nations were well on their way to parity; the third, the use of fertilizer and other chemicals, was one in which the United States was about a decade ahead and required large investments by the Eastern Europeans; the fourth—and here Roswell stuck to his guns—was a farm-to-market road system, in which the United States was "far ahead." Roswell also touched on urea and other protein supplements for livestock and made an appeal for continuing reductions in arms expenditure by both sides. "My hope," he concluded, "is that great progress can be made in both fields—in agriculture and disarmament."

The timing of the publication of the article was impeccable. It appeared in all the major Russian papers on 13 February; Khrushchev gave his speech to the plenary session on agriculture on 14 February. "Comrades," he noted, "I am sure you read in the newspapers yesterday the article by the American farmer Mr. Roswell Garst on the development of agriculture in the Soviet Union and in the United States of America." He did not pretend that it was a coincidence. "I would like to express my gratitude to Mr. Garst, who also 'wished' to include himself in the work of our plenary session, so to speak [*stir in the hall*], even though he is an adherent of the capitalist system and runs his farm well and profitably. . . . Mr. Garst's circumstances have not prevented him from evaluating correctly enough the state of our agriculture."

As Shevchenko told Roswell, Khrushchev in his speech announced an "upsurge" and "intensification" in agriculture, an effort whose centerpiece was to be a program, "unprecedented in scope and significance," Khrushchev said, "for the accelerated development of the chemical industry." A rapid increase in the production of fertilizer was the main goal, but herbicides and chemical additives for livestock feed would also be manufactured on a larger scale. Extensive irrigation projects were to be undertaken, mechanization would continue, efficiency of output would ensure "more products with the same expenditure," and reorganization would create efficient specialization.

Khrushchev used Roswell's article in his speech as a checklist for his own goals. "We must heed the advice Mr. Garst gives on questions of technology and production," Khrushchev noted; they had already taken his advice on hybrid corn and had "accomplished much." Observing that Roswell in his article also emphasized the significance of fertilizers and improved machinery, Khrushchev noted that the new emphasis on chemistry "commanded the respect of Mr. Garst's understanding and sentiments." They were also following his advice in the matter of herbicides and protein feed supplements. Insecticides were still not mentioned.

Three of Roswell's four main points were thus taken up by Khrushchev; the fourth, farm-to-market roads, was to be set aside for the present for financial reasons. "The importance of roads is well known," Khrushchev said. "I have repeatedly listened to Mr. Garst in this connection, and he has fascinated me with his proofs of the need for such construction." However, there was simply not enough money for the capital investment required, Khrushchev concluded. "The large-scale construction of such roads is obviously a matter for the next stage."

Both the speech and Roswell's article caused a stir in the Soviet Union and the United States. "A towering gesture of respect," the *New York Times* reported of the publication of the Garst article. Harrison Salisbury, with Roswell's original text in hand, wrote that the article had been accurately translated, and was "a hell of a good statement," a useful mixture of down-to-earth talk for the Russians, as Salisbury told Roswell, and some good ideas about America. "I'd say you've done more for the 'American image' than all the efforts of our professional propagandists for a long, long time. In this instance you've been once again our most effective 'secret weapon'."

In April, *Izvestia* published another article by Roswell, this time devoted to livestock. There was no further news from Russia until October 1964, when the world learned that Khrushchev had been deposed and forced into retirement, largely, and ironically, according to the Medvedevs, because of his mismanagement of agriculture. Anxious to get a last message through if possible, Roswell wrote to Ambassador Foy Kohler. "How can I extend to Mr. and Mrs. Khrushchev," he wrote, "our thoughts that they served their country and the probability of a more peaceful world well—and that I congratulate them and wish them well?" Kohler suggested a letter to Mikoyan, that accomplished survivor. Roswell never saw Khrushchev again and believed that the abrupt termination of Khrushchev's career also signalled the termination of his connection with the Soviet Union.

El Salvador Experiment

Among his various projects at the close of the fifties, Roswell managed to fit in the beginnings of a book on how to eliminate hunger in the world. It was to be a three-way collaboration: Roswell, Jonathan, and Carl T. Rowan, a Minneapolis-based journalist and free-lance writer interested in the problem of hunger. Rowan was the author of *The Pitiful and the Proud,* a 1956 survey of India, Pakistan, and Southeast Asia, and an admirer of Roswell ("a farmer with a mission," as he characterized Roswell in a presentation copy of his book). Rowan and Roswell started working together in 1959, but the project never got beyond a few chapters dictated by Roswell as grist for Rowan. In 1961 Rowan took a job in the Kennedy administration, and the project in its collaborative form was dropped.

What was finally produced was a book by Jonathan in 1963 entitled

No Need For Hunger, written after his travels in Central and South
America in 1961 and 1962. It did not make much of a splash in the book
world, but it was of central importance to Roswell for the rest of his life.
It celebrated the Coon Rapids achievement and served as a manifesto for
what Roswell hoped to accomplish in the underdeveloped countries
during the sixties. Consequently, it provides an essential prologue to the
El Salvador experiment.

His book, Johnny wrote, was "conceived in anger" over the frustrating knowledge of the gap between the potential available to relieve world
hunger and the failure as yet to fulfill that potential. His book, he said,
was "dedicated to the proposition that almost everybody ought to have all
they want to eat." In style it was only occasionally angry, usually breezily
anecdotal, rather digressive, illustrative of Johnny's ability to present
statistics in readable form and to state arresting thoughts in a catchy,
aphoristic mode. Had it been consistently polemic in tone and more
sharply focused, it might have had more appeal. But then, of course, it
wouldn't have been Johnny.

His formal thesis was that the present world population could be well
fed and that feeding people well was the best way to reduce population
growth. Although there were areas such as South Korea in which population had already outstripped resources, the tropical countries offered
great hope for improving diet and slowing population growth, especially
the Central and South American countries he had most recently visited.
In general, the book moved in two tracks. The first involved a summary
of the progress made in American farming since the turn of the century,
with examples drawn primarily from the Coon Rapids farm; the second,
the means by which that knowledge could be transplanted to the "undeveloped" countries, so that an immediate start on increased production
could be made.

Progress was his theme throughout the book, or, more significantly,
rate of progress. In his chapter on "The Farm at Coon Rapids" Johnny
captured the feeling of acceleration he shared with his brother. We have
had experiments in poor farming for millenia, he wrote, but experiments
in scientific farming for only a hundred years; forty years ago we could
not have fed the entire world, but we can today; in the last ten years the
potential for food production has increased as much as in the entire ten
thousand years of farming in the Western world. Finally, "if you were
away from the coffee table in the Southside Cafe at Coon Rapids for a few
months you hardly knew what they were talking about when you got
back."

Rate of progress was elevated by Johnny into an essential requirement in the successful battle against population growth. Slow, "paltry"
efforts to increase food production were actually dangerous, in his view,

because they merely helped increase the population without raising the standard of living of the poor. They did not create sufficient prosperity to encourage peasants to maintain the level of physical well-being they attained by producing smaller families. However, in South America he saw the opportunity to double food production very quickly, achieving the speed he believed essential. The longer the present circumstance of low yields continued, the more difficult it would be to increase them. "It will be twice as hard in twenty to twenty-five years, because the population will double in that time." The theory that prosperity was the most effective means of reducing population growth was accepted by a number of experts in the field; Johnny's emphasis on speed as an imperative reflected a concept of progress rooted in the history of Iowa cornfields.

Johnny's critique of the present foreign aid program was an extended version of his "send salesman not Ph.D.'s" letters to Roswell. In order to recover the "sources of energy and drive" that had produced America's agricultural achievements, Johnny proposed to shift the balance from governmental intervention to the private entrepreneurial pattern that had worked so well in the Midwest. "We have to work, to some extent at least, on a government-to-government basis," he conceded, but he thought help could be given more effectively by practicing farmers acting as short-term consultants who could get particular programs going in the same way they did at home—a "Food Corps," as Johnny styled it, but with even shorter terms of service than the two years of the Peace Corps.

His second suggestion was the encouragement within the underdeveloped countries themselves of a homegrown entrepreneurial system centered on the agricultural salesman, the kind of structure that made possible the introduction of hybrid seed corn in the thirties. "Here is the road to progress," he wrote, "millions of little salesmen, millions and millions of small sales to small poor operators, financed in all sorts of petty ways." It could not, of course, be a carbon copy of American practice; it would become their system, not our system. "The assumption that because we know better how to produce we also know better how to live is unmitigated arrogance." Nevertheless, Johnny believed it was our best hope for preserving democracy. "A salesman and democracy go together like a fish and water," Johnny wrote. "He has to have customers who are free to choose. He can only persuade, not coerce."

Johnny thought that fertilizer provided the most promising subject for a practical application of these theories in the underdeveloped countries. "Fertilizer," he said, "gets to the bottom of the social scale. The foreign aid cannot all end up in the capital." Its use could be quickly learned by farmers, it required no fundamental change in their pattern of farming, it could be applied by hand, and its results were quickly apparent. In order for its introduction to peasant farmers to be successful, however, it was essential to introduce it on a large scale, Johnny argued. "Fertilizer should have priority in most hungry countries," he wrote, "but priority only if a total job can be done." A small amount would merely increase population. Johnny's analogy was with Europe's postwar recovery: "The reason the Marshall Plan was so successful in Europe was because it was quick and big and fast."

Johnny's suggestions for the techniques of fertilizer distribution came in part from his trip to El Salvador in the spring of 1962 for the USDA to oversee the distribution of a shipment of surplus wheat. Johnny was always critical of the tendency of surplus sales, geared mainly to relieve our own problems, to hurt the small producer of food in the underdeveloped countries by depressing prices and by making the country dependent on imports. Consequently, he worked out a plan with the Salvadorean government to have this shipment of wheat sold to the mills, with the proceeds to be held as credit for the peasant farmers. In this way the farmers could use the credits to buy fertilizer and better seeds and thus help themselves. Mindful of Roswell's use of samples, Johnny discussed the possibility of distributing small bags of fertilizer.

Of course there would be problems. "A program of extending credit to very small, often illiterate farmers," he wrote, "and then collecting the small debts – is slow, difficult, and expensive." Success would also create problems; if yields were dramatically increased, there would be inadequate storage and destabilization of prices. However, it was essential to take the plunge now, to make a start. "This business of reversing the age-old pattern where the rich get richer and the poor have children is hard enough to start without trying to be perfect."

Roswell loved the book. He could embrace its message because he was part of it, the Great Implementer whose farm at Coon Rapids was the source of Johnny's picture of American agricultural progress. It was a celebration and a vindication of his entire career, an eloquent expression of his own aspirations for world agriculture, given a further dimension of satisfaction by the approbation of his two heroes, Johnny himself and Henry Wallace, and that third figure who came to represent much for him, Hubert Humphrey. "The nation and world owe a great deal to Roswell and Jonathan Garst," Wallace had written for the book's dust jacket. "More than anyone else they showed what nitrogen expansion could do to grain yields. . . . *No Need for Hunger* is a splendid book and its essential message is sound." Humphrey's remarks on the jacket were in a similar, if more lengthy, vein. It is, Humphrey wrote, "one of the most exciting books I have seen in the past decade." Roswell regularly took the book off the shelf in his living room to point out the Wallace message in particular and kept another copy upstairs in the bedroom to consult in the evenings. He bought hundreds of copies to send to friends and associates;

Lee Kline, a radio broadcaster on Des Moines' WHO, received five copies
of the book from Roswell over the next decade.

In December of 1963, Roswell had written to Phil Maguire that he was an
Iowa farmer looking for a job. That month passed, and so did January of
1964, without a governmental response to Roswell's offer of service. In
February he got an offer from an unexpected source. A. S. Shevchenko
wrote that during Premier Castro's visit to the Soviet Union just before
Roswell's arrival, Khrushchev had sung Roswell's praises to the Cuban
leader, who was interested in obtaining Roswell's help. "I don't know
whether it is timely," Shevchenko explained, "but I thought wouldn't you
find it expedient and possible to make a trip to Cuba and familiarize
yourself with agriculture there and its possibilities." The request was
timely in a way Shevchenko could not have anticipated. Flattered at first
but then increasingly angry, Roswell, who did not like Castro and would
not have wished to help him, complained to Phil Maguire about the irony
of the request. Khrushchev was anxious to get him to help Castro, he
complained, "and yet I offer to go anywhere in Central or South America
for David Bell—or the Department of State—or Department of Agriculture—and get no use at all out of it." John Chrystal wrote to Bell, an
acquaintance of his, and Roswell decided to go to Washington "and give it
a good big push."

By March things were finally on the move. Roswell's dossier had
found its way to the desk of Dr. Benjamin Birdsall of the Latin American
Bureau of the Agency for International Development (AID). Birdsall set
plans afoot for Roswell to make an exploratory tour of Central and South
America beginning in April. Sandor Rajke of Hungary would see to Castro on behalf of Khrushchev; Roswell had the job he wanted on behalf of
the United States. He became a charter member of Johnny's Food Corps.

Ben Birdsall earned a B.S. in agronomy in his home state at the
University of Wisconsin, his Ph.D. at Michigan State. His first job was
with the United Fruit Company, his first posting abroad to Honduras.
During World War II he entered government service and stayed, devoting
himself to helping Latin American farmers improve their farming techniques. Small and wiry in frame, rich in practical experience, scholarly in
training, enthusiastic about his work, he possessed all the professional
and social attributes Roswell found attractive. The two men immediately
fell into a close working relationship, their wives took to each other, and it
was as a comfortable foursome that Ben and Florence and Roswell and
Elizabeth set off for Latin America in April 1964 to visit government
leaders and agricultural institutions for the next month and a half.

Some large-scale work in promoting the use of fertilizer was already under way in Latin America. In 1961 the United Nations Food and Agriculture Organization (FAO) instituted a program that was largely funded by the contributions of private fertilizer companies. The program operated in seven Latin American countries under the direction of C. H. H. ter Kuile, regional leader, and in 1964 had 3,000 demonstrations in operation. These demonstrations were primarily investigative in nature, designed, as ter Kuile put it, to provide "fertilizer response analysis and economic studies." The demonstrations were not geared especially for small farmers, as were Roswell's, but were complementary in their objectives and would prove an important source of information for the AID program. Roswell and Birdsall included ter Kuile in various meetings in Guatemala, El Salvador, and Costa Rica. Roswell deemed it important to work in cooperation with the FAO as much as possible, and to encourage their fertilizer program. For his part, ter Kuile was happy to cooperate. "I must say," he wrote of Garst and Birdsall to his superiors in Rome, "that they have given us considerable moral support."

Roswell intended to visit Brazil in early June as part of his itinerary, but a revolution in that country forced him to cancel the visit. However, he managed to make a quick trip on his own in July. Roswell had already met in Washington with Richard R. Neuberg, head of the AID agricultural mission to Brazil, and had given him a copy of his pamphlet "Suggestions for Helping Brazil." He saw Neuberg again in Brazil and learned that there was already enough fertilizer on hand for a large number of demonstrations. Roswell also met the director of the country's largest youth organization, who pledged his cooperation, and saw his friend and protegé Antonio Secundino, who pledged enough hybrid seed for 25,000 demonstrations. There was no occasion to use Pioneer seeds because they were unsuited to the tropics; the hybrid seed used in Latin America was developed by the Rockefeller Foundation.

As soon as he returned from his first trip in June, Roswell began lobbying Senator J. William Fulbright, Humphrey, and Thomas C. Mann, assistant secretary of state, on behalf of his plan to establish 5,000 demonstration plots in eight Latin American countries, with Birdsall in charge of the whole project. Although the program was being favorably considered, its scale was immediately called into question. Roswell heard in July via Phil Maguire that Birdsall might not be in charge of the program and thought that both he and Birdsall were going to get nothing more than a bureaucratic shuffle on their program. Roswell wanted one man in charge of the entire operation, he told Maguire, and was ready to come back to Washington to fight for this concept. Roswell also wanted the program to be, as Johnny had described the Marshall Plan, quick and big and fast.

While the shape the demonstrations should take was discussed in Washington throughout the summer and fall of 1964, Roswell continued to do what he could on a personal level. During the Latin American trip, he invited a number of people from the various countries he visited to come to Coon Rapids that fall. In early September Roswell entertained at his own expense guests from five countries for four days, showing them the Coon Rapids operation, the Pioneer research station, and, finally, taking them to Iowa State University to meet with department heads and with Dean Floyd Andre. Later in the month he repeated most of this performance with another, smaller, group.

By this time Roswell had heard that his idea for a regional program had been vetoed by those officials whom Roswell viewed as already committed to it. This was not quite the case, Birdsall informed him in December 1964. It was the project directors for individual countries ("country desk chiefs") who objected to a regional program. "They have had some unfortunate experiences with regionally operated activities," Birdsall said, "and just do not want any more of that sort of management. They want the Country Directors fully responsible with no excuses to get off the hook." Roswell's idea, Birdsall continued, had been accepted in principle, but it would be done first in one country, a country with good prospects for success. El Salvador was the leading candidate. "The idea is still very much alive and the slow process of getting something tangible underway goes forward," Birdsall concluded. By the beginning of the new year, Birdsall and his colleagues had worked out a program for El Salvador, and on 17 February 1965 Birdsall arrived in that country after a nine-day drive to launch the Mass Fertilizer Demonstration Program in the form Roswell had outlined in 1963.

EL SALVADOR had made a deep impression on Johnny during his visit there in 1962. A country about the size of New Jersey, lying entirely on the Pacific coast but running east-west, sprinkled throughout with volcanic cones and crater lakes, it possessed a topography that appealed to the geographer in Johnny. It was also beautiful, with hillsides and plains carpeted with well-trimmed coffee bushes that reminded Johnny of the ornamental plants found in the backyards of his California neighbors. Salvadoreans told him that December was the best month, when the rains had stopped but the country was still green. Johnny loved El Salvador in May when the rains started and the coffee bushes bloomed a bridal white, creating an ever-widening vista of bloom as the rains broke out first in one district, then in another. "Wealth in El Salvador is coffee," he wrote. The old money, the "solid, generation-to-generation wealth" lay in the hands of the owners of the *fincas,* the well-farmed and well-fertilized coffee plantations, intensive in labor but absolutely up-to-date in agricultural technology. In the lowlands along the Pacific Ocean, cotton, the second, smaller and more recent commercial crop also flourished, highly productive and firmly in the hands of the financial aristocracy.

The bad farming in El Salvador took place on the peasant farms, where corn provided the staple diet, supplemented by grain sorghum, bananas, other fruits, and vegetables. "Poor little proprietors," Johnny observed, "patch-farming on the steepest hills, the roughest land, the narrow ridges, scratch a living out of every workable acre." Although El Salvador was the most completely cultivated country in the Western Hemisphere, it was not self-sufficient in its basic diet (corn). In addition, it had a high infant mortality rate and a high rate of population growth. Some people lived well, but the bulk of the population was "engaged in growing an inadequate and dietetically poorly balanced food supply." These were the people the Mass Demonstration Fertilizer Program was designed to help. Johnny saw El Salvador as just stepping into the twentieth century, and saw promise there. "It could be one of the most hopeful" of countries, he wrote, "to work with in finding ways by which small nations can hope to live in prosperity and dignity among giants."

Since November 1964 technical agencies of the El Salvador Ministry of Agriculture had been working on the fertilizer project, but when Birdsall arrived to make the "imperfect" start Johnny had urged, he discovered that, apart from seed corn, none of the materials for the project had yet been acquired. The firm Fertica (Fertilizantes de Centro America, S. A.) was asked in December to supply the necessary amounts of nitrogen and phosphate, but there had been no reply from the company and no follow-up by the ministry. Birdsall spent three weeks in meetings with Fertica representatives, finally persuading the company to hold a board meeting to approve their contribution. On 16 March, with the project already running at least six weeks late, the company advised the minister of agriculture that it would supply the fertilizer.

Birdsall canvassed firms dealing in agricultural chemicals, most of whom offered assistance. Moore Chemical, S. A., agreed to supply insecticide for insects attacking the growing plant and to supply the 3,000 bags for the individual packets. For various reasons it was decided not to use an insecticide for the planting.

Another hitch developed over the fertilizer. The major distributors of Fertica fertilizers had the required fertilizer in stock but did not have the proper size bags for the packets of nitrogen and phosphate (16–20–0). When no supplier could be found who would furnish the bags free of charge, Birdsall finally purchased them with AID funds from the only supplier who could deliver them on time.

By the end of March, and after prodigious effort, Birdsall had collected all the materials and got the packaging process started, with labor and distribution provided for by the Ministry of Agriculture. Roswell's idea had acquired reality in the form of 12,000 individual packets: 3,000 bags of 33.5-0-0 nitrogen fertilizer (11 pounds each); 3,000 bags of 16-20-0 nitrogen phosphate (20 pounds each); 3,000 bags of Sevin insecticide (2.5 pounds each); and 3,000 bags of seed corn (1.5 pounds each). Packaging was completed in late April and distribution began early in May. Birdsall just made it in time for the planting season.

At the same time that he was struggling to find the materials and get them into the appropriate form, Birdsall was trying to create a field organization to distribute four bags each to three thousand farmers, then follow through with technical assistance and advice. The Agricultural Extension Agency, through which he was working, had expanded from thirty-five to fifty in April 1965, which meant that a considerable portion of its staff were inexperienced even in the rudiments of agency work. They were also without transportation. Soon after his arrival, Birdsall completed the first of three rounds of briefings at all the regional offices, set up classes on the project for all the agency employees, and began to seek out the farmers who would benefit most from the demonstration. The Extension Service enlisted the aid of five thousand 4-H Club members and of parish priests to publicize the program and recruit farmers. Peace Corps workers cooperated in the project, and the United States Information Service contributed its publicity service and mobile units. A brochure with pictures of each step in the planting and cultivation process was prepared for each farmer.

The project was aimed at farmers who usually cultivated a *manzana*, or 1.7 acres. The experiment itself was to encompass an area within the manzana of 20 × 30 meters. Birdsall hoped to find farmers who would be able to follow through in succeeding years by obtaining credit from supervised credit agencies, which Birdsall was also helping to establish, and then to purchase enough seed and fertilizer to plant their entire crop in the new way the following year. Birdsall organized a monitoring system to discover which fertilizers worked best, and in what areas. In the initial experiment, he was able to make use of the work done by the FAO Fertilizer Program.

By June, Birdsall had got 3,200 demonstrations of corn and 100 of rice into the ground, and in July his preliminary report to Roswell cited 2,500 as effective. Seven hundred had been ineffective for a variety of reasons but principally because of the inexperience of farmers and agency people. Thus far he had been lucky with the weather. The rains, which he feared might come early, had come late and enabled him to get all the packaging and distribution completed on time. In over half the country there was sufficient moisture to carry the plants through the critical period.

There was still much to do. Birdsall and his assistant, Uriel Chacon, visited all fifty regional agencies during the planting season and in July were in the middle of their second tour. He and Chacon visited fifteen or twenty demonstrations in each of the areas, giving advice, correcting mistakes, collecting information, and working out new research programs for next year. "I have seen most of the country," he wrote laconically, "and some rough roads."

Between his second and third circuit of the country, drought struck the eastern departments of the country, wiping out 60 percent of the corn crop in that area. Fortunately, the bulk of the crop was in the west, and in September, after his third tour, Birdsall could report to Roswell that in areas not affected by the drought the performance of the experimental plots ranged from "fantastic to convincing." A total of 3,220 corn demonstrations had been planted, of which 2,700 had been "effective," and 2,000 of those "outstanding." The national crop that year attained its customary 5 to 15 bushels per acre; the Mass Demonstration Fertilizer Program achieved from 31 to 42 bushels per acre, and in some instances as high as 52 bushels. This constituted an increase in yield ranging from 2.5 to 6 times more than participating farmers had usually obtained. "The results are so significant," Birdsall wrote, "that everybody is interested." Next year, Birdsall hoped for 5,000 demonstrations. Fertica and Esso offered him all the fertilizer he needed, and both the Ministry of Agriculture and private farmers were supplying seed, of which there would be 80 percent more of improved varieties.

Roswell was delighted with the figures and took them to a midwestern seminar in October on U.S. policy toward Latin America. He considered the fertilizer program as proved and immediately began a campaign for AID to implement his original recommendation for 5,000 demonstrations in eight countries, with Birdsall in charge of the entire project.

Roswell did not find acquiescence in this view from AID. Perhaps the most telling opposition to his desire to go quick and big and fast came from Birdsall himself. In November 1965 he wrote Roswell that he thought it would be a mistake for him to divert his attention from El Salvador and spread his efforts over a number of other countries. He did not wish to lose the momentum that had been generated. Consequently, he intended to give the program in El Salvador his full attention through the 1966 crop year and the planning phases for 1967. "We have in the making," he wrote,

a program for approximately 3000 demonstrations on corn; 1000 on grain sorghum; 500 on rice and 500 on beans. This is a sizable effort for this country with their organizational and administrative resource and competence. It will take a lot of doing on my part to put it over. Therefore, I would be strongly opposed as of this writing to having my time dispersed over a number of countries hoping to do a similar amount of work.

There was a personal dimension to his decision. "I have only a couple of more years in this business," he wrote, "and I wish to see this El Salvador program through to the end, without slippage." Roswell gave way, ceased to press for Birdsall's elevation to a regional position, and the program continued its course for two more years.

WHILE Birdsall soldiered on in El Salvador, Roswell turned his attention to another arena of international aid, the grain reserve, as it is called in its statesmanlike international context, or surplus, as it is called when it is seen as a domestic political problem. Although exports of grain to under-developed countries posed the kinds of problems Johnny had described, such traffic was still an essential weapon against the drought and famine that created a formidable obstacle to agricultural progress in the sixties.

This story has a prologue also, which begins in early 1961 as Secretary Freeman investigated the options for dealing with the awesome productivity of American agriculture, which looked very much like a straightforward case of surplus. Even Roswell, since the forties an advocate of high levels of feed grain acreage, thought that there ought to be some restrictions now, but not nearly as much as most people expected. His proposal for the new administration, consistent with his campaign to encourage the production of meat, was for support prices to be placed under pork, broilers, eggs, and possibly beef for about three years. This expansion of the livestock and poultry industry would reduce the excessive size of the surplus and provide more protein for both national and international consumption. The plan would still allow a substantial domestic surplus in these years of rising population. A high level of grain reserves, he wrote in 1960, was "merely prudent."

With these considerations in mind, Roswell launched one of his "swell" campaigns to influence the new agricultural measures about to be drafted. On the Monday after Kennedy's inauguration the campaign got off to a rather inauspicious start in Freeman's office, where Roswell had a preliminary conference with Willard Cochrane of the University of Minnesota, now chief economic adviser to the secretary of agriculture. Cool at the outset to Roswell's proposals, Cochrane unwittingly touched a raw nerve by asking Roswell where he had studied economics. Convinced that Cochrane "had looked down his nose at me," Roswell withdrew to find academic support elsewhere for his proposals. He was willing to carry the ball, he wrote, but "I needed a blocking back."

He chose for this assignment his old friend Ted Schultz at the University of Chicago, a distinguished economist who had lately turned his attention to the problems of the underdeveloped world. He was in broad agreement with Roswell on the need for more protein and the ills of the foreign aid program. Moreover, he was an admirer of Roswell's entrepreneurial imagination ("You take such gigantic steps," he wrote to Roswell four years later. "I admire the extraordinary way in which you cut into a problem.") Together they began drafting a plan for diverting the surplus into the production of pork. Roswell collected figures on grain stocks from the Chicago Board of Trade and figures on pork and its processing from the packing industry. Before long, he wrote, "I knew more figures than they did."

Early in February, Roswell returned to Washington for what he described as "one big week." He presented his plan to Freeman at Agriculture, went over to the White House to perform again for a presidential assistant, and through an arrangement made by Humphrey had "a nice visit" with the president. His next appointment was at the State Department with George Ball, whom Roswell regarded as "a good one." Then he visited Galbraith, who had received a similar accolade some years earlier, and had dinner at Pat Jackson's with George McGovern and Arthur Schlesinger, Jr. "I think I have the whole thing sold," he reported at this stage, "but I am not absolutely sure yet."

His final effort took place a week later at the Farm Forum in Des Moines. Lauren Soth of the *Des Moines Register,* a member of the presidential task force on agriculture, had supported the pork plan in his newspaper editorials and arranged for a joint presentation by Schultz and Garst at this prestigious annual affair. The plan, as it now emerged in public, called for a program of price supports on hogs and soybeans. Grain to feed the porkers created by this financial incentive would come from the present reserve — or surplus — that would be substantially reduced within three years. After butchering, the pork would be purchased by the government and become one of the commodities in its foreign aid program.

It was a "swell" campaign, but it failed. In March 1961 the administration chose instead to inaugurate a program of crop restriction described by the *Wall Street Journal* as "the most ambitious program of controlled farming ever attempted by the Federal Government." By May, enough farmers had accepted the government's incentives to cause 20 million acres of corn and grain sorghum to be removed from active production and transferred into various forms of the Soil Bank. That year, Garst and Thomas cut its seed acreage from 14,000 to 10,000 acres because of the level of compliance with the program.

The prologue was finished, and Roswell took the outcome in good grace. He was not opposed to some reduction in the surplus and found the Soil Bank provisions very useful in the creation of new pastureland. The program of 1961, he wrote a year later, "was popular and effective," and he expected the same to be true for 1962.

However, he also thought that the program would be even more effective in 1962 than the USDA had anticipated, and consequently there would be a greater disappearance of grain over the next few years than expected—a possibility that made him uneasy. Twenty years ago, he told Senator Hickenlooper, the normal carry-over of corn was about 600 or 700 million bushels. "But we have roughly 40 percent more people than we had 20 years ago," he wrote, "so I don't think the carryover of a billion bushels of corn is anything but a good safety hedge—a prudent protection for the consumers of the United States." The poor harvests of 1963 in Russia and elsewhere further disturbed him, and he wrote a series of letters to Freeman, Humphrey, and others expressing his concern that international feed reserves were falling to dangerously low levels and asked for changes in the 1964 program. These were not forthcoming, and throughout 1964 and 1965 the carry-over levels of feed grain continued to fall sharply.

Spurred in part by Roswell's continuing flow of letters and by concern expressed now by others, Humphrey brought the matter up for public discussion in the spring of 1966 in a speech to farm editors. The USDA had projected a 55-million ton carry-over in 1966, but Humphrey thought it would be only 45 million tons. That amount constituted only a four-month supply and "very frankly," Humphrey remarked, "I don't think that's any excess at all. In fact, it is on the borderline of a shortage."

When Roswell saw the report of grain stocks in July 1966, he concluded that the shortage had already arrived and argued in that vein throughout the fall. He was hampered in his efforts, he told Phil Maguire, because "they think at the USDA that I want a big corn acreage." It was "just not true," he insisted. "The thing that is best for corn and sorghums is what I want."

In February 1967 the USDA estimated a carry-over for 1968 of only 25 million tons of feed grains, and in March, Nick Kotz of the *Register*'s Washington Bureau broke the story that a feed grain shortage for 1968 was feared. Officials of the USDA agreed that the surplus was gone and were attempting to increase the 1967 crop to bring as many as 15 million acres back into production. Iowa farmers were expected to plant 11.9 million acres, the highest acreage devoted to corn since 1960.

In its editorial ruminations on the causes of the shortage, the *Register* cited the same two reasons Roswell had been putting forward: the stringent restrictions on acreage since 1961 and the extraordinarily high exports of grain during the last few years to meet a succession of droughts and famines throughout the world.

IN November 1967 Birdsall came in from the field for the last time and sat down at his Washington desk to write his final report on the three years of the Mass Fertilizer Demonstration Program in El Salvador. In 1966 the number of plots had been increased to 6,000, with 4,750 in corn and grain sorghum, the remainder in rice, beans, bananas, and sesame, with results even better than in 1965. In order to increase the efficiency per plot and to find a higher percentage of farmers who could benefit in the long term, the program was reduced to 5,000 in 1967. In spite of another drought, the program in its last year remained successful.

Birdsall estimated that in 1965 and 1966, approximately 50 percent of the farmers in the program obtained some form of credit and put their new knowledge into practice on their entire acreage. By 1967, the use of fertilizer in El Salvador was increasing by 15 percent per year, and corn production was rising correspondingly. Production credit for fertilizer, seed, and insecticide for the medium and small farmer was now reaching 12,000 to 15,000 families who had never before had such assistance. By the seventies, El Salvador was exporting corn.

The expense of the program had been remarkably low. The total cost for three years amounted to $28,800 for private industry, $4,880 for the Ministry of Agriculture above the regular cost of the extension service, and $13,708 for AID above the cost of a full-time technician and administrative support. For the expenditure of $47,388, the program produced 14,385 demonstrations, an average per demonstration of $3.30. It had been a bargain item when considered in the context of U.S. expenditures on foreign aid.

There had also been problems. As expected, there were insufficient storage facilities for the increased harvest, and problems emerged over the price and marketing structure. The road system was inadequate as well, and in general the project suffered in the same way as in Eastern Europe—to achieve its full potential required a commensurate improvement in the web of supporting technology. However, as Johnny observed, perfection was not necessary in order to make a start.

The heartening news of the program's success annoyed Roswell as much as it pleased him; after three years of experimentation, AID was still not prepared to launch the program on the scale Roswell considered essential. To John Strohm, who wanted to write about the project for the *Reader's Digest,* Roswell wrote in 1967 that if AID refused to move with more speed,

then I know I will let you tell the El Salvador story—and let you tell the world that I am trying to get the El Salvador type of thing done in every emergency country in the world—but that bureaucracy in AID is in complete control. . . . You have referred to me in the past as an effective "gad-fly." This is what I am going to try to be in this situation.

His exchanges with AID officials strike some familiar chords. Of one reply he complained that it was "a typical Ph.D. letter! with typical Ph.D. words—more study, technical back stopping, etc., etc." Employees of AID defended their actions in terms of the realities of the situation as they saw them. Herb Waters, assistant administrator for the War on Hunger, assured Roswell that AID was committed to similar goals but pointed out among other things that the agency was going to be hurt by budgetary cuts brought on by the increasing burden of the war in Vietnam. Norman Ward, an agricultural economist with a specific brief to carry on the fertilizer demonstrations, replied at some length to Roswell and sketched out the present state of the program in the fall of 1967. Ward listed 5,339 demonstration plots in operation in Ecuador, El Salvador, Guatemala, Honduras, Paraguay, Peru, and mentioned additional work in Brazil. This was not the total effort, he wrote, but was assembled on short notice "to remind you that AID has listened and is continuing to work on the problem of increasing the production of corn, and in many countries is using the techniques you have suggested." However, progress was contingent upon coping with problems Birdsall had cited in his report. "We agree," Ward concluded,

this program needs to expand and reach more people, but we realize now more than ever, it must be part of an overall plan for increasing agricultural production, including credit, storage, and marketing for basic crops.

Later, Roswell heard from another source, Lester Brown, in 1968 the administrator of the International Agricultural Development Service of the USDA. "Your packets concept," Brown wrote,

including seed, fertilizer and pesticides all in one package, is being widely used in several developing countries. Outside El Salvador, the Philippines has perhaps exploited this idea more than any other country. They were so popular they were commercialized and distributed by commercial firms.

Because it had not been as quick and big and fast as he hoped, Roswell was never able to derive the satisfaction from the program to which he was entitled. In later years, when he reminisced about the program, he talked about his own trip, about Birdsall's splendid work, and the problems with storage. He gave the impression that it had lasted only one year and had disappeared without trace. He did not think that the Mass Fertilizer Demonstration Program had been a failure; he believed that it had never really been tried.

His concern for scale and for rate of progress made him pessimistic over the prospects for world agriculture. To Humphrey he conceded that progress was being made, but "at the best," he remarked, "it will be slow." It would take five years to show any marked increase in yield throughout the underdeveloped countries, and ten years "of the best kind of effort to even make a good start on eliminating malnutrition." These estimates came from Ted Schultz, who presented them to Roswell in a rather different light. "I am probably somewhat more optimistic," he wrote, "that we have turned a corner in many a country in the world to get agriculture moving, but this is going to show results in output more firmly in five to ten years." Schultz also thought that the population curve would begin to move downward, "and not be so appallingly large ten years from now." Lester Brown also found the agricultural situation in Asia "exceedingly encouraging." There was a revolution there in the making and "even bumbling bureaucrats will not be able to stop it."

However, from 1966 through 1968, Roswell could think only in terms of opportunities missed, of the shortfall in his hopes for the sixties, perhaps simply because, as he once remarked, he would not live to see his plans for progress realized. He was greatly moved by a postcard sent him from South America in the fall of 1967 by Dr. Robert de Baca of Iowa State, who was working for AID. "Thousands of tons of bunch grass straw going to waste," de Baca wrote from Paraguay,

cows dying of starvation, steers 4–5 years old when marketed, 40% calf crops, and no one thought of urea and molasses down here. There's still lots of productive land doing nothing while masses starve and nations suffer poverty. There's still lots to do.

In 1968, Roswell sent a copy of the postcard to Lester Brown. "Can any of us read that postcard from Dr. de Baca without embarrassment?" he asked. "Without shame?" His response to his own question reflects his frustration at the gap between available knowledge and actual practice. What Brown should do was to order copies of Garst and Thomas Bulletin Number 5 on cellulose and urea, "and send it everywhere."

The war in Vietnam had a dispiriting impact on Roswell, and early in 1968 he engaged in active opposition. He and Elizabeth went to Des Moines to march in one of the mass protest parades that had become a part of urban life, and he wrote to Humphrey to press for disengagement.

At the same time, it was in Humphrey that he placed his hopes for progress. "In such confused times as these – such sad times as these – such trying times as these," he wrote to the vice president in April 1968, "I refuse to urge anyone to try to become President." However, he continued, "I hope you announce – I hope you are nominated – and elected. . . . I have great confidence in your humane instincts – in your courage – in your intelligence." In a Humphrey presidency Roswell saw hope for a reduction in the arms race, a renewed effort against world poverty, and a stronger commitment to the United Nations. He also saw a way to continue serving his own primary cause as a roving agricultural ambassador, finding out "what went wrong" with the promising programs of the sixties.

Humphrey's narrow defeat was a great disappointment for Roswell. He told friends that if Humphrey lost, he would "take a slow boat to

China," as the song put it. He now had no further expectation of public service. He substituted a long holiday for the slow boat, and at the age of seventy returned home to resume, in whatever form it might take, the job that he had done so well all his life – teaching people how to grow more food with less labor.

CHAPTER TEN

The Last Years

By 1970 ROSWELL HAD FORMALLY RETIRED from Garst and Thomas, but he continued to turn up at his office to write letters on issues that interested him, to keep abreast of the seed corn business, and in general to continue, if at a slower pace, the same pattern of life in Coon Rapids he had maintained during the previous decade.

Roswell involved himself in two events in the early seventies that directly affected the fortunes of Garst and Thomas and the Garst farming operation. The first was the serious epidemic of corn blight, which spread quickly in 1970 and 1971 through the central and western Corn Belt, aided by the uniformity of genetic type recently introduced into seed varieties. Roswell took it upon himself to conduct his own investigation in 1971, visiting corn geneticists, pathologists, and economists at the state universities of Iowa, Kansas, Missouri, and at Purdue University. He published the results of these conversations, along with a recommendation to farmers to plant more grain sorghums, in a 1971 pamphlet entitled "1971 – A Year of Problems and Perhaps a Year of Opportunities."

The second event, the energy crisis, pushed up the price and limited the availability of nitrogen fertilizer, which derives from the fixation of natural gas. Roswell suspected that farmers would "cheat" on their applications of nitrogen in 1973 and 1974 and was among the first to spot the signs of nitrogen deficiency in the corn crop during his daily drives around the Coon Rapids farms. He launched a campaign to convert coal and lignite to gas, which could then be converted into nitrogen. In addition to the technical difficulties involved in this new application of an old process, there was the issue of ecology. Roswell's proposals included the reinstatement of strip coal mining, particularly in the Dakotas. This ecological aspect of the problem does not find its way into Roswell's correspondence. Apart from a few grumbles about Rachel Carson's *Silent Spring*, Roswell chose from the beginning of the controversy over chemical runoff from cornfields to simply ignore it. His kind of ecology was the abundant crop. However, in the matter of the using coal to produce nitrogen fertilizer, he was successful. It was a satisfying conclusion to his last campaign.

His travels in Eastern Europe were not yet over. The seventies brought a rapprochement between Moscow and Coon Rapids, which was signaled on the Russian side by the reinstatement by the Brezhnev regime of Vladimir Matskevitch as secretary of agriculture, and by a decision by the politburo to seek out Western technology on a large scale in the new decade. Brezhnev maintained the general thrust of Khrushchev's agricultural policies, with adjustments to curb the more misguided aspects of Khrushchev's efforts. Such programs as the increased production of fertilizer and further mechanization were pressed forward.

Roswell's own interest in Russia revived with the appointment of Matskevitch, and shortly after Khrushchev's death in 1970, Roswell urged successfully that the Soviet minister of agriculture be invited to the United States. Matskevitch came in 1971, taking home ten bags of grain sorghum he received from Roswell. In 1972 the Russians decided to grow grain sorghum in their dry regions and asked to send a delegation to Coon Rapids. Instead, they immediately accepted Roswell's offer to return to Russia again with John Chrystal. The game was on again: Roswell and John would go in both 1972 and 1974, there would be sales of sorghum, and a continuing dialogue of consultation.

Roswell's reputation in Russia remained undiminished despite the passing of Khrushchev. "I believe they would plant corn upside down if he told them they could do it," John Chrystal remarked after the 1974 trip. "Whatever he said, they believed." In 1972 Roswell and John were taken to an apple orchard of 10,000 acres. It was late October, but five trees were left unpicked, in order to be viewed by the Garst party. Around them was gathered a large group of onlookers. "Do these people know we are Americans?" Roswell asked. "Oh, Mr. Garst," his interpreter replied, "there isn't anybody here who doesn't know who you are." Wherever Roswell went, John reported, there was a crowd, at times as many as three hundred, who would gather after Roswell entered a building. When he emerged, some would produce cameras and take pictures; many would wave at him. Roswell always returned these gestures of affection with his own wave as his car sped away. "He is just like the visiting emperor," John said of Roswell's style in rising to these occasions, "just waving."

There was also recognition at home. In 1973 he was installed by Governor Robert Ray into the Hall of Fame of the Association of Iowa Cattle Growers (and posthumously in 1979 into *Fortune* magazine's Business Hall of Fame). In 1976 his leathery face graced the cover of the February issue of the *Farm Journal* for an article by Dick Seim entitled

"The Salesman Who Changed Agriculture." "The command remains, the electricity," Seim wrote, "even if he now carries his voice in his right hand or stuck in a pants pocket." He still had the presence, Seim said, "that can dominate a crowded cafe, a big meeting, a conversation."

He certainly continued talking. In Des Moines, he lectured the Iowa Banker's Association on "The Dangers of Being Known as a 'Conservative,' " and in Coon Rapids he teamed up with Mary Garst, now in charge of the Garst Company cattle-breeding operation, to conduct several tours per week of the Garst operation. "She breeds 'em and I feed 'em," he liked to say. They were a good act.

During these last years, the part of Roswell's daily life that might be termed routine began in the morning with a stop at the South Side Cafe, followed by his appearance at the office to read his mail and catch up on Garst and Thomas news. About 10 A.M. he walked to the bank, not to deposit money as his father Edward had done, but to visit John Chrystal. From John's office he walked the short distance to the office of Olesen and Reid, where Eddie Reid and his new teleprinter were to be found. There he passed the time of day with Eddie and whoever else happened to be around, while he and Eddie "had a little fun" with the grain futures market, as they had been doing since the twenties. (After Roswell died, Eddie sold the machine because "it wasn't so much fun anymore.") At noon he went home for lunch, then returned to the office to write letters, and later would drive around the corn and cattle circuit. He and Elizabeth often took their evening meal out, sometimes visited the Reids or the Bells, and retired early.

In September 1976 Sandor Rajke brought a Hungarian delegation to the United States to study the feasibility of adopting the cellulose and urea feeding process for his country. Roswell instructed them in Coon Rapids, took the party to Iowa State University, then sent them out with David Garst to the sprinkler country around O'Neill, Nebraska, to see Bill Curry's cattle operation. That same year he received a pamphlet from José Resende Peres, Brazil's secretary of agriculture, describing the "Garst-Peres Method" for feeding molasses and urea with cellulose in three large experimental centers. In the summer of 1977 the son of Alexander Tulupnikov, the man who had "discovered" Roswell for Russia in 1955, came to Coon Rapids to observe the feeding operation his father had seen twenty-two years before.

That summer Roswell's energy began to flag, and he also began to have trouble remembering names. His driving became erratic, not so much from any physical disability as from a change in attitude. With a million miles of driving clocked up at a conservative estimate, Roswell seemed to feel immune from misfortune on the highways. He did not contest other people's right to be on the road, but he did assume that they would make way for him in whatever maneuver he chose to perform, even if it meant coming to a sudden stop on a main highway to look at a cornfield deficient in nitrogen. John Chrystal always arranged to drive when they were out together or in the company of Elizabeth and John's step-mother, Julia. One year John bought a smaller than usual Ford as an economy measure. When Roswell announced that he didn't like the car and proposed to drive his own, John turned in the car the next day for a large one.

In 1977 Roswell and Elizabeth were invited to Hungary to inaugurate the new cattle-feeding operation that had been adopted after Rajke's visit and to celebrate Roswell's contribution to Hungarian agriculture over the last two decades. However, he did not feel up to the trip. At the beginning of November, he suffered a heart attack and was taken to St. Anthony Regional Hospital in Carroll. On the morning of 5 November, apparently well on the way to recovery, he was eating chocolates and reading the impressive accumulation of get-well cards when Elizabeth left the hospital. At home for only a short time that afternoon, she received a phone call from the hospital informing her that Roswell had suffered a second heart attack and was dead. Elizabeth ascribed the second attack to a surfeit of chocolates. Considering the probable state of his arteries after a lifetime of milk, buttermilk, butter, and, of course, chocolates, it was neither an improbable diagnosis, nor perhaps inappropriate. Roswell had lived to be 79 years, 9 months, and 22 days old.

Approximately nine hundred people squeezed into the high school gymnasium to attend the funeral service. Bill Brown of Pioneer International spoke of Roswell as a teacher; Hans Larsen recalled the early days of enthusiasm in Nebraska; Maurice Campbell, who had supervised the first cellulose feeding experiment in Coon Rapids, referred to Roswell's part in the agricultural revolution; Arthur Davis, Roswell's attorney in Des Moines, ascribed Roswell's greatness to passion for ideas. "For those of us not great," Davis concluded, "what a pleasure there was in touching and being touched by someone who was." Roswell's casket was carried by grandsons and grandnephews to its resting place in the Coon Rapids cemetery. Today, the grave is marked by a plain stone monument on which Roswell's signature has been incised, just as it was done for Edward and Bertha.

BIOGRAPHY is an extended form of signature. It fleshes out a name with context and associations, character and events. It must deal with achievement and failure as well, but these matters are only part of its task. In Roswell's case, much of his achievement is clearly discernible, but some of it requires the critical evaluation of specialists in a variety of fields.

Roswell's impact is still fresh, his work needs time to be distilled and measured. Such processes inevitably follow from the touch of greatness.

If last words on Roswell are not in order, closing remarks certainly are. The first of these comes from another veteran campaigner, Nikita Khrushchev, who paid tribute to Roswell's powerful sense of vocation. "I recognized Garst as a human being," Khrushchev wrote in his memoirs, "whom I respected for his energy, his knowledge, his willingness to share his experience and, so to speak, his trade secrets with others, even with us to put to use in our socialist enterprises." It is a sentiment about Roswell to which people of virtually every ideological persuasion have subscribed.

The final remarks bring this book back to the place where it began, the pages of the *Coon Rapids Enterprise*. Drexel Nixon, the publisher of the *Enterprise* at the time of Roswell's death, captured both the sense of loss and the continuity embodied in Roswell's relationship with his town and his land. "The scene will be different in Coon Rapids," Nixon wrote:

Bob will no longer be leading groups on tours at the plants and farms; he will no longer be walking from the G & T office to the South Side Cafe in a blizzard with no headgear; nor will he be coming out of the Garst Store with a sack of candy in his hand.

An era has ended.

S O U R C E S

Abbreviations in correspondence:

AF	ABE FREILER
BB	BENJAMIN BIRDSALL
HAW	HENRY A. WALLACE
HHH	HUBERT H. HUMPHREY
JDP	JOHN DOS PASSOS
JG	JONATHAN GARST
RG	ROSWELL GARST
SB	SCOTT BROMWELL

CHAPTER ONE **TOWN AND FAMILY**

Letters: E. Garst to G. Garst, 31 Jan. 1902; E. Garst to T. Leoon, 3 Feb. 1903. In private hands.

Documents: Horace Garst, "A Short Sketch of the Early Garst Family," 1929; E. and W. Garst, "Recollections of a Half Century," 1929; "Coon Rapids Centennial: 100 Years Proud," 1963. In private hands.

Newspapers: Most of this chapter is based on numerous articles in the *Coon Rapids Enterprise* from 1881 to 1924. Important historical summaries may be found in 1883, 1887, 1892, and 1904. The newspaper is on microfilm in the Coon Rapids Library.

Books: Leland Sage, *A History of Iowa* (Ames: Iowa State Univ. Press, 1974), 224–43; Allen G. Bogue, *From Prairie to Cornbelt* (Chicago: Quadrangle Books, 1963), 1–7, 12–13, 16, 30, 39, 45.

Interviews: Roswell Garst, Elizabeth Garst, Lee Miller, Garst Papers, Iowa State University Library.

CHAPTER TWO **THE EARLIEST YEARS**

GROWING UP: 1898–1922

Letters: E. Garst to G. Garst, 2 Apr. 1908; E. Garst to G. Garst, 11 Apr. 1908; E. Garst to Ida Garst, 29 July 1908; H. Garst to RG, 20 Jan. 1929; JG to RG, 1 July 1918; JG to RG, 19 Oct. 1918.

Newspapers: Coon Rapids Enterprise, 1898, 1909–24.

Books: Jonathan Garst, *No Need for Hunger* (New York: Random House, 1963), 13–14.

Interviews: Roswell Garst, Elizabeth Garst, Charley Rippey, Eddie Reid, Charley Thomas, Garst Papers, Iowa State University Library.

MARRIAGE AND THE DES MOINES YEARS

Books: Russell Lord, *The Wallaces of Iowa* (Boston: Houghton Mifflin, 1947), 144–51, 184–86, 196–201, 285, 305–7, 378; Grant G. Cannon, *Great men of Modern Agriculture* (New York: Macmillan, 1963), 217–28.

Interviews: Roswell Garst, Elizabeth Garst, Garst Papers, Iowa State University Library.

CHAPTER THREE **THE THIRTIES**

FOUNDING GARST AND THOMAS

Letters: RG to G. Carey, July 1944; RG to A. Crabbe, 1947; RG to G. Carey, 1947, Garst Papers, Iowa State University Library.

Newspapers: Coon Rapids Enterprise, Aug. 1933; 21 Feb., 21 Mar., 8 Aug., 7 Aug. 1931; 15 Jan., 22 Apr., 9 Dec. 1932.

Interviews: Roswell Garst, Elizabeth Garst, Charley Thomas, Charley Rippey, Barney Trullinger, Garst Papers, Iowa State University Library.

BRINGING IN THE NEW DEAL

Letters: RG To C. Hamilton, 27 Apr. 1976, Garst Papers, Iowa State University Library.

Newspapers: Des Moines Register, 21 Apr., 27 Apr., 28 Apr., 29 Apr., 2 May, 7 May, 10 May, 18 May, 24 May, 30 May, 31 May, 1 June, 3 June, 9 June, 14 June, 15 June, 22 June, 24 June, 25 June, 27 June, 28 June, 2 July, 4 July, 16 July, 19 July, 26 July, 30 July, 2 Aug., 3 Aug., 6 Aug., 9 Aug., 11 Aug., 13 Aug., 17 Aug., 22 Aug., 24 Aug., 26 Aug., 4 Sept., 1 Sept., 9 Sept., 14 Sept., 23 Sept., 25 Sept., 26 Sept., 8 Oct., 11 Oct., 17 Oct., 18 Oct., 21 Oct., 22 Oct., 26 Oct., 27 Oct. 1933; *Coon Rapids Enterprise,* 30 June, 7 July, 11 Aug., 8 Sept., 27 Oct., 8 Dec. 1933.

Books: Arthur M. Schlesinger, Jr., *The Coming of the New Deal* (Boston: Houghton Mifflin, 1959), 27–49, 50, 63, 62–63; Dean Albertson, *Roosevelt's Farmer* (New York: Columbia Univ. Press, 1961); Theodore Saloutos and John D. Hicks, "Agricultural Discontent in the Middle West, 1900–1939," in *Patterns and Perspectives in Iowa History,* ed. Dorothy Schwieder (Ames: Iowa State Univ. Press, 1973), 361–73, 374.

Interviews: Roswell Garst, Elizabeth Garst, Garst Papers, Iowa State University Library.

BUILDING A SEED CORN PLANT

Newspapers: Coon Rapids Enterprise, 19 Oct. 1 Dec. 1933; 2 Feb., 13 July, 27 July, 3 Aug., 17 Aug., 14 Sept., 7 Dec. 1934; 1 Mar., 10 July, 27 Sept., 4 Oct., 11 Oct., 25 Oct., 20 Dec. 1935.

Interviews: Roswell Garst, Ralph Wheeler, Charley Thomas, Garst Papers, Iowa State University Library.

GOING WEST

Letters: RG to JG, 15 Oct. 1936; RG to JG, 29 Oct. 1936; RG to JG, 5 Nov. 1936; RG to JG, 21 Nov. 1936; RG to JG, 21 Dec. 1936; RG to JG, 15 Mar. 1937; RG to JG, 11 Aug. 1937; RG to JG, 10 Feb. 1938; RG to JG, 6 Apr. 1938; RG to JG, 16 Sept. 1938; RG to A. Ernst, 8 Dec. 1939, Garst Papers, Iowa State University Library.

Newspapers: Coon Rapids Enterprise, 14 Feb., 24 July, 14 Aug., 25 Sept., 13 Nov., 25 Dec. 1936; 1 Feb., 30 Apr., 30 July, 6 Aug., 13 Aug., 17 Sept., 24 Sept., 15 Oct., 22 Oct., 12 Nov., 19 Nov., 3 Dec. 1937; 11 Feb., 18 Mar., 27 May, 5 Aug., 16 Sept., 23 Sept., 14 Oct., 7 Oct., 28 Oct., 16 Dec. 1938.

Interviews: Roswell Garst, Arnold Ernst, Hans Larsen, John Chrystal, Pete Oliver, John Parker, Garst Papers, Iowa State University Library.

POLITICS, FAMILY, AND FRIENDS

Letters: RG to J. Wallace, 29 Oct. 1936; RG to A. Bowman, 12 Nov. 1936; RG to C. Herring, 13 June 1936; RG to G. Jackson, 19 May 1937; RG to N. Kraschel, 21 Dec. 1937; RG to G. Jackson, 18 May 1938; RG to G. Schaller, 25 Apr. 1939; RG to AF, 9 May 1940; RG to JG, 9 July 1940; RG to A. Bowman, 18 June 1940; J. Cowles to RG, 8 June 1940; RG to AF, 17 June 1940; RG to W. Macklin, 28 July 1940; P. Appleby to RG, 20 Nov. 1940; RG to H. Brenton, Sept. 1944; RG to M. Thornbury, Dec.1941; RG to G. Jackson, 1 Nov. 1944; RG to C. Baldwin, 1944, Garst Papers, Iowa State University Library.

Newspapers: Coon Rapids Enterprise, 1 Nov. 1935.

Documents: Roswell Garst, "Radio Talk on Behalf of Governor Kraschel," Oct. 1938.

Interviews: Roswell Garst, Elizabeth Garst, Eddie Reid, Garst Papers, Iowa State University Library.

RECLAIMING THE LAND

Letters: RG to SB, 9 June 1936; RG to SB, 22 July 1936; RG to SB, 17 Mar. 1936; SB to RG, 20 Nov. 1936; RG to SB, 26 Dec. 1936; RG to SB, 22 Dec. 1936; RG to SB, 28 Dec. 1936; SB to RG, 8 Jan. 1937; SB to RG, 13 Dec. 1937; SB to RG, 12 Jan. 1938; SB to RG, 10 Mar. 1938; RG to R. Colwell, 13 Dec. 1943; RG to SB, 10 Dec. 1942; RG to M. Schaumberg, 1 Sept. 1942; M. Schaumberg to RG, 15 Dec. 1943; RG to M. Schaumberg, 23 Dec. 1943; M. Schaumberg to RG, 12 Apr. 1943; M. Schaumberg to RG, 24 Sept. 1943; J. Stein to RG, 7 Oct. 1942; RG to S. Stein, 24 Aug. 1942; S. Stein to RG, 27 Nov. 1942; S. Stein to RG, 21 Oct. 1942; S. Stein to RG, 26 Apr. 1943; RG to S. Stein, 23 Nov. 1943; F. Lehmann to RG, 2 Mar. 1942; F. Lehmann to RG, 17 Dec. 1942; F. Lehmann to RG, 18 Dec. 1942; RG to AF, 7 Dec. 1943; AF to RG, 27 Dec. 1940; AF to RG, 25 Feb. 1941; RG to AF, 11 Dec. 1941; RG to AF, 10 Jan. 1944; RG to AF, 14 Mar. 1946; AF to RG, 10 May 1946, Garst Papers, Iowa State University Library.

Books: Russell Lord, *The Wallaces of Iowa* (Boston: Houghton Mifflin, 1947), 155.

Interviews: Roswell Garst. Garst Papers, Iowa State University Library.

CHAPTER FOUR THE WAR YEARS

BRINGING FERTILIZER TO THE CORN BELT

Letters: RG to "Trail Ammonium Phosphate," 25 June 1942; Consolidated Mining and Smelting to RG, 13 July 1942; Milwaukee and St. Paul Railroad to RG, 4 Aug. 1942; Consolidated Mining and Smelting to RG, 1 Sept. 1942; RG to Consolidated Mining and Smelting, 3 Sept. 1942; RG to W. Ruickbe, 23 July 1942; R. Potts to RG, 6 Aug. 1942; RG to SB, 6 Feb. 1942; SB to RG, 13 July 1942; SB to RG, 13 July 1942; RG to SB, 18 July 1942; SB to RG, 20 July 1942; RG to AF, 3 June 1942; RG to AF, 24 June 1942; AF to RG, 26 June 1942; RG to AF, 9 Dec. 1942; W. Macklin to RG, 29 June 1942; J. Coverdale to RG, 28 Aug. 1942; RG to A. Lang, 23 June 1942; RG to SB, 21 July 1942; RG to C. Charlton, 24 June 1942; RG to Tenants, May or June 1942; RG to M. Schaumberg, Feb. 1943; RG to M. Schaumberg, 23 Dec. 1943; RG to J. Coverdale, 29 Aug. 1942; J. Coverdale to RG, 6 Oct. 1942; T. Roberts to G. Strayer, 21 July 1943; RG to J. Coverdale, 26 July 1943; Rath Packing to RG, 15 Feb. 1943; RG to J. Coverdale, 26 Dec. 1942; J. Coverdale to RG, Dec. 1943; J. Coverdale to RG, 15 Feb. 1943; RG to G. Hoffer, Nov. 1944, Garst Papers, Iowa State University Library.

Newspapers: Fairfield Ledger, 8 Dec. 1942.

Pamphlets and documents: "War-Time Fertilizer Recommendations for Iowa Departments of Agronomy and Horticulture," Iowa State College, 1942; B. S. Pickett, "Report on Meeting of Mid-West Soil Improvement Association with Officials of the Federal Government . . . in Chicago," 21 Oct. 1942; A. W. Kleene, "Putting Fertilizer Down Puts Crops Up," *Crops and Soils,* undated offprint [1941?]. Garst Papers, Iowa State University Library.

Books: George Scarseth, *Man and His Earth* (Ames: Iowa State Univ. Press, 1962), 97–115, 117–37, 138–49, 150–57; Louis M. Thompson, *Soils and Soil Fertility* (New York: McGraw-Hill, 1952), 1–8, 42–52, 131–48, 151–64, 167–77.

Interviews: Roswell Garst, Garst Papers, Iowa State University Library.

PERSONAL RELATIONS

Letters: RG to SB, May 1940; RG to SB, 11 Dec. 1941; RG to A. Bowman, 1942; RG to Guthrie County Rationing Board, 18 Feb. 1943; RG to P. Hendricks, 20 Feb. 1942; RG to J. Stein, 3 Dec. 1943; J. N. Garst to RG, Oct. 1943; RG to Elizabeth Garst, 22 Nov. 1943; RG to W. Macklin, 8 Dec. 1943; RG to D. Garst, Nov. 1943; RG to D. Garst, Oct. 1943; RG to Chicago Board of Trade, 19 Oct. 1943; RG to JG, May 1940; RG to SB, July 1943; RG to J. Davis, 31 Mar. 1943; RG to JG, 16 Sept. 1938; RG to L. McBroom, 19 Feb. 1941; RG to JG, 5 Apr. 1943; RG to AF, Dec. 1941; P. Taylor to RG, 30 Oct. 1940; RG to P. Taylor, 10 June 1941, Garst Papers, Iowa State University Library.

Books: John Dos Passos, *State of the Nation* (Boston: Houghton Mifflin, 1944), 270.

Interviews: Stephen Garst, David Garst, John Chrystal, Eddie Reid, Roswell Garst, Garst Papers, Iowa State University Library.

FEED GRAINS CRISIS

Letters: RG to R. Evans, 17 May 1940; RG to C. Davis, 30 Dec. 1949; M. Ezekiel to RG, 25 Feb. 1942; RG to R. Evans, 6 June 1940; JG to RG, 28 Mar. 1941; RG to A. Bowman, 12 Feb. 1942; RG to L. Bean, 8 Sept. 1941; RG to G. Jackson, 24 Dec. 1941; RG to G. Jackson, 12 Feb. 1942; RG to E. O'Neil, Feb. 1942; B. Baldwin to RG, 23 Feb. 1942; G. Jackson to RG, 5 Sept. 1942; J. Patton to RG, 15 Oct. 1942; J. Galbraith to RG, Oct. 1942; RG to J. Galbraith, Oct. 1942; RG to R. Dixon, 23 Dec. 1942; RG to G. Jackson, 24 Dec. 1942; G. Jackson to RG, 6 Jan. 1943; RG to G. Jackson, 8 Jan. 1943; G. Jackson to RG, Jan. 1943 (telegram); RG to G. Jackson, 9 Jan. 1943; RG to J. Galbraith, 12 Jan. 1943; C.B. Baldwin to RG, 23 Jan. 1943; RG to W. Willkie, 23 Jan. 1943; W. Willkie to RG, 7 Jan. 1943; A. Moore to RG, 11 Jan. 1943; RG to C. Herring, 19 Jan. 1943; C. Hamilton to H. Lee, 26 Aug. 1977; RG to L. Currie, 22 Feb. 1943; R. Uhlmann to RG, 2 Mar. 1943; RG to G. Jackson, 16 Mar. 1943; RG to L. Currie, 15 Mar. 1943; C. Hamilton to RG, 29 Mar. 1943; RG to D. Murphy, 20 Apr. 1943; C. Davis to RG, 24 Apr. 1943; J. Galbraith to H. Lee, Mar. 1977; RG to J. Byrnes, 6 Apr. 1943; RG to M. Oppenheimer, 5 Apr. 1943; M. Perkins to RG, 24 June 1943; RG to C. Davis, 26 June 1943; RG to G. Jackson, 27 June 1943; RG to G. Jackson, 29 June 1943; RG to P. Porter, 15 July 1943; RG to R. Evans, 22 June 1943; RG to E. Pritchard, 25 Oct. 1943; RG to W. McArthur, 22 Nov. 1943; RG to E. Pritchard, 3 Nov. 1943; RG to M. Oppenheimer, 15 Oct. 1943; RG to M. Perkins, 12 Feb. 1944; M. Perkins to RG, 24 Feb. 1944; E. Pritchard to RG, 7 Apr. 1944, Garst Papers, Iowa State University Library.

Newspapers: New York Times, 13 Nov. 1943; *Washington Post,* 7 Jan., 8 Jan. 1943; *Des Moines Register,* 9 Jan. 1943.

Documents: "The Feed Situation," Bureau of Agricultural Economics, July 1941; "Daily Market Letter," Uhlmann Grain Co., 12 Jan. 1943; Roswell Garst, "A Brief Outline of What Should Be Done About the Agricultural Situation," Jan. 1943, Garst Papers, Iowa State University Library.

Books: John Dos Passos, *State of the Nation,* 269–76; Dean Albertson, *Roosevelt's Farmer* (New York: Columbia Univ. Press, 1961), 70, 121–22, 118, 166, 178, 203, 193–94, 204, 217, 218, 224–25, 240, 241–42, 257, 266, 275, 293, 280, 249, 335, 337–40, 348, 349, 355, 359; Walter W. Wilcox, *The Farmer in the Second World War* (Ames: Iowa State College Press, 1947), 129–32, 134, 175, 160, 161, 172; Townsend Ludington, ed., *The Fourteenth Chronicle: Letters and Diaries of John Dos Passos* (Boston: Gambit, 1973), 538–39.

CHAPTER FIVE **COMMERCIAL AND CURIOUS**

LOOKING AHEAD

Letters: RG to W. Albrecht, 19 Dec. 1946; RG to C. Barber, 1945; RG to G. Jackson, 8 Jan. 1945; RG to D. Garst, Mar. 1945; RG to M. Garst, Nov. 1949; RG to JG, Sept. 1955; RG to G. Cannon, Garst Papers, Iowa State University Library.

FINDING ENOUGH FERTILIZER

Letters: RG to JG, July 1945; A. Loveland to L. Smith, 29 June 1945; RG to HAW, 14 July 1945; HAW to RG, 17 July 1945; RG to HAW, 3 June 1946; HAW to RG, 6 June 1946; RG to HAW, 13 June 1946; RG to HAW, 20 June 1946; R. Patterson to HAW, 20 June 1946; HAW to RG, 27 June 1946; RG to HAW, 20 July 1946; HAW to RG, July 1946; RG to C. Anderson, 23 Aug. 1946; R. Steelman to HAW, 6 Aug. 1946; RG to G. Buck, May 1946; G. Buck to RG, June 1946; RG to R. Buchanan, 2 June 1945; RG to G. Hoffer, 11 July 1947; RG to J. Patterson, Jan. 1949; J. Sanders to RG, Sept. 1950, Garst Papers, Iowa State University Library.

Articles and documents: "Memorandum for the Secretary," John Patterson to HAW, June 1946; "15 Ordnance Plants to Manufacture Fertilizers for Starving Countries," War Department press release, 13 June 1946; C. Kenneth Horner, "Ammonium Nitrate – from War to Peace," *Domestic Commerce,* Oct. 1945, 33–34, 42; "Industry Report: Chemicals and Allied Products," Department of Commerce, Aug. 1946; "Fertilizer Position of the United States for 1946–47 Season," Production and Marketing Administration, 31 July, 1946, Garst Papers, Iowa State University Library.

Interviews: Roswell Garst, Hans Larsen, Garst Papers, Iowa State University Library.

COBS FOR CATTLE

Letters: RG to USDA Laboratory, Peoria, 6 Nov. 1943; RG to USDA Laboratory, Ames, 6 Nov. 1943; RG to F. Knoop, 25 Sept. 1948; A. Becker to RG, Nov. 1946; A. Becker to RG, Dec. 1946; RG to *Prairie Farmer,* 20 July 1946; RG to H. Kildee, 3 July 1948; H. Kildee to RG, 10 July 1948; RG to C. Culbertson, 27 May 1949; RG to G. Cunningham, 15 Aug. 1949; RG to P. Gerlaugh, 2 June 1949; M. Baker to RG, Sept. 1948; RG to G. Jackson, Sept. 1949; R. Keenan to RG, Oct. 1949, Garst Papers, Iowa State University Library.

Documents: Roswell Garst (Garst and Thomas), "There's Gold in That Cob Pile!" 1949, 1950; "Progress Report on the Cob Feeding Operation," 1949; "Corn Cobs Have *Real* Feeding Value for Cattle," 1951; "The Use of Corn Cobs, Corn Stalks, and Grain Sorghum Stubble for Cattle Feed," Garst and Thomas bull. 5, 1961; "Feeding Cellulose to Ruminants," (information sheet), 1950; "About Those Corncobs. . . ." (information sheet), 1949; Paul Gerlaugh, Wise Burroughs, L. E. Kunkle, "The Value of Corn Cobs in a Ration for Fattening Steers," Ohio Agriculture Experiment Station, Wooster, mimeo. ser. 52 (c.1947); Maurice A. Campbell, "Report on Cattle Feeding Experiment (Garst Farm)," 18 June 1947; C. C. Culbertson, P. S. Shearer, W. E. Hammond, Scott Moore, "Shelled Ear Corn, Ground Ear Corn. . . . Plus Additional Cob . . . for Fattening Yearling Steers," Iowa State College, AH leaflet 165, May 1947; P. Gerlaugh, W. Burroughs, L. Kunkle, "Corn and Added Cob Meal," (feeding chart, 1945–48); W. M. Beeson, "Corn Cobs for Growing Steers," Purdue University mimeo. AH 39, 22 July 1949; W. M. Beeson and T. W. Perry, "Rations for Wintering Cattle on Corn Cobs," mimeo. AH 43, 11 Nov. 1949; "Wintering Cattle on Corn Cobs," mimeo. AH 48, 21 Apr. 1950, Garst Papers, Iowa State University Library.

Articles: Fred Knoop, "No Privacy for the Rumen," *Farm Quarterly* (Winter) 1948, 40–43, 124–25.

Interviews: Roswell Garst, Wise Burroughs, Maurice Campbell, Garst Papers, Iowa State University Library.

"REVOLUTION ON THE FARM"

Letters: RG to J. Bradley, Apr. 1948; RG to AF, Apr. 1948; RG to AF, June 1949; JDP to RG, 7 June 1945; RG to JDP, 15 Sept. 1947; JDP to RG, 19 Sept. 1947; RG to JDP, 12 Nov. 1947; RG to G. Jackson, 12 Nov. 1947; RG to JDP, 24 Jan. 1948; JDP to RG, 28 May 1948; RG to JDP, 31 July 1948; RG to D. Munro, 7 Aug. 1948; JDP to RG, 6 Aug. 1948; RG to JDP, 26 Nov. 1948; AF to RG, Aug. 1948; RG to JDP, Jan. 1949; JDP to RG, 27 Jan. 1949, Garst Papers, Iowa State University Library.

Articles: John Dos Passos, "Revolution on the Farm," *Life,* 23 Aug. 1948, 95–104.

CHAPTER SIX **CREATING THE YEARS OF ABUNDANCE**

BREAKTHROUGH WITH CELLULOSE

Letters: RG to P. Gerlaugh, June 1949; RG to G. Buck, 1949; RG to F. Andre, Oct. 1949; F. Keenan to RG, 1949; RG to G. Jackson, 1949; RG to L. Bean, 1950; RG to M. Perkins, Nov. 1951; RG to *Farm Quarterly,* 6 Mar. 1952; RG to AF, Feb. 1952; RG to AF, Mar. 1952; RG to G. Bohstedt, Feb. 1951; RG to W. Beeson, Oct. 1951; M. McVickar to RG, 16 Dec. 1952; W. Allstetter to RG, 28 Nov. 1952; G. Bohstedt to RG, Nov. 1951; RG to G. Bohstedt, Nov. 1951, Garst Papers, Iowa State University Library.

Documents: Roswell Garst, "It Needs Seedin'," Garst and Thomas bull., 1949, Garst Papers, Iowa State University Library.

Articles: Jonathan and Perry Garst, "Cow Feed from the Air," *Farm Quarterly* (Summer) 1950; Charles R. Koch, "How Crazy Can a Man Get?" *Farm Quarterly* (Spring) 1952, 30–33, 109; Roswell Garst, *Successful Farming,* 1954; "Early Planting, Soil Fertility are Keys to Corn Yields," *Oklahoma Farmer-Stockman,* Feb. 1949; Warren Garst, "A Country Banker Looks at Fertilizer," *Farm Chemicals* 115, no. 11(1952).

Books: George Scarseth, *Man and His Earth* (Ames: Iowa State Univ. Press, 1962), 109–10.

Interviews: Roswell Garst, Garst Papers, Iowa State University Library.

BREAKTHROUGH WITH NITROGEN

Letters: T. Schultz to RG, 22 Dec. 1949; R. Uhlmann to RG, Dec. 1949; RG to H. Brenton, Jan. 1950; RG to C. Brannan, 3 May 1950; RG to C. Brannan, Dec. 1950; R. Uhlmann to RG, 31 Oct. 1950; RG to P. Maguire, 23 Jan. 1951; RG to H. Larsen, 20 Mar. 1951; C. Brannan to RG, July 1951; RG to G. Hoffer, 21 Oct. 1952; RG to G. Jackson, 31 Aug. 1959; RG to F. Keenan, May 1950; RG to R. Uhlmann, 3 Nov. 1950; RG to G. Jackson, 9 Apr. 1951; O. Wells to RG, 7 Nov.

1950; RG to C. Brannan, 27 Oct. 1950; RG to O. Wells, 28 Oct. 1950; RG to C. Davis, 31 Dec. 1949; RG to C. Davis, 7 Jan. 1950; J. Strohm to RG, 4 Aug. 1951; J. Strohm to RG, 25 Sept. 1951; RG to J. Strohm, 27 Sept. 1951; J. Strohm to RG, 13 May 1952, Garst Papers, Iowa State University Library.

Documents: "The Feed Situation," Bureau of Aricultural Economics, Nov. 1949, Garst Papers, Iowa State University Library.

Articles: Fred Knoop, "New Tricks with Corn," *Farm Quarterly,* 1952, pp. 66–68, 137–40; John Strohm, "This May Revolutionize the Way you Grow Corn," *Country Gentleman,* Feb. 1952, 26–27, 68–70; Grant Cannon, "Nitrogen Will Feed Us," *Atlantic Monthly,* Sept. 1953, 50–53; Roswell Garst, "Legume-Raised Nitrogen Costly," *Crops and Soils,* Jan. 1955, 10–11; "I Believe You Can Make Hay with Your Cornpicker," *Country Gentleman,* Aug. 1954, 39, 60–61; Dick Hanson and George D. Johnson, "The New Era of the Cornstalk," *Successful Farming,* Oct. 1954, 42–48; George D. Johnson, "Can We Throw Away Rotations?" *Successful Farming,* Dec. 1955, 42–43, 99.

Interviews: Roswell Garst, Garst Papers, Iowa State University Library.

AGRICULTURAL PROSPECT

Letters: RG to JDP, 16 Dec. 1950; JDP to RG, 19 Dec. 1950; RG to JG and S. Garst, 7 Nov. 1950; RG to J. Cowles, Feb. 1951; RG to W. Hill, 30 Dec. 1950; RG to G. Cannon, Nov. 1950; G. Cannon to RG, 9 Jan. 1951, Garst Papers, Iowa State University Library.

Newspapers: Des Moines Register, 13 Sept., 18 Sept. 1946.

Articles: Sumner Schlicter, "How Big in 1980?" *Atlantic Monthly,* Nov. 1949, 39–43; Roswell Garst, "The Surplus Is Gone," *Farm Quarterly* (Spring) 1951:32–35, 129-33.

Books: John Dos Passos, *The Prospect Before Us* (Boston: Houghton Mifflin, 1950), 276–87.

Interviews: Roswell Garst, Garst Papers, Iowa State University Library.

CHAPTER SEVEN **BEGINNING THE EAST-WEST DIALOGUE**

BACKGROUND: LIVING WITH THE SURPLUS

Letters: RG to G. Jackson, 31 Aug. 1959; RG to C. Hope, 2 July 1953; RG to L. Soth, 5 Oct. 1953; RG to J. Galbraith, 12 Feb. 1955; J. Galbraith to RG, 15 Feb. 1955; RG to A. Bowman, Apr. 1955; RG to H. Hoover, Jr., 19 May 1955; RG to J. Naughton, 23 June 1955; RG to S. Adams, 27 June 1955; D. Paarlberg to RG, 27 June 1955; A. Stevenson to RG, 7 July 1955; C. Hope to RG, 12 July 1955; HHH to RG, 19 June 1955; RG to HHH, 20 June 1955; RG to T. Schultz, 23 July 1955; RG to D. Paarlberg, 2 July 1955; HHH to RG, 9 Dec. 1955; HHH to RG, 3 Jan. 1956; HHH to RG, 3 Feb. 1956, Garst Papers, Iowa State University Library.

Books: Willard W. Cochrane and Mary E. Ryan, *American Farm Policy, 1948-1973* (Minneapolis: Univ. of Minnesota Press, 1976), (30–31, 89–92, 266–69.)

FIRST AGRICULTURAL EXCHANGE

Letters: RG to HAW, 15 July 1955; HAW to RG, 30 July 1955; RG to B. Hickenlooper, 26 July 1955; RG to J. Mathys, 9 Sept. 1955; RG to J. Fullbright, 10 Dec. 1974; RG to A. Becker, 25 July 1955; RG to G. Schutz, 27 July 1955, Garst Papers, Iowa state University Library.

Newspapers: Pravda, 3 Feb., 11 Feb., 3 Mar. 1955; *Izvestia,* 2 Feb., 3 Feb., 11 Feb. 1955; *Agriculture,* 3 Feb. 1955; *Des Moines Register,* 10 Feb. 1955, Garst Papers, Iowa State University Library.

Books: Edward Crankshaw, *Khrushchev: A Career* (New York: Viking, 1966), 148; Roy and Zhores Medvedev, *Khrushchev: The Years in Power* (Oxford Univ. Press, 1977), 24–37; *Report on the Visit to the USA and Canada of the Soviet Agricultural Delegation* (Moscow, 1955).

Interviews: Alexander Tulupnikov, John Strohm, Lauren Soth, Roswell Garst, Garst Papers, Iowa State University Library.

FIRST TRIP TO EASTERN EUROPE

Letters: R. Moore to A. Andresen, 8 July 1955; RG to V. Matskevitch, 25 July 1955; RG to V. Matskevitch, 5 Aug. 1955; RG to JG and J. Kamps, 31 Oct. 1955; RG to F. Lehmann and J. Wallace, 2 Nov. 1955; RG to V. Matskevitch, 1 Nov. 1955; RG to E. Benson, 12 Dec. 1955; D. Vaughan to JG, 12 Dec. 1955; RG to R. Tugwell, 24 Dec. 1969; RG to P. Maguire, 18 June 1964; RG to M. Cannon, 4 May 1957, Garst Papers, Iowa state University Library.

Newspapers: New York Herald Tribune, 13 Dec. 1955.

Documents: Department of Commerce press release, 3 Nov. 1955, Garst Papers, Iowa State University Library.

Interviews: Roswell Garst, Valerie Tereshtenko, Victor Lischienko, A. Kharchenko, E. Belinskaya, Sandor Rajke, Silviu Brucan, G. Obrejanu, M. Covor, Garst Papers, Iowa State University Library.

WHOSE IRON CURTAIN?

Letters: RG to P. Maquire, 3 Feb. 1956; RG to M. Cannon, 4 May 1957, Garst Papers, Iowa State University Library.

Documents: Department of State: memo of conversation, 24 Apr. 1956 (RG and Francis B. Stevens). FBI memo., 14 Nov., 25 Nov., 30 Nov. 1955; 6 Feb., 29 Mar., 18 Sept., 26 Sept., 3 Oct. 1956; 29 Mar., 29 July, 19 Nov., 20 Nov., 3 Dec., 19 Dec. 1957; 10 Jan., 14 Apr., 28 Oct. 1958; 2 Feb., 25 Sept., 17 Sept. 1959; 23 Feb., 7 Mar., 8 Apr., 4 Aug. 1960, Garst Papers, Iowa State University Library.

Newspapers: New York Times, 11 Nov. 1955.

Articles: Sandor Rajke, "50th Anniversary of the Garst and Thomas Hybrid Corn

Company," *Acta Agronomica* 29(1980):417–24; "From Magyarovar to Martonvasar and Hungarian Plant Breeding," *Acta Agronomica* (Budapest) *academiae scientarium Hungaricae* 30(1981):466–72.

Interviews: Roswell Garst, John Chrystal, Valerie Tereshtenko, Silviu Brucan, Grigor Obrejanu, M. Covor, Sandor Rajke, J. Keseru.

MONTHS OF PROGRESS, DAYS OF DISAPPOINTMENT

Letters: RG to C. Douglas, 20 may 1956; RG to S. Brucan, 4 May 1956; Brucan, Gligor, Obrejanu to RG, 7 Feb. 1956; RG to P. Maguire, 18 June 1964; RG to S. Garst, 1 Sept. 1956; S. Garst to RG, 29 Aug. 1956; S. Brucan to RG, 2 May 1956; G. Zaroubin to RG and B. Brown, 18 Sept. 1956; B. Brown to HAW, 14 Oct. 1956; V. Tereshtenko to RG, 10 Mar. 1958; RG to V. Matskevitch, 29 Sept. 1956, Garst Papers, Iowa State University Library.

Newspapers: New York Times, 12 Apr., 1 May 1956; *Washington Post,* 3 Jan. 1956.

Documents and pamphlets: Department of State, Foreign Service despatch, American Legation, Bucharest, 26 Oct. 1956; Roswell Garst, "Maize: A Reliable Source of Abundance" (Moscow, 1975) (originally "Food Unlimited . . . and Good Food"), Garst Papers, Iowa State University Library.

Books: Miklos Molnar, *Budapest 1956: A History of the Hungarian Revolution* (New York: Crane-Russak, 1971), 82, 96–99.

Interviews: Roswell Garst, Valerie Tereshtenko, Silviu Brucan, Sandor Rajke, Harold Smouse, Garst Papers, Iowa State University Library.

CHAPTER EIGHT STARTING AGAIN

AFTERMATH OF HUNGARY

Letters: RG to M. Cannon, 4 May 1957; RG to V. Tereshtenko, 15 June 1957; P. Maguire to RG, 21 Aug. 1957; RG to P. Maguire, 8 Aug. 1957; RG to J. Krelsnowski, 9 Sept. 1957; RG to J. Brajovic, 4 June 1957; RG to K. Petrzelka, 21 May 1957; "Hranexport" to RG, 6 May 1957; RG to E. Freers, 22 Mar. 1957; RG to V. Tereshtenko, 22 Mar. 1957; RG to R. Spasowski, 14 Feb. 1957; RG to H. Bowen, 14 Oct. 1957; G Reiner to RG, 4 Nov. 1957; H. Salisbury to RG, 21 Oct. 1957; RG to V. Tereshtenko, 9 Jan. 1957; RG to G. Reiner, 9 Jan. 1957; RG to L. Pearson, 28 Mar. 1957; RG to V. Tereshtenko, 7 Mar. 1957; RG to V. Tereshtenko, 10 Jan. 1958; RG to C. Thomas and others, 2 Jan. 1958; RG to V. Tereshtenko (cablegram) 14 Jan. 1958; V. Tereshtenko to RG, 9 Apr. 1958; V. Tereshtenko to RG, 30 May 1958; RG to V. Tereshtenko, 24 Mar. 1958; V. Tereshtenko to RG, 10 Mar. 1958; P. Voutov to RG, 27 Oct. 1958; V. Tereshtenko to RG, 2 Oct. 1957; V. Matskevitch to RG, 24 July 1958; N. Khrushchev to RG (via Soviet Embassy) 26 Dec. 1958, Garst Papers, Iowa State University Library.

Newspapers: New York Times, 10 Sept. 1957; *Minneapolis Tribune,* 27 Sept. 1957.

Interviews: Roswell Garst, Garst Papers, Iowa State University Library.

CONVERSATION WITH KHRUSHCHEV

Letters: RG to HHH, 28 Jan. 1959; RG to N. Khrushchev, 8 Feb. 1959; RG to I. Prumof, 28 Apr. 1959; RG to M. Menshikov, 1 May 1959, Garst Papers, Iowa State University Library.

Newspapers: Des Moines Register, 20 Feb. 1959.

Documents: "Foreign Agricultural Circular," USDA, 2 July 1959; Department of State: memo of conversation, 20 Jan. 1959; Foreign Service despatch from American Embassy, Moscow, 8 Jan. 1960 (includes exchanges of letters between Roswell Garst and Khrushchev published in Soviet press 5 Jan. 1960), Garst Papers, Iowa State University Library.

Books: N. S. Khrushchev, *Khrushchev Remembers: The Last Testament* (New York: Bantam Books, 1976), 449, 450.

Interviews: Roswell Garst, John Chrystal, Garst Papers, Iowa State University Library.

KHRUSHCHEV IN COON RAPIDS

Letters: RG to Dwight Eisenhower, 7 Aug. 1959; RG to Richard Nixon, 8 Aug. 1959; RG to E. Boss, 28 Aug. 1959; E. Boss to RG, 29 Aug. 1959; V. Tereshtenko to RG (cablegram), 25 Aug. 1959; RG to N. Khrushchev, 9 Sept. 1959; RG to V. Tereshtenko, 24 Sept. 1959; RG to V. Tereshtenko, 3 Oct. 1959; V. Tereshtenko to RG (cablegram), 26 Oct. 1959; RG to "whom it may concern," 26 Aug. 1959; RG to N. Khrushchev (cablegram), 6 Aug. 1959; RG to J. Strohm, 30 Mar. 1960; RG to P. Maguire, 7 Aug. 1959; W. Colvin to R. Kintner, 24 Sept. 1959; M. Beatty to W. Colvin, 26 Sept. 1959; RG to N. Khrushchev, 16 Dec. 1959; N. Khrushchev to RG, 31 Dec. 1959; RG to N. Khrushchev, 26 Jan. 1960, Garst Papers, Iowa State University Library.

Newspapers: Des Moines Register, 19 Sept., 24 Sept. 1959; *Washington Post,* 18 Sept. 1959; *New York Times,* 24 Sept. 1959; *Kansas City Times,* 24 Sept. 1959; *Nashville Tennessean,* 24 Sept. 1959; *Nashville Banner,* 24 Sept. 1959; *New York World Telegram,* 24 Sept. 1959; Garst Papers, Iowa State University Library.

Articles: "Corn-Ball Act Down on the Farm," *Life,* 5 Oct. 1959.

Books: N. S. Khrushchev, *Khrushchev Remembers: The last Testament,* 449–54.

Interviews: Garst family, Harrison Salisbury (unrecorded conversations).

CHAPTER NINE **THE SIXTIES**

AGRICULTURE ON THE NEW FRONTIER

Letters: RG to HHH, 25 Feb. 1960; RG to John F. Kennedy, 8 Aug. 1960; John F. Kennedy to RG, 2 Sept. 1960; J. Galbraith to RG, 23 Nov. 1960; HHH to RG, 31 Dec. 1960; RG to JG, 26 Jan. 1961; W. Colvin to RG, 26 Dec. 1963; RG to O. Freeman, 21 Dec. 1960; RG to A. Stevenson, 17 Nov. 1960; B. Hays to RG, 19

Nov. 1959; RG to W. Fulbright, 23 Feb. 1960; RG to B. Hays, 26 Apr. 1960; B Hays to RG, 25 Apr. 1961; RG to P. Maguire, 6 June 1961; HHH to H. Waters, 12 June 1961; McGeorge Bundy to HHH, 27 June 1961; RG to P. Maguire, 4 Aug. 1961; JG to RG, 8 Oct. 1961; B. Hays to RG, 24 Sept. 1961; RG to HAW, 17 Apr. 1962; W. Hangen to RG, 19 May 1962; RG to W. Hangen, 24 May 1962; RG to G. Jackson, 24 May 1962; RG to HHH, 24 May 1962; W. Hangen to RG, 20 July 1963; HAW to RG, 12 June 1963; RG to P. Maguire, 26 Dec. 1963; RG to HHH, 14 July 1965; HHH to RG, 10 Aug. 1965, Garst Papers, Iowa State University Library.

Newspapers: Des Moines Register, 6 Feb. 1961, 22 Mar. 1967; *Wall Street Journal,* 6 Mar. 1961; *New York Times,* 2 July 1964; *Washington Post,* 9 Apr. 1966.

Documents: Roswell Garst, "A New Approach to the Feed Grain Program" (speech), 18 Feb. 1961; T. W. Schultz, "Feed Grain Stocks into Food and Farm Cash" (speech), 18 Feb. 1961; USDA press release on Freeman Program, 24 May 1961; Research Institute Report, 1 July 1966; T. W. Schultz, "Food for One World: Policy Choices," Hearings before the House Committee on Agriculture, 18 Feb. 1966, Garst papers, Iowa State University Library.

Articles: Roswell Garst, "Feeding a Hungry World," *North American Review,* Mar. 1964, 31–36, 75; John Strohm, "Farmer with a Message – and a Method,"*Reader's Digest,* June 1960, 148–52.

BRINGING CATTLE TO THE CORN BELT

Letters: RG to R. Albaugh, 25 Apr. 1958; RH to F. Andre, 18 Apr. 1958; RG to M. Sorkin, 26 Oct. 1959; RG to W. Colvin, 11 Mar. 1960; RG to HAW, 17 Apr. 1962; RG to A. Lee and others, 1 June 1962; RG to A. Lee and others, 26 June 1962; RG to L. Thompson, 21 Feb. 1963; RG to supervisors (Garst and Thomas), 5 Oct. 1962; HAW to RG, 19 Nov. 1962; RG to P. Maguire, 20 Feb. 1963; RG to W. Colvin, 20 Mar. 1962; W. Pierre to RG, 8 Mar. 1963; RG to F. Andre, M. Anderson, and others, 1 Sept. 1964; R. de Baca to RG, 5 May 1966; RG to L. Thompson, 4 Jan. 1968; L. Thompson to RG, 12 Jan. 1968; S. Ewing, M. Anderson, F. Andre to RG, 9 Apr. 1968; S. James to RG, 17 Apr. 1968; RG to S. James, 28 Apr. 1968; S. Ewing to RG, 14 Mar. 1972; RG to F. Andre, L. Thompson, S. Ewing, 24 Apr. 1968; C. Hamilton to RG, 1 Oct. 1968; L. Thompson to RG, 27 June 1969; L. Thompson to RG, 26 Mar. 1969; W. Beeson to RG, 7 Oct. 1969; L. Thompson to RG, 23 Feb. 1970, Garst Papers, Iowa State University Library.

Documents and pamphlets: Roswell Garst, "An Opportunity for Producers of Corn and Grain Sorghums," 24 Jan. 1962; "An Iowa Agricultural Opportunity," 23 Jan. 1962; "A Nebraska Opportunity?" 12 May 1962; "To the American Agricultural Editors' Association" (speech), June 1962; "The Use of Corn Cobs, Corn Stalks, and Grain Sorghum Stubble for Cattle Feed," Garst and Thomas bull. 5, 1961 ed.; "Progress and Opportunities in Corn Growing," Garst and Thomas service bull. 5, 1962; "1964 Agricultural Prospects and Opportunities," Garst and Thomas bull., 1964; "It is Profitable to Fertilize Pastures," Garst and Thomas, 1968. "Stretch Hay Supplies with Ground Corncobs and Chopped Cornstalks," Agricultural Extension Service, Iowa State College pamphlet 232, Sept. 1956; "Feeder Calf Production by Intensive Methods on Iowa Corn Land," Iowa State College, AH 230, Feb. 1958; "Feeder Calf Production under Mid-Western Farm Conditions," Iowa State University, AH R13, Mar. 1960; "Effect of Ground Corn Cobs Fed as a Silage Extender in Wintering Rations for Beef Cows," Iowa State University, AH

R32, May 1961; Solon Ewing, "Where is the Bull Market?" (speech), 17 July 1965; Louis M. Thompson, "A Case for a Land-use Policy for Agriculture" (speech), 13 Aug. 1969; Solon Ewing, "The Role of Corn and Sorghum Refuse Feeds in an Expanding Midwestern Beef Industry" (speech), 10 Dec. 1969; Louis M. Thompson, "Where Will Corn Yields Top Out in the Seventies?" (speech), 14 Jan. 1970; Solon Ewing, "Beef Cows in the Corn Belt" (speech), 29 Sept. 1970; H. L. Self, "Keeping the Beef Industry in Iowa" (speech), 14 Dec. 1971, Garst Papers, Iowa State University Library.

Articles: W. D. Schrader, John Pesek, and W. C. Moldenhauer, "What About Continuous Corn," *Iowa Farm Science* 14, no. 9 (1960):3–5; W. D. Schrader, John Pesek, F. W. Schaller, "Crop Rotations–Fact and Fiction," *Iowa Farm Science* 16, no. 9 (1962):6–9; Roswell Garst, "Bob Garst's Latest 'Crusade,'" *Successful Farming,* July 1962, 32–33, 70–71; Roswell Garst, "More Beef Cow Herds for Iowa?" *Wallaces' Farmer,* Feb. 17, 1962, 30–31; Raymond Ewell, "Feeding the World in 1975," *Crop Life,* Sept. 1963, 58–60, Garst Papers, Iowa State University Library.

Interviews: Roswell Garst, Elizabeth Garst, Garst Papers, Iowa State University Library.

RUSSIA AGAIN, 1960–64

Letters: RG to P. Maguire, 26 Apr. 1962; RG to P. Maguire, 25 Apr. 1962; L. Soth to RG, 8 Aug. 1962; RG to L. Soth, 10 Sept. 1962; RG to A. Stevenson, 10 Sept. 1962; RG to P. Maguire, 12 Apr. 1963; RG to P. Maguire, 12 Apr. 1963 (2d letter); RG to P. Maguire, 11 June, 1963; F. Kohler to RG, 29 June 1963; P. Maguire to RG, 18 July 1963; RG to H. Salisbury, 13 Aug. 1963; RG to P. Maguire, 25 Sept. 1962; RG to C. Streeter, 4 Sept. 1963; V. Tereshtenko to RG, 4 Nov. 1962; J. Chrystal to family, undated, 1963; A. Shevchenko to RG, Jan. 1964; RG to W. Colvin, 7 May 1962; H. Salisbury to RG, 19 Feb. 1964; H Salisbury to RG, 27 Apr. 1964; RG to G. Chaput, 5 Feb. 1964; V. Tereshtenko to RG, 23 Mar. 1964; V. Tereshtenko to RG, 12 Dec. 1964; V. Tereshtenko to RG, 19 Dec. 1965; RG to F. Kohler, 22 Oct. 1964; F. Kohler to RG, 4 Nov 1964, Garst Papers, Iowa State University Library.

Newspapers: New York Times, 17 Aug. 1963, 28 June 1964.

Documents: Department of State: memo of conversation, 11 Feb. 1964 (L. Thompson and P. Maguire); Department of State: aerogram from American Legation, Budapest, 23 May 1963, Garst Papers, Iowa State University Library.

Articles: "Interview with Roswell Garst," *U.S. News and World Report,* 2 Apr. 1962, 78–80; "Exchange of Letters between N. S. Khrushchev and Roswell Garst," *Country Life* (USSR), 28 Dec. 1963; *The Current Digest of the Soviet Press* 14, no. 7, 11 Mar. 1964 (for Khrushchev speech 14 Feb. 1964 and text of RG letter published in *Pravda* and *Izvestia* 13 Feb. 1964), Garst Papers, Iowa State University Library.

Books: Roy and Zhores Medvedev, *Khrushchev: The Years in Power* (New York: Viking, 1966), 127, 159–79; Alec Nove, "Agriculture," in *The Soviet Union Since the Fall of Khrushchev,* eds. A. Brown and M. Kaser (New York: Macmillan, 1975), 1–15; C. Bown and P. Mooney, *Cold War to Detente* (Salem, N.H.: Heinemann, 1977), 57–58.

Interviews: Roswell Garst, John Chrystal, Garst Papers, Iowa State University Library.

EL SALVADOR EXPERIMENT

Letters: C. Rowan to RG, 7 Apr. 1960; A. Schevchenko to RG, 28 Jan. 1964; RG to P. Maguire, 4 Feb. 1964; J. Chrystal to D. Bell, 4 Feb. 1964; BB to RG, 18 Mar. 1964; R. Newburg to RG, 17 Mar. 1964; C. ter Kuile to RG, 30 Apr. 1964; C. ter Kuile to H. Richardson, 30 Apr. 1964; RG to T. Mann, 24 June 1964; RG to R. Burton, 25 July 1964; J. Fulbright to RG, 1 July 1964; T. Mann to J. Fulbright, 13 July 1964; RG to P. Maguire, 24 July 1964; RG to C. Bowles, 5 Aug. 1964; RG to D. Bell, 15 Aug. 1964; D. Bell to RG, 14 Sept. 1964; RG to BB, 18 Sept. 1964; RG to HAW, 12 Sept. 1964; RG to BB, 20 Oct. 1964; RG to BB, 6 Nov. 1964; BB to RG, 16 Dec. 1964; BB to RG, 3 Apr. 1965; BB to RG, 19 July 1965; BB to RG, 15 Sept. 1964; BB to RG, 28 Sept. 1965; RG to S. Markman, 20 Oct. 1965; BB to RG, 3 Nov. 1965; RG to P. Maguire, 13 Dec. 1967; RG to H. Waters, 17 May 1967; H. Waters to RG, 25 Aug. 1967; N. Ward to RG, 28 Sept. 1967; RG to D. Albrecht, 20 Mar. 1967; RG to J. Strohm, 27 July 1967; RG to HHH, 26 Feb. 1968; RG to L. Brown, 9 Apr. 1968; R. de Baca to RG, 11 Sept. 1967; L. Brown to RG, 20 June 1968; RG to HHH, 10 Apr. 1968; RG to J. Strohm, 12 Oct. 1960; RG to G. McGovern, 11 Jan. 1961; RG to A. and H. Lee, 13 Feb. 1961; RG to A. and H. Lee, J. and C. Kamps, 8 Apr. 1961; L. Soth to RG, 13 Feb. 1961; RG to B. Hickenlooper, 21 Mar. 1962; B. Hickenlooper to RG, 24 Mar. 1962; RG to B. Hickenlooper, 26 Mar. 1962; RG to O. Freeman, 13 Nov. 1963; T. Schultz to RG, 26 Mar. 1965; RG to L. Soth, 7 Feb. 1966; RG to O. Freeman, 12 Feb. 1966; T. Schultz to RG, 17 Feb. 1966; RG to HHH, 4 Aug. 1966; L. Soth to RG, 12 Aug. 1966; RG to L. Soth, 17 Aug. 1966; RG to P. Maguire, 18 Oct. 1966; RG to L. Thompson, 8 Jan. 1967; RG to HHH, 11 Feb. 1967; RG to L. Thompson, 23 June 1967, Garst Papers, Iowa State University Library.

Documents: C. ter Kuile, "The FAO Freedom from Hunger Campaign: Fertilizer Program in Latin America" (memo.), 1964; Roswell Garst, "Suggestions for Helping Brazil," 9 June 1964; "Status Report on the MDFF-Mass Demonstration Fertilizer-Corn Program in El Salvador, C.A.," 2 Apr. 1965 (B. Birdsall to C. Dayos); B. Birdsall, "Report on 1965 MDFF Program," 3 Dec. 1965; "Demonstraciones Masivas de Maiz y Fertilizantes," Dirección de Extension Agricola, Santa Tecla, El Salvador, Hoja Divulgata no. 69, 1965; USDA Foreign Agriculture Circular FG 8-65, July, 1965; "Washington Farmletter," no. 1159, 3 Dec. 1965; "The Agricultural Situation," USDA 50, no. 1 (1966); B. Birdsall, "The Mass Fertilizer Demonstration Program in El Salvador, 1965-66-67," 20 Nov. 1967; AID memo.: "Fertilizer Demonstration in Brazil," 20 July 1967. Garst Papers, Iowa State University Library.

Articles: Lester R. Brown, "The Agricultural Revolution in Asia," *Foreign Affairs,* July 1968, 688-98.

Books: Jonathan Garst, *No Need for Hunger* (New York: Random House, 1963), 8-9, 27, 49, 107, 108, 131.

Interviews: Roswell Garst, Benjamin Birdsall, Garst papers, Iowa State University Library; Theodore Schultz, Lester Brown (unrecorded).

INDEX

AAA. *See* Agricultural Adjustment Act
AFL and CIO, 129
Agency for International Development (AID), 235, 269–74, 278–80
Agricultural Act, 1954, 170–71
Agricultural Adjustment Act (AAA), 49, 53–59, 88, 91, 117, 124, 130–32, 141
Production Control Administration, 50
Agricultural exchange, 174–94, 199–206, 208–14, 219–22, 250–52
political aspects, 195–98, 215–19
Agricultural Exhibit, Moscow, 177
Agricultural Experiment Station, Ames, Ia., 147
Agricultural Life, 256
Agricultural Marketing Act, 38
Agricultural Prices (Wallace), 35
Agricultural Reform in the United States (Black), 49
Agricultural Revolution Associates, 234
Agricultural War Board, 121
Agriculture, 178, 180
AID. *See* Agency for International Development
Albertson, Dean, 120
Albrecht, J. W., 102
Albrecht, W. A., 135
Allison, William, 18
American Farm Bureau Federation, 36, 51, 57, 86, 117–18, 122, 181
American Farm Research Association, 163
American Federation of Labor, 129
American Society for the Prevention of Cruelty to Animals (ASPCA), 145
American Society of Agronomy, 156, 159
Amtorg, 206
Anderson, Marvin, 248
Andre, Floyd, 154, 248, 271
Anti-Saloon League, 10
Apple Farm, 24
Apple production, 113
Argentina, 70, 76, 117, 131
Associated Hybrid Producers, 105
Association of Iowa Cattle Growers Hall of Fame, 283
A. Stein and Company, 90

Baker, Raymond, 35
Blancing the Farm Output (Spillman), 49
Baldwin, C. B., 81, 118, 126, 132
Ball, George, 276

Ballachey, Ada Garst, 110
Banner Trophy, 69, 78
Barber, C. A., 136
Bayard, Ia., 64, 77
Beal, J. W., 33, 34
Bean, Louis, 49, 62, 120, 155, 231
Beatty, Morgan, 226–27
Becker, Arthur, 62, 146, 180–84
Beeson, W. M., 154–55, 158, 250
Bell, David, 269
Bell, Jake, 95, 137–38, 162, 284
Bell, Viv, 72, 77, 138, 162, 284
"Belle of the Coon, The," 6–7, 22
Benson, Ezra Taft, 169–71, 196, 230
Beresford, Rex, 154
Berlin wall, 252–54
Birdsall, Benjamin, 269–279
Birdsall, Florence, 269
Black, A. G., 53, 55, 56, 60
Black, John D., 49, 171
Blind Boone, 8, 44
Bliss, R. K., 117
Bohstedt, Gus, 145–47, 155–57
Bonney, Ted, 9
Boone, Ia., 12
Boss, Ed, 224
Bowles, Chester, 257
Bowman, Arden "Red," 82, 99, 122, 131, 171–72, 181
Bowman, Tillie, 172
Bradley, C. C., 47
Bradley, Jim, 149–50
Brannan, Charles, 155, 161–63, 174
Brannan Plan, 170, 173
Bray, Roger, 163
Brazil, 234–35, 270
Brenton, Harold, 31, 82–83, 161
Bressman, Earl, 207
Brezhnev, Leonid, 283
Bromwell, Scott, 90–93, 103, 107, 111
Brown, Bill, 201, 208–9, 212, 285
Brown, Lester, 279–80
Brown, Prentiss, 126
Brucan, Silviu, 190–93, 197–200, 203–4, 262
Bucharest, 190, 198, 203–5, 210, 260–62
Buck, Glenn, 140
Budapest, 193, 210–15, 260
Bulgaria, 216, 220, 222
Bundy, McGeorge, 232
Bureau of Agricultural Economics, 118, 127–28, 155, 161, 166

304

Freeman, Orville, 231–32, 255, 275–77
Freiler, Abe, 90–97, 103, 108, 126, 149, 152, 156–57
FSA. *See* Farm Security Administration
Fulbright, J. William, 270

Galbraith, John Kenneth, 122–23, 126, 129–30, 171, 229–33, 276
  resigns from OPA, 130
Gall, Lorraine, 145
Galloway, Morrie, 93
Galloway farm, 6, 7
Garst, Ada. *See* Ballachey, Ada Garst
Garst, Andrew, 163
Garst, Antonia (Toshia), 84–85, 114, 138
Garst, Bertha (Mrs. Edward Garst), 15–16, 20–24, 28–29, 138, 285
Garst, Charles, 11
Garst, Clara (Mrs. Warren Garst), 17
Garst, David, 110–14, 136–37, 156–57, 204–5, 237, 241, 251, 284
Garst, De Walt, 10–11
Garst, Dorothy (Mrs. Jack Chrystal), 20–23, 28–29, 83–84
Garst, Edward (father of Roswell), 4–22, 26, 29, 284–85
  establishes E. and W. Garst, 5–6, 14
  land acquisitions, 13–14, 17, 28–29
  postmaster, Coon Rapids, 14
  relationship, his children, 20–22
Garst, Eleanor (Mrs. Warren Garst, Jr.), 83–84, 115, 137, 181–82
Garst, Elias, 11
Garst, Elizabeth (Mrs. Roswell Garst), 19–23, 29–31, 39, 44–46, 52, 60–63, 115, 148, 151, 162, 172, 185, 200, 204, 231, 244–46, 259–60, 280, 284–85
  children's births, 28
  courtship and marriage, 27–28
  family life, 83–86
  organizes farm camp, 40–41, 83–84
  tour, Latin America, 269
  tour, Russia and Eastern Europe, 208–14
  visits Khrushchev, 220–22, 225–26
Garst, George. *See* Garst, Goodwin
Garst, Georgianne (Mrs. David Garst), 137, 204–5
Garst, Goodwin, 20–23, 29, 114–15
Garst, Horace, 11, 13
Garst, Jane (Mrs. Clarence Kamps), 28, 46, 110, 126, 137
Garst, John Newton, 114
Garst, Jonathan, 29, 31, 62–63, 70–72, 77–78, 82, 88, 110–12, 119, 124, 127, 137, 140, 145, 165–66, 172, 183–86, 206, 215, 231, 234, 254, 260, 269
  agricultural exchange role, 200
  cattle feed involvement, 155–57
  early years, 20–23
  El Salvador experiment, 265–68, 271–72, 278
  enlists in Army, 24–25
  farming partnership with Roswell, 24, 26
  fertilizer and, 102–4, 141–43, 162, 232
  government posts, 62, 80, 118, 132, 162–63

  on hunger and arms race, 195
  interest in underdeveloped nations, 232–35, 275
  No Need for Hunger, 266
  relationship, Roswell, 23–26, 31, 138–39
Garst, Julia, 115
Garst, Julius, 11, 20
Garst, Laura, 11
Garst, Louise (Mrs. Micko McBroom), 30, 65
Garst, Maria (Mrs. DeWalt Garst), 10–11
Garst, Maria (Mrs. Michael Garst), 11, 13
Garst, Mary (aunt of Roswell), 11, 15
Garst, Mary (daughter of Roswell), 84, 114, 138
Garst, Mary (Mrs. Stephen Garst, daughter of Warren), 137, 181, 204–6
Garst, Michael (Roswell's grandfather), 11–13
Garst, Morrison, 11
Garst, Morrison, Jr., 30
Garst, Nettie (Mrs. Edward Garst), 15
Garst, Perry, 11, 57
Garst, Perry (son of Jonathan), 156
Garst, Roswell, 51, 109–10, 115, 135, 153, 242
  agricultural programs for underdeveloped countries, 232–36, 262, 270–75
  apple production project, 113
  arms race concerns, 255–64, 280
  author of farm bulletins, 149–50, 241–247
  belief in large farming units, 116
  birth and childhood, 20
  builds seed corn plant, 62–70
  cattle production interest, 236–44, 247–50, 256
  children's births, 28
  considers political career, 79
  corn acreage controversy and, 116–17, 119–22, 123–27, 128–33
  corn blight investigation, 282
  corncob feed experiments, 146–49, 153–60, 240
  death, 285
  defender of egalitarian farming, 95
  divided political loyalties, 79–83
  early farming experience, 25–29
  education, 20–26
  enters hybrid seed corn business, 31, 38–47
  exchange visits, Bulgarians, 216, 220
  exchange visits, Russians, 181–90, 196–99, 208–9, 215–22, 250, 255–60, 283
  farm management business, 90–100, 111–12, 134, 137–38
  fertilizer experimentation and research, 100–108, 122, 134–35, 139–43, 282
  Food for Peace involvement, 172, 230–32
  forms Garst Land Company, 30
  founds Garst and Thomas, 42
  friendship, Eddie Reid, 86–88
  friendship, Henry Wallace, 31–32, 38, 52, 79, 82, 141, 168, 245

HAROLD LEE received his B.A. at the University of California, Berkeley, his M.S. at the Columbia Univeristy School of Journalism, and his Ph.D. from Harvard. He has taught at Carnegie-Mellon University and Boston University, and in 1974 became senior lecturer in English Literature and Medieval Studies at the Grinnell College London program. From 1979 to 1982 he was resident director, and remains adjunct professor at Grinnell-in-London. His wife, Antonia, a daughter of Roswell Garst, teaches at the American School in London.

The Lees maintain close links with Coon Rapids. Since 1958 they have been limited partners in the Garst Seed Company (formerly Garst and Thomas). They are the owners of the Garst Store and maintain a residence in Coon Rapids.

JOE MUNROE has been a photographer since 1939, has studied with Ansel Adams, and in 1946 became the first staff photographer for the *Farm Quarterly*. In 1952 he became a free-lance photographer and filmmaker and has subsequently placed his work in every major American magazine. He is especially well known for his agricultural photography. His film documentaries *The Science of Genetics* (based on hybrid corn) and *Dare the Wildest River* (on running the Colorado River) both won the CINE Gold Eagle and other major awards.

Munroe first met Roswell Garst in 1947 on assignment for the *Farm Quarterly* and has been a friend of the family ever since.